Routledge Revivals

The Spirit of Indian Philosophy

First published in 1975 *The Spirit of Indian Philosophy* provides a systematic overview of Indian philosophy. The book is divided into four major parts dealing with Indian epistemology, Indian metaphysics, Indian ethics, and Indian philosophy of religion. It makes a departure from usual method of investigating Indian philosophy by dealing with its different schools individually and separately. It discusses themes like sources of cognition; nature and criterion of true cognition; problem of error; materialism; realism; dualism; Indian theories of causation; reflective morality; the ethics of non-violence; Indian atheism and Indian religion of God, to argue that the usual conception of Indian philosophy in general as religious, spiritualistic and pessimistic is contrary to the fact, that the doctrine of Karma, transmigration and rebirth, strictly speaking is incompatible with the Indian ways of thinking and in deed is an imposition upon them ab extra. This is an essential read for scholars and students of Indian philosophy.

The Spirit of Indian Philosophy

Nikunja Vihari Banerjee

Routledge
Taylor & Francis Group

First published in 1975
by Curzon Press Ltd.

This edition first published in 2023 by Routledge
4 Park Square, Milton Park, Abingdon, Oxon, OX14 4RN

and by Routledge
605 Third Avenue, New York, NY 10017

Routledge is an imprint of the Taylor & Francis Group, an informa business

Publisher's Note
The publisher has gone to great lengths to ensure the quality of this reprint but points out that some imperfections in the original copies may be apparent.

Disclaimer
The publisher has made every effort to trace copyright holders and welcomes correspondence from those they have been unable to contact.

A Library of Congress record exists under ISBN: 0700700781

ISBN: 978-1-032-57250-5 (hbk)
ISBN: 978-1-003-43852-6 (ebk)
ISBN: 978-1-032-57253-6 (pbk)

Book DOI 10.4324/9781003438526

THE SPIRIT OF INDIAN PHILOSOPHY

NIKUNJA VIHARI BANERJEE

CURZON PRESS

Published by
CURZON PRESS LTD.
LONDON AND DUBLIN
1975

SBN 7007 0078 1

Printed in India

CONTENTS

PREFACE 11

PROLOGUE 17

PART I

INDIAN EPISTEMOLOGY

Introduction 50

I The Sources of Cognition 52

A Perception *(Pratyakṣa)* 53

Indeterminate *(nirvikalpaka)* and Determinate *(savikalpaka)* Perception *(Pratyakṣa)* 57

External *(bāhya)* and Internal *(āntara; mānas)* Perception *(Pratyakṣa)* 60

Normal *(laukika)* and Supranormal *(alaukika)* Perception *(Pratyakṣa)* 61

B Inference *(Anumāna)* 65

Varieties of *Anumāna* 69

C Testimony *(Śabda; Āptavacana)* 74

D Comparison *(Upamāna)* 79

E Presumption *(Arthāpatti)* 86

F Non-Apprehension *(Anupalabdhi)* 93

G Minor Sources of Cognition 97

II The Nature and Criterion of True Cognition

A The Nature of True Cognition 99

B Theories of Truth

The Self-evidence Theory *(Svataḥ-prāmānya-vāda)* 108

The Correspondence and Pragmatic Theories *(Parataḥ-prāmānya-vāda)* 114

III The Problem of Error
Introductory Remarks 121
Theories of Error 122

PART II

INDIAN METAPHYSICS

Introduction 133
I Materialism 135
II Realism
A Nyāya-Vaiśeṣika Realism 139
B The Buddhist Schools of Realism
Introduction 157
(i) Vaibhāṣika Realism 158
(ii) Sautrāntika Realism 162
C The Realistic Schools of Mīmāṁsā 166
III Dualism
A The Sāṁkhya Doctrine of Dualism 174
B The Dualistic Metaphysics of the Jainas
(i) Methodology of Metaphysics : The Doctrine of *Anekānta* and *Nyaya* 184
(ii) Jaina Metaphysics 189
IV Idealism
Introduction 196
Vijñānavāda (Idealism) 199
V Absolutism
Introduction 203
A Theistic Absolutism
(i) Pure Non-Dualism *(Śuddhādvaita-vāda)* 206
(ii) Dualistic Non-dualism (Dvaitādvaita-vāda) 210
(iii) The Doctrine of Unthinkable Identity-in-Difference *(Acintyabhedābheda-vāda)* 212

(iv) Dualistic Absolutism *(Dvaita-vāda)* 214

(v) Qualified Non-dualism *(Viśiṣṭādvaita-vāda)* 216

B Non-dualism *(Advaita-vāda)* 221

C Nihilistic Absolutism *(Śūnya-vāda)* 228

VI Concluding Remarks 233

VII Indian Theories of Causation 235

PART III

INDIAN ETHICS

Introduction 243

I Objective Morality 245

Classification of Duties 247

II Reflective Morality 253

A The Psychological Basis of Ethics

(a) Analysis of Volition : Voluntary and Non-voluntary Activities 254

Analysis of Volition and Consciousness of Freedom 255

(b) Analysis of Consciousness of Duty 259

B Virtues and their Classification 270

III The Moral Standards 277

A The Theory of the Moral Standard as Custom or Tradition 278

B Theories of Law as the Moral Standard 279

C The Theory of the Moral Standard as Social Solidarity or Social Good 282

D Theories of the Moral Standard as End 283

(a) Criticism of Hedonism by some of the Anti-hedonistic Schools of Indian Thought 284

(b) Departures from Hedonism 285

IV The Ethics of Non-violence (Ahiṁsā) 288

Part IV

INDIAN PHILOSOPHY OF RELIGION

		Introduction	295
I		Indian Atheism	297
II		Indian Religion of God	306
	A	Proofs of the Existence of God	307
	B	The Nature of God and His Relation to the World and Finite Selves	314
III		Indian Religion as the Way	328
		Introduction	328
	A	Indian Views of Human Bondage	332
	B	Indian Views on Liberation (*Mokṣa*)	338
	C	Indian Views of Mokṣa as the Ideal Way of Life	351
		Selected Bibliography	369
		Index	375

Preface

I was till recently rather reluctant to undertake any systematic work on Indian philosophy. But I persuaded myself to write this book in view of my earnest desire for suggesting the ways of the reorientation which, as I am convinced, the outlook of Indian philosophy is in need of. Accordingly, the plan of this work has been different from that of the numerous works on Indian philosophy by both Indian and Western scholars. In the Prologue, I have disputed the widely current view that the major schools of Indian philosophy have certain common features, and I have tried to show that this view is vitiated by the fault of fitting diverse philosophical systems into a Procrustean bed. In this connection, I have, among other things, argued that the usual conception of Indian philosophy in general as religious, spiritualistic and pessimistic is contrary to fact, that the doctrine of *karma*, transmigration and rebirth, strictly speaking, is incompatible with the Indian ways of thinking and indeed is an imposition upon them *ab extra*, and that the time-honoured division of Indian philosophy into two rival sections respectively designated as *āstika* (orthodox) and *nāstika* (heterodox) is at best unrealistic and at worst irrational.

In particular, I have found it necessary for my present purpose to make a departure from the usual method of investigating Indian philosophy by dealing with its different schools individually and separately. Its investigation by this method, of course, may provide detailed accounts of the results of the different ways of philosophical investigations that have been adopted in India. But, as I have come to realize, it cannot point towards the direction in which the reorientation of the outlook of Indian philosophy should lie. I have, therefore, pursued the novel plan of distinguishing four separate divisions of Indian philosophy respectively called Indian Epistemology, Indian Metaphysics, Indian Ethics and Indian Philosophy of Religion. In this my object has been to bring together the basic ideas of the different schools of Indian philosophy, pertaining to each of these divisions and then try to ascertain how they need to be reconstructed.

It is indeed remarkable that Indian Epistemology, besides concerning itself with the problem of *truth* in common with its counterpart in the West, has dealt with two others, respectively relating to the sources of cognition and the nature of erroneous experience, to which the latter is more or less a stranger. But then, as I have found, its attempts to deal with the problem of truth, like those of Western Epistemology, have failed for two main reasons. One of these consists in their common failure to recognize the *claim to truth* borne by any given instance of cognition in distinction from its truth or falsity as the case may be. The other lies in their ignoring of the distinction between the *truth* of cognition and the *test* or *criterion* of its truth.

As regards the problem of the sources of cognition, Indian Epistemology has betrayed two opposite tendencies towards its solution. One of these is expressed in the unduly strict and rigorous observance of the law of parsimony, resulting in the admission of perception (*pratyakṣa*) as the only genuine source of cognition. The other, on the contrary, disregards the spirit of this law, and, as a result, indulges in indiscriminate inflation of the sources of cognition. The difficulties of the epistemological situation which is thus presented is obviously in need of resolution. Accordingly, I have found it reasonable to uphold the claim of perception (*pratyakṣa*), inference (*anumāna*) and secular testimony (*laukika āpata-vacana*) to be genuine and independent sources of cognition, and reject the similar claim on the part of the rest, including comparison (*upamāna*), presumption (*arthāpatti*) and non-apprehension (*anupalabdhi*).

In its treatment of the problem of erroneous experience, Indian Epistemology is, of course, fully cognizant of the ordinary view that errors of perceptual experience are due to *kāraṇa-dosa*, that is, the defects of its causal conditions, whether physical, physiological or psychological. But it goes further than this view in so far as it comes to realize the need for a deeper analysis of erroneous experience with a view to the determination of the *ontological* status of its *contents*. In this regard, Indian Epistemology has presented a diversity of views, most of which consist in assigning, in one manner or another, a determinate ontological status to the content of erroneous experience. Thus it has been held that this content is unreal or non-existent or a strange mixture of existence and non-existence, reality and unreality or strictly real or existent in the sense of being purely physical or purely mental or both physical and mental. But what else can such conflict of views suggest except that it is utterly futile to make an attempt to assign a *determinate* or *definitive* ontological status to the content of erroneous experience? Hence is evident the exceptional wisdom which Śaṁkara displays in holding the view that, although erroneous experience, like veridical experience, has a content of its own, the ontological status of the content of the former, unlike that of the content of the latter, is indeterminate and indeterminable or indefinable (*anirvacanīya*).

India, as the reader will find, has presented as rich and variegated a corpus of metaphysical doctrines as the West as a whole has done. These doctrines are set in the background of appropriate theories of causation an account of which has been appended to Part II of this work. The metaphysical situation in India, however, has certain unique features, two of which deserve special mention. One of these relates to the role of Materialism in Indian metaphysics. There is, of course, no doubt that Materialism has not wielded as much influence in India as it has done in the West. Even so, it has left its indelible impress upon the metaphysical atmosphere in India in at least two noticeable ways. In the first place, all the so-called heterodox schools and two out of the six so-called orthodox schools of Indian philosophy have come under the influence of Materialism, as is evident from their rejection of the religion of God, together with their recognition, in most cases, of the independent reality of matter alongside that of spirit or soul. Secondly, it is again the influence of Materialism which is, perhaps, responsible for the wide prevalence of the non-absolutistic way of metaphysical thinking in India and the restriction of absolutism to the Vedānta and the Mahāyāna schools of Indian philosophy only. The reason for this circumstance lies in that matter conceived, as Materialism conceives it, to be the Ultimate Reality, is *divisible* and so is amenable to a pluralistic interpretation, whereas the Absolute is, by definition, recalcitrant to any interpretation of this kind.

The other unique feature of the metaphysical situation in India lies in the emergence, under the aegis of Buddhism, of the Mādhyamika doctrine of Vacuity (*Śūnya-vāda*). *Śūnya-vāda* consists in holding that Reality, in the final analysis, is mere Nothing or sheer Non-existence. And this view—although it has been seldom realized—is tantamount to the demonstration of the *reductio ad absurdum* of the metaphysics of Ultimate Reality. But this is far from suggesting the need for the elimination of metaphysics as such. The suggestion here, on the contrary, seems to be that metaphysics is in a class apart from the natural sciences and especially physics which are predominantly, if not exclusively, interested in the *theoretical* problem concerning the *reality* underlying the phenomena of Nature. And this implies that metaphysics, no matter whether it continues to be so called or be given any other name, should have human affairs as its main concern and address itself to the task of solving the fundamental practical problem or problems of human life. Hence arises the demand for an enquiry into ethics and religion which are ordinarily supposed to be especially fitted to deal with the problems of this kind. An attempt has been made to fulfil this demand in Parts III and IV of this work which are respectively concerned with the investigation of Ethics and Religion in the Indian context.

Separate enquiries into Indian ethics have so far been rare rather than common. But my investigation of this branch of Indian philosophy has been considerably facilitated by the work "The Ethics of the Hindus" by my former teacher in the University of Calcutta, the late Professor S.K. Maitra. The scope of my treatment of Indian ethics has, however, been wider than that of Professor Maitra's, on account of my addition of the ethical doctrines of the Cārvākas, the Jainas and the Bauddhas to those advocated by the Hindus, belonging to the so-called orthodox schools of Indian philosophy. In my attempt to present a more or less comprehensive account of the subject-matter of Indian ethics in this manner, it has been one of my objects to show that most of the questions relating to morality which are usually discussed in the philosophical circles in the West have received due consideration in the hands of the philosophers in India. But then, Indian ethics has certain peculiarities of its own, the most outstanding of which lies in the indication of a hitherto undetected characteristic of the role of morality in the conduct of the affairs of human life.

Morality, according to the prevailing Hindu view, consists in the performance of the *varṇāśrama-dharmas* (duties pertaining to one's social class and one's stage in life) and the *sādhāraṇa-dharmas* (common duties enjoined by the scriptures, including the Vedas). That being so, it is apt to be regarded as a means of the maintenance of the *status quo* of the way in which life is ordinarily lived, as distinguished from the way in which it *should be* lived. In other words, morality is liable to be regarded as a means and, maybe, the best possible means, of adjusting oneself to a life of bondage, instead of as the way of the achievement of spiritual freedom (*mokṣa*). This is unmistakably testified to by the doctrine of duty-less-ness upheld by the Sāṁkhya and the Advaita Vedānta of Śaṁkara as well as the widely current Indian doctrine of *ahiṁsā* (non-violence), both of which are conspicuous for their insistence on the all-importance of spiritual freedom in the life of man. The fact of the matter here is, however, that, even granted, as it should certainly be granted, that the Hindu view of morality lacks universality and finality, morality, no matter however else it be conceived, cannot maintain its supremacy, once the idea of spiritual freedom comes to prevail as it actually did in the philosophical atmosphere in India. The reason for this is that morality, while it is certainly wedded to a kind of freedom, conveys no guarantee of immunity from the *potentiality* of bondage which is essential to spiritual freedom.

The question then remains whether religion can overcome the afore-mentioned disability of morality by bringing spiritual freedom within the reach of man. It is precisely this question which constitutes the main subject-matter of discussion in the fourth and the last part of this book. In the treatment of this question with special reference to the Indian situation, I have found it necessary to distinguish between two kinds of religion—the religion of God and religion as the way to spiritual freedom or, in brief, religion as the Way as I have called it. As the reader will see, all the schools of Indian philosophy, with the solitary exception of the Materialists headed by the Cārvākas, regard spiritual freedom as the highest human value, and are of the view that man's realization of this freedom rests upon his initiation into religion as the Way.

It is of interest to note, however, that Buddhism and Jainism on the one hand and the Sāṁkhya and the Mīmāṁsā on the other, while welcoming religion as the Way, reject the religion of God, presumably on the understanding that this religion is not only inadmissible, but irrelevant to man's pursuit of spiritual freedom. And, curiously enough, the Nyāya-Vaiśeṣikas, the Yoga and the Advaita Vedānta of Śaṁkara, which admit both the religion of God and religion as the Way, attach exclusive importance to the latter and treat the former as relatively unimportant with respect to human endeavours to realize spiritual freedom. In this they are, perhaps, under the influence of the idea that the religion of God, like morality, offers no guarantee of immunity from the potentiality of bondage. In view of all this, it sounds rather strange that the various schools of spiritualistic absolutism, otherwise called the Vaiṣṇavites, should—and they actually did—bring about a combination of the religion of God and religion as the Way and regard such a syncretic religion as the way to spiritual freedom. In any case, the attempt on the part of the Vaiṣṇavites to bring the religion of God to bear upon man's endeavour to realize spiritual freedom seems to be un-Indian. In fact, India has demonstrated, through the so-called heterodox schools of philosophy of the Bauddhas and the Jainas, that atheism—of course, unaffected by Materialism—is especially favourable to religion as the Way, man's initiation into which is the *conditio sine qua non* of his achievement of spiritual freedom.

It is most unfortunate, however, that, despite their most serious preoccupation with the ideas of spiritual freedom and their earnest endeavour to discover the way to its realization, most of the schools of Indian philosophy have proved unable to save themselves from the danger of misinterpreting the concepts of highest spiritualistic and humanistic significance such as *mokṣa*, *mukti*, *kaivalya* and *nirvāṇa*. In fact, some of them, as the reader will see, have presented a travesty of the concept of spiritual freedom and have thus belied the promise with which they were informed. Even so, suggestions are available from them and especially the schools of Buddhism which, as I have tried to show towards the end of Part IV of this book, may help the determination of the way of life that is free from the potentiality of bondage and is positively characterized by spiritual freedom *par excellence.* This, as far as I can judge, points towards the conclusion that metaphysics is not dead, but is alive in the garb of religion as the Way impregnated with the humanistic idea of man's spiritual realization in and through the establishment of his essentiality to his fellows in this life and here on earth.

Delhi, January 26, 1974 N. V. BANERJEE

Prologue

Writers on Indian philosophy often start with the assumption that the different schools of philosophy in India share among themselves certain features in common. And some of them have made serious attempts to elaborate this assumption at considerable length. But in this they have, as we shall see below, proved unfaithful to the real task undertaken by them.

One of the features held to be common to all the schools of Indian philosophy is said to consist in the recognition of the *reality* of the world. But this is in a sense true, and in a sense alsois not so. Of course, the world is too palpable a fact to be dismissed altogether as *unreal*. But the reality of the world may be, and in fact has been, understood in more than one sense, and not necessarily in the sense in which commonsense usually understands it, namely, as characterized by *unconditionality* and *absoluteness*. Thus the Advaita Vedānta, for example, holds that the world, including individual selves and material objects, is only *empirically* or *pragmatically* real, but that its reality cannot stand the test of final analysis and so it is, on this account, *unreal*. Moreover, spirituality alone, instead of both spirituality and materiality, may be regarded, as the Advaita Vedānta and Yogācāra Buddhism regard it, as the criterion of reality, with the result that material objects as such, which undoubtedly form part of the world, come to be excluded from the sphere of the *real*. Contrariwise, materiality may be recognized, as the Cārvākas, for example, recognize it, as the sole criterion of reality; so that whatever is ordinarily held to be spiritual such as individual selves can have no legitimate place in the domain of reality. Furthermore, if the real be conceived, as the Advaita Vedānta, for example, conceives it, to be uncompromisingly *unitary*, then reality, regarded, as the pluralists like the Vaiśeṣikas regard it, as finally *multiple*, should be but another name for *unreality*. Conversely, reality conceived to be purely *unitary* should, in the estimation of the pluralists among the Indian philosophers, at best be a figment. It, therefore, follows that it is unwarrantable and indeed misleading to assume that the different schools of Indian philosophy are agreed among themselves in the recognition of the reality of the world.

The observations made above apply *mutatis mutandis* in the case of the admission of the reality of the self, which is said to be another common feature of all the schools of Indian philosophy. Of course, the word 'self', like the word 'world', is not only used by the Indian philosophers, but its use may be indispensable to philosophical investigations as such. But that does not necessarily imply that philosophers in general and Indian philosophers in particular have recognized the reality of the self in one and the same sense, which is meant by the assumption that this recognition is common to all the schools of Indian philosophy. As a matter of fact, while the orthodox schools of Indian philosophy regard the self as a *permanent* entity, the Buddhists hold that it is a 'stream of consciousness' and, consequently, that the self regarded as something permanent is a fiction. Moreover, while the conception of the self as *spiritual* has by and large prevailed among the philosophers in India, there has been no dearth of materialists such as the Cārvākas who dismissed the idea of spirituality altogether and regarded the so-called self as purely bodily, which, from the standpoint of the spiritualists in general, amounted to the denial of the reality of the self. Besides, the view of the self as 'One without a second' advocated by the Advaita Vedānta obviously implies that the pluralistic conception of the self such as that of the Sāṁkhya is false or illusory, being tantamount to the denial of the reality of the self. Conversely, the monistic or singularistic conception of the self would, in the estimation of the advocates of the pluralistic conception of it, amount to the denial of the reality of the self. So the assumption that the recognition of the reality of the self is common to all the schools of Indian philosophy is as arbitrary and misleading as is the assumption that the admission of the reality of the world is a common feature of all the systems of Indian philosophy.

Now, apart from the question of its origin, the doctrine of *karma*, rebirth and transmigration has indeed been an important element in the philosophical outlook in India. But it is not strictly correct to hold, as has been usually held by writers on Indian philosophy, that this doctrine is common to the various systems of philosophy in India. The reason for this, among other things, lies in the obvious fact that the materialists in India headed by the Cārvākas, who conceived the self to be identical with body, naturally proved strangers to this doctrine. Even so it is undeniable that the philosophical atmosphere in India and the Indian mind were and, perhaps, still are very much under the influence of the belief in *karma* allied with transmigration and rebirth. Nevertheless, it would in this connection be of interest to consider whether this belief was really compatible with, or formed an integral part of, the philosophical outlook of those schools of Indian philosophy which entertained it. But before we proceed to deal with this question it would be necessary to have at least a brief account of the doctrine under consideration.

According to this doctrine, actions performed by human beings, while producing immediate visible results, leave behind certain potencies which—in themselves invisible or, to use the more appropriate word, 'unseen' (*adṛṣṭa*)—serve as a causal principle in determining man's character as well as the future course of his actions. But then, it is more likely than not that the effectiveness of these potencies is not exhausted in this life or rather that this life is too short for the complete working out of the *karma* potencies which is necessarily in demand. What then is necessary for the fulfilment of this unavoidable demand is that there must be a rebirth or a succession of rebirths, a life after death or a series of such lives—the nature and quality of the rebirth and transmigration, as held by this doctrine, depending on those of the *karma* potencies concerned.

It may be of interest to mention in this connection that the doctrine of *karma*, rebirth and transmigration is obviously in a class apart from libertarianism, the traditional doctrine of free-will in as much as it regards human conduct as *determined* by *karma* potencies. But it does not admit of identification with necessitarianism either. The reason for this is that it is a form of self-determinism instead of necessitarianism in so far as it holds that the determining factors are not *extraneous* to man, but are only the potencies left behind by his own actions. Nor is the doctrine of *karma* identifiable with fatalism or the doctrine of predestination, because it has its own theory of self-determination to be brought to bear upon the solution of the problem of liberation. According to this doctrine, man, of course, has no escape from the effects of those *karma* potencies which are passing through the process of fructification (*prārabdha*), but can, in virtue of the observance of a certain discipline, neutralize those *karma* potencies that are accumulated (*sañcita*), but have not begun to produce effects, and can thereby prepare himself for the attainment of liberation. This is obviously distinct from fatalism or the doctrine of predestination, and only points to the truth that liberation is a human responsibility, of course, subject to the limits set by the *karma* potencies that are in a state of fructification.

Now, despite the merit to which, as observed above, it has a legitimate claim, the doctrine of *karma*, rebirth and transmigration really implies, and is thus vitiated by, extreme and uncompromising individualism. And, on the other hand, it is a variant of the doctrine of immortality which conveys the most inhuman idea of the indefinite prolongation of the illusory egoity of man and human bondage consequent thereupon. In view of this it would be worth while to consider the question that was raised earlier, namely, whether this doctrine is really an essential element in the philosophical outlook of the much vaunted schools of Indian philosophy which advocated it.

Since the present doctrine is a form of supernaturalism, it is, it may be assumed, inseparably bound up with polytheism as well as theism, owing to the fact that both these are basically supernaturalistic. This assumption may be said to be reinforced by the further fact that the religion of God or gods and the doctrine of immortality usually, if not invariably, go hand in hand. But the difficulty here, in the first place, is that the belief in immortality, which may be said to be essential to religion, whether polytheistic or theistic, is not in every case expressible in the form of the doctrine under consideration, but may, on the contrary, be recalcitrant to the ideas of rebirth and transmigration as is evidenced by the Semitic religions, including Judaism, Christianity and Islam. Secondly—and this is especially important in the present context—Buddhism and Jainism, the two prominent heterodox schools of Indian philosophy on the one hand, and the Sāṁkhya and the Mīmāṁsā, the two influential orthodox schools of philosophy in India on the other, while being altogether divided from religion, whether polytheistic or theistic, are staunch advocates of the doctrine of *karma*, rebirth and transmigration. Hence it follows that this doctrine stands by itself alone and has no necessary alliance with religion in any of the traditional senses.

It is, then, presumable that the belief in *karma*, rebirth and transmigration somehow came into being and entered into the mental atmosphere in India with its most predominant concern with the problem of the destiny of man. And eventually it became easy for it to establish its hold on philosophical thinking in this country, with the exception of that of the materialists and naturalists led by the Cārvākas whose conception of the self was absolutely antithetical to this belief. But this is far from suggesting that the doctrine of *karma*, rebirth and transmigration was essential to, or an unavoidable element in, the different schools of Indian thought with which it came to be associated.

It seems that this doctrine presupposes the conception of the self as characterized by *permanence* and *unchangeability* on the one hand and by gross and unalterable *individuality* on the other, although the converse of this is not true. That being so, it seems to be absolutely incompatible with the Buddhist outlook on man and his future. The reason for this, in the first place, is that, according to Buddhism, the self, like everything else in the world, is ever-changing, being in a state of ceaseless flux; so that it is in no two moments identically the same and, consequently, cannot be spoken of as subject to the law of rebirth and transmigration. But if it should still be held that rebirth and transmigration are possible in its case, then it should be held at the same time that it is reborn and, in a sense, undergoes transmigration at every moment within *this* life, without having to wait for the advent of a life after death as demanded by the present doctrine. Secondly, Buddha himself discounted the importance of *individuality* in so far as he ruled out the idea of individual liberation, and, in virtue of his insistence on the supreme value of Great Compassion (*mahākaruṇā*), conceived of the ideal of human life as the liberation of mankind as a whole.* But, curiously enough, Buddhism, in common with Hinduism, advocated the doctrine of *karma*, rebirth and transmigration, thereby demonstrating that beliefs once set on foot die hard.

As regards Jainism, although, like Buddhism, it is a prominent heterodox system of thought, it is, unlike the latter and like the orthodox schools of Indian philosophy, an advocate of the view that the self is a *permanent* substance characterized by unalterable *individuality*. That being so, the first of the two difficulties with regard to the admission of the doctrine of *karma*, rebirth and transmigration, which, as mentioned above, arises in the case of Buddhism, is indeed out of place in the case of Jainism. And this system of philosophy, whether rightly or wrongly, is equally immune from the second difficulty which has been already found, in the case of Buddhism, to stand against the admissibility of this doctrine. The reason for this is that Jainism insists on the ultimate value of the individuality of the self and so proves to be an exception to the view of human liberation as universal to mankind, instead of being merely individual.

But free from difficulty Jainism is not in the present regard. Strictly speaking, it can no more make room for the doctrine of *karma*, rebirth and transmigration than it is possible for Buddhism to do. Its fundamental difficulty is more or less the same as that of the various orthodox schools of Indian philosophy, and arises out of the view which it shares with the latter—the view, namely, that the self is *eternal* and, consequently, that birth and death are completely out of the question in its case. Since the self is neither born nor dies, and remains unaffected by the mutations of time, it would be a sheer absurdity to hold, as is held by Jainism and all the orthodox systems of Indian philosophy, that it is subject to the law of *karma*, rebirth and transmigration.

These schools of philosophy, including Jainism, however, have tried to overcome this difficulty by admitting, for reasons best known to themselves, the distinction between the self as an *ontological* entity and the same self as an *empirical* reality or, in other words, as it is in its day to day life. While the former is obviously beyond the changes of birth and death, the latter is subject to such changes. The reason for this, according to them, consists in the *association* of the self in itself or the ontological self with the body and the sense-organs and its fall from *eternity* to *temporality* consequent thereupon. As regards this, the question that immediately arises relates to the *rationale* of such association. And the answer in demand

* This is shown by the replacement of the earlier Hīnayāna conception of the ideal of life as Arhatship by the later Mahāyāna conception of it as Buddhahood.

has taken at least three different forms. According to the one which is offered by Jainism, the association in question is *accidental*. But this view is open to at least two fundamental difficulties. In the first place, the view that events or phenomena are due to accidents, of which the present answer of Jainism is an example, is liable to the fault of refusing to account for them or else, as Spinoza would say, taking "refuge in the asylum of ignorance." Secondly, in order that two things may possibly be associated or held together, there should, negatively speaking, be no barrier, and, positively speaking, there should be some kind of *affinity*, between the two. But it is precisely this condition which, on the Jaina view, cannot be fulfilled in the case of the supposed association between the self on the one hand and the body and the sense-organs on the other. The reason for this is that Jainism advocates an uncompromising dualism between the self (*jīva*) and matter (*ajīva*), including the body and the sense-organs. Hence it is evident that the admission of the doctrine of *karma*, rebirth and transmigration on the part of Jainism amounted to its blind surrender to a superstitious belief which somehow came to prevail in the mental atmosphere in India.

Now, as regards the question whether the doctrine of *karma*, rebirth and transmigration is compatible with the various orthodox ways of philosophical thinking in India, it has already been answered in a general way by observing that the conception of the self as a permanent entity, which these share with Jainism and among themselves, is obviously antithetical to this doctrine. But more remains to be said in this regard with reference to the remaining two forms of the answer to the question concerning the *rationale* of the *association* of the self with the body and the sense-organs which, in the view of all the orthodox schools of Indian philosophy, may serve to account for the birth, death, rebirth and transmigration of the self.

One of these two forms of the answer is to be met with in Nyāya-Vaiśeṣika philosophy and may be explained thus. This combined school of philosophy, it may be of interest to note in the beginning, is nearer commonsense than the others belonging to the orthodox circle of Indian philosophy. Accordingly, it admits the Infinite Self on the one hand and a plurality of finite selves on the other, without apprehending, as has been apprehended by the Sāṁkhya and the Advaita Vedānta, the difficulty that may be due to this twofold admission. Nor does it suspect the possibility of any difficulty with regard to the relation between the finite self with its body and sense-organs, despite its conception of the self and matter as disparate from each other. In fact, the Nyāya-Vaiśeṣikas conceive the self as endowed with numerous qualities, including such material or near-material qualities as magnitude.* Hence it is evident that it is virtually divided from the dualism of self and matter, including the body and the sense-organs, which constitutes an essential feature of Jainism and the Sāṁkhya. This is precisely the reason why the *association* of the self with its body and its sense-organs has not, as a matter of fact, posed any problem to this school of philosophy but has been accepted by it as an ultimate datum.

Even so the Nyāya–Vaiśeṣikas are not free from difficulty in respect of their admission of the doctrine of *karma*, rebirth and transmigration. The association of the self with the body and the sense-organs, in their view, is inoffensively natural, and not undesirably accidental as held by Jainism, nor *reprehensible*, being, as in the view of the Sāṁkhya and the Advaita Vedānta, the offspring of *avidyā* (ignorance) or *aviveka* (non-discrimination). That being so, the finite self cannot be conceived, as is conceived by the Nyāya-Vaiśeṣikas, to be in a state of bondage on account of its association with its body and its sense-organs and, consequently, to be subject to the law of *karma*, rebirth and transmigration. And, what is more, there can arise no question of the dissociation of the self from its body and its sense-organs which, according to these philosophers, is essential to its freedom from bondage or liberation. The conclusion which inevitably follows, then, is that the doctrine under consideration is incompatible with the Nyāya-Vaiśeṣika way of thinking.

It still remains for us to consider another view of the *rationale* of the *association* of the self with the body and the sense-organs and its bearing upon the admissibility of the doctrine of *karma*, rebirth and transmigration. This view is most prominently advocated by the Sāṁkhya-Yoga on the one hand and by the Advaita Vedānta on the other. According to the former, this association, as indicated above, is the outcome of the failure on the part of the self to discriminate between itself and its physical or physiological adjuncts (*upādhi*), resulting in its illusory apprehension of itself as inseparably bound up with the latter. But this, in the first place, gives rise to the question concerning the reason for this failure on the part of the self—indeed the question which the Sāṁkhya-Yoga, not to speak of trying to answer it, as it is incumbent upon it to do, does not even take cognizance of. Secondly—and this is especially important—it stands self-stultified for the simple reason that this combined school of philosophy advocates a kind of dualism of self and matter far more radical than that of Jainism and even of Descartes, and, consequently, that it cannot make room for the possibility of the association of the self with the body and the sense-organs,

* It is worthwhile to note in this connection that Jainism, despite its admission of the dualism of the self and matter conceives the self to be co-extensive with the body occupied by it (svadehaparimāna) even as light of a lamp is co-extensive with the room in which it exists.

even regarded as an illusory phenomenon. And this cuts the ground from under the feet of the Sāṁkhya-Yoga view of human bondage and thereby shows its admission of the doctrine of *karma*, rebirth and transmigration to be utterly baseless.

Now as regards the Advaita Vedānta, it falls back upon the concept of *avidyā*, which, according to it, is the individual's share of the Cosmic Ignorance called *Māyā*, and holds that it is under the misleading influence of *avidyā* that the self fails to recognize its true nature consisting in its identity with the Absolute Self, Brahman, and strays into the erroneous apprehension of itself as bound up with the body and sense-organs. This Advaita explanation of human bondage, which may be said to provide the *raison d'etre* of the admission of the doctrine of *karma*, rebirth and transmigration on the part of this school of Indian philosophy, is obviously similar to that of the Sāṁkhya-Yoga, but with this important difference that, whereas, in the view of the Sāṁkhya-Yoga, human bondage is the individual's fall from his spiritual insularity or isolation (*kaivalya*), in the view of the Advaita Vedānta, the fall is from his identity with the Absolute Self or Brahman.

However that may be, the Advaita Vedānta, not being an advocate of any kind of dualism, has an advantage over the Sāṁkhya-Yoga in so far as it is free from that difficulty about the explanation of the self's association with the body and the sense-organs, to which the latter is open on account of its admission of the dualism of self and matter. Nevertheless, it is as incumbent upon this school of philosophy to account for the origin of *avidyā* as it is upon the Sāṁkhya-Yoga to do the same in the case of *aviveka* (non-discrimination). In this regard, it may be said that, whereas the Sāṁkhya-Yoga, as seen above, shirks its present duty, the Advaita Vedānta performs its own by holding that *avidyā* is but the individual's share of the Cosmic Ignorance, *Māyā*. But this is by no means preferable to the shirking of the duty concerned in as much as it really does not offer an answer to the question of the origin of *avidyā*, but puts off that question a step further back, by leaving unanswered the question about the origin of *Māyā*. It may therefore be concluded that the Advaita Vedānta has no justification for the admission of the doctrine of *karma*, rebirth and transmigration in as much as it is unable to account for human bondage which is held to provide whatever reason that there may be with regard to the admissibility of this doctrine.

In view of the prolonged discussion we have already had, it would, perhaps, not be necessary to make an attempt to show that the doctrine of *karma*, rebirth and transmigration cannot enter into a harmonious relation with the ways of thinking represented by the remaining orthodox schools of Indian philosophy, considered individually and separately. What, therefore, remains to be done is to reiterate the consideration which is responsible for the difficulty with regard to the admission of this doctrine on the part of the orthodox schools of Indian philosophy, together with Jainism. This consideration is none other than that which relates to the conception of the self as a permanent entity equally advocated by all these systems of philosophy. This should not, however, be construed as implying that the way to the avoidance of the doctrine lies in the replacement of the conception of the self as permanent by the conception of it as subject to ceaseless change. For, as the example of Buddhism shows, the latter conception of the self, even granted that it is incompatible with the doctrine of *karma*, rebirth and transmigration, cannot be prevented from carrying this doctrine in its trail. Should it then be held that the way in question is to be found in the most radically changed conception of the self as entertained by the Cārvākas, that is, the materialistic conception of it as identical with body and sense-organs? But this question needs to be answered in the negative, and yet it must be observed that it is the Cārvākas and their conféres in India who were most conspicuous for their emphasizing the need for wholesome reform in the philosophical sphere in this country, but that the dismissal of the doctrine of *karma*, rebirth and transmigration on the basis of the materialistic conception of the self is tantamount to the achievement of a goal at a heavy sacrifice—the sacrifice of the peculiarity of the self as such. The reform in demand may then be brought about, among other things, by means of steering clear of the Scylla of this doctrine and the Charybdis of the materialistic conception of the self and thereupon viewing afresh the nature of human bondage as well as human liberation.

The above reference to the concept of liberation brings in another aspect of the assumption which has more often than not influenced the writers on Indian philosophy. The present aspect of the assumption consists in stating that the admission of this concept constitutes a common feature of the various schools of philosophy in India—of course, with the exception of the materialists, including the Cārvākas, who, consistently with their conception of the self as identical with body and sense-organs, dismiss the very idea of liberation as well as human bondage. But the assumption in this case, strictly speaking, is as arbitrary and misleading as we have already found it to be in the case of the admission of the reality of the world or of the self on the part of the various schools of Indian philosophy. The reason for this, as we shall see below, lies in that they understand liberation in different senses, and not in one and the same sense as they should have done in order that they could be said to share this concept among themselves in common.

Now since it is the opposite of human bondage, liberation should be regarded—and the various schools of Indian philosophy also do regard it, as consisting in the negation of the latter. In fact, they hold in common that human bondage primarily consists in the illusory appearance of the self as what it really is not, together with its consequences in the cognitive, affective and active life of the individual, although they differ widely from one another in their view of what the self really is. One important element which is common to their view of the self in bondage consists in holding, however, that it is falsely associated or even identified with its body and sense-organs or rather with its psycho-physical adjuncts.* Since this association or identification is due to endure throughout the individual's life on earth, liberation as the negation of human bondage should naturally be *videha* (disembodied) or, in other words, should take place after death—of course, not automatically, but as a result of the fulfilment of certain disciplinary conditions which are, however, conceived differently by different schools of Indian philosophy. As a matter of fact, the idea of *videha-mukti* came to wield overwhelming influence in the philosophical atmosphere in India, with the result that some of the leading philosophers such as Bhāskara, the founder of the *Bhedābheda* school of the Vedānta, went so far as to affirm that *jīvan-mukti* is absolutely out of the question, and that liberation is, of necessity, consequent upon the termination of life on earth, of course, subject to the the employment of an appropriate means to this end.

But, strangely enough, some of the systems of Indian philosophy, including the Sāṁkhya and the Advaita Vedānta in particular, sought to overcome the sternness and rigour of the view of liberation as *videha* (disembodied) and accordingly admitted the possibility of *jīvan-mukti* at the sacrifice of the prevalent view of human bondage to which they were committed in common with the other systems of philosophy. This shows that there is hardly any unanimity among the different schools of philosophy in India about the meaning of liberation. That the admission of the concept of liberation cannot, then, really be regarded as constituting a common feature of the various trends of Indian philosophy may also be shown by means of an enquiry into the views which have been held regarding the nature of liberation, the peculiarity of the experience in the state of liberation and the means to the achievement of this goal.

Now since human bondage, as previously observed, lies in the false appearance of the self as what it really is not, liberation, as the Indian philosophers in general hold, would consist, not in the self's *becoming* something other than what it really is, but in the

* This is obviously based upon the dualism of spirit and matter consciously advocated by some of the schools of Indian philosophy and unconsciously presupposed by the rest.

termination of its false appearance, together with its return to its pristine purity or, in other words, its coming into its own. But then, the question, in fact, the most important question, which arises in this connection concerns the real nature of the self, the fall from which on its part results in its bondage and its return to which constitutes its liberation. And it is this question which has been differently answered by different schools of Indian philosophy and accordingly the nature of liberation has come to be conceived differently by them.

According to the Vedānta which, in all its forms, admits such a thing as the Infinite and Absolute Reality called Brahman, the (individual) self is real, not in isolation from, but as held in an inseparable relation with, the former. But this relation is conceived by the different forms of the Vedānta in different ways, two of which respectively represented by the Advaita and the Viśiṣṭādvaita schools of this brand of philosophy may be considered for our present purpose. In the view of the Advaita Vedānta headed by Śaṁkara, the individual self's relation with Brahman is that of its *absolute* identity with, and the consequent non-difference and even indistinguishability from, the latter. Accordingly, this school of philosophy comes to conceive liberation as consisting in the elimination of the false appearance of the self as a separate or independent existent and the restoration of its absolute identity with Brahman in the manner of its total absorption in the latter.

But the Vaiṣnava schools of the Vedānta, including the Viśiṣṭādvaita of Rāmānuja in particular, invested with a theistic outlook as they are, recoil from the Advaita conception of the individual self as absolutely identical with Brahman and insist on the recognition of an *eternal distinction* between the two. This, of course, points to an important difference of the Viśiṣṭādvaita conception of the status of the individual self *vis-a-vis* Brahman from that of the Advaita Vedānta. It is therefore expected that the difference between their views of the nature of liberation should be equally pronounced. But, strangely enough, Rāmānuja holds that liberation is that state in the individual in which he transcends empirical life as well as the world of space and time, with the result that his sense of separateness from Brahman disappears and he becomes absorbed in the eternal bliss of union with Brahman regarded as the Deity. Judged from the point of view of the ultimate destiny of the individual, Rāmānuja's view of human liberation, thus, is almost indistinguishable from that of Śaṁkara, except in that it, unlike the latter, is theistic in outlook and includes the conception of liberation as exclusively *videha*. In any case, it seems that the Vedānta, whether Advaita or Viśiṣṭādvaita, on account of its admission of Brahman regarded as the Absolute Reality, hardly has any option but to hold that the ultimate destiny of the individual lies in his annihilation, no matter whether this view is held boldly or half-heartedly. For what else can his absorption in, or union with, the Absolute, that is, Brahman mean except the final end of his personality ? And this points to the most unexpected and indeed queer phenomenon, namely, the meeting of the grossest materialism of the Cārvākas and the most highly developed spiritualism of the Vedānta.

It is, therefore, no wonder that there should arise the need for a corrective of the extravagance of Cārvāka materialism on the one hand and of the Vedāntist spiritualism on the other; so that the destiny of man could be rescued from the dismal prospect envisaged by both of them, no matter whether wittingly or unwittingly. And, as a matter of fact, awareness of the need was aroused in India and attempts were also made to fulfil the need in different ways. One of the ways was rather radical in nature in so far as it was based on the realization that the misunderstanding of human destiny is ultimately due to the admission of such a thing as a supernatural and superhuman being conceived to be absolute and called Brahman or God, and that its removal would depend upon the recognition of nature and man as supreme in their respective spheres and the consequent dismissal of whatever is conceivable as being above man and nature. This brings us to the consideration of the view of liberation held by the Sāṁkhya and Buddhism, both of which are conspicuous for their opposition to the religion of God.

As regards the Sāṁkhya, it not only refrains from admitting anything regarded as being above man or nature or both, but as previously observed, goes further in advocating the most uncompromising dualism by means of treating man and nature as being absolutely disparate from each other, lest the possibility of their being regarded as two distinct aspects of one and the same Ultimate Reality should remain open. It is against this background that the Sāṁkhya comes to conceive the self *(puruṣa)* to be characterized by *pure* consciousness as opposed to the absolute unconsciousness of nature *(prakṛti)* and to be established in a state of isolation from everything else and thus be further characterized by complete *insularity*. While it is thus essentially insular, the self, in the view of the Sāṁkhya, is somehow seized with *avidyā (ignorance)* and, as a result, is thrown into intimate contact with nature and presents itself in the false garb of a *subject of experience (bhoktā)* as well as an *agent (kartā)*. Thus does the self enter into the state of bondage. The self in bondage, according to the Sāṁkhya, is then the self that has fallen from its inherent state of insularity so as to be made into the illusory image of itself as a *bhoktā* and a *kartā*, neither of which it really is. But it is far from the Sāṁkhya and, for that matter, any other school of Indian philosophy which admits such a thing as human bondage, to hold that this state of human life is ever-lasting or irremediable. On the contrary, all these schools of philosophy, including the Sāṁkhya, are definitely of the optimistic view that human bondage is terminable so as to yield place to the culmination of human destiny in liberation. And as far as the Sāṁkhya in particular is concerned, in view of its own conception of human bondage, it holds that liberation of the self consists in its return to its pristine purity characterized by pure consciousness, as distinguished from empirical consciousness or *experience* as well as by complete insularity. But this calls for the following critical observations.

In the first place, the Sāṁkhya view of human bondage is absolutely untenable on account of its being inconsistent with the dualistic standpoint initially adopted by this school of philosophy. For, as previously seen, the possibility of the self's being associated with *prakṛti* in general and body and sense-organs in particular, no matter whether veridically or illusorily, is precluded by the dualism of *puruṣa* and *prakṛti*. Strictly speaking, it is not the association of *puruṣa* with *prakṛti*, but the dualistic relation between them postulated by the Sāṁkhya which is really illusory. So what is regarded by this school of philosophy as human bondage is really one of the normal and by no means undesirable relations in which the self may be held. Secondly, the Sāṁkhya conception of human liberation is as objectionable as its conception of human bondage is thus found to be. The reason for this is that pure consciousness, as distinguished from empirical consciousness, that is, consciousness *of* this or that which the Sāṁkhya regards as the essence of the self, seems to be an abstraction and so is merely conceivable, but cannot have an *existential status*, either as a quality or as the essence of any kind of existence. Moreover—and this is especially important—insularity *(kaivalya)*, which the Sāṁkhya regards as the characteristic peculiarity of the self in itself or the liberated self, is, strictly speaking, another name for the self's *egoity* and as such betrays the self's bondage, instead of constituting its liberated state. Thus the Sāṁkhya not only differs from all forms of the Vedānta in its conception of liberation, but like the latter, views liberation in a wrong perspective. It remains to be noted, however, that the requirement of the proper understanding of the nature of liberation is to steer clear of the absorption of the self in the Absolute as envisaged by the Vedānta as well as the development of the self into egoity as suggested by the Sāṁkhya. This brings us to the consideration of the Buddhist view of liberation as *Nirvāṇa*.

As has been already mentioned, Buddhism, like the Sāṁkhya, is opposed to the religion of God. It, therefore, easily finds itself in a position to avoid the misunderstanding of the nature of liberation in which the Vedānta, whether Advaita or theistic, is inextricably involved. And it is conspicuous for its special endeavour to get rid of the kind of misunderstanding which, as seen above, is consequent upon the Sāṁkhya view of the self as essentially insular. The result of this endeavour is the emergence of the view of the nature of liberation in the form of the doctrine of *Nirvāṇa* which is unique in the history of Indian philosophy.

Now, since no clear and unambiguous statement of the doctrine of *Nirvāṇa* is available in the canonical texts which are said to contain the teachings of Buddha, it is difficult to ascertain, with any measure of certainty, what he exactly meant by *Nirvāṇa* in the sense of human liberation. But a clue to the discovery of his real meaning in this regard seems to be provided by his doctrine of 'no-self' (*anāttā*). As far as I can judge, this doctrine is not intended to convey an *empirical* statement about the self, but a *valuational* assessment of the empirical fact of the self's assertion of its *individuality* or egoity. What is meant thereby is that, although the self in its ordinary day to day life is, as a matter of fact, presented to itself as well as to others as an insular being characterized by individuality or egoity, it *should* rise above its ordinary way of life by means of the elimination of its accustomed individuality, with a view to the fulfilment of its ultimate destiny. Judged in this light, *Nirvāṇa* is not the extinction or annihilation of the self itself as it is sometimes construed to be with reference to casual statements in the Pali Canon. It really conveys the most urgent demand for a complete change of the way of life as lived under the overmastering influence of the biological urges. It is, of course, predominantly negative. But what else should it be when the fact is that there is no way to the achievement of the final goal of human life except through the undoing of the ill-effects carried by the ordinary way of life in its trail, which may be summed up in human suffering ?

In fact, the starting-point of Buddha's treatment of the problem of human liberation lies in his recognition of human suffering as a fact and, moreover, as an evil which is only fit to be put an end to. The removal of human suffering, then, is, in his view, the ultimate goal of life, irrespective of whatever it may positively be. Be it noted, however, that it was far from Buddha to deny that the goal of life has a positive content. But he seems to have felt that the question of its positive content, like the question concerning the existence of God, is interminably controversial and so is in need of being avoided in order that the question of the removal of human suffering, which is not controversial and really is in urgent need of decision, may not come to be ignored. That being so, it would be as arbitrary to construe Buddha's view of *Nirvāṇa* as the view of it as an eternal state of happiness or bliss as it would be to suggest that *Nirvāṇa*, in his view, is the annihilation of the self itself.

But before beginning to consider the question as to how human suffering can be removed altogether, one should recognize, as Buddha himself seems to have recognized, the fact that some of human suffering is not due to anything that man does or does not do and as such is beyond human control. So the question of the removal of this kind of suffering does not come within our purview. But there are various kinds of suffering for which man himself is responsible, and it is precisely these which are amenable to removal. But in order that the question of their removal may be satisfactorily decided, it is necessary, as a first step, to enquire into their cause or causes. It is precisely this enquiry which Buddha undertook as a testimony to the fact that he stood out as the most scientifically-minded among the ancients. The kinds of human suffering for which man himself or mankind itself is responsible are, however, too many to be mentioned, and their causes at first sight seem to be too many and various to be taken account of. But these causes, however various they may be, are, according to Buddha, ultimately reducible to, or deducible from, just a few which reside in man's mind, instead of in his physical environment.

As regards the causes in question, they seem to be none else than the effects produced in the human mind by man's biological urges or vital drives purely on their own account. These effects, according to Buddha, are *desires* and especially those which know no satisfaction, but go on producing further desires in an unending succession. And it is from such desires that there arise the passions, called 'flames' in the Pali Canon, such as greed, hate, anger and delusion and also the impurities of the mind (*āsavas*), comprising sensuality, the will-to-be-born and ignorance. It is these psychological phenomena and others of their kind produced by man's vital drives which, in the view of Buddhism, constitute his individuality, that is, egoity. Liberation conceived to be *Nirvāṇa* is, then, but another name for the elimination of these psychological phenomena, together with their net result in the form of egoity, which, as Buddhism rightly holds, is at the root of all kinds of human suffering for which mankind itself is responsible. But this gives rise to two important questions: (a) What are the means of the elimination of egoity or the achievement of *Nirvāṇa* ? (b) Is the realization of Nirvāṇa a sure guarantee for the elimination of the *insularity* of the individual which, as previously mentioned, is the last vestige of human bondage ?

As regards the former of these two questions, we shall consider it in due course. And as far as the latter is concerned, it may be immediately observed that mere elimination of the egoity of an individual may at best entitle him to *arhatship*, and that the *arhat's* liberation or freedom which, according to Early Buddhism, is of the highest order, is, after all, a sort of self-sufficiency, one's sufficiency unto oneself and, as such, is not the denial, but, on the contrary, a way of the affirmation, of one's insularity. That being so, the Early Buddhist conception of liberation is not free from the difficulty which we have already noticed in the case of the Sāṁkhya conception of it. This was eventually realized by the Buddhists themselves and, as a result, the highest ideal of human life signifying man's perfect liberation came to be conceived by the Mahāyāna school as *Buddhahood*—indeed the ideal which amounts to the admission of the breakdown of all barriers between the individual and his fellows and the consequent liberation of all and not merely of this individual or that individual, in the manner of their realization of their *essentiality* to one another. This view of liberation as subject to the all or none principle is obviously such that, had it been translated into practice, heaven would have descended on earth. But not to speak of its being turned to account, it has not so far been worked out in detail nor even has its importance been realized in the philosophical world.

We have so far considered the chief Indian views of the nature of liberation and noticed their differences. We have also found how they fall short of a proper understanding of the ultimate destiny of man. Nevertheless, as has been indicated above, it was singularly creditable on the part of Buddhism to have finally arrived at an idea of liberation which seems to be the closest approximation to perfection. But then, this idea was in need of being worked out in detail and of being put to practice with a view to the safety of the future of mankind. Such is the misfortune of the history of the human race, however, that this twofold need has remained unfulfilled till this day. This is enough to indicate that the remaining Indian views of the nature of liberation can hardly have any advantage over those which we have already brought under review.

As regards the Jaina view of the nature of liberation, the understanding of it is dependent on the consideration of the view of human bondage held by this heterodox school of Indian philosophy. The bondage of the human individual, according to Jainism, is due to the penetration of *karma*-matter into the inmost recesses of his very existence. Liberation should, then, as this system of philosophy comes to hold, consist in a gradual process of the individual's purging itself of the impurities produced in it by *karma*-matter. The means to this end is *tapas* (penance) and the end, as is further held, finally consists in *dravyamokṣa* (objective liberation), as distinguished from *bhāvamokṣa* (subjective liberation), the state in which the individual is said to be completely self-determined in the sense of being free from relations to other selves and the material world. Liberation thus conceived, strangely enough, is regarded by Jainism as *divine*, while the fact remains that its view of liberation proceeds from the most crude conception of human bondage, and that it lays itself open to the same difficulty which, as we have previously seen, vitiates the Sāṁkhya view of liberation on account of its understanding of the liberated self as essentially insular.

The Nyāya-Vaiśeṣika system of philosophy, like other orthodox schools of Indian philosophy, holds that human bondage is the offspring of the self's association with body and sense-organs. And holding further that this association is the invariable source of pain, this system of philosophy comes to regard pain as the essential feature of human bondage. That being so, liberation, in the view of the Nyāya-Vaiśeṣikas, should, and, in fact, does consist in the elimination of pain and be realizable in the event of the dissolution of the self's association with body and sense-organs, or, in other words, in the event of death. Having thus arrived at the view of liberation as *videha* (disembodied), this combined school of philosophy takes into account all the implications of this view and employs them in its final understanding of liberation. Thus the liberated self comes to be conceived by it to be not only denuded of pain, but also of other kinds of mental phenomena that are due to the self's association with body and sense-organs, namely, cognition, pleasure, desire, aversion, volition, merit, demerit, impression, etc.* The state of the self's liberation understood in this way, however, seems to be a complete vacuum, not far removed from its annihilation. Hence is evident the affinity, detectable in a deeper analysis, which subsists between the Nyāya-Vaiśeṣika and the Vedānta on the common ground of the understanding of liberation as annihilation.

It is important to notice, however, that the Mīmāṁsā (or rather Pūrva-Mīmāṁsā) school of philosophy is, from our present point of view, an exception to the orthodox schools of Indian philosophy as well as the heterodox schools of Buddhism and Jainism. This is due to the fact that it emphasizes the all-importance of *dharma* (performance of rituals enjoined by the Vedas) and its effect called *abhyudaya* (prosperity), as distinguished from *apavarga* (*mokṣa* or liberation). This indifference on the part of Mīmāṁsā to the ideal of liberation is evident from the fact that its outstanding leaders such as Jaiminī, Sabarasvāmin and even Prabhākara have not spoken of such a thing as *mokṣa* (liberation). But this indifference could not last long. The idea of the completion of the Mīmāṁsā system of thought as a parallel to other systems of Indian thought became dominant in course of time, and a section of influential thinkers belonging to the Mīmāṁsā school such as Kumārila, Sālikanātha and their foll-

* A few Naiyāyikas, for example, the Saiva Naiyāyika Bhāsarvajña, hold that liberation consists in the experience of eternal happiness, on the understanding that, although knowledge is the cause of happiness, the absence of knowledge in the state of liberation does not affect the existence of eternal happiness in that state. But outstanding Naiyāyikas such as Vātsyāyana and Udayana have argued at length to show that liberation is incompatible with eternal happiness.

owers such as Pārthasārathi Miśra undertook the enquiry into the nature of liberation as a part of their philosophical investigations.

It is, however, Kumārila who initiated this enquiry by emphasizing that liberation cannot be a temporary phenomenon, but must be an *eternal* state in order to be worth the name. But then, it can be eternal provided that it is not *positive*, but purely *negative*. For, as Kumārila argued, if, for example, it be held, positively, to consist in the enjoyment of happiness, it would be associated with heaven, and, consequently, be perishable for the simple reason that heaven, as the scriptural authority would have it, is itself perishable. Having thus arrived at the view of liberation as a pure negation, Kumārila proceeds further to deduce the implications of this view. In the first place, there must be complete destruction of merits and demerits followed by the destruction of the present body and the complete cessation of rebirth and transmigration. Secondly, this being given, it inevitably follows that liberation as a state of the self is eternally emptied of all kinds of empirical experience such as cognition, pleasure, pain, desire, aversion, etc. Thus Kumārila is in agreement with other orthodox schools of Indian philosophy, with the exception of the Sāṁkhya and the Advaita Vedānta, in holding the view that liberation is exclusively *videha* (disembodied). On the other hand, he, like the Nyāya-Vaiśeṣikas, is of the view that the transcendental state of liberation is a complete vacuum, and so he, like the latter, has no means of distinguishing the self's liberation from its annihilation.

Our next task is to consider the different views held by the different schools of Indian philosophy with regard to the nature of the experience which is peculiar to the state of liberation. These views may, for the sake of brevity, be brought under two main heads : one of these is based on the understanding that experience as such is necessarily *empirical*, and consists in stating that the state of liberation, being obviously transcendental and not empirical, is empty of all experience and is a mere state of *being* which is *a fortiori* one of non-being. The most prominent representatives of this view, as has been already evident, are the Nyāya-Vaiśeṣika and Mīmāṁsā schools of philosophy. As regards the other view, it is not only not opposed to the possibility of such a thing as transcendental experience or rather consciousness, but, on the contrary, admits its possibility and, what is more, regards it as the essence of the state of liberation, on the understanding that it is consciousness *par excellence*. This view has been advocated, among others, by the Sāṁkhya and Vedānta schools of philosophy. According to the Sāṁkhya, the consciousness which is peculiar to the state of liberation is, negatively speaking, in a class apart from empirical experience of all kinds, namely, cognitive, affective and conative. In other words, it is devoid of pleasure, pain, desire, anger, hate, etc.

as well as of the experience of being a *knower (bhoktā)* and an *agent (kartā)*. Positively speaking, it is pure consciousness otherwise called *knowledge (jñāna)* as opposed to *ajñāna* or *avidyā* (ignorance). Thus the Sāṁkhya holds a purely intellectualist view of the state of liberation and accordingly comes to conceive the liberated self as at best a *self-illumined* existent, besides being self-sufficient or insular.

The conception of the liberated self as essentially pure consciousness or self-illumined is not, however, peculiar to the Sāṁkhya, but is equally shared by the Vedānta. But then, according to the Vedānta, the self regarded as a self-sufficient or insular entity, far from being self-illuminated, is steeped in darkness, that is to say, is held in a state of bondage. So the self, in the view of the Vedānta schools of philosophy, is self-illuminated in so far as it is conscious of itself as being held in an inseparable relation with the Brahman in one way or another.* But this is not the only difference between the Sāṁkhya and the Vedānta in the present context. Another difference—indeed an important one—between the two lies in that, whereas the Sāṁkhya entertains a purely intellectualist or, let us say, theoretical view of transcendental consciousness regarded as essential to the state of liberation, the Vedānta views it from the theoretical as well as the practical standpoint, and accordingly conceives it to be of the nature of self-illumination (*ṣvayaṁprakāsa*) and also to be impregnated with bliss (*ānada*). The present Vedānta view, it may be of interest to note, conveys the idea of the realization of both theoretical and practical demands of human life in the state of liberation.

Besides the two mutually opposed views with regard to the possibility of transcendental consciousness which we have considered above, there is another which is peculiar in that it, in a sense, agrees with, and also in a sense, differs from, those of the Nyāya-Vaiśeṣikas and the Jainas on the one hand and those of the Sāṁkhya and the Vedānta on the other. This view is none else than that of Buddhism. Buddhism agrees with all the above-mentioned systems of philosophy in holding that the state of liberation is necessarily devoid of empirical experience, whether cognitive, affective or conative. But it differs from the Nyāya-Vaiśeṣikas and the Jainas and agrees with the Sāṁkhya and the Vedānta in so far as it is of the view that there is such a thing as transcendental consciousness, and that its proper place is in the state of liberation. Even so it differs from both the Sāṁkhya and the Vedānta in a fundamental respect. For the Sāṁkhya and the Vedānta agree with each other in holding that the consciousness in question is *determinate*, being merely self-illumination or pure consciousness in the view of the former and

---

* This relation is conceived to be identity or substance-attribute or unity-in-difference as the case may be.

both pure consciousness and bliss in the view of the latter.

Buddhism, on the other hand, affirms that transcendental consciousness, that is, the consciousness which may be said to belong to the state of liberation, is, from the nature of the case, *indeterminate* and *indeterminable* and accordingly declares its exact nature to be *inconceivable.* And in this Buddhism indeed displays unique and unparalleled philosophical insight. For, pure consciousness which both the Sāṁkhya and the Vedānta regard as essential to the state of liberation is at best empirical cognition abstracted from its objective side. And bliss, which in the view of the Vedānta, is equally essential to this state, seems to be, after all, the empirical mental phenomenon of *happiness* in abstraction from its unavoidable perishability. Thus both the Sāṁkhya and the Vedānta may be said to have failed to conceive liberation to be disparate from human bondage as it should have been conceived to be. And it is this failure on the part of the two most highly developed orthodox schools of Indian philosophy which Buddhism has tried to overcome by eschewing both direct and indirect reference to *experience* or empirical consciousness in its attempt to understand the nature of the consciousness which is peculiar to the state of liberation. Thus has Buddhism conformed to a maxim of inestimable philosophical significance, namely, that it is wiser to leave a question undecided than to decide it at any cost.

Now, as regards the question concerning the means to the attainment of liberation or *sādhana* as it is called in the philosophical and religious literature in India, it is naturally of common concern to all those schools of Indian philosophy which admit the concept of liberation. But this is far from suggesting that all these schools are agreed among themselves about the nature of *sādhana.* On the contrary, as we shall see below, they differ among themselves in their understanding of *sādhana* as widely as they have already been found to do in their understanding of liberation. The various views regarding the nature of *sādhana* held by the different schools of Indian philosophy may be brought under four distinct heads according as *jñāna* (knowledge) or *viveka* (discrimination) as opposed to *ajñāna* or *aviveka* (ignorance or lack of discrimination), or *bhakti* (devotion) or *karma* (prescribed duties) or the unity of all these three together is regarded as the primary means to the realization of liberation. The first among these views is advocated especially by the Nyāya-Vaiśeṣika, the Sāṁkhya and the Advaita Vedānta systems of philosophy. As previously mentioned, bondage, in the view of the Nyāya-Vaiśeṣika, is due to the false association or identification of the self with body and sense-organs. That being so, the means to the realization of liberation should naturally be that which can bring this falsity to an end. In this connection this combined school of philosophy recognizes the importance of the practice of Yoga, together with certain austerities, the performance of obligatory *(nitya)* as well as occasional (*naimittika*) duties, abstension from sin and the like. But it regards these as mere aids to *tatvajñāna* (true knowledge of the self) which, in its view, is alone competent to put an end to the self's illusory apprehension of itself as identical with body and sense-organs and thereby bring about its liberation. Thus does the Nyāya-Vaiśeṣika school of philosophy advocate a predominantly intellectualist view of the means to the attainment of liberation.

As regards the Sāṁkhya, it, like the Nyāya-Vaiśeṣika, holds that human bondage is due to the false identification of the self *(puruṣa)* with matter *(prakṛti)*, including body and sense-organs, although, as previously mentioned, the possibility of such identification is precluded by the doctrine of dualism of *puruṣa* and *prakṛti* advocated by this school of philosophy. The question then arises as to how the false identification in question may be eliminated in order that liberation may be achieved. In its answer to this question, the Sāṁkhya, like the Nyāya-Vaiśeṣika, recognizes the importance of a number of measures, including the practice of Yoga. But then, these measures, however useful and important in themselves they may be, cannot, according to this system of philosophy, put an end to the various kinds of suffering (*duḥkha*) which, as the Sāṁkhya philosophy further holds, are the invariable concomitants of human bondage and the elimination of which constitutes liberation. These are, in the view of the Sāṁkhya, only ancillary to the primary and indeed the specific means to the realization of liberation. And as regards the means in question, this school of philosophy, like the Nyāya-Vaiśeṣika, holds a predominantly intellectualist view about it by stating that it is none else than discrimination (*vivekakhyāti*), that is, intuitive apprehension, as distinguished from discursive knowledge, of the distinction of the self (*puruṣa*) from matter (*prakṛti*).

Now, as far as the Advaita view of the means to the attainment of liberation is concerned, it is prominently represented by Śaṁkara, the most outstanding protagonist of this school of philosophy. Like most philosophers belonging to the orthodox schools of Indian philosophy, Śaṁkara holds that human bondage consists in the illusory identification of the self (*ātman)* with the not-self resulting from *avidyā* (ignorance), and that the demand of liberation, from the nature of the case, should be the elimination of *avidyā* together with the false identification consequent thereupon. The fulfilment of this demand, in the view of Śaṁkara as in the view of the Nyāya-Vaiśeṣikas and the Sāṁkhya, is possible through the means of *vidyā* or *jñāna* (knowledge) as opposed to *avidyā* or *ajñāna* (ignorance). What then is the nature of this *vidyā* or *jñāna*? As regards this question, Śaṁkara's answer to it agrees with, and yet differs rather fundamentally from, those of the Nyāya-Vaiśeṣikas and the

Sāṁkhya. There is agreement among all these three in so far as they hold in common that *ātmajñāna* is the primary means to the attainment of liberation. But their difference relates to the nature of the self, the knowledge of which is held to be the means in question. Both the Nyāya-Vaiśeṣikas and the Sāṁkhya understand the self in an individualistic or particularistic sense, that is, the sense in which it is a *jīva* as conceived by the Advaita Vedānta, which is an illusory appearance of Brahman or the *Ātman* properly so called. That being so, that which, in the view of the Nyāya-Vaiśeṣika and the Sāṁkhya, is *ātmajñāna* and, consequently, the means to the realization of liberation, is, according to the Advaita Vedānta, not only not that, but is the very basis of human bondage.

The fact, however, is that the Advaita Vedānta understands *ātmajñāna* with reference to Brahman regarded as the veritable *Ātman* and accordingly holds that it is none else than the direct and immediate apprehension of all beings in Brahman and of Brahman in all beings. What is of special importance in the case of *ātmajñāna* as conceived by this school of philosophy is, then, that the individual loses its individuality and is absorbed in the Absolute that is Brahman. In its attempt to steer clear of such misunderstandings of the means to liberation as those of the Nyāya-Vaiśeṣika and the Sāṁkhya, the Advaita Vedānta thus comes to misconstrue the ultimate destiny of the human individual as his annihilation. And the ground is prepared for this dismal future of man in terms of the code of moral and spiritual discipline which this school of philosophy prescribes for the observance of the aspirant for liberation (*mumukṣu*).* The reason for this is that the formulation of this code is obviously governed by the spirit of asceticism and that asceticism points towards annihilation in the disguise of spiritual excellence. Moreover, liberation consequent upon *ātmajñāna* in the Advaita Vedānta sense is, in one of its aspects, *actionlessness*** which is but an approximation to annihilation.

The consequence of the intellectualist view of the means

* This refers to the well known fourfold requirement for ātmajnāna, namely, (1) capacity for the discrimination between the eternal and the non eternal; (2) freedom from desire for pleasure and aversion to pain in this life or hereafter; (3) acquisition of the spirit of renunciation, fortitude, faith, etc.; (4) desire for freedom or liberation.

** The reason why we have characterized the Nyāya-Vaiśeṣika, Sāṁkhya and Advaita Vedānta views of the means to liberation as intellectualist is mainly that all these three schools of philosophy and especially the last among them have underestimated the importance of action (karma) in the individual's endeavour to attain liberation.

to the attainment of liberation, especially in its most developed form in the Advaita Vedānta, is, as seen above, not only unfavourable but definitely suicidal. How, then, can this view be countered and replaced by another which can show the way to the fulfilment of human destiny? It is in connection with this question that there arises the need for the consideration of the importance of *bhakti* (devotion) regarded as the primary means to the realization of liberation. Be it borne in mind, however, that the concept of *bhakti* is as old as the *Vedas*. This is evident from the fact that traces of it are to be found in ths Vedic hymns to Varuna. It is also to be found later in the Epics and especially the Mahābhārata. Not only that; it has received considerable developement in the Gītā where it signifies the mystic and emotional mood expressible in adoration and worship and, what is more, surrender (*prapatti*) to divine grace (prasāda). In any case, *bhakti* has an advantage over *ātmajñāna* in that, unlike the latter, it can easily appeal to the popular mind. This is precisely the reason why the *Purāṇas*, especially represented by the *Bhāgavata* and *Visṇu-Purāṇa,* the main object of which was to inspire the common people and not to propound any philosophical doctrine, had a leaning towards *bhakti*. However that may be, it was left for the *Vaiṣnava* or theistic schools of the Vedānta to make attempts, under the lead of the Gītā, to establish the supremacy of *bhakti* as a means to the attainment of liberation.

The most important point to be noticed about the concept of *bhakti* is, however, that it is affiliated to religion in the ordinary sense and is bound up with theism in so far as it understands the relation of man to God in terms of the notion of unity-in-difference. Once man is thus conceived to be *different* from God, this relation in its concrete manifestation is man's *adoration* and *worship* of God, which is an essential element in *bhakti*. But this does not exhaust the connotation of *bhakti*. The reason for this is that the ideas of adoration and worship are not peculiar to theism to which the concept of *bhakti* is affiliated but is common to any form of religion, whether polytheistic, deistic or theistic. In fact, the characteristic peculiarity of *bhakti* is brought out by the concrete manifestation of the relation of man's *unity* with God alongside his *difference* from Him, which, as mentioned above, is man's surrender to God for the sake of His Grace. And this brings to light the crux of the whole situation which may be briefly stated as follows.

As previously seen, the view of *ātmajñāna* as the primary means to the attainment of liberation has, in the hands of the Nyāya-Vaiśeṣikas and the Sāṁkhya, resulted in the understanding of man's liberation as his return to his intrinsic state of insularity which is but another name for his bondage. And the use of the same view by the Advaita Vedānta on the basis of the conception of man as being held in the relation of unity or rather identity with Brahman has amounted to the flagrant misunderstanding of human liberation as the annihilation of man. What, then, was left to be done for the completion of the misunderstanding of human liberation was to impart religious significance to the master-slave relation which prevailed in many earlier societies and thereby construe human liberation as solely dependent upon *bhakti*, consisting primarily in man's surrender to divine Grace. Of corse, *Nimbārka*, *Vallabha* and *Caitanya*, the respective founders of the *bhedābheda*, *suddhādvaita* and *acintyabhedābheda* schools of Vaiṣnavism, held that God presents Himself to man in His *mādhurya-rūpa*, that is, the form in which He is a human being, without transcending the limitations of ordinary manhood. Accordingly, they went further to hold the view that in *bhakti* man is held in the relation of friendly love with God. But this view seems to be untenable in as much as it is incompatible with the conception of *bhakti* as surrender on the part of man to divine Grace. The reason for this is that, even if it be said to involve an element of surrender, love would be out of the question if the surrender concerned is not mutual, but only one-sided as it is bound to be in the case of man *vis-a-vis* God. It is, therefore, no wonder that Rāmānuja and Madhva, the respective founders of the Viśiṣtādvaita and Dvaita schools of Vaiṣnavism emphasized the importance of God's transcendent majesty (*aiśvarya*), greatness and glory and accordingly regarded reverence, awe and submission as the essential features of *bhakti*, thereby conveying the veiled suggestion that the relation between God and man is the religious analogue of the obnoxious socio-economic relation between master and slave.

We may now proceed to consider whether *action* (*karma*) may serve as a means to the attainment of liberation. In this regard it is of interest to note that the concept of action has been of considerable importance in the field of philosophy in India on account of its bearing upon the doctrine of rebirth and transmigration which has influenced the philosophical outlook of both the orthodox and the prominent heterodox philosophers in this country. This seems to be the reason why this concept acquired a rather negative value in the context of the question of human liberation. Since liberation, as was held by the majority of Indian philosophers, is, at least in one of its aspects, the conquest over rebirth and transmigration, action was naturally regarded by them as a hindrance rather than a help in respect of the fulfilment of human destiny. This presumably proved unfavourable to the material progress of the Indian people. However that may be, we are at present concerned with action, not in its wide sense, but in the restricted sense of the performance of the various kinds of duties which usually devolve upon man. And the question which we are especially required to consider relates to the important Indian views about the bearing of action in this sense upon the realization of liberation.

Let us first take up the case of the empirical duties (*kāmyakarma*), including those which relate to rituals enjoined by the Vedas. These duties are all-important in the estimation of that section of the Pūrva Mīmāṁsā school of philosophy which, as we have previously observed, ignores the ideas of liberation and regards *prosperity (abhyudaya)* as the supreme goal of life. But it is precisely this kind of duties which the majority of the orthodox schools of Indian philosophy and the heterodox schools of Buddhism and Jainism regard as absolutely irrelevant to the realization of liberation. Their reason for this is that these duties are at best the means to the fulfilment of egoistic desires, the desires for pleasure, power and authority which are really reprehensible from the point of view of the genuine interest of the aspirant for liberation *(mumukṣu)*.

As regards the duties pertaining to castes *(varṇa)* and stations in life (*āśraṁa*) known as *varṇāśramadharmas*, even supposing that they are useful for the maintenance of social order, they cannot be regarded as the means to the realization of liberation. This has been argued by Advaita Vedānta on the basis of the assumption that *vidyā* or *ātmajñāna* (true knowledge of the self) is the only means to the attainment of liberation and by stating that the *vidyā* in question is by no means dependent upon *varnāśrama* duties. But this radical view of the Advaita Vedānta has not met with universal approval among the various schools of Indian philosophy. On the contrary, the teaching of the doctrine of *svadharma* (one's specific duties) by the Gītā led to the recognition, on the part of the theistic or *Vaiṣnava* schools of the Vedānta, of the importance of the *varṇāśramadharmas* as a means of spiritual realization.* This has, however, contributed to the estabilshment of the legitimacy of the offensive caste system, although the comparatively inoffensive idea of *āśramadharmas* (duties corresponding to the different stages of life, namely, the life of the seeker after truth, of the householder, of the hermit and of the recluse) has gradually lost its importance.

The divergence of opinion about the bearing of duties upon the realization of liberation, which we have noted above, equally holds good in the case of other kinds of duties, including the *nityakarmas* (daily duties of a religious kind such as prayer, worship, meditation, etc.) and the *naimittikakarmas* (occasional duties). Thus the Advaita Vedānta and the Sāṁkhya in particular, while not ruling out the need for the performance of these duties, hold that they have no direct

* This indicates that the achievement of the Gītā consists, among other things, in vitalizing Hindu orthodoxy.

part to play in the realization of liberation. The Gītā and the systems of philosophy influenced by its practical teaching, on the other hand, are of the view that these duties as well as others form part of an entire code of discipline, the observance of which is the only way to spiritual realization and its culmination in the attainment of liberation.

But then, while emphasizing the importance of duties in any scheme of spiritual realization, the Gītā lays down a proviso which is, perhaps, intended to meet the opposition of those philosophers or schools of philosophy which underestimate the importance of duties and even go further as does Śaṁkara or the Sāṁkhya in holding that the state of liberation as such is characterized by *karmasanyāsa* (actionlessness). This proviso primarily consists in the insistence on the importance of the doctrine of duty for duty's sake which conveys the idea of the performance of duties in complete disregard of its consequence. And it further adds that duties are properly done when their performance is dedicated to the will of God. Duties performed in the spirit of such dedication and without any selfish motive, as the Gītā holds, contribute to the moral and spiritual welfare of mankind *(lokasaṁgraha)* and indeed do good to the entire sentient creation *(sarvabhutahita)*. Thus does the Gītā come close to Buddhism in advocating the doctrine of universal liberation. It is, then, evident that the outstanding merit of the Gītā lies in its bringing the neglected cause of activism to the forefront of practical philosophy and its insistence on the need for the spiritual regeneration of mankind as a whole.

The importance of the Gītā, as we shall presently see, is also evident in connection with the question which is still left for our consideration—the question whether the unity of *jñāna* (knowledge), *bhakti* (devotion) and *karma* (action) may be a more suitable means to the realization of liberation than any one of these taken individually and separately. As regards this question, those who advocate the intellectualist view of the means to the attainment of liberation such as Saṁkara or the philosophers belonging to the Sāṁkhya school would, for obvious reasons, answer it in the negative. Thus the Sāṁkhya, for example, holds that *action* is phenomenal (*māyika*) like a dream and, consequently, that it is incapable of producing a positive result. That being so, the combination of knowledge with action *(jñāna-karma-smuccaya)*, in the view of the Sāṁkhya, cannot bring about liberation if, of course, *jñāna* alone is supposed to be unable to do the same. But this does not imply that action has no part to play with respect to the realization of liberation. Of course, it has not been held by any philosopher in India or any school of Indian philosophy that action, besides being able to contribute to happiness, power and prosperity, is also sufficient to bring about liberation. But it has been widely held by philosophers in India that the performance of certain kinds of duties *indirectly* serves the cause of spiritual realization by way of purifying the mind or helping the development of knowledge. What is thus held about the importance of action may be held with equal justification about the importance of *bhakti*. And this brings us to the consideration of the attempt made by the Gītā to resolve the conflict among the schools of Indian philosophy regarding the way *(mārga)* to spiritual realizâtion.

According to the Bhagavad Gītā, the goal of human life is the union *(yoga)* of the individual with God or Brahman. And as regards the way *(mārga)* to the establishment of this union, the Gītā is of the view that it is neither single nor simple, but manifold and composite, being the integration of three different ways respectively called the *karmamārga* (the way of action), the *bhaktimārga* (the way of devotion) and the *jñānamārga* (the way of knowledge). Accordingly, the union of the individual with God has three distinct aspects, namely, *karmayoga*, *bhaktiyoga* and *jñānayoga*. Even so, it seems that the Bhagavad Gītā is predominantly activistic in its practical outlook and attaches special importance to action or rather duty regarded as a means to spiritual realization. And its opposition to the philosophy of inaction in general and the doctrine of renunciation *(sanyāsa)* in particular is most pronounced. But then, as previously mentioned, it makes room for a welcome relief from the excess of activism in so far as it advocates the doctrine of *niṣkāmakarma* (disinterested action) or, in other words, the doctrine of duty for duty's sake. Not only that; it puts a further check upon activism by its proclamation that no action is worth while or is properly done which is not a dedication to the will of God, and is not a means of binding the agent with God by the strongest of all bonds, the bond of *love*. And this points towards another dimension of the union of the individual with God which, according to the Gītā, is none other than *bhaktiyoga* (union through devotion).

The Gītā, however, takes great care to distinguish genuine devotion from the spurious ones. Some are devoted to God when they are in a state of distress and pray to Him for their deliverance from distress. Some, on the other hand, are devoted to God with the sole object of knowing His nature. There are still others who are devoted to God out of a selfish motive and pray to Him for the satisfaction of their desires. And in distinction from all these three kinds of pseudo-devotees, there is a fourth kind consisting of *wise* and indeed genuine devotees who *know* God and pray to Him for His sake and out of love of Him, born of knowledge of Him. This leads the Gītā to hold that *bhakti*, strictly speaking, is inseparably bound up with *jñāna* just as *karma* properly so called does not tolerate separation from *bhakti*. *Jñānamārga*, *bhaktimārga* and *karmamārga*, according to the Gītā, are then the three factors which together constitute the high way that leads to spiritual realization in its culmination in liberation. While this seems to be the final view of the Gītā with regard to the question of the means to the attainment of liberation, it has greatly complicated its position in this regard by occasionally shifting its main interest from one to the other among the three traditionally recognized ways of the realization of liberation. This only shows that the problem of liberation is extremely difficult and, consequently, that there are bound to be differences among different schools of philosophy and even within one and the same system of thought regarding its solution.*

Another feature which is usually held to be common to the different schools of Indian philosophy—of course, with the exception of the materialists headed by the Cārvākas—is the pessimistic outlook on life. This is due to the fact that the majority of philosophical systems in India admit such a thing as human bondage, and hold that human bondage is the invariable source of suffering, and that suffering is, as a matter of fact, universal to mankind. This is precisely the view to which optimism is diametrically opposed, and its opposition is due to its refusal to admit the unquestionable fact of human suffering on the most inhuman understanding that suffering is not real or else is pregnant with the mystery of happiness. That being so, the admission of human suffering as a fact on the part of Indian philosophy, instead of making it liable to condemnation, speaks of the seriousness of its purpose, as distinguished from levity to which philosophy, unfortunately, is usually prone.

It should be noted, however, that the so-called pessimistic outlook is not equally prominent in all the schools of Indian philosophy. It is Buddhism among the heterodox schools and the Sāṁkhya among the orthodox schools in which this outlook plays a dominant role. Buddha himself declared : "Birth is painful; decay is painful; disease is painful; union with the unpleasant is painful; separation from the pleasant is painful." And the Sāṁkhya began its philosophical investigations with the recognition of three kinds of human suffering : (a) suffering due to bodily diseases and mental ailments (*ādhyātmika*); (b) suffering due to the agency of other men and animals (*ādhibhautika*); (c) suffering due to supernatural agency (*ādhidaivika*). Having thus recognized the reality of human suffering, both Buddhism and the Sāṁkhya have addressed themselves to the task of discovering the means of putting an end to the suffering of mankind. In this is expressed their most earnest concern with the problem of liberation, in fact, the problem which has equally occupied the main attention of other prominent schools of Indian philosophy, whether orthodox or heterodox.

* We shall return to the question of human bondage and liberation in the last part of this work entitled Indian Philosophy of Religion and shall be required to deal with it at length even at the cost of repetition.

It may be mentioned, however, that there was no dearth of the display of the optimistic outlook in the philosophical literature in India. Thus the *Taittirīya Upaniṣad*, for example, upheld optimism by means of its boldest declaration : "All creatures spring from bliss, are substained by bliss and are reabsorbed in bliss" and "Who would live if Brahman were not bliss ?" But this neither presupposes nor amounts to the denial of human suffering. It only conveys the truth that suffering, despite its prevalence among mankind is not a permanent feature of human life, but is removable and can be removed* and, consequently, that the destiny of man may find its fulfilment in the joy of living *(ānanda)*. Judged in this light, the outlook of Indian philosophy is neither pessimistic nor optimistic. It is not optimistic for the simple reason that it affirms the reality of human suffering, instead of denying it as optimism does. It is not pessimistic either, because it is inspired by the *confidence* that human suffering can be removed, instead of entertaining, as pessimism entertains, the belief that the life of man is a weary battle where suffering in its ever-changing form holds the field, driving happiness into the future or else into the past. Hence it is evident that neither *hope* inspired by the optimistic outlook on life nor *despair* engendered by pessimism, but *self-confidence* set in the background of a humanistic reorientation of the view of human destiny which seems to be the key-note of Indian philosophy in general.**

Now, of the many and various misunderstandings about the nature of Indian philosophy, which are prevalent among Western orientalists and even Indian scholars, one consists in holding that the outlook of Indian philosophy is by and large religious and spiritualistic and, what is more, is governed by the spirit of world-negation. Let us first deal with the first part of this view. We may begin here by observing that, not to speak of the materialists and naturalists led by the Cārvākas, even some of the orthodox schools of philosophy cannot be regarded as religious or spiritualistic. Thus the Sāṁkhya and the Mīmāṁsā, while being included among the orthodox schools of Indian philosophy, are in agreement with Buddhism and Jainism in having nothing to do with belief in the existence of God. Moreover, no school of Indian philosophy, with the exception of some of the Vedāntic systems of thought and Yogācāra Buddhism, can be said to regard reality as ultimately or exclusively spiritual. The fact which should be noted in this connection is, however, that philosophical orthodoxy in India meant

* Most significant in this connection is Buddha's teaching of the four Noble Truths (āryasatyāni) : (1) there is suffering; (2) there is a cause of suffering; (3) there is cessation of suffering; (4) there is a way to the termination of suffering. The last among these truths points towards his doctrine of Nirvāṇa.

***Vide* my *Glimpses of Indian Wisdom;* Munshiram Manoharlal, New Delhi, 1972; pp. 34-35.

nothing but belief in the authority of the Vedas, which was not bound to vindicate religion in its ordinary sense nor conveyed any guarantee for the development of spiritualism; it was at best a demand for a rational consideration of the ideas contained in the Vedas and the allied scripture.

As regards the second part of the view mentioned above, it may be observed that it is positively improper to regard the Indian philosophical thought as governed by the spirit of world-negation. Of course, there is no denying the fact that the idea of renunciation (*sanyāsa*) found an important place in the ethico-religious thought in India. But good life was never identified with a life of unmitigated renunciation. And when it was conceived to be essential to good life, renunciation was regarded as the final stage (*āśrama*) in the individual life following upon three preceding stages respectively called *brahmacarya* (the life of a student or the seeker after truth), *gārhaṣthya* (the life of a householder) and *vānapraṣtha* (the life lived in seclusion and dedicated to quiet meditation). Even so, renunciation, despite the fact that it was understood in the sense of detachment from worldly affairs, was not intended to mean a retreat from the world in disgust. On the contrary, it was, as in the case of Buddha, conceived to be something positive, being devoted to the discovery of the possibility of a better world for man to live in than the world in which he is ordinarily condemned to live and being vested with the responsibility for suggesting the ways and means of translating this possibility into an actuality.

The Indian conception of *mokṣa* (liberation) as *videha* (dependent on the termination of man's earthly existence), may, however, be said to have contributed to the view of Indian thought as imbued with the spirit of world-negation. But then, it should be noted that the idea of *jīvanmukti* (liberation during man's life on earth) figured prominently alongside that of *videhamukti* in the history of religious thought in India. Moreover, *mokṣa* was not the only value to have been recognized by Indian philosophers. In fact, besides the spiritual value called *mokṣa* and the social value known as *dharma* (principles of individual and social conduct), two mundane values respectively designated as *artha* (wealth) and *kāma* (happiness) received due recognition and found a proper place in the well known Indian doctrine of fourfold value. The recognition of the mundane values as values properly so called was, however, subject to the proviso that their pursuit should be governed by *dharma* and should at the same time conform to the requirement of *mokṣa*. But this, far from revealing the spirit of world-negation, conveys the demand for the establishment of a wholesome world-order in which conflicts among individuals, communities and nations should be replaced by perpetual peace.

We may now bring our present discussions to a close with a brief comment upon a characteristic which is held to be common to the so-called orthodox schools of Indian philosophy, and to which the so-called heterodox ways of thinking in India are regarded as being conspicuous exceptions. In this regard it is of foremost importance to note that all the six systems of philosophy held to belong to the so-called orthodox group, namely, the Nyāya, the Vaiśeṣika, the Mīmāṁsā, the Sāṁkhya, the Yoga and the Vedānta, quote the authority of the Upaniṣads in support of some of their views, and take care to see that they are in harmony with, instead of being opposed to, the teaching of the Vedas. But this presents a fiction which has produced a misleading impression about the nature and mutual relations of these six systems of philosophy. The point raised here may be discussed as follows.

Although they are of considerable philosophical importance, the Upaniṣads are not systematic philosophical works. They contain ideas which not only are not always coherent with one another, but are sometimes mutually conflicting. This accounts for the fact that two schools of philosophy, say, the Sāṁkhya and the Vedānta, which are radically different from each other, could yet justifiably cite the authority of the Upaniṣads in support of their divergent views. But they cannot, on this account, be said to be dependent upon one and the same authority for the confirmation of their respective views. Consequently, their affiliation to the Upaniṣads cannot be regarded as a tie to bind them together so as to provide justification for their being designated as orthodox in common. And what is thus true about the question of the dependence of these systems of philosophy upon the Upaniṣads is *mutatis mutandis* true about the question of their harmony with the Vedas. The reason for this is that the Vedas, like the Upaniṣads, contain conflicting ideas and especially that the philosophical importance of the Vedas is definitely much less than that of the Upaniṣads.

The fact which needs to be especially noted in this connection is, however, that the differences among the so-called orthodox systems of philosophy are no less acute or radical than their differences from the so-called heterodox systems of philosophy. This is particularly evident from the fact that the Vedānta, for example, does not rest content with its dispute of the views of Buddhism and Jainism, but carries its controversy into the territory of the Sāṁkhya and the Nyāya with a view to vindicating its philosophical position in one respect or another. The case is similar with any of the so-called heterodox schools of Indian philosophy. Moreover, even a casual student of Indian philosophy may easily be able to find out that the divergence of a so-called orthodox system of Indian philosophy, say, the Sāṁkhya from another of its kind, for example, the Vedānta, is no less serious than its divergence from one of the so-called heterodox systems of philosophy, say, Buddhism. On the contrary, it may well be held that the Sāṁkhya is nearer Buddhism than the Vedānta. In view of all this it would be advisable not to insist on the distinction between orthodox and heterodox schools of Indian philosophy but to judge them on their own account and without reference to any discriminatory label arbitrarily imposed upon them. In any case, far be it from us to conceive the six major systems of Indian philosophy to be orthodox and thus construe them in terms of scholasticism.

We may now sum up the results of the foregoing discussions briefly as follows. In the first place, it is a fact that all the schools of Indian philosophy, with the exception of the materialists most prominently represented by the Cārvākas, have admitted the doctrine of *karma*, rebirth and transmigration. But this doctrine cannot be said to form an integral part of, or even be compatible with, the central philosophical position of any of these schools. It, therefore, seems that it had its origin outside the philosophical circles in India, but somehow entered into them without being offered any resistance. The reason for this was that it had a bearing upon the question of the destiny of man with which philosophers in India, with the solitary exception of the materialists, were most earnestly concerned. But this is far from suggesting that the question of the destiny of man is spurious, and that the materialists were justified in ignoring this question as well as the doctrine under consideration. What, then, was really in demand was the admission of the question of the destiny of man and its treatment, but with due concession being made to the materialist standpoint by way of separating it from the doctrine of *karma*, rebirth and transmigration.

Secondly, it is definitely improper to characterize the different schools of Indian philosophy as pessimistic. Of course, the majority of them refrained from admitting that kind of irrational optimism which is advocated by materialism on the one hand, and certain types of idealism on the other, by means of the ignoring of the fact of human suffering. But their admission of this fact, together with their firm conviction that suffering is not an inalienable feature of human life, but is amenable to removal in a suitable manner, divides them from the irrationality of optimism and at the same time provides them with relief from the depressing effect of pessimism. And, positively speaking, it enables them to inculcate upon their adherents the feeling of *confidence*, at once distinct from hope and despair, which philosophy may well be held to have the prerogative to do. In fact, Indian philosophy is as recalcitrant to its characterization as pessimistic as it is to its characterization as religious or spiritualistic. It seems, however, that the ascription to Indian philosophy of such adjectives as 'pessimistic', 'religious' or 'spiritualistic' is based upon the consideration of the erstwhile political, economic, scientific and industrial backwardness of India. But it is lacking in justification for the simple reason that its basis is unsound, being extra-logical and hence inapposite.

Thirdly, it is equally improper to take the step which has been actually taken in dealing with the schools of Indian philosophy, namely, to divide them into two separate groups, and to characterize one of them as orthodox (*āstika*) and the other as heterodox (*nāstika*). The reason for this is mainly that the recognition of the authority of the Vedas on the part of the former group which is held to constitute its *orthodoxy* is, after all, *nominal* and not really *real.* So the so-called orthodox schools of Indian philosophy are not far removed from the so-called heterodox schools, despite their open disregard of the authority of the Vedas which is held to constitute their heterodoxy. Strictly speaking, the distinction between orthodoxy and heterodoxy in the field of Indian philosophy as anywhere else is too insignificant and unimportant to deserve serious notice. Unfortunately, however, philosophical heterodoxy acquired undeserved opprobrium in a predominantly Hindu atmosphere just as heresy at one time did in the Christian world.

Fourthly, as far as the concept of liberation is concerned, it is, of course, admitted by almost all the major schools of Indian philosophy. But they disagree among themselves as to the content of this concept. And their disagreement in this respect is sometimes so radical that what is liberation in the view of one of them may well signify human bondage in the estimation of another. So it would be extremely unreasonable and indeed misleading to hold, as writers on Indian philosophy usually hold, that the concept of liberation is one of the ties which bind the different schools of Indian philosophy together.

Lastly, as regards the views held by the various schools of philosophy in India about the ontological status of the world and the self, they are so bewilderingly diverse that it would amount to the most objectionable oversimplification to hold, as has often been held by writers on Indian philosophy, that there is a fundamental agreement among them, consisting in their common recognition of the *reality* of both. The fact in this respect is, however, that the conception of reality, whether in the case of the world or in that of the self, varies from one school to another so much so that what is reality in the view of one may well be its contrary in the view of another. Hence it is evident that the schools of philosophy in India are ontologically diverse. And similar diversity, as we shall now proceed to show, is conspicuous for its presence in their epistemological situation.

PART 1

Indian Epistemology

INTRODUCTION

The title of this part of our work calls for the following observations. In the first place, the use of the adjective 'Indian' is intended merely to express the specific geographical origin of the epistemology which we are about to investigate. Secondly, the word 'epistemology' is not used here in the sense of an enquiry into the *possibility* of knowledge variously characterizable as mathematical, scientific and metaphysical, that is, the sense which it has acquired in the West since the time of Kant. As far as we are at present concerned, this word means an enquiry into the nature, kinds and sources of knowledge. Thirdly, the meaning of the word 'knowledge' which is thus held to be the subject-matter of a special investigation is in need of clarification in order that the confusions which usually prevail in the field of Epistemology may be removed.

Now the English word 'knowledge' means true or veridical *cognition,* it being understood that, whereas cognition may be either true or false, knowledge *qua* knowledge is true, although its inherent truth-value is in no need of indication by means of the addition to it of the adjective 'true'; nor does the distinction between truth and falsity hold good in its case. Knowledge thus understood is the same as what is called *pramā* or *yathārtha-jñāna* (veridical cognition) in Indian philosophy. And the distinction between *knowledge* and *cognition* may be said to correspond to the distinction between *pramā* and *jñāna.* The question then arises as to the nature of the task which epistemology is required to perform. The answer would obviously depend upon whether epistemology is held to be concerned with knowledge or cognition or both.

Let us first enquire whether any problem arises in connection with knowledge understood in the sense mentioned above. In this regard it is most important to note that knowledge *presupposes* cognition in as much as it marks the final point in a process in which cognition is its immediate precedent. This process may be called a causal nexus, but subject to the proviso that *causality* in this case does not have the same sense as it has in the purely physical sphere. What is meant here is that that which precedes cognition in this nexus, if it must be called a cause, may, to use a terminology familiarized by the French philosopher Guelincx, be said to be its *occasional* cause, and that cognition, in its turn, may be called the *occasional* cause of knowledge. But to say that knowledge is due to cognition regarded as its occasional cause seems to be the same as to say that it is *sui generis*. That being so, it appears that no problem can arise in connection with knowledge properly so called. For that which is *sui generis* in some sense or other is immune from the attack of any problem and indeed is in need of being accepted as an ultimate datum.

Nevertheless, the fact remains that that which is taken at a given time to be an instance of veridical cognition or knowledge may really be an instance of false or erroneous cognition. And this gives rise to a problem. But this problem does not, as is usual to hold that it does, concern knowledge as such. It really relates to aberrations from, or exceptions to, knowledge. In other words, the problem in question is that of *error*, not of *knowledge*. That this is really so has been seldom realized by philosophers in the West. On the contrary, it is usual with them to mix up truth and falsity in the most arbitrary manner and thereby raise the fantastic problem of the *possibility* of *knowledge* and make attempts to solve it by falling back upon the equally fantastic doctrine of 'ideas', 'sense-data' or 'sense' as the case may be. The schools of Indian philosophy, on the other hand, have displayed sufficient philosophical insight in so far as they have concerned themselves with the problem of error and have made serious attempts to solve it in their respective ways. But apart from the question how far or whether at all their attempts in this direction have been successful, there is no gainsaying the fact that these have contributed to the enrichment of epistemology in a manner to which there is no parallel in the history of Western philosophy.

One of the concerns of epistemology, then, is the problem of *error*, instead of the problem of *knowledge*, which has figured as the epistemological problem *par excellence* in the history of Western philosophy since the time of Kant. But is this problem, it may be pertinently asked, the only one which this branch of philosophy is required to deal with or is there any other which may have a legitimate place within its scope ? This demands the consideration whether any problem strictly so called can arise in connection with *cognition (jñāna)* and, if so, what that problem is.

In this regard it is necessary to remind ourselves that cognition is due to certain preceding conditions regarded as its *occasional* causes just as knowledge is due to cognition regarded as its occasional cause. But, unlike knowledge, it occupies only an intermediate and not the final point in a causal nexus. Moreover, unlike the latter, it is open to the distinction between truth and falsity. Both these circumstances together stand in the way of the treatment of cognition as *sui generis* and at the same time lead to the question regarding its source or sources. This question, it is hardly necessary to emphasize, is as essential to epistemology as is the problem of error. But it is the various schools of Indian philosophy which have taken keen interest in this question as well as in the problem of error, whereas Western philosophy in general has proved rather indifferent to the former as well as the latter. It is most important to note, however, that Indian philosophy, including the various schools into which it is divided, has created a great deal of confusion in so far it has called the sources of cognition *pramāṇas*, having meant thereby that these are instrumental to the emergence of *pramā* (knowledge or true cognition), instead of mere cognition which is open to the distinction between truth and falsity. Hence it is evident that Indian philosophy has, at least by implication, missed the truth that the sources concerned, for example, perception *(pratyakṣa)*, inference, etc yield cognition *(jñāna)* which may prove to be *pramā* (knowledge) in one set of circumstances or *apramā* (error or false cognition) in another.

As previously observed, no problem arises in connection with knowledge as such. What is meant thereby is that knowledge (*pramā*) is recalcitrant to any problem which demands its self-transcendence. But that does not preclude the need for an enquiry into the nature and the criterion of the truth of true cognition which is knowledge. This enquiry, it may be of interest to observe, is not peculiar to Indian philosophy, but has also received a well deserved treatment in the history of Western philosophy. However that may be, as far as Indian epistemology is concerned, its main object is threefold : (1) to deal with the problem of error; (2) to investigate the sources of cognition; and (3) to enquire into the nature and the criterion of the truth of true cognition, that is, knowledge (*pramā*). Our study of Indian epistemology may conveniently begin with the consideration of the results of the investigations of the sources of cognition made by the different schools of Indian philosophy.

I

THE SOURCES OF COGNITION

In any enquiry into the Indian theories of the sources of cognition miscalled doctrines of *pramāṇa*, it is necessary to note at the very outset that there is no unanimity among the different schools of Indian philosophy about the *number* of these sources. The minimum number is *one*, standing for perception (*pratyakṣa*) which is regarded by the materialists and naturalists led by the Cārvākas as the only source of cognition. The next higher number is *two*, including perception (*pratyakṣa*) and inference (*anumāna*) which, in the view of Buddhism and Kanāda, the founder of the Vaiśeṣika school of Indian philosophy, are the only two sources of cognition. The Sāṁkhya goes further in admitting *three* sources of cognition, including *testimony* (*śabda; āptavacana*) in addition to perception and inference. One section of the Nyāya is in agreement with the Sāṁkhya in admitting these three only, but another section adds to this number by recognizing *comparison* (*upamāna*) as a separate source of cognition. Further addition to the number is made by the Mīmāṁsā school, with the result that the sources of cognition become *five* in number, including *presumption (arthāpatti)* over and above the four recognized by the Nyāya. But even then, the process of the increase of the number of the sources of cognition did not come to an end. For in the hands of the Vedānta and the section of Mīmāṁsā philosophy headed by Kumārila, the number increased to *six* with the addition of *non-apprehension* (*anupalabdhi*) to the list admitted by the Mīmāṁsā school as a whole. One wished, however, that the tendency to multiply the sources of cognition came to an end at least at this stage. But that did not happen. For it was left for the Paurāṇikas (believers in the authority of the semi-historical branch of Sanskrit literature known as the *purāṇas*) to increase the number of the sources of cognition to *eight* by means of the addition of *tradition* (*aitihya*) and *inclusion* (*sambhava*). But even this was not the end of the matter. Mention has been made in Indian philosophical literature of two more sources of cognition respectively called *gesture* (*ceṣṭā*) and *elimination* (*pariśeṣa*).

We are now required to consider whether the sources of cognition listed above are all genuine and independent of one another. We shall deal with them separately and in an order in which perception should come first. For the claim of perception to be recognized as a source of cognition, psychologically speaking, is too strong to be ignored. But even otherwise, perception is especially important in as much as it is presupposed by, and indeed constitutes, the basis of, several other sources of cognition. On these accounts, all the schools of Indian philosophy, in the fitness of things, admit perception as a source of cognition; and, what is more, the Indian materialists and naturalists led by the Cārvākas took the arbitrary step to regard it as the only independent source of cognition.

A

PERCEPTION (*PRATYAKṢA*)

Almost all the schools of Indian philosophy are agreed among themselves in the recognition of the undeniable fact of the physical, physiological and psychological conditionality of perceptual experience. Accordingly, they hold in common that perception is a process which is initiated by the *contact* (*sannikarṣa*) of an object with the sense-organs (*jñānendriyas*) and culminates in the arousal of the awareness of the object on the part of the self. According to them, such contact is of exceptional importance in the case of perception in as much as it constitutes the differentia of this source of cognition, distinguishing it as it does from other sources of cognition such as inference, testimony, etc. It may be mentioned, however, that the Nyāya school of Indian philosophy, especially in its later developement, which took exceptionally keen interest in, and made valuable contributions to, epistemology and logic, made a searching enquiry into the phenomenon of *sannikarṣa* and came to distinguish six kinds of it respectively called *saṁyoga* (conjunction), *samavāya* (inherence), *saṁyukta-samavāya* (inherence in that which is conjoined), *saṁyukta-samaveta-samavāya* (inherence in the inherent with that which is conjoined), *samaveta-samavāya* (inherence in that which is itself inherent) and *viśeṣaṇa-viśeṣya-bhāva* (the relation of qualification and the qualified).

This distinction of the contacts (*sannikarṣas*) is based on the recognition of the fact that the different kinds of sense-organs come into contact with their appropriate objects, not in one and the same manner, but in different ways. Thus when we are aware of a concrete object such as a cup, as a result of its contact with one of our sense-organs, the contact is obviously of the nature of a temporary conjunction of the object and the sense-organ concerned, because the two are separable and indeed are separate from each other. This means that the contact in question is *saṁyoga* (conjunction). As regards the contact called *samavāya* (inherence), the Naiyāyikas hold that it is illustrated in the auditory perception of *sound*. Their reason here derives from their assumption that sound is an *inherent quality* of ether (*ākāśa*), and that *ākāśa* which fills the cavity of the ear is an essential constituent of this organ of hearing. This, in their view, suffices to indicate that in the case of the perception of sound, the sound is perceived as a *quality* of the ear and, consequently, that the *sannikarṣa* in this case is characterizable as *samavāya*, it being understood that a quality can only *inhere* in that of which it is said to be the quality. It may be of interest to note in this connection that Prabhākara and others belonging to his school of Mīmāṁsā philosophy are in agreement with the Naiyāyikas in regarding *samavāya* as one of the ways of *sannikarṣa*, although they differ from them in holding that the kinds of *sannikarṣa* are not *six*, but only *three* in number. However that may be, the fact that we hear a sound, not always, but only when it strikes upon our sense of hearing from outside is enough to refute the present assumption of the Naiyāyikas and counter their view that *samavāya* needs to be counted as one of the various kinds of cognitive relations. Moreover, this view is incompatible with the thorough-going epistemological realism advocated by them.

The third kind of *sannikarṣa* in our list, namely, *saṁyukta-samavāya* is, in the view of the Naiyāyikas, a twofold contact which obtains in the case of our perception of something which is held in the relation of *samavāya* (e.g. the *quality* or the *genus*) with something else (e.g. a jar) which is, however, held in the relation of mere conjunction (*saṁyoga*) with the sense-organ, say, the eye. Thus the *sannikarṣa* involved in the case of our perception of the *colour* of a jar is, according to them, *samavāya* on the one hand and *saṁyoga* on the other and so is characterizable as *saṁyukta-samavāya*. But even granted that the relation of the jar to its colour or its genus is *samavāya*, it does not follow that our *awareness* of its colour or its genus involves the same relation. On the contrary, the relation involved in this awareness is *saṁyoga* in as much as it is dependent upon, and is mediated by, our awareness of the jar itself which involves the relation of mere conjunction (*saṁyoga*). Hence it is evident that in construing the perception of qualities and genera as involving the relation of *saṁyukta-samavāya*, the Naiyāyikas have laid themselves open to the fault of confusing the *ratio essendi* and the *ratio cognoscendi* in the matter.

One of the three remaining kinds of *sannikarṣa* recognized by the Naiyāyikas is *saṁyukta-samaveta-samavāya* (inherence in that which is itself inherent in that which is conjoined) which, according to them, involves a threefold contact as is illustrated in our direct awareness of *colour in general* (*rūpasāmānya*) in the case of our perception of a piece of coloured cloth present before us. The contact between our eyes and the genus 'colour' apprehended by us is threefold, being (1) *saṁyoga* (mere conjunction) of the eyes with the piece of cloth; (2) samavāya (*inherence*) of the particular colour of the cloth in the cloth itself; and (3) the relation of *samavāya* of the particular colour of the cloth with the 'genus' colour (*rūpa-sāmānya*). In other words, the piece of cloth in this example is conjoined (*saṁyukta*) with the eyes, the colour of the piece of cloth is *samaveta* (inherent) in that piece and the genus 'colour' is held in the relation of *samavāya* with the particular colour concerned. But this, despite the complications presented by it, makes no secret of the difficulty in which it is involved. The difficulty is none other than that which we have already noticed in the case of the *sannikarṣa* known as *saṁyukta-samavāya*, namely, that which consists in the cofusion of the *ratio essendi* and the *ratio cognoscendi*.

The next in the list of the *sannikarṣas* is *samaveta-samavāya* (inherence in that which is itself inherent) which, according to the

Naiyāyikas, is twofold, as is illustrated in the case of our direct apprehension of the genus 'sound' in the case of our apprehension of a particular sound by means of our ears. The peculiarity of this twofold *sannikarṣa*, however, lies in that it is, as the Naiyāyikas hold, *samavāya* (inherence) in either case, the relation between the genus 'sound' and any particular sound being *samavāya* and the relation between the ear and a particular sound being likewise *samavāya*. But even granted that their conception of the former relation as *samavāya* is justifiable, there is no doubt that their conception of the latter relation also as *samavāya* is as crude as it is absurd.

Lastly, let us consider the *sannikarṣa* called *viśeṣaṇa—viśeṣya-bhāva* (the relation between qualification and the qualified). This kind of 'contact' is most peculiar in view of the fact that its nomenclature provides no judication of its indentity, and that the Naiyāyikas' characterization of it is as astounding as it is arbitrary and unwarranted. According to them, this kind of contact *(sannikarṣa)* is involved in our perception of the *non-existence* of an object. This may be clarified thus. When we do not perceive an object where it usually remains or is expected to remain, what happens, according to them, is not that there is total absence of perception, but that we have the perception of the place where the object is not present for the time being, together with the *notion* of the non-existence of the object concerned. And this is construed by them in terms of the view that the notion of the non-existence of the object becomes the qualification *(viśeṣaṇa)* of the place which is actually perceived and thereby presents the latter as *viśeṣya* (qualified). But this is open to several difficulties, the most important among which are as follows.

In the first place, nothing can be said to *qualify* something else and thus become the latter's *viśeṣaṇa* (qualification) which is not *positive*, so that the notion of the non-existence of an object, being purely negative in import, cannot be regarded as the *viśeṣaṇa* of the that place from which the object concerned is absent, despite the fact that that place is actually perceived. Secondly, not to speak of the *notion* of non-existence, even non-existence as such cannot possibly come into contact with a sense-organ which is essential to the very possibility of perception *(pratyakṣa)*. That being so, the Naiyāyika view, which consists in construing the notion of non-existence as having a bearing upon perception, is tantamount to the denial of the peculiarity of perceptual experience which serves to differentiate it from other kinds of sources of cognition. It is, perhaps, in view of this that the Vedānta and the Bhātta school of the Mīmāṁsā, both of which regard non-eixstence as a legitimate object of cognition, recognize *anupalabdhi* (non-apprehension) in distinction from perception and treat it as a separate and independent source cf cognition. Thirdly, the understanding of *sannikarṣa* in terms of the relation of *viśeṣaṇa*-

viśeṣya seems to be as incompatible with the epistemological realism advocated by the Nyāya as is the understanding of it in terms of the relation of *samavāya*. In fact, any understanding of *sannikarṣa* except in terms of the relation of *saṁyoga* (conjunction) is not only antithetical to epistemological realism, but amounts to the ignoring of the peculiarity of perception as an independent source of cognition.

It is then evident that the Naiyāikas, despite their laudable attempt to conduct the most thorough-going investigation of perceptual experience, suffer the untoward consquence of their excessive zeal for the attainment of intellectual perfection, consisting in jeopardizing their own epistemological position on the one hand, and inviting a gross misunderstanding of this kind of experience on the other. In any enquiry into perception, it would, therefore, be enough to take cognizance of the contact (*sannikarṣa*) of the object of perception with one sense-organ or another, without undertaking the unnecessary task of ascertaining whether such contact is of one kind or of many kinds. For this enquiry, after all, is mainly concerned with the understanding of perception regarded as an *accomplished fact* in the form of a way of cognition. And this goes to indicate that the main demand of epistemology with regard to perception is the *analysis* of perceptual experience as such. Accordingly, we may proceed to the consideration of the distinction between *nirvikalpaka* (indeterminate) and *savikalpaka* (determinate) perception which has been of considerable importance in the analysis of perceptual experience in the field of Indian epistemology.

INDETERMINATE *(NIRVIKALPAKA)* AND DETERMINATE *(SAVIKALPAKA)* PRECEPTION *(PRATYAKṢA)*

The distinction between *nirvikalpaka* and *savikalpaka pratyakṣa* is well known in the field of Indian epistemology. As regards the former of these two, it is usually taken to mean the awareness of a sensible object together with those of its qualities that are actually sensed, but without its name and genus and also without those of its qualities that are left unnoticed.* This is obviously in conformity with the strictest understanding of perception as *wholly* and *entirely* due to the contact of an object with one or more sense-organs as the case may be. In any case, *nirvikalpaka pratyakṣa* is non-relational, being lacking in the discrimination between the *substratum* and the *qualities* of the object and also in the recognition of the *relations* sub-

* Some philosophers and especially Prabhākare, the founder of one of the two main divisions of the Mīmāṁsā, hold that indeterminate perception includes the awareness of the generic as well as the specific features of the object, but that it does not involve the apprehension of the object as actually belonging to a genus and as characterized by the specific features. But this hardly makes any substantial difference to the view of indeterminate perception explained above.

sisting among its parts and its qualities. On this account it may also be called *non-judgmental* apprehension of sensible objects. William James's conception of 'immediate experience' seems to be the Western analogue of the Indian conception of *nirvikalpaka pratyakṣa*. So in the light of his characterization of immediate experience, *nirvikalpaka pratyakṣa* may be regarded as 'a simple *that* which is not yet any definite *what*', and which 'only new-born babes, or men in semi-coma from sleep, drugs, illness, or blows, may be assumed to have'.

Standing in contrast with *nirvikalpaka pratyakṣa* as it does, *savikalpaka pratyakṣa*, on the other hand, is the apprehension of a sensible object, together with its name, genus and those of its qualities that are not actually sensed in addition to those that are. Hence it is evident that it involves the discrimination between the substratum and the qualities of the object and the recognition of the relations in which its parts as well as its qualities are held. Thus *savikalpaka pratyakṣa* is relational and *judgmental*, being of the nature of 'knowledge about', as distinguished from the mere 'enjoyment of acquaintance' which constitutes the essence of *nirvikalpaka pratyakṣa*.

It is important to note, however, that all the major *āstika* (orthodox) systems of Indian philosophy, with the exception of the schools of the Vedānta respectively headed by Madhva and Vallabha, recognize the distinction between *nirvikalpaka* and *savikalpaka pratyakṣa*. But while most of them regard this distinction as the distinction between two separate and independent forms of perceptual experience, some of the Naiyāyikas hold that the two are but two different stages in the development of one and the same perceptual experience, *nirvikalpaka pratyakṣa* and *savikalpaka pratyakṣa* being respectively the lower and the higher stages. But the question arises whether the present distinction in either of these two senses is justifiable or not. It is precisely this question which seems to have been raised by the two prominent *nāstika* (heterodox) schools of Indian philosophy, namely, Buddhism and Jainism. And both of them answered it in the negative. But then, their answers were mutually opposed in as much as Buddhism rejected *savikalpaka pratyakṣa* as spurious and regarded *nirvikalpaka pratyakṣa* as perceptual experience *par excellence* and Jainism, on the other hand, dismissed the possibility of *nirvikalpaka pratyakṣa* as a source of cognition and treated *savikalpaka pratyakṣa* as the only genuine form of perceptual experience.

Now Buddhism's dismissal of *savikalpaka pratyakṣa* and its view of *nirvikalpaka pratyakṣa* as perceptual experience properly so called are obviously based upon its strictest adherence to the understanding of perception as *wholly* due to the *contact (sannikarṣa)* of some sensible object or other with one or more sense-organs. But then, this understanding is vitiated by the admission of a hypothetical abstraction from the ordinary perceptual experience of normal adult human beings with reference to the unverified and unverifiable experience of babes and men in semi-coma from sleep, drugs, etc. In view of this it is necessary to realize that, while dependence upon *indriyasannikarṣa* (contact with sense-organs) is essential to perceptual experience, it is no demand of the possibility of this kind of experience that this dependence should be total or uncompromising. In fact, constituted as we human beings are, our perceptual experience in our normal adult life is bound to cover much more than what is provided for by mere *indriyasannikarṣa.* It is, therefore, extremely wise on the part of Jainism and the two schools of the Vedānta respectively founded by Madhva and Vallabha to hold that *nirvikalpaka pratyakṣa* is a figment of imagination, and that *savikalpaka pratyakṣa,* in spite of its *partial* dependence on *indriyasannikarṣa,* is perceptual experience properly so called. It may be mentioned in this connection that to deny, as Buddhism denies, the *perceptual* character of *savikalpaka pratyakṣa* on the ground that its dependence on *indriyasannikarṣa* is only partial is no less improper than it would be to hold, on the same ground, that perception regarded as *savikalpaka pratyakṣa* is not an independent source of cognition but is the same as *inference.*

We may bring the present discussion to a close by mentioning that some of the Indian philosophers, including even those who belong to the ancient Nyāya school, hold that the question of *validity* is as relevant in the case of *nirvikalpaka pratyakṣa* as it is in the case of *savikalpaka pratyakṣa.* William James, to whom reference has been already made, however, goes further in observing thus about 'immediate experience' : "In this *naïf* immediacy it is of course *valid*; it is *there*, we *act* upon it."*

But, strictly speaking, *nirvikalpaka pratyakṣa* or 'immediate experience' can not only not be regarded as being *valid* in itself, but is also recalcitrant to the question of the distinction between its validity and its invalidity, its truth and its falsity. The reason for this is that this question, as the modern Naiyāyikas urge, can arise only in connection with statements of *relations* or *judgements,* and that *nirvikalpaka pratyakṣa* or 'immediate experience', not conforming to this characterization, remains unaffected by the distinction between truth and falsity. The Buddhists, who, as previously seen, regard *nirvikalpaka pratyakṣa* as the only kind of perceptual experience, may, however, have no option but to hold—and they actually hold—that this kind of experience is characterized by validity. But this leads to a most curious situation, namely, that they have no means of admitting any such thing as invalidity or falsity, and,

* William James, *Essays in Radical Empiricism,* Longmans, Green and Co., New York, 1922, pp. 23-24.

consequently, that validity, being the correlate and indeed the opposite of invalidity, should *eo ipso* be at best a word without meaning. All this points towards the muddle which has come about in the field of Indian epistemology in consequence of the introduction of the distinction between *nirvikalpaka* and *savikalpaka pratyakṣa*. But more of this unseemly situation of Indian epistemology will come within view in the course of our consideration of the other distinctions which have been brought to bear upon the understanding of perceptual experience.

EXTERNAL (*BĀHYA*) AND INTERNAL (*ĀNTARA; MĀNASA*) PERCEPTION (*PRATYKṢA*)

Of the remaining distinctions admitted by most of the major schools of Indian philosophy with regard to their understanding of perceptual experience, one concerns the difference between two distinct kinds of sensible objects and correspondingly between two distinct kinds of sense-organs. It is the distinction between internal perception and external perception. It may be of interest to mention in this connection that among the philosophers in the West who admitted the present distinction, the most prominent were the British philosopher John Locke and the German philosopher Immanuel Kant. But neither Locke nor Kant succeeded in establishing the parallelism between external perception and internal perception as both of them very much wished to do. One of the reasons and, in fact, the main reason for their failure to do so was their inability to point to anything that could be regarded as an internal sense-organ properly so called, in distinction from the many and various kinds of external sense-organs such as the eye, the ear, etc. But this is a difficulty from which the philosophers in India tried to free themselves by means of the admission of *manas* (mind) or *antaḥkaraṇa* as the internal sense-organ.*

In their view, *antaḥkaraṇa* is required to function in the case of internal perception as well as in the case of external perception. For the self's awareness of an object, no matter whether internal or external, necessarily presupposes the self's contact with the *antaḥkaraṇa*. But, while in the case of external perception, the self must be in direct contact with the *antaḥkaraṇa* and in indirect contact with some external object or other through the intermediary of the *antaḥkaraṇa*, in the case of internal perception, the *antaḥkaraṇa* itself serves as the means of direct intercourse bet-

* The position of the Advaita Vedānta is exceptional in this regard, owing to the fact that this school of philosophy rejects the view of manas as the internal organ and, consequently, holds that our awareness of pleasure, pain, etc, while being a fact, is non-sensuous, not being dependent upon the function of any sense-organ

ween the self and the internal objects which are but the phenomena of the human mind itself, namely, cognition, pleasure, pain, desire, aversion, volition, etc. Since our internal sense-organ is only one in number, our awareness of all these diverse mental phenomena, as the Indian philosophers hold, is naturally of one and the same kind. Our awareness of external objects, according to these philosophers, is, on the other hand, of different kinds, its differences depending on the differences of the outer sense-organs as well as of the objects with which they are respectively concerned. And having been unaware of the existence of sense-organs other than the well known five major ones they have recognized only five kinds of external perception, namely, visual (*cākṣusa*), auditory (*srautriya*), tactual (*spārśana*), gustatory (*rāsana*), and olfactory (*ghrānaja*).

The question, however, remains whether the Indian philosophers have succeeded any more than Locke and Kant in making out a case for the admission of internal perception in distinction from external perception. Of course, it is far from us to deny the possibility of our awareness of such things as pleasure, pain, desire, aversion, etc. But must our awareness of these phenomena be understood on the analogy of our awareness of colour, smell, taste, etc and be construed as being, like the latter, *perceptual* in character? The proper answer to this question should be in the negative for the simple reason that the phenomena in question constitute the self-conscious or rather self-illumined, but contingent and transitory, states of the self's *being*, having hardly anything to do with the act of *knowing*. But philosophers, whether in the East or in the West, have, on the other hand, proceeded on the tacit and, maybe, unconscious acceptance of an affirmative answer to it. This accounts for their admission of internal perception on the analogy of, and in distinction from, external perception, no matter whether or not they succeed in inventing an internal sense-organ such as *antaḥkaraṇa*. In this, they, at least by implication, take the arbitrary step of insisting on the *paradigmatic* character of perceptual experience in the usual sense of the term. But they are, on this account, no less to blame than are the Cārvākas on account of their view of perception as the only source of cognition. This will be further borne out by the consideration of another distinction which some philosophers in India have admitted in connection with the understanding of the scope of perceptual experience—the distinction, namely, between *laukika* (normal) and *alaukika* (supranormal) *pratyakṣa* (perception).

NORMAL (*LAUKIKA*) AND SUPRANORMAL (*ALAUKIKA*) PERCEPTION (*PRATYAKṢA*)

Laukika pratyakṣa is held to comprise all those kinds of perceptual experience which are due to *indriyārtha-sannikarṣa* (contact between objects and sense-organs). Thus it seems to correspond to what Jainism calls *saṁvyavahārika pratyakṣa* (empirical perception). Since the sense-organs, according to most Indian philosophers, are either *external* or *internal* and since the former are five in number, namely, the visual, the auditory, the tactual, the gustatory and the olfactory and the latter only one, being *manas* or *antaḥkaraṇa,* the scope of perceptual experience should, in their view, be confined to six kinds of perception, five of them being external and one internal. But, strangely enough, they and especially the Naiyāyikas and the members of the Sāṁkhya school extend the scope of perceptual experience by including within it certain kinds of cognition that are not due to *indriyārtha-sannikarṣa* and so are called *alaukika* (supranormal) or, as Jainism would say, *pāramārthika pratyakṣa* (transcendental perception). In this they are obviously open to the charge ef arbitrarily relinquishing the view of perceptual experience as due to the contact between objects and sense-organs, which is above reproach. But, what is more, they are unavoidably caught in the grip of the difficult question as to whether the different kinds of *alaukika pratyakṣa* admitted by them are all really *alaukika* and whether all of them are genuine modes of cognition.

Now according to the Nyāya, *alaukika pratyakṣa* is of three kinds respectively called *sāmānyalakṣaṇa*, *jñānalakṣaṇa* and *yogaja.* As regards the first, it is held to be the apprehension of the *jāti* (genus) of an object. When, for example, we are aware of the general nature of the horse at the sight of a particular horse, this awareness on our part is, according to the Naiyāyikas, characterizable as *sāmānyalakṣaṇa pratyakṣa.* As regards this, apart from the controversy among the advocates of realism, conceptualism and nominalism with regard to the status of the *universal,* it seems that the awareness in question is bound up with, if it is not the same as, the *savilkalpaka pratyakṣa* of a horse. And since *savikalpaka pratyakṣa,* despite the fact that it is not *wholly* due to *indriyārtha-sannikarṣa,* is *laukika* (normal) on account of the partial contact of its object with some sense-organ or other, the awareness of *jāti* (genus) is in need of being regarded as an instance of *laukika pratyakṣa* and not one of *alaukika pratyakṣa* as the Nyāya conceives it to be.

Let us next consider the case of the so-called *jñānalakṣaṇa pratyakṣa* which the Naiyāyikas regard as *alaukika.* This kind of perceptual experience is illustrated in those cases in which we are immediately aware of a quality of an object which is not nor can be said to be in contact with the sense-organ or sense-organs operating in connection with our awareness of it. Our awareness of the quality of coolness of snow at the mere sight of snow is a concrete example of *jñānalakṣana pratyakṣa* as conceived by the Naiyāyikas.

But why should the kind of perception which is thus exemplified concretely be regarded, as these philosophers regard it, as *alaukika ?* Since the apprehension of the coolness of snow in this case is bound up with the visual sensation of snow, these two elements together form part of the *savikalpaka pratyakṣa* of snow; so that the former element cannot be considered separately from, and be regarded as *alaukika* in contrast with, the latter. It, therefore, follows that *jñānalakṣaṇa pratyakṣa*, like *sāmānyalakṣaṇa pratyakṣa*, is organically related to some *savikalpaka pratyakṣa* or other and as such is *laukika* (normal) instead of being *alaukika* (supranormal).

As regards *yogaja pratyakṣa*, it is peculiar and indeed is in a class apart from all other kinds of perception, whether normal or supranormal, in that it is neither directly nor indirectly dependent upon *indriyārtha-sannikarṣa* (contact between objects and sense-organs). In other words, it is not brought about by the intercourse between objects and sense-organs in any sense whatsoever. On the contrary, as its designation indicates, *yogaja pratyakṣa* is the outcome of the illumination of the mind by intense meditation (*yoga*). The objects of this kind of perception are obviously not those that are *present* and are capable of being sensed as they must be in the case of *laukika pratyakṣa*. They are, according to the Nyāya and the Sāṁkhya, past, future, remote or subtle, precisely the objects which elude the grasp of *laukika pratyakṣa*.

It may be of interest to note, however, that *yogaja pratyakṣa* as understood by the orthodox schools of Indian philosophy resembles what the heterodox school of Jainism calls *mukhya* or *pāramārthika pratyakṣa*. According to Jainism, *pāramārthika pratyakṣa* is independent of the operation of the external sense-organs as well as the internal sense-organ *manas* or *antaḥkaraṇa*. It is the self's direct apprehension of certain kinds of objects as a result of the elimination of the *karma*-matter which covers it and thereby obscures its knowledge of things. *Pāramārthika pratyakṣa*, however, as Jainism holds, is mainly of two kinds : *vikala* (partial or incomplete) and *sakala* (whole or complete). The former is again of two kinds : *avadhi* and *manaḥparyāya*. *Avadhi pratyakṣa*, according to Jainism, is the perception of ordinary sensible objects independently of the operation of the sense-organs and *manas;* so that the possibility of the apprehension of *remote* sensible objects definitely opens up. *Manaḥparyāya-jñāna*, on the other hand, is concerned, not with sensible objects, but with other minds. It is, as held by Jainism, telepathic knowledge of the minds of one's fellows which is characterized by *directness* and *immediacy* (*sākṣātkāritva*). As regards *sakala pāramārthika pratyakṣa* (complete transcendental perception), Jainism regards it as the highest development of perceptual experience and holds that it is due to the elimination of the entire crust of *karma*-matter with which the self is covered, resulting from right intuition, right faith and right conduct of the most perfect kind. Thus understood, transcendental perception of this kind is, in the view of Jainism, but another name for omniscience, it being the immediate knowledge (*kevalajñāna*) of all things and all their modes and all their aspects.

It now remains to observe that the recognition of *alaukika pratyakṣa* and especially *yogic pratyakṣa* among the orthodox circles of Indian philosophy and of *pāramārthika pratyakṣa* on the part of the heterodox school of Jainism seems to be based on the belief that the scope of the source of direct and immediate cognition called perception is amenable to unexpected and even unimaginable enlargement beyond the limits set by the operation of external and internal sense-organs, and, consequently, that there arises the possibility of one's direct and immediate apprehension of things with their modes and aspects which elude the grasp of sense-perception, that is, perception due to *indriyārtha-sannikarṣa.* This belief in its turn has been engendered by another belief, namely, the belief in the extraordinary efficacy of the spiritual discipline commonly known as *yoga*, which came to prevail in the sphere of Indian philosophy, both orthodox and heterodox. Even so it may be observed as follows.

In the first place, apart from the question whether or not it is ascribable to God, *omniscience* cannot be ascribed to man for the simple reason that the ascription of it to him would amount to the surrender of the idea of man as a human being and the consequent absurdity, consisting in the view that mankind were, as it were, non-existent. Secondly, the apprehension of what is *past* is indeed possible at least in some cases, if not in all. But it should be due to *historical investigations* which, while not being confined to sense-perception, are, in a sense, at least partly dependent upon this source of cognition. And this accounts for whatever measure of reliability the results of historical investigations may command. The so-called direct and immediate apprehension of the past supposed to be provided by *yogaja pratyakṣa* or *pāramārthika pratyakṣa*, on the other hand, is of questionable value in as much as its reliability cannot be tested by any means whatsoever.

Thirdly, there cannot be any such thing as cognition of the *future*, whether direct and immediate or indirect and mediate. For what is attainable in the name of the apprehension of the future is only *prophesy* which is distinct from scientific *prediction* on the one hand and from perception or cognition on the other, and, as such, is, like the so-called *yogaja pratyakṣa* of the past, of dubious value. Fourthly, as far as *subtle* things such as atoms (*aṇus* or *paramāṇus*) are concerned, they are indeed *discoverable*--discoverable, not by means of direct and immediate perception, whether *yogaja* or *pāramārthika*, but by means of *scientific analysis.* And as regards scientific analysis, it is important to note that, while not being coextensive with, or confined to sense-perception, it takes serious notice of relevant data provided by sense-experience and is, on this account, entitled to verifiable reliability which seems to be out of the question in the case of *yogaja* or *pāramārthika pratyakṣa*. Lastly, there is at present no dearth of scientific devices which enable us to have some apprehension of *remote* things, that is, things that are beyond the reach of our sense-organs. But the apprehension thus provided is not altogether independent of the operation of our sense-organs. On the contrary, sense-perception, while not being the sole constituent of it, has an important bearing upon it. This is precisely the reason why the apprehension in question is characterized by a reasonable measure of reliability. But it is doubtful whether the same may be the case with the so-called *yogaja* or *pāramārthika pratyakṣa* of remote objects.

It may be of interest to mention in conclusion that one of the remarkable trends of Indian thought is to suggest the possibility of an extraordinary development of human capacities by means of the observance of the spiritual discipline commonly called *yoga*. This accounts for the admission, among both orthodox and heterodox circles of Indian philosophy, of such things as the various kinds of *alaukika* or *pāramārthika pratyakṣa*. Judged from the strictly scientific point of view, this suggestion, however, is, as we have seen above, of doubtful value. But even then, the significance of the challenge which it poses to science is not lost but, on the contrary, remains in force.

B

INFERENCE *(ANUMĀNA)*

It may be mentioned at the outset that Indian philosophers usually distinguished two kinds of cognition—the direct (*pratyakṣa* or *aparokṣa*) and the indirect (*parokṣa*). Among the various sources of cognition, perception is the only one which provides direct cognition, whereas the rest, including *anumāna* can only yield indirect (*parokṣa*) cognition. As regards *anumāna*, it is important to observe, however, that it is at once a source of cognition and a way of reasoning as such. Thus it has an *epistemic* and a *logical* aspect, both of which should be kept in view in its investigation.

Anumāna, as held by the major schools of Indian philosophy and the Nyāya in particular, is the indispensable means (*karaṇa*) of inferential knowledge (*anumiti*).* As regards inferential knowledge, it is obviously the knowledge of something which does not present itself to the knower through the intermediary of any sense-organ.

* The use of word 'knowledge' in this context may be excused.

In other words, it is the knowledge of something which may be said to be *absent*. But then, the question naturally arises as to how an absent object may at all be brought to anyone's awareness. The answer should be, and as given by philosophers and, perhaps, even laymen, indeed, is that this is possible in virtue of the *consideration* (*parāmarśa*) of a mark or sign (*linga*) which signifies, or rather serves as a pointer towards, the object concerned. Even so the question still remains as to how one thing can serve as a sign of, or a pointer towards, another. This question is indeed crucial in the present context, and the answer offered to it by philosophers should naturally be of paramount importance in the understanding of *anumāna* as a source of cognition. This answer consists in stating that the *linga* can serve as a pointer towards the object of *anumiti* provided that the two have been repeatedly perceived *together* in a state of coexistence or succession as the case might be, and, in consequence, the relation of *invariable concomitance* (*vyāpti*) has been established between them. Once this relation is established, the sensuous presentation of that which is the sign or mark (*linga*, *sādhana*, *sādhaka* or *vyāpya*) leads to the indirect (*parokṣa*) awareness of that which is *lingī*, *sādhya* or *vyāpaka*. Thus, for example, one in whose experience smoke and fire have been held together in the relation of invariable concomitance (*vyāpti*) will have the indirect awareness of the existence of fire wherever one happens to perceive actually existing smoke. In this example, smoke is the *linga*, *sādhana*, *sādhaka* or *vyāpya* and fire the *lingī*, *sādhya* or *vyāpaka*. And *vyāpti*, in virtue of which the actual sight of smoke leads to the apprehension of the unperceived fire, is the relation of invariable concomitance between smoke and fire, resulting from the repeated sense-experience of these two together as coexistents.

As seen above, *vyāpti* is the very foundation of *inferential knowledge*. That being so, if the possibility of this relation be ruled out, as it has been ruled out by the Cārvākas, the claim of *anumāna* to be regarded as a legitimate source of cognition would necessarily come to be negatived. But since we actually make use of inference even in the conduct of the affairs of our day to day life and since inference forms an essential part of the subject-matter of an academic discipline of great repute, namely, logic, it would be worth while to enquire into the arguments advanced by the Cārvākas for the dismissal of *vyāpti* as an impossibility.

The Cārvākas' arguments for the dismissal of *vyāpti* may be said to have proceeded on two distinct lines, one of which concerns the question whether *vyāpti* can at all be established, and the other relates to the question as to whether it can be *known*, even granted that it is somehow established: The former obviously concerns the *essendi*, and the latter the *cognoscendi*, of *vyāpti*. Let us first consider the argument put forward by the Cārvākas against the possibility of the establishment of *vyāpti*. The main point in their present argument is that *vyāpti* (invariable concomitance) is a relation which, from the nature of the case, must not be subject to any condition (*upādhi*), but that one can never be sure about the required *unconditionality* of *vyāpti*. For even if particular care be taken to establish a *vyāpti* in freedom from all the conditions that are so far known, the possibility of its still being subject to hitherto unknown conditions is not necessarily precluded. Moreover, the relation of invariable concomitance can be established between the *linga*, for example, smoke and the *lingī* or *sādhya*, for example, fire, provided that the former is *identically the same* and not merely *similar* in the various instances in which it is found to coexist with the latter. But this proviso, as the Cārvākas contend, is difficult of fulfilment. Thus arguing the difficulty, if not the impossibility, of the establishment of *vyāpti*, the Cārvākas arrive at the conclusion that *anumāna*, based on mere *generalizations* as it, according to them, must be, can yield only *probability* and not, as held by the major schools of Indian philosophy, *certain knowledge*.

The argument advanced by the Cārvākas against the possibility of *vyāpti* with reference to its *knowability* may be stated as follows. Since *vyāpti* is a *universal relation*, it cannot be known by means of external perception. For this kind of perception can only convey information about the relation between one *particular* and another *particular* and certainly not about the relation between two sets, each comprising *all* relevant particulars, whether past or present or future—precisely the relation which is said to be *universal*. It may be replied, however, that *vyāpti* is the relation of invariable concomitance between two *classes*, for example, the class or genus of smoke on the one hand and the class or genus of fire on the other. Even then, the Cārvākas argue that class-characters cannot be known by means of perception. But even granted that perception is competent to serve as a means of the knowledge of class-characters, that would not serve any real purpose in this context. For the invariable concomitance between the class-characters of the *linga* and of the *lingī* does not necessarily entail the relation of invariable concomitance between their respective particular instances. If external perception is thus unable to yield the knowledge of *vyāpti*, internal perception, as the Cārvākas further argue, is equally unable to do the same. The reason for this, according to them, lies in that the internal sense-organ *manas* is not independent of, but, on the contrary, is helplessly dependent upon, external sense-organs in apprehending outer objects, and that, with regard to this kind of apprehension, its importance lies only in the elaboration of the material supplied by external perception.

If it is held, however, that *vyāpti* can be known by means of inference, this would, according to the Cārvākas, lead to the fault of *infinite regress* (*anavasthā*). For this view would imply that one *vyāpti* is known by means of an inference, which is *ex hypothesi* based on another *vyāpti*, and that the latter *vyāpti* in its turn should be known by means of another inference and so on *ad indefinitum*. But it may still be contended that where both perception and inference fail, *testimony* can succeed, and that it rests with testimony to provide the knowledge of *vyāpti*. But then, the Cārvākas can easily fall back upon the Vaiśeṣika view of testimony as dependent upon, and inseparably bound up with, inference, and, accordingly, hold that testimony is as unable to provide the knowledge of *vyāpti* as is inference. But even granted that testimony is independent of inference, there is no gainsaying the fact that it is dependent upon the words of a reliable person, and especially that words, after all, are signs of meanings. That being so, the comprehension of the meanings of words would presuppose the knowledge of the relation of invariable concomitance between words and meanings. Thus testimony supposed to be the source of our knowledge of *vyāpti* is found to be itself dependent upon the same kind of knowledge. It, therefore, follows that the view of testimony as the source of the knowledge of *vyāpti*, as the Cārvākas would object, is involved in circular reasoning. Moreover, the acquisition of the knowledge of *vyāpti* from someone's statement that there subsists the relation of invariable concomitance between the *linga* and the *lingī* is tantamount to blind submission to authority, which is antithetical to the true spirit of philosophical investigations.

If testimony is thus unable to provide the knowledge of *vyāpti* may it not be, it may be asked, that another source of cognition, say, comparison (*upamāna*) can serve as the means of the attainment of that knowledge ? But as far as the Cārvākas are concerned, their answer should naturally be in the negative for the following reason. Comparison is the knowledge of an object, for example, a *gavaya* (a wild cow) brought about by the indication of a statement of a dweller in the forest, namely, that 'a *gavaya* is like a cow'. Thus it depends upon the universal relation between words such as 'a *gavaya* is like a cow' and objects signified by them such as a *gavaya*. Since comparison itself is, then, dependent upon the knowledge of invariable concomitance (*vyāpti*), it cannot be regarded as the source of this kind of knowledge.

The main point which the Cārvākas have really in view in disputing the possibility of inferential *knowledge* is that the so-called *vyāpti* on which it is said to be based is at best an inductive generalization derived from simple enumeration (*bhuyodarśana*) which can by no means yield the required necessary connection or invariable concomitance between the *linga* and the *lingī*. That being so, the indirect apprehension of the *lingī*, consequent upon the direct perception of the *linga*, as they find it easy to realize, cannot be characterized by *certainty* so as to deserve to be called *knowledge* in the strict sense of the term. In this the Cārvākas discovered a truth which was little known to the philosophers in the West until Hume and later J.S. Mill came to rediscover it in comparatively modern times.

It may be mentioned, however, that the Naiyāyikas, who among the philosophers in India, were most anxious to rescue inferential knowledge from the onslaught of the Cārvākas, contended that generalization is based not only on simple enumeration, but on the supersensible apprehension of the universal aspect of things (*sāmānyalakṣaṇa pratyāsatti*) on the part of an expert, and, consequently, that *vyāpti* is really the relation of invariable concomitance between the *linga* and the *lingī* and as such guarantees the legitimacy of inference as a source of cognition strictly so called. But the difficulty here is that the Naiyāyikas, in their opposition to the Cārvākas, do not meet them on a common ground, but, on the contrary, bring an extra-logical consideration to bear upon the controversy in so far as they admit the possibility of the supersensible apprehension of *universals*. Moreover, the admission of this possibility on their part, instead of providing them with an advantage over the Cārvākas, leads them into the vexed controversy among the realists, conceptualists and nominalists with regard to the status of the *universal vis-a-vis* the *particular*.

It is important to note, however, that while the majority of the Cārvākas hold that inference is of no avail in our concern with the sensible world or the domain of phenomena as well as with the supersensible world or the domain of noumena, a few of them, known as *suśikṣita* (*refined*) Cārvākas, are of the view that inference is indeed a source of knowledge in so far as its operation is confined to phenomena only. Moreover, the refined Cārvākas admitted another distinction between two kinds of inference, namely, inference respectively concerning the *past* and the *future*. And they held that inference concerning the past is useful and indeed legitimate, but that in its reference to the future, inference is absolutely useless and in fact spurious. Nevertheless, they did not fail to realize, at the same time, that the cognition yielded by inference in relation to the phenomenal world is only *probable* and by no means *certain*. And they upheld the pragmatic standpoint in their realization that inference is primarily of practical importance, and that the probable cognition which it yields is enough for the purposes of our day to day life.

VARIETIES OF ANUMĀNA

As previously indicated, among the schools of Indian

philosophy it is the Nyāya which is especially interested in a searching enquiry into *anumāna* in its epistemic as well as its logical aspect. This is evident, among other things, from the fact that this school has taken pains to distinguish different kinds of *anumāna* from different points of view. One of these points of view relates to the question: For whom is the *anumiti* (inferential knowledge) needed? The answer, as the Naiyāyikas have realized, would consist in stating that the need is either for *oneself* or for *others*. Accordingly, they distinguish between two kinds of *anumāna* respectively called *svārthānumāna* (inference for one's own sake) and·*parārthānumāna* (inference for the sake of others).

As regards *svārthānumāna*, negatively speaking, it is unconcerned with the formal demonstration of truths discovered by means of the inferential process. So it is in a class apart from what inference is from the logical point of view. Positively speaking, it conveys a psychogenetic account of inferential knowledge with a view to showing *how* an individual comes to apprehend an *unperceived* object on the basis of his *perception* of something else. Judged in the light of these two considerations, it is an *epistemological* process comprising the following factors: (a) knowledge of the relation of invariable concomitance between one thing called a *linga*, for example, smoke and another thing called a *lingi*, for example, fire, resulting from repeated observation of the coexistence of the two things, and expressible in the statement 'whatever is smoky is fiery'; (b) Perception of the former, namely, 'smoke' on a hill conjoined with the remembrance of the relation of invariable concomitance in question; and (c) The consequent apprehension that the hill is fiery or that there is fire on the hill. A concrete illustration of *anumāna* regarded as an epistemological process may, then, be stated as follows :

Whatever is smoky is fiery
The yonder hill is smoky
Therefore, it is fiery

It is most important to bear in mind, however, that not only propositions like those that have been cited above, but also the *order* in which they have been presented are essential to *anumāna* in the sense of an epistemological process. But the situation cannot, for obvious reasons, remain the same in the case of *anumāna* in the logical sense, that is, in the sense of a process of the formal demonstration of truths discovered by means of inferential knowledge (*anumiti*). This does not necessarily mean that the *nature* and *number* of the propositions which constitute *anumāna* in the logical sense should be different from what they are in the case of *anumāna* in the epistemological sense. But the *order* of the propositions cannot be the same in the two cases. The reason for this is that the discovery of truths with which *anumāna* in the epistemological sense is concerned is radically different from the *formal demonstration* of the truths discovered which is the primary object of *anumāna* as a logical process. Since in the process of the discovery of a truth, the truth should mark the culminating point in the process, the proposition conveying the conclusion should naturally be placed last among those which constitute *anumāna* as an epistemological process. But when the object of *anumāna* is to provide the formal demonstration of the truth already discovered, the truth in the form of a thesis to be established should naturally be the starting point of the process and stand in need of vindication. So, in their view, the concrete examples of the propositions which we have been making use of in our present discussion should, in the case of inference in the logical sense, be placed in the following order :

The yonder hill is fiery
Because it is smoky
And whatever is smoky is fiery

But then, this is not all that the Naiyāyikas and their Indian conferers have suggested with regard to the understanding of *parāthānumāna*, that is, inference in the logical sense, in distinction from *svārthānumāna*, that is, inference in the epistemological sense. Among the other suggestions that they have made in this connection, the following deserve to be carefully noted. In the first place, the first proposition in the list given above has been most appropriately designated by them as *pratijñā* (the thesis to be established). Secondly, they have equally properly called the second proposition in the same list *hetu* (reason). Thirdly, difficulty arises with regard to their understanding of the nature and status of the third proposition in the list. The reason for this is that they add to the end of this proposition the words 'for example, a kitchen' and call it *udāharaṇa* (example). But in this they fail to realize that the third proposition should not be an *example*, but a *reason* and, in fact, the *major* reason as distinguished from the *minor* reason as represented by the second proposition. Strictly speaking, the addition amounts to imposing an unnecessary psychological burden upon the logical relation of invariable concomitance between the *linga* and the *lingī* and so is uncalled for from the logical point of view.

Fourthly, the Indian logicians have gone further in adding two more propositions to the three we have mentioned above, respectively occupying the fourth and the fifth places in the list and being respectively designated as *upanaya* and *nigamana*. The former of these two propositions is intended to show the application of the universal proposition, for example, 'whatever is smoky is fiery' to a particular instance, for example, 'the hill is smoky'. It may therefore, be illustrated thus : 'The hill has smoke which is invariably accompanied by fire'. And as regards the latter, it is, in fact, the *pratijñā* stated over again, not as a *pratijñā* as such, but in the state of its establishment as the conclusion (nigamana). In the light of these considerations, a concrete example of the five-membered process of logical inference as conceived by Indian logicians may be given as follows :

1. The hill is fiery (*pratijñā*)
2. Because it is smoky (*hetu*)
3. Whatever is smoky is fiery, for example a kitchen (udāharaṇa)
4. The hill has smoke which is invariably accompanied by fire (*upanaya*)
5. The hill is fiery (*nigamana*)

A careful consideration of the above propositions would easily reveal that the fourth among them is the statement of the combination of the second and the third. But this combination would have been absolutely unnecessary had it been realized that the third proposition is not an *udāharaṇa* (example), but a reason (*hetu*) and indeed the major reason alongside the minor reason as represented by the second. So the introduction of the fourth proposition into the logical process of inference amounts to committing the fault of prolixity. Further, the addition of the fifth proposition would have been equally unnecessary if the third were regarded as a reason and, consequently, the question of the addition of the fourth would not have arisen at all. In any case, once the *pratijñā* is established in virtue of the minor and major reasons provided respectively by the second and thc third propositions, its restatement in the shape of a conclusion would be unnecessary.

The fact of the matter here is, however, that the Indian logicians, despite the fact that they were, unlike Aristotle and his followers, aware of the distinction between the epistemological and the logical sense of inference, proved unable to keep this distinction constantly in view and, as a result, arrived at a view of the logical process of inference which really amounted to the admission of the unwarrantable mixture of the epistemic and logical aspects of that process.. This is clearly evident from the fact that the first three propositions in the list (without the addition of the words 'for example, a kitchen' to the third) may together well represent inference as a logical process, and that the last three propositions with suitable changes can constitute inference in the epistemological sense. Thus, while Aristotle mistook inference in the epistemological sense for inference in the logical sense, the Indian logicians erroneously conceived logical inference to be a strange mixture of two distinct aspects of inference, the epistemic and the logical.

Other classifications of *anumāna,* unlike the one we have considered above, pertain to inferential knowledge as such, irrespective of the distinction between the epistemic and the logical aspects of the inferential process. One of these classifications has been made with reference to the view that the *vyāpti* which is the foundation of inferential knowledge, is, at least in some cases, traceable to, or deducible from, the principle of uniformity of nature, whether causal or non-causal. This classification, according to Gautama, the founder of the Nyāya school of Indian philosophy, comprises three kinds of *anumāna* which he respectively designated as *pūrvavat, śeṣavat* and *sāmānyatodṛṣṭa.** The first two of these are based on the causal form of the principle of uniformity of nature, and the last on the non-causal form of this principle. Thus *pūrvavat anumāna*, according to Gautama, yields the apprehension of an unperceived *effect*, for example, future rainfall, on the basis of the perception of its cause, for example, dense clouds. *Śeṣavat anumāna* is just the opposite of the former and consists in the apprehension of an unperceived *cause*, for example, rainfal, on the basis of the perception of its effects, for example, the fulness of the river, the muddiness of its water and the swiftness of its current. *Sāmānyatodṛṣṭa anumāna*, on the other hand, consists in the apprehension of an imperceptible object, for example, the movement of the earth, on the basis of the perception of a mark which is known to be, not causally but merely uniformly related to it, for example, the different positions of the sun in the sky.

It may be of interest to note, however, that Vātsyāyana, the commentator on the Nyāya-Sūtra of Gautama, understands these three kinds of *anumāna* in two senses, in the same sense as does Gautama as well as in a different sense. Thus *pūrvavat anumāna*, according to his new interpretation, is based on previous experience of the invariable concomitance of two perceived objects, for example, smoke and fire, and consists in the apprehension of an unperceived object, for example, fire at the sight of smoke and on the ground of the uniform relation between the two experienced in the past. *Śeṣavat anumāna* as newly interpreted by Vātsyāyana consists in the indirect apprehension of something by means of a process of elimination (*pariśeṣa*). Thus one may come to know that *sound* is a *quality*, by means of gradually eliminating the possibility of its being a *substance* (*dravya*), action or motion (*karma*), community (*sāmānya*), particularity (*viśeṣa*), inherence (*samavāya*) or non-existence (*abhāva*). Lastly, as regards *sāmānyatodṛṣṭa anumāna*, he holds that it consists in the apprehension of an unperceived object on the perception of a mark, although the relation between the object and the mark is not perceived. This, according to him,

* Iśvarakṛṣna has also admitted these three kinds of anumāna in his authoritative work on Sāṁkhya philosophy called Sāṁkhya—Kārikā. Vacaspati Miśra, in his commentary on this Kārikā, has brought these three under two categories, namely, yīta and avīta, the former being held to include both pūrvavat and sāmānyatodṛṣta anumāna and the latter only śeṣavat anumāna.

is well illustrated in the admission of the existence of the soul as a substance in view of the direct awareness of the qualities of cognition, pleasure, pain, etc. and on the logical, as distinguished from the empirical, ground that the qualities concerned must inhere in a substance.*

In the subsequent history of the Nyāya school of Indian philosophy, it is important to note, the present classification of *anumāna* lost its original importance, if it did not definitely come into disfavour. This is evident from the fact that Uddyotkara, who wrote *Nyāyavārtika* on Vātsyāyana's Nyāyabhāsya, rejected the ideas of the inference of an effect from a cause and, conversely, the inference of a cause from an effect respectively meant by *pūrvavat* and *śeṣavat anumāna.* In this he seems to have expressed his difference from all those logicians in India and abroad, including modern logicians in the West, by ruling out the importance of the causal principle as a basis of inductive inference. This seems to be the reason why *sāmānyatodṛṣta anumāna*, not being based on causal uniformity, but merely on the uniformity of coexistence, was acceptable to him as a genuine form of inference. The importance of Uddyotkara in the history of Indian Logic, however, lies in his introduction of a new classification of *anumāna* under three heads which he called *anvayī*, *vyatirekī* and *anvayīvyatirekī*, but which were redesignated as *kevalānvayī*, *kevalavyaterekī* and *anvayavyatirekī* by later logicians such as Varadarāja, Gangesa and others.

C

TESTIMONY (*ŚABDA; ĀPTAVACANA*)

It may well be presumed that perception and inference together cannot yield whatever knowledge we are in need of, and that at least some of it must come from other sources, including *śabḍa.* Although it literally means 'word', *śabda* is used in this connection in the technical sense of statements regarded as an independent source of cognition. But then, words must be uttered by someone or come from some source. And, what is more, the person who utters the words or the source from which they originate must be reliable in order that they can yield knowledge worth the name. In view of this, *śabda* is understood in the philosophical literature in India in the sense of *āptavacana* (true or reliable statements). All the orthodox (āstika) schools of Indian philosophy, with the exception of the Vaiśeṣika, admit *śabda* as an independent source of

* To start with the dogmatic view, as is done by the Nyāya School, that cognition, pleasure, pain, etc., are qualities of the self and then argue that the soul must exist in order that these qualities may have something to inhere in are tantamount to circular reasoning.

cognition. But then, as we shall see below, they are not agreed among themselves with regard to the *scope* of testimony.

Śabda is sometimes said to be of two kinds—the *dṛṣta* and the *adṛṣta*. The former is held to include the testimony of reliable persons as well as the scriptures, concerning *perceptible* objects or this-worldly matters. The latter is, likewise, regarded as comprising both human and scriptural testimony, but about *imperceptible* objects or other-worldly matters, including supersensible realities such as God, soul and immorality. But a more convenient classification of *śabda* would consist in its subsumption under the two heads *laukika* and *alaukika* or *Vaidika*, the former including the statements of reliable persons, that is, persons who are in the habit of speaking the truth (*yathārtha-vaktā*), and the latter being confined to scriptural statements.

Now it is the Naiyāyikas who gave the widest scope to *śabda* regarded as an independent source of cognition. According to them, the Vedas are created by God and indeed are made up of the words of God who is omniscient and veracious to the highest degree. So they are undoubtedly the most reliable source of knowledge. Human testimony (*āptavacana*), including statements concerning secular matters, as they further hold, are also competent to yield knowledge properly so called. But it is this view of the Naiyāyikas which does not meet with the approval of the Sāṁkhya-Yoga, the Mīmāṁsā and the Vedānta schools of philosophy. The reason for this, as the Sāṁkhya in particular came to realize, lies in that human testimony is dependent upon perception and inference and, so, while being competent to provide knowledge, cannot be regarded as an independent source of cognition. Scriptural testimony, according to these schools of philosophy, is, on the other hand, the most invaluable means of the direct revelation of truths regarding supersensible realities and so it eminently deserves to be regarded as an independent source of cognition. But then, they hold this view, not because scriptural testimony, as the Naiyāyikas hold, is God's creation or the embodiment of His words, but because it is *apauruṣeya* (not created by any person, whether human or superhuman), and indeed is the repository of eternal truths.

Thus three orthodox (*āstika*) schools of Indian philosophy suggested the restriction of the scope which the Naiyāyikas assigned to testimony held to be an independent source of cognition. Nevertheless, they still recognized its independence especially with a view to making room for the possibility of knowledge about other-worldly matters or supersensible realities. But granted that both human and scriptural testimony or, in other words, *śabda* in the widest sense, as the Naiyāyikas hold, can yield knowledge strictly so called, why, it may be pertinently asked, should it be regarded as an *independent* source of cognition? It is precisely this question which the later Vaiśeṣikas asked, and they answered it in terms of their view that the ultimate basis of the knowledge derivable from both human and scriptural testimony is the knowledge of the relation of invariable concomitance (*vyāpti*) between words and their meanings; so that testimony, while being able to provide knowledge, is not an independent source of cognition, but derives from inference.

It may be objected, however, that testimony is not dependent upon inference in as much as the relation between words and their meanings cannot be construed as *vyāpti*. The reason for this may be briefly stated as follows. The same word may have different meanings in different contexts, so that there can be no relation of invariable concomitance between a word and its meaning as there is, for example, between smoke and fire. This point may be specifically expressed by stating that the relation between a word and its meaning is not inherence (*samavāya*) nor even conjunction (*saṁyoga*) like the relation between smoke and fire, and, consequently, that the possibility of its being treated as *vyāpti* is ruled out. Moreover, if the relation between the two is said to be the same as the relation which subsists between the *indicator* and the *indicated*, the difficulty would be that this relation owes its existence to the comprehension of meaning and not *vice versa*; so that it cannot be of the same kind as is the relation of invariable concomitance, say, between smoke and fire, which constitutes the basis of inference.

But against objections such as the above, the Vaiśeṣikas, including Śrīdhara in particular, reply as follows. Of course, whereas the relation between smoke and fire, for example, is universal, the relation between a word and its meaning, as Śrīdhara admits, is not so, owing to the fact that it is limited to place, time and especially the intention of the speaker. But that does not really matter. For the latter relation, as he holds, is as *natural* as is the former, and—this, in his view, is particularly important—the word uttered by a certain person is the *linga* (sign) from which the appropriate meaning is *inferred*. So the comprehension of the meaning of a word, he concludes, is the result of an inferential process; and this goes to establish that testimony, in an ultimate analysis, is a variant of inference and not an independent source of cognition.

Even so, the same word, it may be reiterated, may have different meanings in different contexts, and, consequently, that the relation between a word and its meaning can not only not be universal, but cannot be *natural* either. The fact of the matter here is, however, that the relation of invariable concomitance which is said to constitute the foundation of inference should not only be universal, but also natural. For if it is not natural, but *conventional* as is the relation between language and meaning, then the transition from the former to the latter should be determined *ab initio* and be by no means dependent upon the process of inference. So a word, while being a *symbol* of a meaning, is not, as in the view of the Vaiśeṣikas it is, a sign (*linga*) from which a meaning may be inferred. In fact, a linguistic symbol is in a class apart from what is called *linga* (sign; mark) in logic; so that to treat, as the Vaiśeṣikas treat, the former as *functionally* the same as the latter is tantamount to an unpardonable confusion.

But granted as it should be that the question of testimony is connected with the question of the relation between language and meaning, it does not follow that testimony derives from inference and is not an independent source of cognition. This is so, not merely because the passage from language to meaning, as seen above, is not inferential, but also because it is, unlike perception and yet like inference, a source of *indirect* cognition. If such a thing as a source of indirect cognition should, as it must, be admitted in consideration of the possibility of inferential knowledge, then testimony, obviously not being perceptual nor, as has been already argued, being inferential, must be recognized as an independent source of indirect cognition.

Nevertheless, the Sāṁkya, the Mīmāṁsa and the Vedānta schools of Indian philosophy may be said to have done a signal service to epistemology by suggesting the restriction of the scope of testimony as against the Naiyāyikas who set no limit to it. But then, their suggestion proved misleading in so far as it consisted in the expression of preference for scriptural testimony to the exclusion of human testimony, including statements concerning perceptible objects or secular matters. For this was certainly the outcome of the non-human attitude of *indifference* to this-worldly matters which most deservedly came in for condemnation by the Cārvākas. But then, the Cārvākas went to the other extreme not only in their rejection of the claim of inference to be an independent source of cognition, but also in their ruling out the same claim on the part of testimony. But this was not due to their heterodoxy, consisting in the rejection of the authority of the scriptures, including the Vedas. For heterodoxy, however it may affect the philosophical position of its adherents, seems to have hardly any bearing upon their epistemological theory. This, as we shall see below, is evident from the fact that Jainism, which is as uncompromisingly heterodox as is the materialist school led by the Cārvākas, admitted testimony as an independent source of cognition. So it seems that it is scepticism, the outcome of their extreme empiricism, which has led the Cārvākas to exclude not only inference but also testimony from the usual list of the independent sources of cognition.

As regards Jainism, testimony (*āgama*), according to it, comprises propositions (*vacana*) composed of sentences, words and letters, and it yields knowledge on account of the fact that words signify objects in virtue of their inherent *denotative power* as well as *convention.* Thus the Jainas, while holding that a word naturally points to an object, display a great philosophical insight by adding, in disagreement with many other philosophers, that this natural phenomenon is subject to the limitation imposed by convention. However that may be, Jainism recognizes two kinds of testimony respectively called *laukika* (secular) and *lokottara* (non-secular) and regards both as independent sources of cognition. But as regards secular testimony, it is of the view that its validity is not guaranteed, and that its truth or falsity would depend upon the excellence (*guṇa*) or imperfection (*dosa*) of the speaker. And as far as non-secular testimony is concerned, the Jainas, being heterodox and, consequently, not being believers in the authority of the Vedas, hold that its only source is the *Tīrthankaras*, the rarest among human beings, who have attained perfection and omniscience. Hence it is evident that, in the view of Jainism, the testimony of the *Tīrthankaras* (*lokottara āgama*) is, unlike secular testimony, characterized by unquestionable validity. Jainism then differs from the Sāṁkhya, the Mīmāṁsā and the Vedānta in holding that secular testimony is, in a sense, an independent source of cognition. But in so far as it rejects the authority of the Vedas and yet admits non-secular testimony as an independent source of cognition, it lays itself open to the possible objection of the Cārvākas which, as previously mentioned, is applicable to the Sāṁkhya, the Mīmāṁsā and the Vedānta schools of philosophy in their admission of scriptural testimony as an independent source of cognition.

It is perhaps in view of this that Buddhism, the most prominent among the heterodox schools of Indian philosophy, denied epistemological value to testimony and remained content with the admission of perception and inference as the only independent sources of cognition. The reason why testimony is not admissible as an independent source of cognition, as the great Buddhist logician Diṅnāga observes, is that the validity of testimony depends upon the reliability of the speaker, and that our knowledge of his reliability is derivable either from our *perception* of the fact stated by him or from *inference* based upon our knowledge that his other statements have proved true. In any case, on account of its dismissal of testimony as an independent source of cognition, Buddhism may be said to have been free from the possible objection of the Cārvākas already referred to. And on account of its admission of inference as an independent source of knowledge alongside perception, it was, on the other hand, free from the extremism of the Cārvākas consisting in their rejection of inference as an autonomous source of cognition. But it was not altogether free from the extremism set on foot by the Cārvākas. This was due to its ignoring the importance of secular or human testimony as a source of cognition. What is implied thereby is that statements of reliable persons (*āptas*), whether orally transmitted or written or preserved in historical records, have an epistemological value of their own so as to deserve to be recognized as an independent source of cognition in addition to perception and inference.

D

COMPARISON (*UPAMĀNA*)

It seems that philosophers usually admit perception, inference and testimony as separate and independent sources of cognition, and that nowhere else outside India have they cared to consider the possibility of there being sources of cognition other than these three. It is especially in view of this that it would be worth while to try to ascertain whether Comparison (*Upamāna*), Presumption (*Arthāpatti*), etc., which have come to be recognized as additional independent sources of cognition within the field of Indian philosophy, really deserve to be so recognized. Let us then begin the consideration of *Upamāna* (Comparison), it being kept in view, however, that there is a fundamental difference between the Nyāya on the one hand and the Mīmāṁsa and the Vedānta on the other, with regard to the understanding of the nature of this source of cognition.

According to the Nyāya, *Upamiti* (that is, knowledge resulting from the employment of *Upamāna*) is not, as it would perhaps be natural to hold that it is, the knowledge of the *resemblance* of one thing to another. On the contrary, in the view of this school of philosophy, it has for its object the denotative relation between a word or a name standing for an unfamiliar object and the unfamiliar object itself, on the ground of the resemblance of that unfamiliar object to an already familiar one. This may be illustrated as follows. Let us suppose that a person, who very well knows the animal called the *cow*, is told by another person that there is a kind of animals living in the forest which *resembles* the cow and is called *gavaya*. He then happens to go to the forest and actually *perceives* an animal which is hitherto unknown to him, but which resembles the cow. Thereupon he comes to *remember* what he was told before, namely, that the *gavaya* resembles the cow. And, as a result, he acquires the knowledge that *gavaya* is the name of the strange animal concerned.

Upamāna thus understood by the Nyāya is obviously a highly complicated process involving other ways of knowing such as perception, testimony and memory or recollection. On this account as well as for other reasons, several schools of Indian philosophy, as we shall see later, have found it difficult to recognize it as an independent source of cognition. Moreover, resemblance or similarity, the concept to which *Upamāna* owes its very designation, is, strangely enough, thrown by the Nyāya into the background, instead of being treated by this school of philosophy in a more plausible manner in terms of the view of it as the object of *Upamiti*. It is, perhaps, in consideration of this drawback of the Nyāya that both the Mīmāṁsā and the Vedānta have put forward an alternative view of the nature of *Upamāna*. No matter whatever its foundation be, the knowledge of the denotative relation between a word and its meaning cannot, in the view of the Mīmāṁsā and the Vedānta, be, as in the view of the Nyāya it is, the kind of knowledge called *Upamiti*. The reason for this, according to the two former schools of philosophy, is that this relation as such is the object of another way of knowing, namely, *testimony*. But this, according to them, is far from implying that *Upamāna* is not a genuine source of cognition. On the contrary, as both Prabhākara and Kumārila, respectively the founders of the two distinct branches of the Mīmāṁsā school, have observed, there remains the possibility of our knowledge of the *resemblance* or *similarity* of an *unperceived* or rather *remembered* object, for example, a cow, to a *perceived* object, for example, a *gavaya*. And accordingly, they, together with other prominent members of the Mīmāṁsā school, including Sabara and Pārthasārathi Miśra, find in the realization of this possibility the achievement of *Upamāna* regarded as an independent source of cognition. Thus does the Mīmāṁsā assign to resemblance or similarity what seems to be its due place, by means of rescuing it from the subordinate status to which it is condemned by the Nyāya and recognizing it as the veritable object of *Upamiti*.*

It is necessary to note, however, that the Vedānta goes further than the Mīmāṁsā in holding that the knowledge of the similarity of the remembered cow to the *gavaya*, which, according to the latter, is sufficient unto itself and is an example of *Upamiti* as a complete process, is really not so. For this knowledge, in the view of the Vedānta, is characterized by a certain dynamism and, in consequence, inevitably leads to its correlate consisting in the knowledge of the similarity of the *perceived gavaya* to the *remembered* cow. In this the Vedānta is perhaps trying to bring to light the whole truth about *Upamiti* by means of emphasizing that this kind of knowledge is indeed the knowledge of the relation of mutual similarity between two similar objects. But then, mutuality in

* Prabhākara regards similarity as an independent category, whereas Kumārila does not do so. But that does not affect the identity of their views of the nature of Upamāna.

this case is of a *logical* character, signifying mutual implication and does not admit of being construed, as is construed by the Vedānta, in terms of the relation between *cause* (*karaṇa*) and *effect* (*phala*).*

Now the three schools of Indian philosophy, which have recognized *Upamāna* as an independent source of cognition in their respective ways, have done that, not arbitrarily, but with at least a show of reason. Thus the Nyāya argues that Comparison is distinct from Perception on the ground that, while the wild cow and its resemblance to the domestic cow are actually perceived, the knowledge that the wild cow bears the name *gavaya*, which, in the view of this school of philosophy, is an example of *Upamiti* properly so called, is obviously not *perceptual*. But the argument of the Mīmāṁsā and the Vedānta in this regard is different from that of the Nyāya, owing to the difference between the two former schools of philosophy and the latter in respect of the understanding of the nature of *Upamāna*. Consistently with its view that it is resemblance or similarity which is the object of *Upamiti*, the Mīmāṁsā argues that *Upamāna* cannot be the same as *Pratyakṣa* (perception) in as much as the object known to be similar, for example, the domestic cow is not in the present case in contact with any sense-organ, being *ex hypothesi* an object of memory or recollection. But this, according to the Mīmāṁṣā, does not warrant the conclusion that *Upamāna* is the same as recollection. For, while the domestic cow is, in the present context, an object of recollection, its similarity to a perceived object, for example, the wild cow, is not an object of the same kind. The line of argument thus followed by the Mīmāṁsā is the same as that which is pursued by the Vedānta in its attempt to show that *Upamāna* is distinct from *pratyakṣa*.**

Cannot *Upamāna* then be a variant of *Anumāna* (Inference)? As regards this question, all the three schools of Indian philosophy, namely, the Nyāya, the Mīmāmsā and the Vedānta, answer it in the negative. The reason offered by the Nyāya for its negative answer is mainly that *Upamāna* does not involve what is absolutely essential to *Anumāna*, namely, *Vyāpti* (invariable concomitance). This, according to this school of philosophy, is evident from the fact that the knowledge that the unfamiliar object in our previous example is a *gavaya*, resulting from its similarity to a familiar cow, is not based upon an invariable connection between 'similarity to a familiar cow' and the name *gavaya* established by previous experience of the two together. On the contrary, whereas *Anumāna* is based on *Vyāpti*, *Upamāna*, in the view of the Nyāya, has a basis of an altogether different kind, namely, the testi-

* Vide Vedānta-Paribhāṣā; Section on Upamāna.
** Vide Vedānta-Paribhāṣā; Section on Upamāna.

mony that the unfamiliar animal is similar to the domestic cow and is called *gavaya*. The argument of the Mīmāṁsā in this regard, however, is different from that of the Nyāya on account of the difference between their respective ways of understanding the nature of *Upamāna*. Since it is the similarity between two objects, for example, the wild cow (*gavaya*) and the domestic cow which, according to the Mīmāṁsā, is the object of *Upamiti*, *Upamāna* could be regarded as a variant of *Anumāna* had it been the case that the knowledge of the similarity between the two has its foundation in the relation of invariable concomitance between them established as a result of previous perception of them together. But this is certainly not the case in as much as the wild cow and the domestic cow in the present example were never perceived together in the past.

Be it noted, however, that the Vedānta, while agreeing with both the Nyāya and the Mīmāṁsā in holding that *Upamāna* is distinct from *Aunmāna*, seeks to establish this view in a way different from those of the latter. In fact, the Vedānta's main object is to show that the knowledge of the resemblance existing in the remembered domestic cow to the perceived wild cow, which, as previously observed, is the correlate of the knowledge of the resemblance existing in the perceived wild cow to the remembered domestic cow, is not *inferential*. To this end the Vedānta begins by observing that in an inference properly so called that which is the *linga* (sign or mark) must be present in the *pakṣa* (minor term). In the present case the *linga* is the 'resemblance existing in the perceived wild cow to the remembered domestic cow', and the *pakṣa* is 'remembered domestic cow'. But then, as is contended by the Vedānta, the former is not present or does not exist in the latter in fulfilment of the legitimate demand of *Anumāna*, with the result that the relevance or logical propriety of the major term, namely, 'the resemblance existing in the remembered domestic cow to the perceived wild cow', is not established. And this leads the Vedānta to the conclusion that the knowledge of the resemblance existing in the remembered domestic cow to the perceived wild cow cannot be acquired by means of *Anumāna*.

We may now proceed to enquire how the three schools of philosophy seek to defend *Upamāna* against the possibility of its being construed as a form of Testimony (*Śabda*; *Āptavacana*). As far as the Nyāya is concerned, its argument in this regard is as follows. *Upamāna*, of course, involves verbal testimony, for example, the statement by a knowledgeable person that there lives in the forest a kind of animals which resembles the cow and is called *gavaya*. But then, the Nyāya contends, this testimony alone cannot yield the knowledge that 'this animal bears the name *gavaya*'. In order that this knowledge may be an accomplished fact, the wild animal must be *perceived*. So while *Upamāna* actually involves testimony, *Upamiti* does not derive from testimony alone, but is the result of the combined function of both testimony and perception. Hence follows the Naiyāyika's conclusion that *Upamāna* is no more identifiable with testimony than with perception and, consequently, that it is an independent source of cognition. As far as the Mīmāmsā and the Vedānta are concerned in this connection, they are not required to make any special effort to show that *Upamāna* is not a form of testimony. The reason for this is that they recognize the centrality of *resemblance*, and eschew all reference to testimony, in their understanding of the nature of *Upamāna*.

But despite whatever attempt has been made to establish the independence of *Upamāna* as a source of cognition, quite a few among the schools of Indian philosophy have been left unconvinced about the truth of the view that *Upamāna* is coordinate with the more or less universally recognized sources of knowledge such as Perception, Inference and Testimony. The Cārvākas who admit perception (*pratyakṣa*) as the only source of cognition, the Buddhists, according to whom perception and inference (*Anumāna*) are together sufficient as the means of the provision of whatever knowledge we do have or require, and lastly, the Jainas who admit testimony alone in addition to perception and inference are obviously unconcerned with the question of the possibility of *Upamāna* as an independent source of cognition. Among the orthodox schools of Indian philosophy, it is the Vaiśeṣika and the Sāṁkhya-Yoga which have not only not admitted *Upamāna* as a separate source of knowledge, but have entered into a controversy with the Nyāya, the Mīmāṁsā and the Vedānta schools with a view to showing that their view of *Upamāna* is, to say the least, untenable.

Now as far as the Vaiśeṣika school is concerned, its contention is that the knowledge of the relation between a word, for example, *gavaya* and its meaning or rather the object meant, namely, the wild cow, which the Nyāya regards as *Upamiti* properly so called, really derives from the testimony of a reliable person to the effect that a kind of animals living in the forest resembles the domestic cow and is called *gavaya*. In this the Vaiśeṣika obviously ignores the Naiyāyika's view that *Upamiti*, while being dependent upon testimony, is not, as previously seen, solely dependent upon it, but is partly due to perception for its being an accomplished fact. But granted that the Vaiśeṣika is not to blame on this account, there is no doubt that this school of philosophy goes beyond legitimate limits in its criticism of the Naiyāyika view of *Upamāna* in so far as it holds that this source of cognition is, in the final analysis, a form of Anumāna (Inference). For in holding this view the Vaiśeṣika falls back upon its understanding of testimony as ultimately reducible to *Anumāna* which, as we have previously observed, is arbitrary and unwarranted.

The Vaiśeṣika, however, proceeds further in finding fault with the views regarding the nature of *Upamāna* held by the Mīmāṁsa and the Vedānta. As previously indicated, neither the Mīmāṁṣā nor the Vedānta makes any room for testimony within the structure of *Upamāna* and, what is more, both of them regard *resemblance* or *similarity* as the object of *Upamiti*. That being so, the Vaiśeṣika's objection against the Naiyāyika view of *Upamāna* is obviously inapplicable in the case of the views of this source of cognition held by the Mīmāṁsā and the Vedānta. And yet the Vaiśeṣika is as anxious to refute the latter view as it is to refute the former. Accordingly, this school of philosophy adopts the simple device of affirming the very thing which the Mīmāṁsā (and also the Vedānta) find it necessary to deny, namely, that the similarity of the *remembered* cow existing in the *perceived gavaya* is the object of memory or recollection. As previously seen, the Mimāṁsā tries to make out a case for the recognition of *Upamāna* as an independent source of cognition by arguing that, while a thing itself, say, a domestic cow, may be the object of recollection, its similarity to a perceived thing, for example, the wild cow, need not be an object of the same kind. It is precisely against this argument that the Vaiśeṣikas and especially Śrīdhara contend that similarity, unlike *conjunction*, is confined to one individual, instead of abiding in two or more individuals which are similar to each other; so that the recollection of the domestic cow is conjoined with the recollection of its similarity to whatever is found to be similar to it. And this leads the Vaiśeṣikas to the conclusion that *Upamāna* even as understood by the Mīmāṁsā and the Vedānta is not an independent source of cognition, being but a form of recollection.

From the account of the dispute between the Vaiśeṣika on the one hand and the Nyāya, the Mīmāṁsā and the Vedānta on the other which we have given above, it seems that the dispute is not resolvable in favour of either of the two sides, and that its resolution calls for fresh thinking over the problem of our knowledge of the denotative relation between words and the objects meant by them as well as of the similarity between two or more objects. Let us then proceed to enquire whether the Sāṁkhya's objections against the possibility of the recognition of *Upamāna* as an independent source of cognition conveys any indication of the fulfilment of this demand.

The Sāṁkhya's object is to show that, no matter whether it is understood in the Naiyāyika's sense or in the sense admitted by the Mīmāṁsā and the Vedānta, *Upamāna* is not a distinct source of cognition. First as regards the Naiyāyikas' view of *Upamāna*, the Sāṁkhya attempts to counter it by arguing as follows. The knowledge derived from the statement of a reliable person, for example, that the wild animal called *gavaya* is similar to the domestic cow is indeed an instance of *testimony.* That being so, the knowledge that the word *gavaya* denotes the wild cow resembliug the domestic cow is at best a derivative from this testimony and so is *inferential,* being devoid of any claim to be regarded, as the Nyāya regards it, as an independent source of cognition called *Upamāna.* But in this the Sāṁkhya obviously understands Inference in a loose or vulgar sense and not in the strictly technical sense in which it is understood by most of the schools of Indian philosophy, including itself. It cannot, therefore, be said to have much of an advantage over the Nyāya in its opposition to the latter's view of *Upamāna.*

The view of *Upamāna* held by the Mīmāṁsā and the Vedānta being different from that which is held by the Nyāya, the objection of the Sāṁkhya against the former should naturally be different from its objection against the latter. The question which is all-important here, however, is: What kind of knowledge is that which has, for its object, the similarity between two things, one of which is *perceived* and the other unperceived or rather *remembered?* Both the Mīmāṃsā and the Vedānta answer this question by stating that it is none else than *Upamāna* regarded as an independent source of cognition, whereas the Sāṁkhya's answer consists in its view that it is a form of Perception (*Pratyakṣa*). Now in holding this view the Sāṃkhya ultimately depends on the assumption that similarity is not, as in the view of the Nyāya it is, confined to one individual but abides in two or more individuals which are similar to one another. In consequence, it finds itself in a position to affirm, and rightly too, that the remembered domestic cow's similarity to the perceived wild cow amounts to the same thing as the perceived wild animal's similarity to the remembered domestic cow. That being so, the knowledge of the latter similarity should be *perceptual* and not derivable from any source other than perception, for the simple reason that the knowledge of the former is unquestionably due to perception. Thus does the Sāṁkhya arrive at the conclusion that *Upamāna* as understood by the Mīmāṁsā and the Vedānta is out of place among the independent sources of cognition.

The foregoing discussion may now be brought to a conclusion as follows. Let us first remind ourselves that *Upamāna,* in the view of the Nyāya, is the source of our knowledge of the denotative relation between a word (or a name) and an unfamiliar object meant by it, through the intermediary of our knowledge of the similarity of that unfamiliar object to a familiar one which is yielded by Testimony. Now as far as the Vaiśeṣika is concerned, it emphasizes the importance of Testimony which the Nyāya regards as an integral part of Upamāna, and thereby, as a first step, it comes to hold that what the Nyāya calls Upamāna should really be *Āptavacana* (Testimony).

Finally, by falling back upon its view of Testimony as ultimately reducible to Inference (*Anumāna*) it dismisses Upamāna altogether and allows Anumāna to take its place. But in this the Vaiśeṣika, as we have previously observed, commits the mistake of denying the undeniable independence of Testimony as a source of cognition.

It needs to be mentioned in this connection, however, that both the Mīmāṁsā and the Vedānta seem to be right in holding as they do that what the Nyāya calls *Upamāna* is really a variety, indeed a complex variety, of Testimony. Not only that; both of them have been able to realize an important point about the nature of *Upamāna* which the Nyāya has missed altogether, namely, that *Upamāna*, as its very designation indicates, should be none else than the source of our cognition of the similarity between two things, one of which is *perceived* and the other *remembered*. But then, the view of *Upamiti* held by the Mīmāṁsā seems to be inadequate in so far as this school of philosophy confines it to the knowledge of the similarity of the remembered object to the *perceived* one, leaving out of account the knowledge of the similarity of the *perceived* object to the *remembered* one, which seems to have an equally legitimate claim to be an object of *Upamiti*. It is precisely this inadequacy which the Vedānta seeks to remove by holding that *Upamiti* is made up of both these items of knowledge. But this is most significant in that it points towards the truth of the view held by the Sāṃkhya, namely, that *Upamāna*, understood in either of the two senses respectively admitted by the Mīmāṁsa and the Vedānta, is not an independent source of cognition, but is at best a variant of Perception (*Pratyakṣa*). The reason for this, according to the Sāṁkhya, is that the two items of knowledge are not really separate from each other, but are two aspects of one and the same thing and, consequently, that both of them must be *perceptual*, one of them, namely, the knowledge of the similarity of the *perceived* object to the *remembered* object being unquestionably so. And this leads to the decision of the main point at issue in terms of the view that *Upamāna* has no claim to be recognized as an independent source of cognition.

E

PRESUMPTION (*ARTHĀPATTI*)

As we have mentioned earlier, among the schools of Indian philosophy, it is the Mīmāṁsā (including the two branches respectively headed by Prabhākara and Kumārila Bhatta) and the Vedānta which alone recognize Presumption as a separate or independent source of cognition. In the view of the former, the admission of Presumption is a necessity when there arises a conflict between two well known facts followed by a demand for its resolution. Accordingly, the prominent members of the Mīmāṁsā school, including Sabara, have defined Presumption as the assumption of an unperceived fact apart from which the conflict between two actually perceived or known facts cannot be resolved. The typical example of Presumption which has been of common use in the Mīmāṁsā school of philosophy is as follows. If we know that Devadatta is alive and at the same time find that he is absent from home, there arises a conflict between his being alive and his being absent from home, which cannot be resolved except on the *assumption* that he lives somewhere away form home.

Prabhākara and Kumārila, however, differ from each other in their understanding of the nature and function of Presumption. According to the former, Presumption involves an element of *doubt*, the doubt about the truth of two well known facts on account of their mutual conflict. And it is the removal of this doubt which, in the view of Prabhākara, is the specific function of Presumption. The recognition of doubt as an element in Presumption, he further holds, is not only of use in the understanding of the nature and function of Presumption, but serves the additional purpose of showing that this source of cognition is distinct from Inference. As regards the latter point, Prabhākara explains it as follows. In the case of Inference, the *linga* (sign or mark), for example, smoke, is such that its existence is *beyond doubt*; so that from the undoubted perception of smoke one can *immediately* infer the existence of fire. But the situation is different in the case of Presumption in as much as the undoubted perception of Devadatta's absence from home, of course, may lead to his unperceived existence somewhere outside his home, but it can do that not *immediately* but only *mediately* by way of removing the doubt about his being alive.

Kumārila, on the other hand, holds that Presumption primarily and indeed exclusively involves the conflict (*virodha* or *anupapatti*) between two well known facts; so that any additional element such as *doubt* must be out of place within the structure of this source of cognition. In any case, the recognition of doubt as an element in Presumption, according to Kumārila, is not, as according to Prabhākara it is, called for in view of the distinction between Presumption and Inference. Kumārila's reason for this is that this distinction can be very well explained solely with refercnce to the conflict involved in Presumption. With a view to the explanation of the distinction between Presumption and Inference, it would, in the view of Kumārila, be sufficient to observe that, whereas Presumption involves an element of conflict and at the same time is required to resolve the same, Inference is free from this element and, consequently, does not have the same function te perform as is incumbent upon Presumption to do. Besides, the recognition of doubt as an element in Presumption, Kumārila observes further, would adversely affect the performance of the proper function on the part of this source of cognition. For if the knowledge or rather information about a fact, for example, Devadatta's being alive, were doubtful, Presumption would certainly be left without a sound basis to stand upon. Kumārila thus frees this source of cognition from the additional burden, the burden of doubt which Prabhākara imposed upon it and seeks to show that, rid of its complexity, Presumption can very well maintain its distinctness from Inference.

Now the Vedānta, the other advocate of the view of presumption as an independent source of cognition, may be said to differ from Parbhākara and be in agreement with Kumārila in not recognizing *doubt* as an element in this source of cognition. Even so, be it noted that it understands Presumption in a way different from that in which the Mīmāṁsā understands it, although it may be that their separate understandings ultimately amount to one and the same thing. The Vedāntist view of Presumption differs from that of the Mīmāṁsā in making no mention of such a thing as the conflict between two known facts and, consequently, being unconcerned with the idea of the resolution of the conflict of this description, In the view of the Vedānta, there is only one fact which is said to be well known, namely, that something presents itself to be inexplicable or stands unexplained and so is in need of explanation. This points to the function, the performance of which is the very essence of Presumption. And the function, according to the Vedānta, is none other than the framing of an assumption or *supposition* (*Kalpanā*) which provides the explanation in demand. Thus Presumption is regarded by this school of philosophy as comprising the knowledge of the fact to be explained (*Upapādya-jñānaṁ*) and the supposition or, let us say, knowledge of something that provides the required explanation (*Upapādaka-jñānaṁ*). Then by calling the former knowledge *karaṇaṁ* (instrumental cause) and the latter *phalaṁ* (result or effect), the Vedānta arrives at the definition of Presumption as the framing of an explanatory hypothesis (*Upapādaka-kalpanaṁ*) on the basis of the knowledge of the fact to be explained (*Upapādya-jñānaṁ*).* This seems to indicate that the Vedānta makes an improvement upon the position of the Mīmāṁsā in so far as it presents Presumption (*Arthāpatti*) in a clearer, scientific light by regarding it as the framing of explanatory hypotheses instead of as a source of cognition in the ordinary sense. Thus the situation, for example, that a person who desists from eating during daytime is still stout (*pīna*), is, in the view of the Vedānta, one which primarily calls for an explanation, instead of

* Vide Vedānta-Paribhāṣā; Chapter on Arthāpatti.

the acquisition of the knowledge of something or other. And the explanation in demand, as is held by this school of philosophy, is to be found in a hypothesis which is likely to be that the person concerned eats at night.

It would be worthwhile to mention, however, that the Vedānta has made an attempt to enquire into the various situations which call for their explanation and has, accordingly, come to admit several kinds of Presumption (*arthāpatti*). But since we are not at present concerned with the detailed investigation of the Vedāntist view of this source of cognition, we need not enter into the discussion of the classification of *arthāpatti* admitted by some of the members of the school of Vedānta philosophy. What, then, is necessary for our immediate purpose is to enquire whether *arthāpatti* as understood by both the Mīmāṁsā and the Vedānta is reducible to any of the primary sources of cognition, including Inference in particular.

Now since it is primarily concerned with the framing of hypotheses, and since hypotheses relate to something as yet unperceived, Presumption needs to be regarded as a source of *parokṣa* (non-perceptual) and not *aparokṣa* (perceptual) cognition. So the question of its reducibility to perception cannot arise. And its reducibility to either Testimony or Comparison, on account of their being sources of *parokṣa* cognition, is obviously out of the question. The only source of *parokṣa* cognition, its reducibility to which may be characterized by some measure of plausibility, should be none other than Inference. But, as we have seen earlier, both Prabhākara and Kumārila have argued the distinctness of Presumption from Inference in their respective ways. The Vedānta also does the same in the following manner. This school of philosophy, be it noted in the beginning, holds that in the case of Inference strictly so called, the universal major premise must be based on positive concomitance (*anvayavyāpti*), and that the Inference in which negative concomitance (*vyatirekavyāpti*) constitutes the basis of its universal major premise is really no Inference as such, but is another name for Presumption.* Judged in this light, Presumption, as the Vedānta argues, is distinct from Inference for the simple reason that a universal major premise based on positive concomitance is not available in its case, the proposition, for example, "wherever there is stoutness (*pīnatvaṁ*)

* The foremost among the schools of Indian philosophy which admit the possibility of Inference with a universal major premise based on negative concomitance is the Nyāya. The typical example of such Inference as given by this school of philosophy is :

Earth is distinct from other elements ;

Because it is endowed with smell as its attribute and because whatever is not of this description, is not of this description.

The Vedānta's contention in this connection is, however, that he who draws this conclusion is definitely aware that he is not inferring anyithing, but is only supposing something.

there is the condition of eating at night (*rātribhojanaṁ*)" being contrary to fact. But this really brings to light the crux of the whole situation by leaving behind the demand for a fresh enquiry into the possibility of Inference with a universal major premise based on negative concomitance (*vyatirekavyāpti*). Hence arises the necessity for the consideration of the attempts made by the Vaiśeṣika, the Nyāya and the Sāṃkhya to show that Presumption, in the final analysis, is a form of Inference.

Let us begin by observing that Prabhākara's attempt to account for the distinction between Presumption and Inference with reference to his admission of the presence of an element of *doubt* in the former and the absence of it in the latter proves a failure in the light of Kumārila's finding that Presumption, as a matter of fact, does not have to bear the burden of any such thing as *doubt*. Even so, Kumārila is as insistent on the recognition of this distinction as is Prabhākara, and finds the reason for this recognition in his view that Presumption differs from Inference in that, whereas the former involves the conflict between two known facts, the latter is free from such involvement. But then, any attempt to argue the distinction between the two sources of cognition under consideration, not with reference to their respective peculiarities as ways of cognizing, but with reference to the element or elements supposed to be involved in them, is undoubtedly superficial and cannot really serve the purpose which it is intended to serve. This seems to have been realized by the Vedānta as is evident from the fact that, instead of undertaking the useless task of ascertaining the factors likely to be involved in Presumption, it straightaway takes notice of the peculiarity of this way of cognizing and accordingly states that it is none but the act of framing hypotheses with a view to explaining situations which call for explanation. Thus has the Vedānta, as it seems to me, offered the most realistic interpretation of the nature of Presumption, which, as will be explained later, hardly leaves any scope for asking the question whether this source of cognition is reducible to any other and especially Inference. But the question has been actually asked. And this is due to two circumstances: the failure on the part of the Vedānta to realize the full significance of its view of Presumption as an act of framing hypotheses, and its folly, consisting in its attempt to show that this source of cognition is recalcitrant to its identification with Inference.

As previously indicated, the Vedānta, while dismissing the possibility of the interpretation of Presumption as identical with that kind of Inference in which the universal major premise is based upon positive concomitance, does not rule out, but, on the contrary, admits the possibility of its being regarded as the same as the kind of Inference in whose case the universal major premise is based on negative concomitance. Even so, it seeks to rescue Presumption from its absorption in Inference by declaring the Inference of the latter kind to be nothing but Presumption in disguise. But this is too simple and easy a way of vindicating the independence of this way of cognizing to produce any salutary effect upon the Vaiśeṣika, the Nyāya and the Śaṁkhya schools of philosophy which, consistently with their respective epistemological positions, are intent upon establishing the identity of Presumption with Inference. It is, therefore, no wonder that all of them should try to show that Presumption is indistinguishable from Inference in one form or another. It is, however, the philosophers belonging to the Vaiśeṣika and the Nyāya schools who have taken the greatest interest in the performance of this task. The main points in their argument against the views of Presumption held by the Mīmāṁsā and the Vedānta schools may, then, be noted as follows.

As previously mentioned, the Vedānta recognizes several kinds of *Arthāpatti* which, according to it, come under two broad heads: (1) *dṛstārthāpatti* (that which is based on the *perception of some* fact), and (2) *śṛutārthāpatti* (that which is based on knowledge derived from verbal testimony). That being so, in their opposition to the Mīmāṁsā and the Vedānta, the Vaiśeṣika and the Nyāya seek to show that both these kinds of *arthāpatti* are indistinguishable from Inference. As regards *dṛstārthāpatti*, Udayana puts forward the curious argument that, though the existence of a living person outside his home is not in conflict with his absence from home, being alive and being absent from home are in conflict with each other, and, consequently, that the Presumption of a living person's being outside his home does not really deserve to be so called, but should be regarded as an opposing Inference (*virodhī anumāna*). Śrīdhara and Śaṁkara Miśra, on the other hand, offer a more plausible argument in favour of the view that *dṛstārthāpatti* is identical with Inference. According to them, the Presumption that Devadatta lives outside his home is really inferential knowledge in as much as it is dependent on the invariable concomitance (*vyāpti*) between a *probans*, namely, the non-existence at home of Devadatta as a living person, and a *probandum*, namely, his existence outside his home. It is to be noted, however, that the invariable concomitance referred to here is *positive* (*anvayī*) and not *negative* (*vyatirekī*). That being so, the Vedānta seems to lose its point in so far as it holds that Presumption may be shown to involve negative concomitance, but never the concomitance of the positive kind. But, as we shall immediately see, the present controversy is really pointless and there really does not arise any question about the gain or loss on either side.

As far as *śṛutārthāpatti* is concerned, it is well illustrated in the Presumption of Devadatta's eating at night on the basis of the knowledge derived from verbal testimony, namely, that he is fat, but eats no food during the daytime. With regard to Presumption of this kind, Udayana holds that it is not an independent way of cognizing, but involves a twofold inference—the inference of Devadatta's fatness from the verbal statement that he is fat and then the inference concerning his eating food at night from his being fat. In view of this, he calls *śrutārthāpatti* an inference derived from an inferred fact (*anumitānumāna*). Śaṁkara Miśra also agrees with Udayana in holding that this kind of *arthāpatti* is not a single inference but consists of two inferences. But this procedure, it may simply be stated, is, on the one hand, vitiated by the prejudiced view of the Vaiśeṣika that Testimony is a form of Inference. On the other hand, it betrays the crudity of its conception of Inference in so far as it regards Devadatta's eating at night as inferentially derivable from the so-called inferential knowledge about his being fat.

It would, however, be unnecessary for our immediate purpose to consider further details regarding the attempts that have been made to establish the identity of Presumption with Inference. What needs to be especially noted in this connection is, however, that it is as unwarranted and futile to try to defend the independence of Presumption as a way of cognizing as it would be to try to show that, as a way of cognizing, Presumption is indistinguishable from Inference. The question as to which of the two sides is preferable to the other is, therefore, absolutely idle. The reason for this is that Presumption cannot be said to be a way of knowing unless the verb *to know* is used in the widest sense and knowing is regarded as consisting in making assertions, including fictitious assertions like 'Desdemona loves Cassio'. But since fictitious assertions cannot really be said to be items of knowledge, the sense in which the verb 'to know' needs to be understood should be *reasonably* restricted. The word 'reasonably' is of special importance in this connection. For, if the restriction is not reasonable, the scope of knowledge may come to be regarded, as the Cārvākas and extreme empiricists in general have regarded it, as too narrow to leave room for any kind of knowledge other than that which is perceptual.

Even so, the Cārvāka view of knowledge as exclusively perceptual, no matter whether it is acceptable or not, is important in that it stands as a warning to those who are loath to set any limit to the scope of knowledge, but, on the contrary, are anxious to widen it as far as possible. To obey this warning and yet not to be misled by the extremism of the Cārvākas would, perhaps, result in the admission of Perception, Inference and (secular) Testimony as the only genuine ways of cognizing, it being a fact that Inference and secular testimony, while being sources of *parokṣa* cognition, are based on the solid foundation of Perception. But then, to be based on Perception would not be enough for an instance of apprehension to be recognized as an item of cognition, unless the *act* involved in the apprehension concerned is characterizable as cognizing. This is one of the reasons, if not the only reason, why Presumption, while having its basis in Perception, is not a way of cognizing. Indeed, *supposing*, in which Presumption as an act consists, is certainly not the same as act of cognizing.* It may lead, and it is really intended to lead, to the emergence of cognition, but it is not itself a way of cognizing. So the question whether Presumption is distinct from, or identical with, the way of cognizing called Inference is absolutely ill-conceived. The conclusion which forces itself upon us, then, is that the proper place for Presumption is not among the ways of cognizing, but among the methods of scientific investigation which are intended to explore the region of facts with a view to explaining whatever lies unexplained within it.

F

NON-APPREHENSION (*ANUPALABDHI*)

Another source of cognition in addition to the five which we have already surveyed, has been admitted by the Vedānta and some of the members of the Mīmāṁsā school of philosophy, including Kumārila and his followers. It is called *Anupalabdhi* (Non-Apprehension) which conveys the apparently paradoxical idea that just as the positive apprehension of some existent through any of the accredited sources such as perception, inference, etc. is a way of cognizing, the non-apprehension of something or other is likewise another way of cognizing. This obviously presents a curious epistemological situation which needs to be investigated as follows.

The admission of *Anupalabdhi* as an independent source of cognition is primarily based on the presupposition that *abhāva* (non-existence or negation) is a separate category, parallel to, and coordinate with, *bhāva* (existence), That being so, those philosophers who do not admit *abhāva* as a separate category do not and also, from the nature of the case, cannot recognize any such thing as *Anupalabdhi* regarded as a way of cognizing in any sense whatsoever. To this class of philosophers belong the members of the Sāṃkhya and Yoga schools and Prabhākara, the head of one of

* It would be most appropriate to not the view of the Vedānta in this connection the view, namely, that when I perform the act of presuming, I am aware that I am supposing (kalpayāmi), and not that I am inferring (rnuminomi). Vide Vedānta-paribhāṣā; Chapter on Arthāpatti.

the two main branches of the Mīmāṁsā school. The Sāṃkhya-yoga, on one hand, and Prabhākara, on the other, dismiss *abhāva* in any of its four forms, namely, *prāgabhāva* (prior non-existence) *dhvaṁsābhāva* (non-existence after destruction), *anyonyābhāva* (mutual non-existence) and *atyantābhāva* (absolute non-existence), as an ontological category, and come to treat the non-existence of a thing, say, the table, as identical with a particluar state (*avasthāviśeṣa*) of its locus (*adhikaraṇa*), for example, the ground. Accordingly, they hold that the so-called *Anupalabdhi* is really a variant of perception and not a separate source of cognition.

But this is far from suggestiug that those who recognize *abhāva* as a separate ontological category are bound to recognize or do, as a matter of fact, recognize *Anupalabdhi* as a distinct source of cognition. On the contrary, the fact is that the Nyāya and the Vaiśeṣika schools of philosophy, which admit *abhāva* as an ontological category, hold that it is *perception* (*pratyakṣa*) which is the source of our cognition of the non-existence of things, and thus rule out the necessity for the admission of any such thing as *Anupalabdhi*. Their reason for holding this view may be illustrated by stating that the apprehension of the non-existence of the table on the ground is never cut off from, but, on the contrary, retains its continuity with, the *perception* of the ground with the table upon it, and, consequently, that the former, like the latter, is, in a sense, *perceptual.** But this, however ingenious it may be, involves the arbitrary mixing up of existence and non-existence together and, in particular, the treatment of the latter as ancillary to the former, which obviously militates against the view of non-existence as a separate ontological category held by the Vaiśeṣika and the Nyāya themselves. So it seems that the recognition of non-existence as a category by itself is not compatible with the view that *perception* is the common source of our cognition of both existence and non-existence. This must have been realized by the Vedāntists as well as Kumārila and, accordingly, they have, as we shall see below, argued the need for the admission of a unique source of cognition under the title of *Anupalabdhi*, in vindication of their view of non-existence as an independent category.

The Vedānta does not deny, but, on the contrary, admits, the possibility of the apprehension of non-existence (*abhāva*) through some of the accredited means of the acquisition of cog-

* According to both Udayana and Śaṁkara Miśra what Kumārila and the Vedāntists call non-apprehension is perception in some cases and inference in others. Thus, in this view, the so-called non-apprehension of the table on the ground, as mentioned above, is really an instance of perception. On the other hand, the non-existence of a cause, as both of them hold, is inferred from the non-existence of an effect on the ground of the invariable concomitance between the non-existence of a cause and the non-existence of an effect.

nition (*jñānakaraṇa*) such as inference. But then, it holds at the same time that there are cases in which the apprehension of non-existence cannot be due to *jñānakaraṇa*, but must be a kind of unique (*asādharaṇa*) experience (*anubhuti*) in the form of *Anupalabdhi*. Thus, according to the Vedānta, *Anupalabdhi* is not a mere void, being empty of all kinds of experience, but certainly is *non-apprehension*, the word 'apprehension' being understood in the ordinary sense, namely, as being due to *jñānakaraṇa*. With a view to distinguishing the non-apprehension of *abhāva* from the apprehension of the same due to *jṇānakarañа*, the Vedānta observes, however, that the former needs to be qualified by the adjective '*yogya*' (appropriate). What is really meant thereby is that *Anupalabdhi* is not properly so called except in so far as it is characterized by a certain 'appropriateness' (*yogyatā*). The question then is : How or under what conditions can *Anupalabdhi* be characterized by this quality? The answer of the Vedānta, negatively speaking, is that the quality concerned would not belong to *Anupalabdhi* or, in other words, that *Anupalabdhi* would be a sheer misnomer if the non-existence with which it is concerned is that of some supersensible object or other, for example, merit (*dharma*), demerit (*adharma*), God, immortality or the like. For the non-existence of such things, as the Vedānta holds, is open to inferential knowledge which is due to *jñānakaraṇa*. Positively speaking, the Vedānta's answer consists in stating that *Anupalabdhi* is 'appropriate' (*yogya*) in so far as the non-existence with which it is concerned is that of an object belonging to the same order of reality as its locus (*adhikaraṇa*) which is *perceived*. Stated otherwise, the answer is that the non-existence, the *anubhuti* (as distinguished from *knowledge*) of which is not produced by any positive *karaṇa*, but is due to the negative condition of non-apprehension, is not absolute negation nor the negation of anything supersensible, but should be the negation of something *perceptible*.

It is then evident that the application of *Anupalabdhi*, in the view of Vedānta, is confined to epistemological situations expressible in statements such as 'there is no jar on the ground' (*bhutale ghataḥ nāsti*) which are set in the background of perception. But does this not lend support to the view held by the Nyāya and the Vaiśeṣika, namely, that, the jar being as perceptible as is the ground on which it stands, the apprehension of its absence on the ground should, like the apprehension of its presence on the ground, be *perceptual*? The Vedāntist as well as Kumārila, however, reply that the apprehension of the presence of the jar on the ground is one thing and the apprehension of its absence on the ground is quite another. Had both of them been the same, the absence of the jar, as these philosophers further contend, would be perceived even when it is present, which is really an impossibility. In this the Vedāntist and Kumārila definitely have an advantage over the Nyāya and the Vaiśeṣika resulting in the demonstration of the untenability of the latter's view that the non-existence of an object whose locus is perceptible is itself *perceptible.* But the crux of the situation is conveyed through the question which naturally arises in this connection—the question whether the refutation of the Nyāya-Vaiśeṣika view of the apprehension of non-existense by the Vedāntist and Kumārila has anything to do with the establishment of their doctrine of the non-apprehension of non-existence.

The answer to the question posed above should naturally be in the negative. For granted as it must be that the non-existence of perceptible objects like the jar cannot be the object of perception, nor can it, for obvious reasons, be the object of any other accredited way of cognizing such as inference, it does not follow, as according to the Vedāntist and Kumārila it does follow, that there must be some unique way of cognizing to claim it to be its special object. Strictly speaking, anything that cannot be said to be the object of any of the usually accepted ways of cognizing is precisely that about which the question of its cognizability is irrelevant. To hold as the Vedāntist and Kumārila do hold, that such a thing is the object of a unique way of cognizing called *Anupalabdhi* is really as wrong and misleading as it is to hold, as Kant does hold, that it is unknown and unknowable. The former, to use a Spinozistic phraseology, amounts to taking, refuge 'in the asylum of ignorance' in one way and the latter does the same in another. But merely to say all this is not the end of the matter.

What still remains to be observed is that statements such as 'there is no jar on the ground' involve the *negating* of the deliverance of some perceptual experience or other, which is a *pure act* in itself and, consequently, is recalcitrant to its interpretation as an act of apprehending or as an act of not *apprehending*, both being tantamount to the ignoring of the inherent peculiarity of the act of negating which is all-important in the epistemological situation under consideration. Hence we are led to the conclusion that it is, perhaps, a greater mistake to recognize *Anupalabdhi* as a way of cognizing than it is to accord the same recognition to either *Upamāna* or *Arthāpatti*. And this, it is most important to note, bears the reflection of the decision of the underlying basic issue concerning the status of non-existence—the decision which is expressed in the view that non-existence or negation is not a category by itself, but is the offspring of the arbitrary and unwarrantable conversion of the act of negating into an independent *entity*.

G

THE MINOR SOURCES OF COGNITION

Our enquiry into the sources of cognition which have come to be recognized within the field of Indian philosophy as a whole is still in need of being extended further lest the minor sources of cognition which have found mention in philosophical and semi-philosophical literature in India should be left out of account. As previously listed, these are Tradition (*Aitihya*), Inclusion (*Sambhava*), Gesture (*Ceṣṭā*) and Elimination (*Pariśeṣa*). First as regards *Aitihya*, it has been regarded as a source of cognition by the *Paurānikas* and is taken to mean a traditional belief or a body of such beliefs which have originated from unknown sources and have been handed down from generation to generation. But, considering that the sources of these beliefs are unknown and, consequently, that we have no means of ascertaining whether they are reliable or not, *Aitihya* is, in principle, unacceptable as a source of cognition in any sense whatsoever. Supposing, however, that the sources in question are somehow discovered to be reliable, *Aitihya* would, of course, be admissible, not as an independent source of cognition, but as a variant of testimony (*Āptavacana*). In any case, Tradition is no addition to our list of independent sources of cognition comprising Perception, Inference and Secular Testimony.

Sambhava (Inclusion) is regarded as the process of knowing something, not directly and immediately, but, indirectly and mediately, on account of its being included in something else which is already known. In order to ascertain whether or not *Sambhava* admits of recognition as an independent source of cognition, it is necessary to note, however, that it may be of two different kinds: (1) possible inclusion, and (2) certain inclusion. As regards the first, for example, a Brahmin may possess holiness, it is uncertain and so, as Udayana rightly observes, cannot be regarded as a source of cognition at all. As far as the second is concerned, it finds illustration in such cognitive judgments as "a thousand includes a hundred" which are valid. That being so, *Sambhava* of the second kind is acceptable as a source of cognition. But then, the question is whether it is fit for recognition as an independent source of cognition or is reducible to, or is a variant of, another source of cognition. The answer, of course, lies in stating that it is a form of inference. But then, the inference concerned is not, as according to the Mīmāṁsā, the Sāṁkhya and the Nyāya-Vaiśeṣika it must be, *syllogistic*, but is of an altogether different kind, being solely dependent upon the application of the principle of *implication*. Thus it is found that our own list of the independent ways of cognizing is still in no need of enlargement.

The third among the minor sources of cognition in our list is *Ceṣṭā* (Gesture) which is regarded by the Tantras as having a special epistemological significance. Now Gestures, which, strictly speaking, are non-verbal, consist of certain bodily movements and facial expressions which normally convey certain meanings or else serve as directions to the performance of certain *actions*. As regards Gestures of the former kind, they are obviously a source of cognition. But it is not independent, but, on the contrary, is a form of inference based on the invariable concomitance between the gestures concerned and their meaning. As regards Gestures of the latter kind, they being primarily and indeed exclusively concerned with *action*, instead of cognition, there arises no question about their being a source of cognition in any sense whatsoever. So we see how very difficult it is to make out a case for the addition of a new source of cognition to the list of the three which we have found it reasonable to recognize as characterized by independent epistemological significance.

Lastly, we come to the consideration of Elimination (*Pariśeṣa*) regarded as a source of cognition. As is indicated by its very designation, *Pariśeṣa* is the process of knowing something by means of the elimination, from a group of objects, of those which are known to be distinct from, or unidentifiable with, it. Judged from this point of view, there is no doubt that things are sometimes cognized in this way, and, consequently, that the process of cognition under consideration is genuine. But why should it be called independent and irreducible? To all intents and purposes, it is, after all, the same as the process of perceiving subject to the exercise of circumspection and discrimination. Thus our enquiry into the minor sources of cognition leaves us with no better conclusion than that these are as unable to serve the cause of the expansion of the scope of cognition as *Upamāna*, *Arthāpatti* and *Anupalabdhi* have already been found to be.

What, then, was really needed for the determination of the identity and number of the sources of cognition was the judicious employment of the principle represented by the law of parsimony. The Cārvākas are, perhaps, the only group of Indian philosophers who accepted this principle whole-heartedly. But then, the trouble with them was that they went too far in their employment of this principle, with the result that philosophy was impoverished in their hands in many respects, including the epistemological, with which we are at present especially concerned. This is evident from their rejection of all sources of cognition except perception. Among the major schools of Indian philosophy, the Vedānta and the Bhātta school of Mīmāṁsā philosophy, on the other hand, paid no heed to the principle under consideration at least in respect of their treatment of the sources of cognition. As a result, they indiscriminately inflated their number so as to recognize as many as six of them. As regards the remaining schools of Indian philosophy, they sought to steer clear of the Scylla of the extremism of the Cārvākas and the Charybdis of the counter-extremism of the Vedānta and the Bhātta school of Mīmāṁsā philosophy. Accordingly, the number of the sources of cognition admitted by them ranged between two and five. But it was given to the Sāṁkhya school alone to arrive at a statisfactory decision with regard to the identity and number of the sources of cognition. This is evident from the fact that Perception, Inference and Testimony, the three sources of cognition which they have admitted are each independent of the others, and, what is more, they together constitute the entire corpus of unquestionably legitimate sources of cognition.

II

THE NATURE AND CRITERION OF TRUE COGNITION

A

THE NATURE OF TRUE COGNITION

We have already investigated one of the three parts of Indian epistemology, which is especially concerned with the enquiry into the sources of cognition. Of the remaining two parts of it, one, as we have previously indicated, deals with the problem of truth and the other with that of error or falsity. As far as we are at present concerned, we shall undertake the investigation of the former of these two parts of Indian epistemology, leaving the latter for subsequent treatment.

Let us first acquaint ourselves with the principal views of the nature of true cognition which are noticeable within the field of Indian philosophy. It does not, however, seem necessary to mention them in any particular order. We may start with any one of them we may choose. The Sāṁkhya view of the nature of true cognition may then be our starting point. According to this school of philosophy, true cognition is the apprehension of an object (*viṣaya*) which is above *doubt* (*asaṁdigdha*), free from error (*aviparita*) and has not been previously known (*anadhigata*) and so falls outside the scope of memory (smṛti). The Vedānta agrees with this view in ruling out the role of memory, but substitutes its own concept of *abādhitatva* (uncontradictability) for the Sāṁkhya concept of *asaṁdigdhatva* (indubitability) in its characterization of true cognition. Thus the Vedānta is in substantial agreement with the Sāṁkhya with this difference, however, that this substitution on its part serves to rescue truth from the subjectivity which is consequent upon the application of the concept of *asaṁdigdhatva* by the Sāṁkhya in its understanding of the nature of true cognition.

Mention may next be made of the Mīmāṁsā view of the nature of true cognition. In this connection it would be worth while to note that, while it is not alone in holding that cognition *as such* is true, the Mīmāṁsā is most conspicuous for its laying the greatest emphasis on this view.* This view, as we shall see later, is one of the two rival views which have figured most prominently in the discussion of the question regarding the *criterion* of truth. However that may be, in the present context, the Mīmāṁsa is almost at one with the Sāṁkhya and the Vedānta. For both the branches of the Mīmāṁsā respectively led by Prabhākara and Kumārila, like the latter, dissociate true cognition from memory or recollection. Not only that; they go so far as to hold that recollection as such is lacking in truth for the simple reason that it consists in the apprehension of that which has been already apprehended by means of perception. Moreover, some of the members of the Mīmāṁsā school and especially Pārthasārathi Miśra, like the Sāṁkhya and the Vedānta, hold that a cognition is true in so far as it remains uncontradicted (*abādhita*) by another cognition.

Jainism, despite its heterodoxy, is in partial agreement with the orthodox schools of Sāṁkhya, Vedānta and Mīmāṁsā in its view of the nature of true cognition. In the first place, it, like the latter, regards true cognition as being in a class apart from memory or recollection.** Secondly, some of the Jaina philosophers such as Siddhasena display their community with these orthodox schools of Indian philosophy in recognizing *abādhitatva* as an essential feature of true cognition. But then, Jainism is of the view that true cognition is invariably the cognition of itself as well as of some external object or other. In holding this view it is, on the one hand, opposed to the Nyāya, the Mīmāṁsā, etc., according to which true cognition is the cognition of external objects only, and not of itself in addition. On the other hand, it is opposed to those Buddhists who hold that true cognition is that cognition which consists in the apprehension of itself only and of no external object whatsoever in as much as such objects, in their view, are non-existent. In this twofold opposition, Jainism obviously bases itself on the assumption that cognition of itself and cognition of external objects are inseparable correlatives and, consequently, that the one apart from the other is a false abstraction.

* "It is strange, indeed, how a cognition is said to apprehend an object, and yet be invalid", says Sabara.

** Some of the definitions of true cognition given by Jaina philosophers like Vādi Deva Suri and Siddhasena do not, however, exclude recollection from the field of this kind of cognition.

Moreover, in course of the further development of its view of the nature of true cognition, Jainism comes to recognize certain additional features of this kind of cognition, which reveals its agreement with some of the schools of Indian philosophy and its difference from others. Thus it holds that true cognition must be *determinate* (*savikalpaka*), and not *indeterminate* (*nirvikalpaka*). This view, as we have previously seen, is set in the background of Jainism's rejection of any such thing as indeterminate cognition and, consequently, is a pointer to its opposition to all those schools of philosophy, including the Nyāya, which admit the distinction between determinate and indeterminate cognition. But the real point here is that in holding the view under consideration, Jainism gives vent to its strongest opposition to Buddhism which agrees with it in rejecting the distinction between determinate and indeterminate cognition, but admits the latter to the exclusion of the former, and, what is more, proclaims that cognition as such is unavoidably indeterminate, and that indeterminate cognition is true cognition *par excellence*.

Jainism, however, goes still further in admitting two more features of true cognition, one of which indicates its realistic tendency and the other expresses its pragmatist outlook. Thus it arrives at the view that cognition is true in so far as it is characterized by correspondence (*avisaṁvādakatva*) with its object* and is at the same time endowed with *practical efficiency* or the capability of leading to the attainment of the intended object (*arthaprāpakatva*). In viewing true cognition from the realistic point of view, Jainism is, of course, in agreement with most of the schools of Indian philosophy with the exception of the Yogācāra school of Buddhism, according to which external objects are non-existent and, consequently, the correspondence of cognition with external objects is out of the question. But in so far as it understands true cognition from the pragmatist point of view, its agreement with other schools of Indian philosophy is rather limited, and does not go much further than the Nyāya-Vaiśeṣika.

The above reference to the schools of the Nyāya and the Vaiśeṣika brings us to the consideration of the view of true cognition held by them. Be it noted in the beginning that these schools are no exceptions in dissociating true cognition from memory or recollection. Thus, negatively speaking, true cognition, according to the Nyāya-Vaiśeṣika, is something unaffected by memory. And, positively speaking, it is, as held by the most prominent members of this combined school of philosophy, including Uddyotkara, Udayana, Varadarāja and others, characterized by correspondence with its object and thus is the certain apprehension of the real

---

* As this view implies, truth and its opposite, that is, falsity are, according to Jainism, extrinsic and not intrinsic features of cognition.

nature of its object (*arthapariccheda*). This idea of 'correspondence' is, however, understood in a rather complicated way by Gangeśa, the founder of the school of Navya Nyāya. According to him, true cognition is the apprehension of what exists in its object. What this means, as Visvanātha points out, is that in the case of true cognition, the content of apprehension is the generic character of the object as abiding in the object itself. The content thus characterized may otherwise be called the cognized mode (*prakāra*) of the object. That being so, the 'correspondence' which the Nyāya-Vaiśeṣika regards as essential to true cognition is, in the view of the Navya Nyāya, the correspondence of the cognized mode to the object. Now, apart from the question whether it is right or wrong and also apart from the more fundamental question whether or not the truth of cognition has anything to do with the idea of 'correspondence', this view of the Navya Nyāya, it must be admitted, is an attempt to introduce a definite meaning into this idea which is left absolutely vague by the school of the Nyāya-Vaiśeṣika as well as the others which have made use of it in their understanding of the nature of true cognition.

In further elaboration of its view of the nature of true cognition, the Nyāya-Vaiśeṣika comes to agree with the Sāṁkhya in separating it from *doubt* and *error* and takes a step ahead in ruling out the admixture of hypothesis with it, and thereby lends support to its view of the impossibility of *Arthāpatti* regarded as a source of true cognition. It remains to be observed, however, that the Nyāya-Vaiśeṣika shares with Jainism the pragmatist outlook, and holds that *practical efficiency* is a characteristic mark of true cognition. But then, it keeps the distinction between truth itself and the test or criterion of truth clearly in view,and holds that reference to practical efficiency is called for in the understanding of the *test* or criterion of truth, but not in the case of the understanding of the nature of truth itself. We may now bring our enquiry into the Nyāya-Vaiśeṣika view of the nature of true cognition to an end by highlighting the fact that, whereas the Mīmāṁsā regards the relation of truth to cognition as *internal* or *intrinsic*, this combined school of philosophy is of the view that it is *external* or *adventitious*.

Lastly, as regards Buddhism, in its understanding of the nature of true cognition, it emphasizes the importance of the harmony or correspondence of cognition with its object. But then, it does not understand 'correspondence' in the sense in which the Nyāya-Vaiśeṣika understands it, but in the light of its pragmatist outlook. Accordingly, it holds that cognition is in correspondence with its object and so is true in so far as it leads to the attainment of its object. In its elaboration of this point, Buddhism in the first instance emphasizes the importance of the role of recollection in true cognition—recollection which, as we have already seen, has been completely left out of account by the majority of the schools of Indian philosophy in their understanding of the nature of true cognition. Once the importance of recollection is restored, Buddhism, however, moves forward to hold that true cognition gives rise to the recollection of an object perceived in the past, that this recollection gives rise to a desire which in its turn leads to a certain action, and finally that this action serves to bring about the attainment of the object concerned. Besides, Buddhism, like Jainism, holds in this connection that true cognition is naturally directed towards desirable objects and tends to avoid undesirable ones.

As previously observed, Buddhism rejects the claim of determinate cognition to be regarded as true. Its reason for this is that the determinations (*vikalpas*) of determinate cognition are not real features of objects, but are ideal constructions of the mind superimposed upon indeterminate or unqualified objects. While determinate cognition is thus shown to be false, indeterminate cognition, according to Buddhism, is unquestionably true in as much as it is, on the one hand, free from the burden of ideal constructions and, on the other, is such that in its case there is similarity (*sārūpya*) between the form of cognition and the form of the object. But then, Buddhism, strangely enough, holds that the truth of cognition is not one of its *intrinsic* features. On the contrary, cognition, according to it, is intrinsically false and is in need of being validated by extraneous conditions. When it just comes into existence, cognition is uncertain and so is liable to be contradicted and hence, argues Buddhism, should be regarded as false. And it is only later that its truth may be established by the knowledge of the excellence of its causes, or the knowledge of its correspondence with the real nature of its object or again the knowledge of a fruitful action to which it has led.

It may be reiterated in conclusion that one of the several respects in which Buddhist epistemology stands unique relates to the Yogācāra view that true cognition is cognition of itself only, having nothing to do with the so-called object for the simple reason that it does not exist. This view, as previously indicated, divides Buddhism, on the one hand, from Jainism, according to which true cognition is at once cognition of itself as well as of its object and, on the other, from the Nyāya-Vaiśeṣika, Mīmāṁsā and others on account of their view that cognition of itself is an obvious impossibility, and, consequently, that true cognition is the exclusive apprehension of its object.

The foregoing account of the views held by the major schools of Indian philosophy about the nature of true cognition calls for a number of critical remarks, only a few of which may conveniently be mentioned here as follows. In the first place, it is indeed strange that almost all the major schools of Indian philosophy, with the exception of Buddhism,* should look upon *memory* as foreign, or even antithetical to true cognition. That even perceptual cognition in our day to day life, irrespective of its distinction between the true and the false, unavoidably involves the role of memory or recollection is a truth which is unmistakably testified to by psychological evidence. That being so, the ignoring of the importance of memory on the part of most of the schools of Indian philosophy in their understanding of the nature of true cognition cannot be accounted for except on the assumption that they have, whether consciously or unconsciously, accepted the view of perceptual cognition as *paradigmatic*, together with the additional view that perception is *wholly* due to *indriyārtha-sannikarṣa* (contact of the object with some sense-organ or other). But this twofold view, curiously enough, seems to be, on the one hand, due to the misleading influence of the Cārvākas, according to whom perception is the only source of cognition. On the other hand, it is the outcome of an unduly exaggerated view of the importance of *indriyārthasannikarṣa* with regard to possibility of perceptual experience. This is indeed strange in view of the fact that all these schools of Indian philosophy are avowedly opposed to the Cārvāka view of perception as the only source of cognition, and that most of them admit the possibility of *savikalpaka pratyakṣa* (determinate perception) and so are precluded from holding that perception is wholly due to *indriyārthasannikarṣa*.

Secondly, the recognition of the unduly exaggerated importance of *indriyārthasannikarṣa* in the case of perceptual experience is responsible for the admission of the arbitrary and unwarrantable distinction between determinate and indeterminate perception which has produced a prejudicial effect upon the understanding of the nature of true cognition. The dismissal of this distinction on the part of Jainism has, however, been of considerable help in the understanding of the nature of cognition in general and true cognition in particular. In fact, by holding that there can really be no such thing as indeterminate cognition and that cognition as such is determinate, Jainism has done a signal service to Indian epistemology by bringing out the truth that the truth of cognition is inseparable from its determinateness. But Buddhism, on the other hand, has taken the indiscreet step of dismissing determinate cognition as spurious and recognizing indeterminate cognition as cognition properly so called and, moreover, as characterized by

* Buddhism's recognition of the importance of memory or recollection for the possibility of true cognition is, however, misleading. For memory, according to Buddhism, does not really enter, as from the psychological point of view it does enter, into the structure of cognition as such, but is only an item in a chain which leads to the emergence of the practical results of cognition.

truth. In this Buddhism obviously ignores the fact that indeterminate cognition is at best a hypothetical abstraction and at worst a figment of imagination.

Thirdly, whereas it is ordinarily held and is also held by the Nyāya-Vaiśeṣika, the Mīmāṁsā and others, that the object of true cognition is some external object or other, Jainism, as we have already seen, is of the view that the object of such cognition is both itself and some external object or other. But the position thus upheld by Jainism is obviously neither purely idealistic nor purely realistic, but seems to be an attempt to mix up both idealism and realism in the vain hope of the neutralization of their respective shortcomings as a result of their impact upon each other. So the way out of the predicament thus presented lies either in the admission of pure realism, together with the view that the object of true cognition is nothing but some external object or other or in having recourse to idealism and holding the view that the object of true cognition is nothing but itself. But as regards the latter alternative, it can be definitely said that it leads from the present predicament to a new one called ego-centric predicament. The former, on the other hand, seems to be preferable in view of the consideration that it steers clear of the Scylla of the hybrid of idealism and realism and the Charybdis of the ego-centric predicament.

Lastly, we may take up the consideration of the question whether the relation of truth to true cognition is intrinsic or extrinsic, the question which has led to a great deal of controversy among most of the schools of Indian philosophy. This question, it is important to note, has a significant bearing upon the idea of the correspondence of cognition with its object and the idea of the practical efficiency of cognition which have been made use of by some of the schools of Indian philosophy in their understanding of the nature of true cognition. As previously mentioned, Sabara, a prominent member of the Mīmāṁsā school of philosophy expressed his utmost surprise about the possibility of the recognition of any given instance of cognition as false. And thereby he insisted on the truth of the doctrine of the intrinsic truth (*svataḥprāmānya*) of cognition. But once this doctrine comes to be accepted, as it is accepted by the Mīmāṁsā, the ideas of 'correspondence' and 'practical efficiency' are obviously out of place in the understanding of the nature of true cognition. And, as a matter of fact, the Mīmāṁsā rules out both these ideas in this kind of understanding on its part. In this it takes its stand on the assumption that the truth of cognition is known by the cognition itself and not by a separate cognition of its correspondence with its object or of the utility which has been its outcome.

But apart from other difficulties of the Mīmāṁsā doctrine of the intrinsic truth of cognition, the one that is most obvious and indeed the most fundamental lies in the inability of this school of philosophy to admit such a thing as false cognition. But, curiously enough, the Mīmāṁsā does admit the possibility of false cognition with the proviso that the falsity of false cognition, unlike the truth of true cognition, is extrinsic and not intrinsic. Thus does the Mīmāṁsā come to add the doctrine of *parataḥaprāmānya* (extrinsic falsity) of false cognition to the doctrine of *svataḥprāmānya* (intrinsic truth) of true cognition. But this device, it is hardly necessary to mention, puts the initial difficulty of the Mīmāṁsā a step further back, instead of offering its solution. It is, therefore, no wonder that the Sāṁkhya, which agrees with the Mīmāṁsā in advocating the doctrine of the intrinsic truth of true cognition, should reject the Mīmāṁsā doctrine of the extrinsic falsity of false cognition and admit that of the intrinsic falsity of false cognition. But then, if true cognition, as the Sāṁkhya holds, is intrinsically true and false cognition is likewise intrinsically false, the distinction between these two kinds of cognition cannot be ascertained without reference to extraneous conditions, which would obviously lead to the overthrow of the twofold Sāṁkhya doctrine of the intrinsic truth of true cognition and the intrinsic falsity of false cognition.

But still more fantastic than either of the two views considered above is the Buddhist view about the truth of true cognition which is diametrically opposed to that of the Mīmāṁsā. As previously mentioned, it consists in holding that cognition as such is intrinsically false but that the possibility of true cognition is not precluded on that account. On the contrary, true cognition is within our reach, but, it is further held, the truth of true cognition is extrinsic, being determinable with reference to extraneous considerations. As regards this view, its difficulty is just the opposite of that of the Mīmāṁsā and consists in stating that it has no means of recognizing such a thing as true cognition just as the latter has no means of admitting the possibility of there being any such thing as false cognition. The only other alternative way of the understanding of the nature of the truth and falsity of cognition which is still open should then lie in the view that neither of these two is intrinsic and that both are *extrinsic*, being determinable with reference to some extraneous mode of cognition or other. This view, as is well known, is precisely the one which is upheld by the combined school of Nyāya-Vaiśeṣika and is diametrically opposed to the Sāṁkhya view, according to which both truth and falsity, as mentioned above, are intrinsic features of cognition. But then, this Nyāya-Vaiśeṣika view, apart from the other difficulties to which it may be open, is undoubtedly vitiated by the fault of infinite regress. For the extraneous cognition, on which a prior cognition would be required to depend for the determination of its truth or else its falsity should, according to the present view, be in its turn required to depend upon another cognition for the fulfilment of a similar object and so on *ad indefinitum.*

The difficulties with regard to the understanding of the nature of true cognition in which the various schools of Indian philosophy are thus found to be involved seem to be ultimately due to their having been misled by the unpardonable confusion between what may be called the *claim to truth* and *truth itself.* Sabara's surprise to which reference has been already made would have been thoroughly justified had he realized that it is not truth itself, but the claim to truth which is essential, or is intrinsically related to, cognition as such. What this implies is obviously that cognition as such is not, as held by the Nyāya-Vaiśeṣika, *neutral* nor, as in the view of the Mīmāṁsā, intrinsically true or extrinsically false. It also is not, as according to the Sāṁkhya it is, intrinsically true or equally intrinsically false. Nor is it, as Buddhism holds, intrinsically false but extrinsically true. All these ways of understanding the nature of true cognition are, in fact, the different ways of answering the irrelevant question as to whether truth and its opposite falsity are intrinsic or else extrinsic features of cognition, instead of the relevant question as to whether the claim to truth which cognition as such invariably bears stands intact and, consequently, the cognition concerned is acceptable as true or else it is negatived, with the result that the cognition concerned shows itself to be false.

It then follows that in the understanding of the truth or the falsity of cognition it is absolutely necessary to recognize that cognition as such is intrinsically endowed with the claim to truth, together with its implication that it *is* true if this claim on its part remains uncontradicted (*abādhita*) and falls if the same claim comes to be sublated (*bādhita*) by a subsequent cognition.* This is, perhaps, all that is required to be admitted with regard to the understanding of the nature of true cognition. So the reference to the distinction between determinate and indeterminate cognition, the foreignness of memory to true cognition, the correspondence of cognition with its object and the practical efficiency of cognition, etc., which has led to unnecessary complications in the Indian theories of truth, seems to be uncalled for. But then, there remains

* This is a remineer of the wisdom which the Vedānta and its followers among the other schools of Indian philosophy have displayed by emphasizing the importance of abādhitatva (uncontradicted-ness) as a feature of true cognition. Yet it must be said that in its treatment of memory as antithetical to true cognition, the Vedānta, like many other schools of Indian philosophy, has betrayed gross ignorance of an important finding of the psychology of cognition.

the question of the *test* or *criterion* of truth as distinguished from truth itself. And we have yet to see whether the ideas of 'correspondence', 'practical efficiency' and the like, which are really foreign to the understanding of the truth of cognition, have any bearing upon the understanding of the *test* or *criterion* of truth.

B

THEORIES OF TRUTH

As we have already seen, the truth of cognition needs to be understood in one way and one way only, namely, by means of holding that cognition as such is inherently endowed with the claim to truth, and that it *is* true in so far as this claim on its part is not negatived or sublated by a counter-cognition. But then, the question arises as to how one is to ascertain whether the claim to truth borne by a given cognition is liable to be negatived or not. It may be that so far as our present knowledge goes, it is not negatived. But that is no guarantee that it will not be negatived in the distant or even the near future. Can it, then, be ascertained that the claim to truth on the part of a given cognition is not liable to be negatived at any time or in any circumstance? This question really concerns the test or criterion of truth and needs to be distinguished from the question concerning the nature of truth itself. And unlike the latter which should be answered in one way only, the former admits of several alternative answers, each of which may be said to constitute an independent *theory* of truth. As far as Western philosophy is concerned, it has found place for a number of theories of this kind, the best known among which are the self-evidence theory, the correspondence theory, the coherence theory and the pragmatic theory. But as regards Indian philosophy, it recognizes three of these to the exclusion of the coherence theory if, of course, the distinction between the coherence and correspondence theories be insisted on as is done in the West. Our present task, then, is to enquire into the three Indian theories of truth respectively called the self-evidence theory, the correspondence theory and the pragmatic theory. In the performance of this task the repetition of at least some of the things that have been previously mentioned will naturally be unavoidable.

THE SELF-EVIDENCE THEORY

(*Svataḥ-Prāmānya-vāda*)

The most prominent advocates of this theory known as *svataḥprāmānya-vāda* in India are the Mīmāṁsā, the Sāṁkhya and the Vedānta. According to the Vedānta, the word *svataḥ* applies in the case of the *origin* of true cognition as well as in the case of our *knowledge* of its truth. But then, the former application of this word does not mean that true cognition originates of itself or is not due to any cause. On the contrary, its origin, as the Vedānta holds, is due to certain causes, but the causes concerned are the usual ones and not anything extraordinary characterized by the quality of *excellence* (*guṇa*) as held by the Nyāya-Vaiśeṣikas. But it may be objected that this view is not compatible with the admission of any such thing as false cognition in distinction from true cognition in as much as false cognition must be said to owe its origin to the same usual causes as are responsible for the origin of true cognition. To this objection the Vedānta's reply is that, although false cognition and true cognition are equally due to the usual causes of cognition as such, these causes in the case of true cognition are free from defects or, in other words, are characterized by the want of defects (*dosābhāva*), whereas in the case of false cognition they are characterized by the presence of defects (*dosa*). And since the want or absence of defects (*dosābhāva*), being a pure negation, has no causal efficiency, the view that true cognition is produced by the usual causes alone, as the reply of the Vedānta continues, remains intact and, consequently, the application of the word *svataḥ* in the case of the origin of true cognition stands vindicated.

It is strange, however, that the question of the origin of true cognition should at all be raised, as the Vedānta raises it, in connection with the propounding of *svataḥprāmānya-vāda* (the self-evidence theory of validity). For the very asking of this question presupposes the admission of the causal view of cognition, which is, perhaps, the greatest hindrance to the understanding of the real nature of cognition. It is, therefore, most unfortunate that almost all the schools of Indian philosophy are in agreement with Western philosophy in general in making use of this view in their enquiry into the nature of cognition or, let us say, knowledge. But apart from this, the view of true cognition as an *effect* produced by certain causes even conceived to be free from defects seems to be unnecessary, if not altogether out of place, in the understanding of the truth of true cognition as self-evident. What this understanding implies is, perhaps, nothing more than that the knowledge of the truth of true cognition is inherent in that cognition itself,

It is important to note, however, that since the falsity of false cognition is due to the *presence* of defects (*dosa*) in the usual causes of cognition in general, irrespective of its distinction between the true and the false, the falsity (*aprāmānya*) of false cognition, in the view of the Vedānta, should naturally be, and, in fact, is *parataḥ* and not *svataḥ*. The Mīmāṁsā as represented by

Kumārila is in agreement with this Vedāntist doctrine of the *paratahaprāmānya* of false cognition. It also agrees with the Vedānta in holding that true cognition is generated by the usual causes of cognition in general, unaffected by anything extraneous to them such as *guṇa* (excellence), and, consequently, that its truth is intrinsic (*svataḥ*). And yet both Kumārila and Prabhākara hold in common that agreement with its object is a characteristic feature of true cognition whereas disagreement with its object is a distinguishing feature of false cognition. This shows that the Mīmāṁsā, despite its agreement with the Vedānta in admitting *abādhitatva* (uncontradictedness) as essential to true cognition, has ultimately proved unable to resist the influence of the Nyāya-Vaiśeṣika which is most conspicuous for its insistence on the supreme importance of correspondence in the case of the determination of truth. But then, while it is thus at one with the Nyāya-Vaiśeṣika in advocating the realistic theory of knowledge, it desists from the attempt to combine realism with pragmatism which is peculiar to the latter.

The Sāṁkhya, like the Mīmāṁsā, agrees with the Vedānta in advocating the doctrine of the intrinsic truth of true cognition and in holding that the truth of true cognition is generated by the usual causal conditions of cognition in general, and not, as held by the Nyāyā-Vaiśeṣika, by any additional quality or excellence (*guṇa*). But then, it differs from both the Mīmāṁsa and the Vedānta in its treatment of falsity (*aprāmānya*) as equally intrinsic, and thus comes to admit the doctrine of the intrinsic falsity (*svataḥaprāmānya*) of false cognition in addition to the doctrine of the intrinsic truth (*svataḥprāmānya*) of true cognition. But in this the Sāṁkhya, unlike the Vedānta and the Mīmāṁsā, must have ignored the question of the origin of false cognition. For had it raised and answered this question, it would, like the latter, have had no option but to regard the falsity of false cognition as extrinsic, instead of as intrinsic. If the question of the origin could then be left out of account in the case of false cognition as was done by the Sāṁkhya, it could with equal plausibility be set aside in the case of true cognition, with the result that the enquiry into the truth or falsity of cognition could be emancipated from the influence of the causal view of cognition which, as has been previously observed, is prejudicial to the proper understanding of the nature of cognition in its various aspects. But as far as the Sāṁkhya is concerned, since it has gone into the question of the origin of true cognition, it has hardly any justification for ignoring the question of the origin of false cognition and thereby treating falsity as intrinsic.

But even granted that the falsity of false cognition is as intrinsic as is the truth of true cognition, and also that we, as the Sāṁkhya itself holds, can have direct and immediate apprehension of the truth of true cognition as well as of the falsity of false cognition, the question arises whether in this event we could recognize true cognition in distinction from false cognition or the latter in ditinctions from the former. This is precisely the question which Pārthasārathi Miśra of the Mīmāṁsā school has raised and has answered it rightly by stating that for the recognition of this distinction we shall be required to refer to certain other conditions, besides our direct and immediate apprehension of the truth as well as the falsity of cognition. And, as a matter of fact, the Sāṁkhya, while eschewing reference to 'correspondence', speaks of the capacity of true cognition to lead to fruitful action and the incapacity of false cognition to do the same, thereby, giving an indication of its predilection for the pragmatist view of truth and falsity. And yet it makes no secret of its unflinching adherenc to its original standpoint by proclaiming that the truth of cognition is not dependent upon fruitful action, nor is the falsity of cognition upon unfruitful action. So the difficulty of the Sāṁkhya under consideration remains where it was.

It remains to observe, however, that if the falsity of false cognition, as held by the Vedānta and the Mīmāṁsā, is due to some defect or other that exists in its causes, it is difficult to understand why the truth of true cognition should not be held by them, in agreement with the Nyāya-Vaiśeṣika, to be due to a certain quality of its causes. Since truth and falsity are mutually opposed, it would, perhaps, be more appropriate to hold that these two are respectively due to the excellence and the defect of the causes of the cognitions concerned than to hold that the former is, ultimately, due to the usual causes of cognition as such, unaffected by any extraneous thing or quality, and the latter owes its origin to some defect or other existing in the causes of the cognition concerned. However that may be, it seems that the resolution of the present conflict between the Vedānta and the Mīmāṁsa on the one hand and the Nyāya-Vaiśeṣika on the other should lie in the surrender of the causal view of cognition and the consequent attempt to understand the difference between truth and falsity with reference to the difference of the causal conditions of the cognitions concerned.

Let us now proceed to the consideration of the application of the word *svataḥ* in the case of our *knowledge* of the truth of true cognition which, according to the Vedānta and its confréres, is as necessary a mark of the intrinsic truth of true cognition as is the application of the same word in the case of the *origin* of this kind of cognition. In this connection it is necessary to note that the possibility of the direct and immediate knowledge (*svataḥ-jñāna*) of the truth of true cognition, according to the Vedānta, presupposes the absence of defects (*dosābhāva*) in the causes of the cognition in question. Given this absence, there arise modifications of the inner sense (*cittavṛtti*) corresponding to the object of cognition, together with the apprehension of these modifications (*vṛtti-jñāna*) characterized by truth (*prāmānya*). And once this comes about, the ground is fully prepared for the transcendental subject or the Witness (*Sākṣī*) to appropriate the *vṛtti-jñāna* together with the *prāmānya* (truth) inherent in it. Thus, according to the Vedānta, the truth of true cognition comes to be known. The knowledge of such truth is, in the view of the Vedānta, direct and immediate (*svataḥ*) in a rather unusual sense in as much as it is not the case that nothing intervenes between the knower of the truth and the truth itself. On the contrary, as has been already evident, this knowledge, in the view of the Vedānta, is a complicated process, involving several factors which affect the truth and its knowledge. What the Vedānta, then, means by the directness and immediacy of the knowledge of the truth is that it is not, like inference or any other source of *parokṣa* (indirect) knowledge, derivable from extraneous considerations, but is similar to the direct and immediate knowledge yielded by perception.

The Vedānta's application of the word *svataḥ* in the case of our *knowledge* of the truth of true cognition is thus similar to its application of the same word in the case of the *origin* of that kind of cognition. And the similarity consists in that just as the origin of true cognition cannot be due to any extraneous causal condition, the knowledge of the truth of true cognition is not derivable from any extraneous consideration or, in other words, is not *parokṣa* (indirect). However that may be, both the Mīmāṁsā and the Sāṁkhya are in substantial agreement with the Vedānta in holding that our knowledge of the truth of true cognition is direct and immediate and not derivable from any subsequent knowledge such as the knowledge of the absence of a contradictory cognition or of fruitful action to which the cognition concerned has led. But then, the fact remains that neither the Mīmāṁsā nor the Sāṁkhya adheres to the doctrine of the intrinsic truth (*svataḥ-prāmānya*) of true cognition as faithfully as does the Vedānta. For, as previously mentioned, the Mīmāṁsā refers to the knowledge of cognition's correspondence with its object and the Sāṁkhya attaches considerable importance to the workability of cognition in their respective attempts to account for the possibility of the knowledge of the truth of true cognition. But this is perhaps due to the overwhelming influence of the Nyāya-Vaiśeṣika upon these two schools of philosophy. As far as the Sāṁkhya in particular is concerned, there seems to be in its case an additional reason for the relaxation of the strictness of adherence to the doctrine of the intrinsic truth of true cognition. This may be explained as follows.

As has been already evident, the Sāṁkhya stands alone in advocating the doctrine of the intrinsic falsity of false cognition.

And it may and, perhaps, does admit that false cognition involves the knowledge of its own falsity just as it does admit that true cognition involves the knowledge of its own truth. But, in view of the fact that this doctrine, unlike the doctrine of the intrinsic truth of true cognition, has not been admitted by any other school of Indian philosophy, the Sāṁkhya must have felt somewhat doubtful about the propriety of the former. Accordingly, while not definitely dismissing it, the Sāṁkhya proceeds on the assumption that the falsity of false cognition, as it were, showed itself to be extrinsic and, consequently, admitted of being known indirectly from some extraneous knowledge such as the knowledge of the unworkability of the cognition concerned. And once the Sāṁkhya allowed itself the latitude of relaxing the strictness of its own doctrine of the intrinsic falsity of false cognition, no insuperable obstacle could remain to prevent it from treating the doctrine of the intrinsic truth of true cognition in a similar way and holding, as it actually did hold, that our knowledge of truth is derivable from some extraneous knowledge such as the knowledge of the workability of the cognition concerned.

Thus we see how the self-evidence theory of truth has suffered stultification in the hands of two of its own advocates, the Mīmāṁsa and the Sāṁkhya. The former, like the Vedānta, of course, admitted the doctrine of the extrinsic falsity of false cognition in the name of securing plausibility—for what else could it be? —for the doctrine of the intrinsic truth of true cognition. But the influence of the Nyāya-Vaiśeṣika upon it proved too strong to allow it to maintain its agreement with the Vedānta and to remain faithful to the self-evidence theory of truth. The Sāṁkhya, in this respect, was placed in the same predicament as the Mīmāṁsā. But, in addition, it had to pay the penalty for its mistaken enthusiasm displayed by its advocacy of the doctrine of the intrinsic falsity of cognition.

The trouble with the self-evidence theory of truth, however, lies in holding, as the Vedānta holds till the end, that our knowledge of the truth of true cognition is not derivable from any other knowledge, but is direct and immediate, whereas our knowledge of the falsity of false cognition can by no means be direct and immediate, but must be derivable from some extraneous knowledge or other such as the knowledge of its being contradicted by another cognition. But then, this view—although this is not obvious—is really such that its inner logic, far from allowing it to retain its identity, unavoidably leads to its liquidation. For once it is granted, as this view certainly grants, that our knowledge of the falsity of false cognition is indirect and mediate, there can be no argument or reasoning to prevent the view that our knowledge of the truth of true cognition should likewise be indirect and mediate. The view that false cognition involves the apprehension of its own falsity or any other device of its kind can only reinforce the predicament of the self-evidence theory of truth, instead of providing any remedy for it.

The real fact of the matter in this connection is, however, that *self-evidence* seems to be too subjective to deserve to be regarded as a criterion of truth and so may be taken to be synonymous with 'no-evidence'. The way in which the advocates of the self-evidence theory of truth, including the Vedānta in particular, understands the criterion of falsity should then be regarded as a model to which the way of determining the criterion of truth should conform. This brings us to the consideration of the theories of *parataḥ-prāmānya* (extrinsic truth), comprising the correspondence theory and the pragmatic theory.

THE CORRESPONDENCE AND PRAGMATIC THEORIES

(*Parataḥ-Prāmānya-vāda*)

We have just finished our enquiry into the theory of truth known as the self-evidence theory and found that it does not really serve the purpose which it is intended to serve. The reason for this, as has been already made plain, is that self-evidence in the sense in which it has been understood is notoriously subjective and so is unable to provide any guarantee of the uncontradictedness (*abādhitatva*) of a given cognition endowed with an inherent claim to truth, which constitutes the vindication of this claim on its part. It seems then that we have no option but to admit that the criterion in question must be somehow *objective* and to enquire what it must be or how it should be understood to be. In this regard it needs to be borne in mind that the failure of the self-evidence theory amounts to the demonstration of the impossibility of any *direct* and *immediate* knowledge of the truth of true cognition. That being so, in our search for an objective criterion of the truth of true cognition we are required, as a preliminary step, to ascertain what kind or kinds of knowledge there should be from which the knowledge of the truth of true cognition may be derived.

One of these kinds of knowledge, perhaps, is that of the absence of defects (*doṣābhāva*) in the causal conditions of the cognition under consideration. But one of the difficulties in this regard is that this kind of knowledge is not easily available inasmuch as the detection of the absence of defects in the causal conditions of a given cognition would demand prolonged and painstaking investigations. Another difficulty here is that, even granted that we can somehow be sure that the causal conditions of a given cognition are free from all defects, that cognition may still be false for a reason lying outside its causal conditions. The kind of knowledge under consideration, then, is not the one from which the knowledge of the truth of a true cognition may be certainly derived. May not the knowledge in demand, it may be asked, then be that of a given cognition's being uncontradicted by another cognition? The answer, it may at once be stated, should be in the negative. The reason for this is that uncontradictedness, as we have previously held, is essential to true cognition as such, but that it cannot be regarded as the criterion of the truth of true cognition, it being undeniable that it is itself in need of being determined with reference to a criterion.

Another alternative, which at first sight seems to be more plausible than either of the two mentioned above, is the knowledge of the correspondence of cognition with its object. That being so, it may accordingly be held that our knowledge of the truth of true cognition is derivable from our knowledge of its correspondence with its object. This view, as already mentioned, has been entertained even by the Mīmāṁsā, one of the advocates of the doctrine of the intrinisic truth of true cognition. And as regards those who have either refrained from admitting this doctrine or else have deliberately rejected it, have almost invariably regarded the truth of cognition as consisting in its correspondence with its object, and have thus advocated or else have lent support to, the correspondence theory of truth, which is one of the important forms of *parataḥ-prāmānya-vāda.* Thus Jainism, as previously mentioned, regards correspondence (*avisaṁvādakatva*) as a characteristic feature of true cognition and thereby points towards the plausibility of the view of correspondence as a *criterion* of truth. And Buddhism which, as we have seen earlier, holds the curious view that, whereas falsity is intrinsic, truth is extrinsic, obviously proves to be an advocate of *parataḥ-prāmānya-vāda.* And, like Jainism, it affirms that our knowledge of the truth of a given cognition is derivable, among other things, from the knowledge of the correspondence of that cognition with the real nature of its object. Although it is not the sole criterion of truth, 'correspondence', according to Buddhism, is thus one such criterion. Hence it is evident that Buddhism joins the company of those schools of philosophy which either advocate, or are sympathetic to, the correspondence theory.

But among the schools of Indian philosophy, the one that is most conspicuous for its advocacy of the correspondence theory is the combined school of Nyāya-Vaiśeṣika. As seen earlier, the Nyāya-Vaiśeṣikas hold that a given cognition is in itself neither true nor false, but is *neutral*, and that both truth and falsity are equally adventitious characteristics of cognition, not being due to anything belonging to the cognition itself. Truth, then, as held by this combined school of philosophy, is due to the excellence (*guṇa*) of the causal conditions of the cognition concerned, whereas falsity owes its origin to the defect (*dosa*) of its causal conditions. But, as the Nyāya-Vaiśeṣikas fully realize, there arises the difficult question as to how the alleged twofold fact can be ascertained. They feel sure, however, that the difficulty is overcome by the answer that the presence of the correspondence of a given cognition with its object and the absence of its correspondence with the latter are respectively the means of the determination of truth and falsity. Thus do the Nyāya-Vaiśeṣikas arrive at the view that the correspondence of cognition with its object is at once the content and a *criterion* of truth, which is the very essence of the correspondence theory.

But, despite the support which it has received from many philosophical quarters in India, the correspondence theory seems to be fatally vulnerable on at least two grounds. One of these relates to the question regarding the meaning of 'correspondence'. As previously indicated, the majority of the philosophers and schools of philosophy, which speak of the correspondence of cognition with its object, seem to be using words without having any definite meaning in view. For the relation between cognition and its object seems to be expressible by the statement that the latter is, if we may say so, the *accusative* (that is, object in the grammatical sense) of the former, which can by no means be taken to convey the sense of correspondence between the two. Of course, one may admit the distinction between the object as cognized and the object in itself and thereupon speak of the correspondence between the two and regard this correspondence as the same as the correspondence between cognition and its object. This seems to be the basis of the understanding of 'correspondence' by the Navya-Nyāya to which reference has already been made.

Even so the difficulty still is that, once the distinction between the object as cognized and the object in itself is admitted, the cognition of the latter should necessarily be an impossibility. In consequence, the correspondence of the object as cognized with the object in itself would altogether fall outside the field of knowledge. And this brings in the other difficulty of the correspondence theory which consists in stating that, even granted that the word 'correspondence', in the present context, has a determinate meaning, the correspondence between cognition and its object is something unknown and unknowable and so is as good as nothing. This is precisely the difficulty from which the correspondence theory seems to have no escape, so that the attempt to establish 'correspondence' as an independent criterion of truth to which this theory amounts is doomed to failure. But granted, and the Nyāya-Vaiśeṣika and its confreres do readily grant, that 'correspondence' does not admit of direct and immediate knowledge nor can it be an independent criterion of truth, it, in their view, does not, on that account, lose, but, on the contrary, retains its importance with regard to the determination of the truth of cognition. For what else can the *workability* or practical efficiency of cognition be but the manifestation of its correspondence with its object and what else does the practical efficiency of cognition serve to show except the truth of the cognition concerned? It is a question like this which points towards the view held by the Nyāya-Vaiśeṣika and the allied schools of Indian philosophy, according to which the correspondence theory as a theory of truth realizes itself through its absorption in the pragmatic theory and, accordingly, correspondence as a criterion of truth finds its culmination in the practical efficiency of, or the successful activity (*pravṛttisāmarthya*) following upon, cognition. Hence it is evident that the correspondence and the pragmatic theories are respectively the preliminary and the final stages in the development of *parataḥprāmāṇyavāda*.

Now it is sometimes held that pragmatism as a philosophical outlook is natural to practically minded people such as the Americans, but is likely to be out of place in an atmosphere dominated by the speculative tendency and relatively free from the burden of practical considerations such as that which is said to prevail in India. But this is belied by the fact that Pragmatism is not a peculiar possession of America, but did earlier have its day in Western countries with highly developed speculative atmospheres such as Germany and Italy. On the other hand, the fact is also that there is hardly any school of Indian philosophy which has not attached at least some importance to the pragmatic way of thinking in certain matters. Among the schools of Indian philosophy with affiliations to the self-evidence theory, it is the Mīmāṁsā with alone refrains from having recourse to pragmatism in accounting for the truth as well as the falsity of cognition. The Sāṁkhya, despite its advocacy of the self-evidence theory, does, on the other hand, attach considerable importance to the consideration of the *workability* (*arthakriyākāritva*) of cognition in the determination of its truth. It also holds that the unworkability of cognition is a determination of its falsity. Thus the Sāṁkhya shows itself to be inconsistent with its original position with regard to the nature of truth and falsity on account of its advocacy of pragmatism alongside the self-cvidence theory.

As regards, the Vedānta, it, of course, sticks fast to the self-evidence theory and keeps pragmatism at a safe distance in its understanding of the nature and criterion of truth. But when it comes to the consideration of the question of the criterion of falsity, it deliberately falls back upon the pragmatic way of thinking and accordingly holds that the falsity of cognition needs to be determined with reference to *pravṛtti-visaṁvāda* (the failure of the activity prompted by cognition). But in this connection, it may be pertinently suggested that the Vedānta might as well depend on the parity of reasoning and hold, like the Sāṁkhya, that both truth and falsity are equally intrinsic or, like the Nyāya-Vaiśeṣika, that both of them are alike extrinsic, being determiable with reference to *pravṛtti-saṁvāda* (the success of the activity prompted by cognition) and *pravṛtti-visaṁvāda* (the failure of the activity following upon cognition) respectively. But the fact that the Vedānta did not adopt either of these two alternatives seems to indicate that it was seized with a kind of dogmatism and was lacking in the openness of outlook which is of inestimable value in philosophical investigations.

But it was outside the circle of the advocates of the self-evidence theory that the pragmatic way of thinking could establish its sway without let or hindrance. Besides the orthodox school of Nyāya-Vaiśeṣika, about whose intimate concern with pragmatism we have already had some account, the heterodox schools of philosophy, including the materialist school led by the Cārvākas, Jainism and Buddhism, had no hesitation in having recourse to the pragmatic way of thinking in many respects and especially in their discussion of the problem of truth and falsity. Nevertheless, it must be admitted that pragmatism has not been developed into a brand of systematic and comprehensive philosophy in India as has been done in the West in the hands of philosophers like William James and John Dewey. But one may, perhaps, venture to state that the philosophy of the Cārvākas betrays the development of an unbridled pragmatic outlook, of pragmatism let loose and gone astray. But Jainism and Buddhism, with their poignant concern with the problem of the ultimate destiny of man, are naturally free from any manner of excess of enthusiasm about the pragmatic way of thinking and yet do willingly have recourse to it if and when this is in demand.

Now, as far as Jainism is concerned, while it does not go so far as the Nyāya-Vaiśeṣika in definitely advocating the pragmatic theory of truth, it certainly holds that the capacity to lead to the attainment of the intended object (*arthaprāpakatva*) is indeed an essential characteristic of true cognition, and thus demonstrates its sympathy for, nay, agreement with, this theory. Not only that; Jainism lends added support to the pragmatic theory of truth by holding that true cognition is that cognition which is endowed with the capacity to lead to what is good and to avoid whatever is evil. But Buddhism goes further than Jainism in espousing the cause of the pragmatic theory of truth. This is evident from the fact that it proceeds in the manner of the Nyāya-Vaiśeṣika in arguing the need for the understanding of the truth of true cognition in the pragmatist way. Thus Dharmottara, for example, holds that a given cognition can be true if it is in correspondence with its object. But how can it be known that the cognition concerned is in correspondence with its object? His answer is that this can be known if it is known that it leads to the attainment of its object. Thus in the view of Buddhism, as in the view of the Nyāya-Vaiśeṣika, the pragmatic theory of truth serves to establish the correspondence between cognition and its object which at first sight seems to be the criterion of truth. May it not then be said that the search for the criterion of truth reaches fulfilment in the pragmatic theory which holds that cognition is true if it *works* or, in other words, successfully leads to the attainment of the object it has in view?

The consideration of the question posed above, prehaps, may most suitably take the place of an enquiry into the vexed controversy in which the major schools of Indian philosophy have been involved with no other object in view than the refutation of one another's theory of truth. It is, therefore, incumbent upon us to discuss whether the pragmatic theory *works* better than the self-evidence theory in the Vedāntist version, it being understood, however, that the correspondence theory is not a theory of truth by itself but is only a stepping-stone to the former of these two theories. In this regard it is first necessary for us to realize that the self-evidence theory as presented by the Vedānta seems to be very much under the influence of the idea of the *theoretical* or rather rational determination of the truth of cognitive statements, which is essential to mathematics and logic. This seems to be the reason why the Vedānta, unlike the Sāṁkhya, eschews all reference to the practical efficiency of cognition. But then, the Vedānta certainly does not understand self-evidence in the sense in which it is understood by mathematics and logic. According to the latter, a cognitive statement is said to be self-evident if its contradictory is *inconceivable*. By the self-evidence of a given cognition the Vedānta, on the other hand, means its being inseparably bound up with the *knowledge* of its own truth, which obviously has nothing to do with self-evidence in the mathemetical and logical sense. In consequence, the initial apriorism of the Vedānta disappears, yielding place to empiricism. And the evidence of the employment of empiricism presents itself even within the sphere of the Vedānta's influence. This is verified by the Mīmāṁsā's recognition of the importance of the knowledge of 'correspondence' and the Sāṁkhya's insistence on the importance of the workability of cognition in their respective attempts to understand the nature of truth. And once empiricism thus gains a foothold in the epistemological field, the attempt to understand the nature and criterion of the truth of cognition is bound to be led to its logical culmination in the emergence of the pragmatic theory.

If it is true, as it seems to be, that the self-evidence theory as constructed by the Vedānta, the Mīmāṁsā and the Sāṁkhya is, by the sheer force of its inner logic, transmuted into the pragmatic theory, it would be worthwhile to enquire what should really be the fate of the pragmatic theory itself. In this regard, it is necessary, in the first place, to note that, while the self-evidence theory, at least in principle, presupposes the recognition of the all-importance of *a priori* propositions at the cost of the importance of empirical propositions, the pragmatic theory, as a matter of dialectical necessity, is antithetical to the former in that it leaves *a priori* propositions completely out of account and attaches undue importance to empirical statements. In consequence, the question of the truth of *a priori* propositions falls beyond the scope of the pragmatic theory. The reason for this is that the question of workability or practical efficiency is absolutely irrelevant in connection with the truth of *a priori* propositions. It is then plain that the pragmatic theory loses one-half of its importance as a theory of truth on account of its inapplicability in the case of *a priori* propositions.

Secondly, since the pragmatic theory, according to its Indian advocates such as the Nyāya-Vaiśeṣika and Buddhism, serves to establish the correspondence between cognition and its object and thereby acquires the status of a theory of truth, that status cannot be said to belong to it or, in other words, it cannot be regarded as a theory of truth properly so called. The reason for this is that the correspondence in question, as we have previously argued, is, to all intents and purposes, spurious. But let us waive this objection as we should, perhaps, do, and ask the straight question whether the practical efficiency or workability of cognition, no matter whether or not it serves to establish the correspondence of the cognition concerned with its object, can be said to be the invariable criterion of its truth. As regards this question, it would, perhaps, be quite relevant to refer to those whose name is legion and who, out of their bitter experience of the ordinary ways of the conduct of human affairs, proclaim that falsehood pays much more than truth and are more or less convinced about the truth of this proclamation. Of course, it may be contended that the proclamation in question involves the misunderstanding or misuse of the idea of the workability or practical efficiency of cognition. But this contention conveys the invitation of the question as to what the criterion of workability or practical efficiency of cognition should be. Hence follows the liquidation of the pragmatic theory as an independent and finally formed theory of truth. Thus has the pragmatic theory to share the same fate as that of the self-evidence theory on the one hand and the so-called correspondence theory on the other.

The attempt to ascertain the criterion of the workability of cognition would, however, be as much a wild goose chase as it would certainly be to try and find out the criterion of the correspondence of cognition with its object. For it seems that the endeavour to determine the criterion of the truth of cognition should come to a dead end on reaching the pragmatic theory or else should be in need of being continued *ad indefinitum* so as to be vitiated by the fault of infinite regress. In view of this, we, perhaps, have no option but to rest content with a position such as the following. Since propositions come under either of the two heads, the *a priori* and the *empirical*, and since these two are absolutely disparate, the criterion of truth cannot be one and the same in the two cases. As regards *a priori* propositions, the criterion of truth in their case should naturally be self-evidence—self-evidence, not in the sense in which it is understood by the Vedānta, the Mīmāṁsā and the Sāṁkhya, but in the sense in which it is understood in the field of mathematics and logic. In the case of the empirical propositions, on the other hand, the criterion of truth should, from the nature of the case, be workability or parctical efficiency. Even so, neither of the two criteria should be regarded as *absolute*, but, on the contrary, should be taken to be at best *contingent* in view of the possibility of their inapplicability in their respective fields under as yet unknown circumstances. What is really meant here is that cognition or, as we should rather say, knowledge is, after all, venturesome and, consequently, that what is taken at one time to be knowledge or true cognition may at some other time prove to be no knowledge at all, but error instead.

III

THE PROBLEM OF ERROR

Introductory Remarks

Let us begin by reminding ourselves that it is in connection with the aberrations of, or exceptions to, knowledge, presenting themselves in the form of error, and not in connection with knowledge as such that a problem or problems may arise. The reason for this is that we can have no means of recognizing error as error, and, consequently, affirming that there is such a thing as error, if knowledge, in contrast with which alone such recognition and such affirmation are possible, be not regarded as an *ultimate datum.* In this context, it would, perhaps, be of interest to observe that for the sake of the enlivening of our interest in things usually regarded as genuinely valuable, philosophy, of all the activities of the human mind, should be well advised in devoting its special attention to the *negations* of such things. This is, perhaps, the reason why Indian philosophy, unlike philosophy in the West, has taken great pains in dealing with the practical problem of human suffering and the theoretical problem of error.

Now the problem of error, be it noted at the outset, relates exclusively to the field of perception, and conveys the demand for the investigation of the aberrations of perceptual knowledge. Judged in this light, this problem obviously calls for an enquiry into the physical and physiological conditions of erroneous perception. And as regards the major schools of Indian philosophy which have undertaken the investigation of the phenomena of error, they hold in common that these phenomena are due to some defect or other in their causal conditions (*kāraṇadosa*). But, as they have rightly realized, the admission of these defects is not enough for the explanation of the origin of erroneous perception. Accordingly, they have come to hold the view that over and above defects in the physical and physliological conditions of perception, there must be certain psychological factors which play an important part in the occurrence of the phenomena of error. Nevertheless, they do not stop there, but go further in understanding erroneous perception, in contrast with perceptual knowledge properly so called, in terms of the view that in the case of the former, unlike in the case of the latter, there is no correspondence between the cognition concerned and its object, nor is the cognition capable of leading to fruitful action.

But then, most of the schools of Indian philosophy have realized that what is especially important for the explanation of the phenomena of error is to take into account the psychological factors involved in erroneous perception and, what is more, to enquire into the *ontological* status of the content of erroneous perception. As regards the latter requirement, it seems that by admitting it, Indian philosophy has displayed exceptional originality with regard to its treatment of the problem of error. However that may be, our immediate task is to investigate how the major schools of Indian philosophy have dealt with this problem in fulfilment of this twofold requirement.

Theories of Error

As there arises no question of the investigation of the theories of error in any particular order, we may begin with any one of them according to our own choice. Let us then first take up the theory of error advocated by the Mādhyamika school of Buddhism, which is known as *Asatkhyātivāda* (the doctrine of the apprehension of the non-existent) and seems to be the simplest of its kind. This doctrine, as its very designation indicates, consists in holding that erroneous perception is the apprehension of a non-existent thing as existent. Now this view seems to be above reproach in so far as it is regarded merely as a statement of the *fact* concerning our erroneous perception of something, for example, 'nacre' (*sukti*) as what it really is not, for example, 'silver' (*rajata*). But considered as an attempt to *explain* the fact concerned, which it is really intended to do, it seems to be a failure. For, in the first place, it has no satisfactory answer to offer to the question regarding the exact nature of the alleged apprehension of the non-existent. The apprehension is obviously supposed to be perceptual. But it can by no stretch of imagination be said to be perceptual, because the non-existent is recalcitrant to *indriyasannikarṣa* (contact with sense-organs), and because in the total absence of *indriyasannikarṣa* there can be no perceptual experience. This obviously points towards a psychological as well as epistemological drawback from which the Mādhyamika theory of error suffers.

Secondly, the Mādhyamika provides no explanation of why 'nacre' should be mistaken for 'silver' and not anything else and how 'silver' which is not perceived should come into the picture at all. These two shortcomings of the *asatkhyāti* theory betray the inadequacy of its psychological analysis of erroneous perception, it being understood that the *memory* or *recollection* of something *resembling* that which is actually presented is an important psychological factor in this kind of perception. Thirdly,—and this is especially significant—it seems to be absolutely arbitrary and unwarrantable to hold, as the Mādhyamika does hold, that the immediate content of erroneous perception is, ontologically, non-existent. The reason for this is that, apart from the difficulty consisting in the impossibility of the perception of anything non-existent, which has been already mentioned, the supposed apprehension of something non-existent is the same as the total *absence* of apprehension which erroneous perception certainly is not. The fact of the matter here is, however, that the Mādhyamika's explanation of the fact about the phenomena of error bears the reflection of its misleading ontological theory which holds that the Non-existent (*Śūnya*) is ultimately real and that what is called *existence* derives from the Ultimate Reality conceived to be Non-existence. So it seems that the Mādhyamika has been led to misinterpret erroneous perception by its fantastic idea that the phenomena of error bears an unmistakable testimony to the vindication of its ontological theory known as *Śūnyavāda* (the doctrine of the Void or Vacuity).

The inadequacy of psychological analysis and the misconception of the ontological status of the content of erroneous perception persist in the theory of error known as *Ātmakhyātivāda* (the doctrine of the apprehension of one's own ideas) advocated by the Yogācāra school of Buddhism. The philosophers belonging to this school are supporters of *Vijñānavāda* (subjective idealism), according to which there are no such things as external objects, and one's own ideas alone exist or are real. Accordingly, whereas the Mādhyamika, in its explanation of erroneous perception, holds that we directly and immediately apprehend something non-existent, but misconstrue it as existent, the Yogācāra is of the view that, in the case of erroneous perception, the direct and immediate object of our apprehension is an idea of our own, but that that idea is misconstrued as something external. Now in holding this view, the Yogācāra, of course, realizes the truth which the Mādhyamika misses, namely, that erroneous perception consists in the apprehension of something *existent* as something other than itself. But then, it, on the other hand, misses the truth on which the Mādhyamika lays special stress, namely, that the object of erroneous perception, for example, 'silver' is, after all, non-existent.

Moreover, the apprehension of ideas, which the Yogācāra obviously regards as perceptual, cannot really be called the process of perception, the erroneousness of which is under consideration, it being an instance of inner apprehension or *introspection* as opposed to *extrospection* which perception really is. This shows that the Yogācāra's attempt to account for the phenomena of error is vitiated by a mistaken view of the psychology of perception. Besides, perception, which is, in the view of the Yogācāras, the apprehension of some idea or other, must, according to them, be invariably erroneous or invariably veridical as the case may be inasmuch as this school of philosophy seems to have no means of distinguishing between those cases of perception in which the idea is construed as *external* and the others in which it is not so construed. All these difficulties of the *Ātmakhyāti* theory of error advocated by the Yogācāras are, however, ultimately due to their mistakenly ego-centric view of the ontological status of the contents of perception, whether veridical or erroneous—the view, namely, that these are one's own ideas.

Let us now proceed to the consideration of another typical theory of error which is known as *Akhyātivāda* (the doctrine of non-apprehension) or *Vivekākhyātivāda* (the doctrine of the non-apprehension of distinction) which is advocated by the Mīmāṁsā school and is especially associated with the name of Prabhākara. According to him, in the case of an erroneous perceptual judgment, for example, 'this is silver', there are two distinct cognitions, one of which is the perception of 'this' and the other the recollection of 'silver'. But, continues Prabhākara, the distinction between these two cognitions is not apprehended or, in other words, there is non-apprehension (*akhyāti*) of this distinction (*viveka*). This, as he concludes, is due to the obscuration of the element of recollection or memory (*smṛtipramosa*), and constitutes the error or illusion.

Now this theory seems to be an improvement upon the *Asatkhyātivāda* of the Mādhyamika and the *Ātmakhyātivāda* of the Yogācāra in this, that erroneous perception, according to it, does not, as it does in the view of the Mādhyamika, lose its cognitive character altogether, nor is it reduced, as the Yogācāra reduces it, to a process of inner apprehension or introspection. So it is, in a sense, more satisfactory than the other two from the psychological point of view. But then, Prabhākara's view that erroneous perception, as distinguished from veridical perception, involves two distinct cognitions—one *presentative* (that is, perceptual) and the other *representative*, being memory or recollection—seems to be untenable from the strictly psychological point of view. The reason for this is that perception, no matter whether it is veridical or erroneous, is never purely presentative at least in our adult life, but is a whole in which the presentative and the representative elements are blended into a unity; so that the question of the non-apprehension of the distinction between the two kinds of elements does not arise at all, and in any case is not, as according to Prabhākara it is, relevant to the understanding of erroneous perception.

What, then, is at fault in the case of erroneous perception as illustrated in the apprehension of 'nacre' as 'silver' is not the non-apprehension of the distinction between the perceived 'this' and the recollected 'silver', but the recollection of silver instead of anything else and the positive blending of this representative element with the given presentative one. This indicates at least an aspect of the truth about the fact of erroneous perception which the *Vivekakhyātivāda* of Prabhākara has missed altogether. This drawback on his part is at least partly attributable to his misconception of the ontological status of the immediate content of erroneous perception which finds expression in his view that it is a mere 'this', that is, indeterminate existence.

We may next take up the theory of error advocated by the Sāṁkhya school of philosophy which may be called either *Akhyātivāda* (the doctrine of non-apprehension) or *Vivekākhyātivāda* (the doctrine of the non-apprehension of distinction) or *Sadasatkhyātivāda* (the doctrine of the apprehension of the real and the unreal). Now from the first and the second designations of this theory it appears that the Sāṁkhya and the Mīmāṁsā are in agreement with each other in their explanation of the phenomena of error. But this is in a sense true and in a sense also not so. Their agreement, in the first place, lies in that, according to both of them, an erroneous perceptual statement, for example, 'this is silver' is based upon two separate cognitions, namely, the perception of 'this' and the recollection of 'silver'. Secondly, they agree in holding that erroneous perception involves the non-apprehension (*akhyāti*) of the distinction (*viveka*) between the two elements of cognition. But then, there is an important difference between them which may be stated thus. The Mīmāṁsā regards the perceived *this* as real and treats the 'silver' merely as something recollected without declaring it to be either real or unreal. And thereupon it holds that the error in question owes its origin to the failure to apprehend the real 'this' in distinction from the recollected 'silver'. The Sāṁkhya, on the other hand, while holding in agreement with the Mīmāṁsā that the perceived 'this' is real, differs from the latter in regarding the recollected 'silver' as unreal. Consequently it arrives at the *Sadasatkhyātivāda* (the doctrine of the apprehension of the real and the unreal) in terms of the view that error is due to the apprehension of the real, together with the unreal. Thus the Sāṁkhya is, on the one hand, in agreement with the Mīmāṁsā, and, on the other, propounds a theory of error which, unlike that of the latter, is more positive than negative.

Now the Sāṁkhya theory of error is, for obvious reasons, open to the same objections as is that of the Mīmāṁsā in so far as it is in ageeement with the latter. And, as mentioned earlier, these objections are ultimately traceable to the misconception of the ontological status of the immediate content of erroneous perception which they admit in common—the misconception which consists in holding that this content is none but indeterminate existence signified by the mere 'this'. But the Sāṁkhya theory of error is open to an additional difficulty in so far as it holds, in disagreement with that of the Mīmāṁsā, that the recollected 'silver' is unreal. The reason for this is that the question whether they are real or unreal is irrelevant in the case of memory-images as such. And judged from this point of view, the Sāṁkhya is not only at fault, but shows itself to be rather naive in its treatment of the recollected 'silver' as unreal, whereas the Mīmāṁsā displays its wisdom in virtue of its view that memory-images, including the recollected 'silver', are in need of being treated merely as memory-images and in any case are recalcitrant to the question as to whether they are real or unreal.

It would certainly be of interest to make, at this stage, a brief critical enquiry into another theory of error which is just the contrary of that of the Mādhyamika and may be called Satkhyātivāda (the doctrine of the apprehension of the real or existent). It has been propounded by Rāmānuja, the founder of the *Viśiṣṭādvaita* school of the Vedānta and consists in holding that erroneous perception does not involve any *ideal* or imaginary construction, and that its object, like that of veridical perception, is objectively real (*sat*). The reason for this, according to Rāmānuja, is that the function of perception, no matter whether it is called erroneous or veridical, is not to *create* anything, but to *reveal* that which it has for its object. This, of course, contains an element of truth in so far as there is no denying the fact that error or illusion invariably has an objective foundation. Thus in the case of our erroneous perception of 'nacre' as 'silver', the silver may be said to be objectively present in the sense that the 'nacre', owing to the resemblance of some of its qualities to those of the 'silver', were, as it were, a bit of the silver itself. But the difficulty in this connection, among other things, is that Rāmānuja mistakes objective reality in a figurative sense for the same in a literal sense. For the identity of the nacre with a bit of silver is only verbal or figurative and not real or literal.

Rāmānuja is, however, careful enough to admit that the object of erroneous perception is not, as that of veridical perception is, wholly objectively real; it is only partially real. This obviously implies the view that there can be no error or falsity which ultimately is not some *degree* of truth. Hence is evident Rāmānuja's alliance, whether conscious or unconscious, with the advocates of the coherence theory of truth, of which the doctrine of degrees of truth is an essential aspect. This goes to show that Rāmānuja is one of those philosophers who have been led to misconstrue the essentially *qualitative* distinction between truth and error as merely *quantitative*. And the factor which may be said to be mainly responsible for his being misled in this manner is his misconception of the ontological status of the content of erroneous perception as real or existent (*sat*), together with his mistaken view that erroneous perception and veridical perception as psychological processes are identically the same.

We may next pass on to the consideratoin of the theory of error propounded by the Nyāya-Vaiśeṣika which is known as *Anyathākhyātivāda* (the doctrine of the apprehension of one thing as adother) or *Viparitakhyātivāda* (the doctrine of the apprehension of something as other than what it is in itself). This theory, as indicated by its designations, consists in holding that erroneous or illusory perception is the apprehension of something as something else. This view, it is important to note, amounts to the *positive* statement of a truth about the fact of erroneous perception, the *negative* statement of which constitutes the essence of the *Asatkhyātivāda* of the Mādhyamika. For to say, as the Mādhyamika says, that erroneous perception is the apprehension of what is non-existent is the negative way of expressing what is positively expressed by saying, as the Nyāya-Vaiśeṣika says, that the object of this kind of perception is something other than itself. But that does not mean that either of these two alternatives is sufficient as the statement of the whole truth about the fact of erroneous perception. On the contrary, each is partial and indeed complementary to the other; so that both of them together are needed for the complete expression of the truth in question. Hence it is evident that the *Anyathākhyātivāda* of the Nyāya-Vaiśeṣika is as incomplete and one-sided a theory of error as is the *Asatkhyātivāda* of the Mādhyamika. And at the same time the mistake of the Nyāya-Vaiśeṣika conception of the ontological status of the content of erroneous perception comes within view—the mistake which is conveyed by the view of this content as existent (*sat*).

The misunderstanding, on the part of the Nyāya-Vaiśeṣika, of the ontological status of the content of erroneous perception referred to above brings in its train at least two serious difficulties. In the first place, since the content of erroneous perception is, in the view of this combined school of philosophy, existent (*sat*) as must be that of veridical perception, there can really be, as in the view of Rāmānuja, no difference between these two kinds of perception. And this brings out the *reductio ad absurdum* of *Anyathākhyātivāda* as well as the *Satkhyātivāda* of Rāmānuja. Secondly, whereas Rāmānuja holds the absurd view that all the qualities of the object of erroneous perception are actually presented to the senses, the Nyāya-Vaiśeṣika is of the view that some of them are, of course, presented to the senses in the ordinary way, but that the others are somewhere else. Even then, the latter, being, like the former, existent (*sat*), cannot, in the view of this combined school of philosophy, be regarded as objects of memory or recollection but must be viewed to be sense-contents. This raises the question as to how the qualities of objects that are absent or exist elsewhere can be *sensed* here and now. To this question the Nyāya-Vaiśeṣika has no reply to offer, the Naiyāyika's outlandish concept of *Alaukikapratyakṣa* (extraordinary perception) being of no avail in this connection. This seems to be, ultimately, due to the inadequacy of the psychological analysis of erroneous perception which is consequent upon the extreme realism advocated by the Nyāya-Vaiśeṣika, the epistemological theory which insists on the all-importance of *indriyasannikarṣa* (contact with sense-organs), and rules out the role of memory or ideal construction, with regard to the possibility of perceptual experience, irrespective of its distinction between the true and the false.

In this connection it is necessary to observe, however, that the Yoga system of Indian philosophy, in spite of its intimate alliance with the Sāṁkhya, differs from the latter and agrees with the Nyāya-Vaiśeṣika in its admission of a theory of error which is a variant of *Anyathākhyātivāda* (the doctrine of the apprehension of one thing as another). That the Yoga is an advocate of *Anyathākhyātivāda* is evident from its understanding of the nature of *avidyā* (false cognition) in disagreement with the Sāṁkhya. Unlike the Sāṁkhya, it defines false cognition (*avidyā*) as the apprehension of one thing as a different thing. But then, there is an important difference between the Yoga and the Nyāya-Vaiśeṣika interpretations of the *Anyathākhyātivāda*.

As we have already seen, in the view of the Nyāya-Vaiśeṣika, one object is erroneously perceived as another in virtue of the apprehension of a remote external object, for example, 'silver' as a present object, say, 'nacre'. According to the Yoga, on the other hand, the actual situation in the case of our erroneous perception of 'nacre' as 'silver' is different in the following manner. The 'silver' is not, as according to the Nyāya-Vaiśeṣika it is, a remote external object, but, on the contrary, is directly and indeed internally related to us, being an idea of our mind. And it is this idea of 'silver' that is attributed to the 'nacre' which is presented to us through the intermediary of our sense-organs. Thus does the Yoga come to the rescue of the *Anyathākhyātivāda* from the ill-effects produced upon it by the extreme realism of the Nyāya-Vaiśeṣika, by way of introducing an element of ideal construction or mental manipulation into the psychology of erroneous perception. But this is far from suggesting that the *Anyathākhyātivāda* of the Nyāya-Vaiśeṣika as modified by the Yoga is an ideal theory of error. The psychological analysis of erroneous perception done by the Yoga is, of course, an improvement upon that of the Nyāya-Vaiśeṣika, Rāmānuja, the Mādhyamika and the Yogācāra in so far as it, unlike the latter, recognizes an element of ideal construction as essential to this kind of perception. But the effect of this improvement is neutralized by the mistaken view of the ontological status of the content of erroneous perception held by the Yoga—the view, namely, that this content is something *ontologically determinate*, being a *reality* which is a curious mixture of the physical and the mental.

At long last we are approaching the end of our present discussions, having been left with the only remaining task of enquiring into the theory of error which has been propounded by the Advaita Vedānta and is known as *Anirvacanīyakhyātivāda* (the doctrine of the apprehension of what is unspeakable, indefinable or indeterminate). The first and the foremost prerequisite of the understanding of this theory of error is the consideration of the view of the nature of perception held by this school of philosophy. Now, according to the Advaita Vedānta, perception, no matter whether it is veridical or erroneous, must have an object which is *fit* (*yogya*) to be perceived. And in the case of external perception, when the object comes into contact with a sense-organ, the *citta* or *antaḥkaraṇa* (mind) goes out to the object through that sense-organ and is modified into the form of the latter (*vṛtti*). Once this happens, the mental modification (*cittavṛtti*) of the object (*viṣaya*) arouses the I-consciousness or subject-consciousness (*pramātṛcaitanya*) and, as a result, there comes about the identification of the object (*viṣaya*) with the subject-consiousness which, according to the Advaita Vedānta, constitutes perceptual experience.

But then, the Advaita Vedānta soon realizes that this characterization of perception is in need of a suitable modification which can make room for erroneous perception, as distinguished from veridical perception or for the latter in distinction from the former. Accordingingly, it comes to hold that the object (*viṣaya*) mentioned in the description of the perceptual process should be qualified by the adjective 'uncontradicted' (*abādhita*) in the case of veridical perception, and by the adjective 'contradicted' or 'sublated' (*bādhita*) in the case of erroneous perception. But then, the 'contradictedness' or 'sublation' of the object in the case of erroneous perception is obviously a phenomenon which demands explanation. And the Advaita Vedānta has offered the required explanation which, as we shall see below, provides a way of the psychological analysis of erroneous perception as well as a view of the ontological status of the object of erroneous perception.

Be it noted, however, that the reason why the object of erroneous perception is liable to be contradicted or sublated cannot be explained except by saying that the perception concerned is erroneous (*mithyā*). But even then, the question remains as to how erroneous perception is erroneous. And it is precisely this question which the Advaita Vedānta seeks to answer by way of offering a psychological analysis of this kind of perception and a view of the ontological status of its object.

Now, since in the case of our erroneous perception of the 'nacre' as 'silver', it is the 'nacre' and not the 'silver' that is presented to us, the question naturally arises as to how the silver in particular comes into the picture and is attributed to the nacre. As we have already seen, the answer of the Nyāya-Vaiśeṣika which constitutes its *Anyathākhyātivāda* is unsatisfactory, and the Advaita Vedānta also realizes that this is so. Accordingly, this school of philosophy holds that the silver in question is not that which exists here or elsewhere, but is the *false appearance* of silver produced now and here (*tatkalotpanna*). Of course, as the Advaita Vedānta admits, in this case there is no real silver to give rise to the apprehension of itself. But that does not matter in connection with the question of the erroneous perception of silver, as distinguished from the veridical perception of the same. The Advaita Vedānta then holds that there are at least two contributory factors in the production of the false appearance of the silver. One of these is some disease or other by which the eyes of the percipient are affected. The other is the visual sensation of the 'brightness' (*chākchikya*) of the nacre, having a resemblance to that of the silver. And it is this factor in particular which brings the silver into the picture.

But then, the silver's coming into the picture by itself alone cannot account for the erroneous perception of the nacre as silver. For this erroneous perception cannot be an accomplished fact if the false appearance of the silver remains a floating entity and does not become an *object* (*viṣaya*) of cognition. Hence arises the necessity for the discovery of the epistemological condition of the erroneous perception under consideration, in addition to its physiological and psychological conditions mentioned above. To this end the Advaita Vedānta brings its epistemological analysis of perception to bear upon the understanding of the erroneous perception of the nacre as silver. Accordingly, it holds that the 'bright this', resulting from the perception of the 'bright' nacre, under the handicap of the disease of the eyes, is modified into *cittavṛttis* (mental modes) which *eo ipso* come to bear the reflection of this-consciousness (*idaṁabacchinna-caitanya*). And once this comes about, the this-conciousness and the mental-mode-consciousness (*vṛtticaitanya*) become identified with each other and with the *pramātṛcaitanya* (subject-consciousness). As a result, there emerges an *avidyā* (ignorance) in the shape of the nacre, which means that the identity of the nacre is hidden (*āvarita*). And, as the Advaita Vedānta continues, it is the *avidyā* in the shape of the nacre which assumes the shape of the silver in virtue of the visual sensation of 'brightness' and at the same time gives rise to the false perception of silver.

The above analysis of erroneous perception, despite its formidable subtlety, leaves no room for doubt about the fact that it is entirely determined by the Advaita metaphysical doctrine with its emphasis on the concept of Māyā or Avidyā. Since Māyā regarded as the cosmic principle of illusion is, according to the Advaita Vedānta, endowed with the capacity for the covering of reality under a cloak (āvaraṇa) as well as for the projection (*vikṣepa*) of the false appearance of reality, erroneous perception in which the working of this cosmic principle is illustrated in a small measure must have a share of the twofold capacity in question. This is precisely the reason why, in the view of the Advaita Vedānta, our erroneous perception of the nacre as silver consists in the hiding of the identity of the former on the one hand, and the projection of the false appearance of the latter on the other. This view, despite its bearing the stigma of being metaphysically oriented, seems to be the most satisfactory among the theories of error we have so far had occasion to examine—and this owing to its providing the most realistic and faithful account of the fact about erroneous perception.

Another point which is especially favourable to the theory of error advocated by the Advaita Vedānta also derives from its doctrine of Māyā and concerns the ontological status of the content of erroneous perception. It relates to the Advaita view that this content cannot be regarded as real, because it is liable to be contradicted or sublated, whereas that which is real is not so liable. Nor, as the view continues, it can be held to be unreal, because it *appears* and because that which is unreal is incapable of appearing. In view of this predicament the Advaita Vedānta arrives at the conclusion that the content of erroneous perception cannot come under either of the two categories of reality or existence and unreality or non-existence, and so needs to be regarded as *anirvacanīya* (unspeakable, indefinable or indeterminable). This conclusion, it is important to note, divides the Advaita Vedānta, on the one hand, from the Mādhyamika which regards the content of erroneous perception as unreal or non-existent and, on the other hand, from the remaining schools of Indian philosophy which conceive this content to be a strange mixture of both existence and non-existence, reality and unreality or else to be real or existent in the sense of being purely physical, purely mental or both physical and mental as the case may be. The fact of the matter is, however, that in their attempt to determine the ontological status of the content of erroneous perception, the schools of Indian philosophy other than the Advaita Vedānta indulge in vanity by having recourse of half-truths which are worse than falsities. The Advaita Vedānta in its attempt to do the same, on the other hand, demonstrates humility in conformity with the true spirit of philosophizing, by desisting from offering definitive, well-defined or clear-cut solutions of difficult philosophical problems at the cost of truth.

PART 2

Indian Metaphysics

INTRODUCTION

It is hardly necessary to mention that there is no such thing as Indian Metaphysics in the singular. As is evident even to a casual student of the history of Indian thought, metaphysical thinking in India has been bewilderingly various, instead of having been characterized by any manner of uniformity. As we have tried to show earlier, the ordinary view that the different schools of Indian philosophy have a number of features in common with one another is merely verbal, having no foundation of fact to stand upon. And it would certainly be too much to expect that the pattern of thought should be uniform in a vast country like India where climate, language, custom, culture, etc. vary from one local region to another and where, in particular, indigenous culture has, almost throughout its history, borne the impact of culture from abroad. But, not to speak of a big country like India, even a small country such as Greece of ancient times evolved, not a single or uniform type, but diverse types, of metaphysical thinking. This indicates that the differences of individuals or of groups of individuals have no less important an effect to produce upon the nature and quality of metaphysical speculations than the differences of geographical region, climate, language and culture may be said to have. It is, therefore, no wonder that in India, metaphysics, like any other branch of philosophy, should come to be diversified on group lines and result in the emergence of a few distinct types of metaphysical doctrines.

Our immediate task is to ascertain what the distinct types of metaphysical doctrines are which form part of Indian philosophy in general. To this end it is first necessary to repudiate the view held by some Western Indologists and even some Indian intellectuals, that Indian philosophy in general and Indian metaphysics in particular have been dominated by a religious, spiritualistic or other-worldly outlook. This view, as we shall see in due course, is definitely countered by the fact that there has been no dearth of materialistic, anti-spiritualistic and anti-religious thinking in the domain of Indian metaphysics. Secondly, the charge of dogmatism, which Kant brought against all kinds of metaphysics in the history of Western philosophy before his time, is not applicable in the case of Indian metaphysics any more than it was really applicable in the case of Western philosophy. For his view that the enquiry into the nature, conditions and limits of knowledge should have precedence over the enquiry into the nature of Ultimate Reality seems to be the expression of a dogma which he himself, perhaps, did not succeed in practising and which is, to all intents and purposes, impracticable.

The fact that deserves to be especially taken into account in this connection is, however, that philosophy in India proceeds on the assumption that knowledge is an ultimate datum and, consequently, that there arises no need for the enquiry into its possibility which is usually regarded as the epistemological enquiry *par excellence.* The point which Indian philosophy has in view in this connection may be figuratively expressed by stating that the world for us is illumined and not steeped in darkness. Of course, one may still refer to the charge of dogmatism which is often made against Indian philosophy in general and Indian metaphysics in particular, on the ground of their alleged dependence upon the authority of the Vedas and allied scriptures.* But in this regard we have only to refer to our earlier argument to show that this charge is baseless and unjust.

Be it noted, however, that the motive of metaphysical thinking in the Indian situation has been, in a sense, *practical*, and not predominantly *theoretical* as it has been in the West ever since the beginning of philosophy in ancient Greece. Here in India concern with the problems regarding man and the universe and all important matters relating thereto, which is usually regarded as essential to the metaphysical venture, has been subordinated, either overtly as in the case of Buddhism and the Sāṁkhya or implicitly as in the case of the majority of the remaining schools of Indian philosophy, to the concern with the most human of all human problems, that of the ultimate destiny of man and its fulfilment. Whether this was proper or not from the strictly metaphysical point of view need not be discussed here. Philosophical modernism is, of course, more likely than not to be in favour of a negative answer to this question. But all that may be said in this regard is that modern knowledge, in spite of the tantalizing effect it has succeeded in producing, is, after all, no rival of ancient wisdom. However that may be, the question that is especially important in this connection is whether metaphysical thinking may possibly be autonomous and be freely diversified in the circumstance of its being invariably motivated in one and the same way. As regards this question, it may, with reference to the Indian situation, be answered emphatically in the affirmative in view of the fact that the metaphysical doctrines propounded by the different schools of Indian philosophy, as we

* This charge is levelled against the orthodox (āstika) schools of Indian philosophy only.

shall see later, are so diverse from one another that hardly any trace is noticeable about their having been determined by a common motive.

So it is plain that there was no insuperable obstacle to interfere with the freedom of the metaphysical pursuit in India and prevent the growth of diversity with regard to its findings. This is definitely borne out by the fact that the field of Indian metaphysics is replete with almost as many and as diverse metaphysical doctrines as one may be able to notice in the metaphysical sphere in the West supposed to be imbued with the spirit of freedom. And of the many and various metaphysical doctrines universally recognized, materialism, significantly enough, found not an inconspicuous place in the intellectual *milieu* in India. We may, therefore, be well advised in beginning with the consideration of materialism in India in our enquiry into the Indian metaphysical doctrines.

I

MATERIALISM

According to some scholars, materialism is the earliest among the metaphysical doctrines which have been propounded in India, while others are of the view that it is the latest among them. The truth in this regard, however, seems to lie midway between these two extremes and consists in stating that it is almost contemporaneous with the others of its kind. But then, it is absolutely certain that Indian materialism is not so well known, nor is it known in all its details at home or abroad as are other metaphysical doctrines which originated in India. This is mainly due to the fact that the original literature relating to materialistic metaphysics has been lost beyond recovery, and that the critical references to this brand of metaphysics made by its adversaries as well as certain stray references to it to be found here and there are the main sources of our knowledge about it. Another thing to be noted about Indian materialism is that it is not so widely known that it has passed through a gradual process of development from a state of crudity to a state of refinement, and that the views of the Cārvākas, which are ordinarily regarded as its sole constituents, are really not so.

The beginning of Indian materialism is marked by the emergence of *Bārhaspatya*, the school of philosophy founded by a person called Bṛhaspati whose identity remains undiscovered till this day. To begin with, the Bārhaspatya was purely negative and destructive, with no positive contribution of its own towards the enrichment of philosophic thought. To oppose the views of other schools of philosophy, to refute the authority of the Vedas and to harp on the futility of the performance of the rituals enjoined by the Vedas were the sole occupation of the immediate followers of Bṛhaspati. But the purely negative attitude of the Bārhaspatya eventually underwent a modification in the manner of the incorporation within it of the doctrine of *svabhāva* (*svabhavavāda*), according to which effects are self-existent, being neither the products of other things as causes nor, obviously, of themselves. As a result, Indian materialism in the shape of the Bārhaspatya became conspicuous for its rejection of the principle of causality and of the good and evil consequences of actions. In fact, this twofold rejection remained its main feature. Thus Indian materialism in the hands of the immediate followers of Bṛhaspati retained its original negative and destructive tendency. It was, therefore, in need of the incorporation within itself of a few positive elements in order that it could establish its claim as a metaphysical doctrine properly so called. And the fulfilment of this need came about as a result of the transition from the Bārhaspatya to the Lokāyata school at a time when famous materialists like Ajita Keśakambalin, Kambalāsvatara and Purāṇa Kāśyapa were engaged in intensive philosophical activity.

The Lokāyata School, initially equipped with naturalism and, consequently, committed to the rejection of the principle of causality and of the good and evil consequences of actions, soon became positively oriented and admitted the authority of *perception*. In consequence, it came to advocate the most extreme form of empiricism, holding as it did that nothing can be said to exist or be real which is not perceivable. And this ruled out the possibility of inference, because inference must have a universal proposition (*vyāpti*) as its major premise, and because perception is incapable of yielding universal propositions, being unavoidably limited to the exploration of *particular* matters of fact. Solely dependent upon the deliverances of perception and deprived of the help of inference in its understanding of man and the universe as it was, the Lokāyata had no option but to regard *life* and *consciousness* as ancillary to, or derivatives of, matter which alone is open to perception. According to it, life is the result of the collection or mixture of material atoms (*bhuta*) in a certain proportion and according to a certain order. Consciousness, likewise, is inseparable from matter, being none but the function of the living body. This, as the Lokāyata observes, is conclusively established by innumerable facts concerning the relation between the body and the mind. Since consciousness, as ordinarily held, is the essence of what is called the soul or self, and since it is the function of the living body, the soul, as the Lokāyata further holds, is indistinguishable from, and indeed is identical with, the living body.

Given the above view of the situation of man regarded as a living being with a soul, the Lokāyata, with a view to forming itself into a sort of philosophical system, seeks to derive its necessary corollaries as follows. Since consciousness is the essence of the soul and is at the same time the function of the living body, the perishing of the body amounts to the complete cessation of consciousness and the consequent termination of the existence of the soul. And in this the Lokāyata finds all the reason for the dismissal of belief in immortality and, in particular, the doctrine of *karma* and transmigration which has played a dominant role in Indian philosophy through the ages. And once this doctrine comes to be rejected, the consequences which necessarily follow are: the denial of the supposed reality of other worlds (*paraloka*), whether heaven (*svarga*) or hell (*naraka*); disbelief in the theory of *karmaphala*, signifying the effectiveness of the consequences of good and bad action in future life and the denial of any such thing as *adṛṣta* (unseen agency; fate) regarded as the determinant of the future of man. All this led the Lokāyata to the defiance of the authority of the Vedas, the supposed source of the guiding principles of human life and conduct and to the revaluation of the prevailing religion.

In bitter criticism of the Vedas, the Lokāyata observes that statements contained in them suffer from the faults of repetition, ambiguity, contradictoriness, absurdity and even meaninglessness. Moreover, in some cases a line of action prescribed by one Vedic text is condemned by another, and it sometimes happens that the sacrifices enjoined by the Vedas as productive of a certain result turn out to be fruitless. And, what is more, some of the sacrifices enjoined by the Vedas, for example, the horse sacrifice recommended for the performance of the queen, involve certain obscene rituals. In view of all this, the Lokāyata holds that the authors of the three Vedas cannot be regarded as anything better than hypocrites (*bhanda*), knaves (*dhurta*) and demons (*niśācara*).

Traditional religion, like the Vedas, receives the most vituperative criticism at the hands of the Lokāyata. It is said to be as harmful as an intoxicant such as opium. Prayer is regarded as the resort of those who are mentally weak and are lacking in the will to undertake hard work. And what is worship but the expression of the egoistic idea of one's enjoyment of heavenly happiness or else one's safety from the tortures of hell? Moreover, who can think of the prophets except as the greatest and the most mischievous liars among men? All religious rites and ceremonies and all human endeavours to placate the gods by prayer and offerings are, therefore, vain and illusive. Religion, as the Lokāyata concludes, is the invention of individuals seized with the evil design of the exploitation of their fellowmen in order to further their selfish end and fulfil their personal ambition.

The kind of thinking which went into the Lokāyata attack upon some of the important aspects of the prevailing state of human affairs could, however, have resulted in something better than that in which it actually resulted, namely, the philosophy of 'eat, drink and be merry', which, obviously, treats the fulfilment of desires (*kāma*) as the *summum bonum* of human life. Nevertheless, it would be a mistake to hold that this sums up the entire achievement of the Lokāyata. On the contrary, it should be admitted that this school of philosophy brought about the Indian *Aufklärung* (Illumination) similar to the Greek *Aufklärung* which the Sophists introduced into the outlook on life in ancient Greece. In fact, the distinguishing feature of the Lokāyata lay in that it was a reformist movement with a poignant concern with the social, political and religious aspects of Indian life of its time. It was conspicuous for its appeal for the shift of interest from the wanton waste of human energy and resources over other-worldly affairs to the urgent need for the realization of earthly welfare. In a deeper analysis, it was the harbinger of freedom, freedom from the shackles which had bound people through the ages.

It is on account of its championing the cause of freedom that the Lokāyata could prepare the ground as it actually did for the rise of Buddhism and the Buddhistic culture, This is evident from the fact that Buddha's views against the authority of the Vedas and the Vedic sacrifices, the caste system, the worship of the deities, mortifications and other ascetic practices are similar to those of the Lokāyata. And the influence of the freedom movement inaugurated by the Lokāyata was so comprehensive that people did not rest content with freedom only in the social and religious spheres, but became conscious of the need for political freedom. This need was eventually fulfilled when the mutually hostile states of India were brought together under the common sovereignty of the Maurya Empire at first by Chandra Gupta and then by Asoka. In any case, the Lokāyata, while ignoring those academic disciplines which deal with the supersensible, attached considerable importance to those branches of knowledge which bear upon earthly welfare, including politics and economics. This is evident from the fact that their earlier view of pleasure or happiness (*kāma*) as the highest good of life was changed and they came to regard *artha* (wealth) as a good of human life in addition to happiness. But this was not all that came out of the movement that was the Lokāyata. It is most probable that it was during the period of Indian history occupied by Indian materialism that several sciences and innumerable fine arts came into existence and were widely propagated. All this serves to indicate that the Lokāyata was not an evil as it is ordinarily considered to be, but was pregnant with the promise of the inauguration of an ideal state of human affairs—but a promise which has been left unfulfilled partly owing to its degeneration and partly owing to the revival and revitalization of Brahmanism to which it was sharply opposed.

The Lokāyata in its degenerate form came to be newly designated as Cārvāka, although it still retained its old designation as Bārhaspatya. The most outstanding feature of the Cārvāka consisted in its laying undue stress on the importance of pleasure as an object of human pursuit and thereby evolving the grossest form of hedonism, with the result that the freedom, the cause of which was espoused by the Lokāyata, was replaced by licentiousness. It was therefore no surprise that the Buddhists and the Jainas, despite their being united with the Indian materialists by the tie of common heresy, became hostile to the latter. In consequence, the already existing opposition of the orthodox schools of Indian philosophy to Indian materialism was considerably reinforced. In this circumstance the position of Indian materialism became rather shaky and so it was compelled to yield to anti-materialistic criticism as far as possible. Thus the materialists surrendered their old *dehātmavāda* (the doctrine of the identity of the self with the body) by first identifying the self with the sense-organs, then by identifying it with the principle of life and lastly, by identifying it with the mind. They were also compelled to withdraw step by step their view of inference as a source of knowledge. At first they conceded that inference is useful in so far as it can yield *probability*, instead of certain knowledge. Then it came to admit that inference is a source of (certain) knowledge about what has taken place, but not about what has not taken place or, in other words, has not been perceived such as Heaven, God, Soul, etc. Thus was enacted the tragedy of a way of thinking which was full of the promise of a better future for man and society, but which was misled by its own folly on the one hand and was put to torture by reactionary trends of thought on the other.

II

REALISM

A

NYĀYA-VAIŚEṢIKA REALISM

We may next proceed to enquire into a group of metaphysical doctrines which are peculiar in that they are nearest to materialism and yet are not identifiable with the latter. The reason for this is that they admit such a thing as spirit or mind or soul in distinction from matter or the latter in distinction from the former; but they do not view the relation between the two *dualistically*. That being so, they cannot be called materialistic nor spiritualistic nor dualistic. For want of a better designation for them to bear, they may, therefore, be brought under the category of Realism, although the word 'realism', it must be admitted, is more epistemologically than metaphysically significant. The most salient examples of this kind of metaphysical doctrines are provided by the two schools of Vaiśeṣika and Nyāya. Let us, then, have an account of the realistic metaphysics which have been produced by them.

Although the Vaiśeṣika and the Nyāya have separate founders, the founder of the former being Kanāda and that of the latter Gautama, and they also differ from each other in several respects, they are very intimately allied with each other and are usually treated as the two parts of one philosophy. We may, therefore, deal with the metaphysical doctrines of the two schools together, treating them as one and the same and noting their differences wherever necessary.

The first thing to be noticed about the Nyāya-Vaiśeṣika metaphysics is that its authors, like Aristotle, seek to work it out in accordance with a plan previously determined. The plan consists in the classification of the supposed realities underlying the universe under a few categories (*padārthas*) in order that the treatment of them might be convenient as well as comprehensive. The Vaiśeṣika recognizes seven such categories. One of them called *abhāva* (non-being) stands for all kinds of non-existence or negative facts. The remaining six respectively called *dravya* (substance), *guṇa* (quality), *karma* (action), *sāmānya* (community), *viśeṣa* (particularity) and *samavāya* (inherence) represent the various kinds of being (*bhāva*). Be it noted, however, that the Nyāya has admitted as many as sixteen categories which are respectively designated as *pramāna* (means of knowledge), *prameya* (objects of knowledge), *saṁśaya* (doubt), *prayojana* (end), *dṛṣṭānta* (example), *siddhānta* (doctrine), *avayava* (members of syllogisms), *tarka* (hypothetical argument), *nirṇaya* (ascertainment), *vāda* (discussion), *jalpa* (wrangling), *vitaṇḍā* (cavilling), *hetvābhāsa* (fallacies of inference), *chala* (quibbling), *jāti* (futile objections) and *nigrahasthāna* (points of defeat in a debate).

Now the categories admitted by the Nyāya are obviously related to Epistemology and Logic, and have hardly anything directly to do with metaphysics, whereas those of the Vaiśeṣika are of undoubted metaphysical significance. This suffices to indicate that the realistic metaphysics of the Nyāya-Vaiśeṣika is primarily the contribution of the Vaiśeṣika. Let us, however, begin our investigation of the Nyāya-Vaiśeṣika scheme of metaphysical construction with the consideration of its admission of *abhāva* (non-existence) as a metaphysical category. The reason why *abhāva* (non-existence) should at all be regarded as a metaphysical category seems to be more psychological than otherwise, it being rooted in the dread of destruction and death. It is, perhaps, this dread which induced several schools of Indian philosophy, including the Nyāya–Vaiśeṣika, to admit this category. And it is equally probable that it is again this dread which is responsible for the admission of the supreme importance of Nothingness on the part of the existentialist thinkers of our time like J. P. Sartre who became most sensitive to the horror of destruction following in the foot-steps of the greatest calamity that befell mankind in the shape of the Second World War. In any case, as we have tried to show earlier, neither the Nyāya-Vaiśeṣika nor even the Advaita Vedānta and the Bhāṭṭa school of Mīmāṁsā which, unlike the former, admit *anupalabdhi* (non-apprehension) as the specific source of our knowledge of non-existence, are justified in recognizing *abhāva* as a separate metaphysical category. The reason for this is that that recognition is liable to the fault of the arbitrary conversion of the mere *act* of negating into an independent *entity* called non-existence (abhāva).*

While, as seen above, it has no justification for its recognition of *abhāva* as a metaphysical category, the Nyāya-Vaiśeṣika scheme of metaphysical construction stands on a sounder footing than many others of its kind such as that which has been handed down since the time of Plato, in so far as it admits the six categories of *bhāva* (being; existence). Following in the foot-steps of Plato and Aristotle, the modern rationalists in the West headed by Descartes proceeded in their metaphysical venture on the assumption that the two categories of *substance* and *attribute* are together sufficient to represent the universe as a whole and in all its aspects. But then, as is well known, the world as conceived by Descartes and his followers in terms of the categories of substance and attribute, for example, presents itself to be something weird, being essentially lacking in temporality and being devoid of colour, smell, etc. as well as many other things with which the universe of our day to day experience is richly endowed. The Nyāya-Vaiśeṣikas, on the other hand, are, as we shall see below, free from such defects of the interpretation of the universe by the Western followers of Plato and Aristotle.

Substance (*dravya*), according to the Nyāya-Vaiśeṣika metaphysics, is the substratum of *qualities* and *actions* and, moreover, is the material cause of effects. Thus conceived, it is, obviously, *dynamic* and not static as it is in the view of Descartes. On the other hand, being the substratum of qualities, it cannot be, as in the view of the realist schools of Buddhism it must be, a mere aggregate of qualities; nor can it be a complex of *ideas* (*vijñāna*) as held by the Yogācāra school of Buddhism. In fact, substance, according to the Nyāya–Vaiśeṣika, does not admit of being understood in terms of qualities or actions in as much as the latter depend for their existence upon, and inhere in, the former. Substance regarded as a category is not,

* It is of interest to note that Kaṇāda, the founder of the Vaiśeṣika school, did not admit the category of abhāva (non-existence). It was Śridhara, Udayana and others who later added the seventh category of abhāva to the list of the padārthas finally recognized by the Vaiśeṣikas.

however, a mere entity, but, as this combined school of Indian philosophy holds, is something in which *dravyatva* (the genus of substance) inheres. This is important in that it opens up the possibility of the recognition of various kinds of substances. Accordingly, the Nyāya-Vaiśeṣika admits the existence of many substances and is of the view that they exist in themselves and independently of one another. They are, of course, *namable* and *knowable*. But their existence does not consist in their being named or known. Their namability and knowability are accidental to their existence. Hence it is evident that the metaphysical doctrine of the Nyāya-Vaiśeṣika is realistic pluralism.

Broadly speaking, substances, according to the Nyāya-Vaiśeṣika, come under two heads, the eternal and the non-eternal. As regards the latter, they are of a compositive character and as such are made of parts, so that they are produced by means of the combination of their parts and are destroyed as a result of their separation. The non-eternal substances are the concrete objects of our day to day experience and indeed are too many and various to admit of enumeration as well as classification. This difficulty does not, however, arise in the case of the eternal substances. So the Vaiśeṣika finds itself in a position to recognize nine kinds of eternal substance, namely, *pṛthivi* (earth), *jala* (water), *tejas* (fire), *vāyu* (air), *ākāśa* (ether), *kāla* (time), *dis* (space), *ātman* (soul) and *manas* (mind). Now the first four substances, according to the Vaiśeṣika, are of an *atomic* character. On this account, they are not perceivable, and their existence can only be *inferred*. The question of the inferability of the existence of atoms (*paramāṇu*) has given rise to a controversy among the members of the Vaiśeṣika school into which it is not necessary for us to enter. We would rather have a brief account of the Nyāya-Vaiśeṣika theory of atomism as follows.

According to the Nyāya-Vaiśeṣika, the atoms of earth, water, fire and air are the indivisible and minutest elements which are globular and partless, and constitute physical substances. But they are in themselves inactive or motionless, and their motion is due to an external agent. But in this regard, the Vaiśeṣika had recourse to anthropocentricism at the cost of the apparently scientific character of their attempt to interpret the physical universe. The earlier Vaiśeṣikas held that motion is imparted to the atoms by the unseen agencies (*adṛṣta*) residing in the individual souls. The later Vaiśeṣikas went further in holding the view that it is God who imparts motion to the atoms and combines them into concrete objects in accordance with the merits and demerits of the individual souls for their enjoyment or suffering as the case may be. This, obviously, amounts to the admission of a sort of teleological view of the evolution of the universe, according to which the universe is not the product of the fortuitous combination of atoms governed by the mechanical principle of causality, but is a sphere full of opportunities for individual souls to realize their moral aspirations. This, while having some resemblance to Anaxagoras's view of reason (*nous*) as the determining principle of the evolution of the universe, is completely opposed to the view of the Greek atomists such as Leucippus and Democritus who relegated the evolution of the universe to the agency of *chance*.

Another respect in which the Vaiśeṣika atomic theory differs from the atomism of the Greeks as well as the Jainas in India relates to their view of the different kinds of atoms as *qualitatively* distinct from one another. Whereas the latter hold that all atoms are qualitatively alike, but are only quantitatively different, that is, different in shape, size and magnitude, the former admit their qualitative differences in addition to the quantitative ones. Accordingly, the Nyāya-Vaiśeṣika proceeds to determine the qualities of the four kinds of atoms as follows. The qualities of earth are seven in number, namely, odour, taste, colour, touch, acquired fluidity, gravity and velocity. Those of water are taste, colour, touch, natural fluidity, viscidity, gravity and velocity. Fire has four different qualities, including colour, touch, aquired fluidity and velocity. And lastly, the qualities of air are only two in number, being touch and velocity. Moreover, all these four kinds of atoms possess, in common, the general qualities of number, magnitude, distinctness, conjunction, disjunction, remoteness and proximity. All this is, however, apt to create the impression that, while the Greek atomists committed the fault of oversimplification in their understanding of the universe as ultimately *quantitative*, the Vaiśeṣikas committed the opposite mistake of conceiving the ultimate structure of the universe to be almost a replica of the variegated contour of the world of our day to day experience.

As seen above, the qualities which belong to the four atomic substances, namely, earth, water, fire and air do not include *sound* as one of them. The reason for this is that sound, as the Nyāya-Vaiśeṣika holds, cannot be regarded as a quality of any of these four atomic substances, and, further, that none of the remaining four substances, namely, space, time, self and mind can have sound as one of their qualities. But then, since the reality of sound as a quality cannot be doubted, there must be a substance of which it is the quality. Arguing on this line, the Nyāya-Vaiśeṣika, like some classical scientists in the West, admitted ether (*ākāśa*) as a substance. Ether, like the atomic substances, then, is not an object of perception; it is inferable from the existence of sound. But it is not itself atomic. On the contrary, it is not only eternal but ubiquitous (*vibhu*), despite the fact that it is the substrate of sound. Moreover, it is homogeneous and only one of its kind, it being understood that all sounds, despite the differences of their loudness as well as the apparent differences of their quality, are of the same kind. But in this, the position of the Nyāya-Vaiśeṣika is far from being satisfactory. It is, therefore, no wonder that scientists should eventually find no justification for the admission of such a thing as ether.

Space (*dis*), according to the Nyāya-Vaiśeṣika, is an external reality and does not admit of being construed as subjective in any sense whatsoever. It is, like ether, non-atomic, unitary and ubiquitous. And it agrees with other eternal substances in that it is not perceivable, but is *inferable*—inferable, among other things, from the fact that it can produce the determinate cognitions of directions such as the east, the west and the like. But in this connection it would be wrong to argue that there are different cognitions of the east, the west, etc. in different places and, consequently, that there exist many spaces instead of one only. The reason for this, according to the Vaiśeṣika, is that one and the same object may be perceived as situated to the east of another object and to the west of a third object, which would not have been possible, had there been many spaces and not one only. Hence the Nyāya-Vaiśeṣika arrives at the conclusion that space is not only eternal, but is one, despite the fact that it appears to be many owing to its limiting conditions (*upādhi*). In further characterization of space, the Nyāya-Vaiśeṣika holds that it has no specific qualities, and all its qualities are generic ones, namely, number, magnitude, distinctness, conjunction and disjunction. It is of special importance to note, however, that space alone is in conjunction with corporeal substances and thereby serves to determine their spatial positions.

Time (*kāla*), according to the Nyāya-Vaiśeṣika, is not only eternal as all substances are, but is, like space, non-atomic, unitary and ubiquitous. It is also an external reality as is space and so is recalcitrant to the conception of it as subjective in any way whatsoever. Moreover, it shares a common characteristic of all eternal substances in so far as it is imperceptible and can be known only inferentially. In the first place, time, according to the Vaiśeṣika, is inferable from the cognitions of temporal determinations such as remoteness and proximity, simultaneity and succession, slowness and rapidity. Secondly, production, persistence and destruction are phenomena, the possibility of which presupposes the objective reality of time. Thirdly, our notions of duration, whether short or long, such as hours, days, months, etc. are all set in the background of time and so presuppose its reality. But these arguments advanced by the Vaiśeṣika failed to produce any positive effect upon the Nyāya in as much as this school of philosophy definitely held the view that time is perceptible on the ground that it is perceived as a quality (*viśeṣaṇa*) of effects produced, but not as an independent reality. The Vaiśeṣika's reply to this objection is, however, far from being satisfactory, because it consists, on the one hand, in admitting that time is perceptible and, strangely enough, in holding, on the other hand, that this does not affect its being inferable at the same time.

The Vaiśeṣika seems to be equally unsuccessful in meeting the objection of the Buddhists conveyed by their view that time is not a separate or independent reality, but is identical with change or action. For this school of philosophy approves of this view and yet holds that time must be said to be presupposed by, and not to be identical with, action. But this amounts to having recourse to *apriorism* in defiance of the verdict of experience and thereby setting aside the legitimate claim of empiricism. It may be of interest to note in this connection, however, that the Vaiśeṣika seeks to avoid the mistake involved in the conception of time in terms of space, which has been committed by many a philosopher in the West, by having recourse to the view that it is *action* only which holds the key to the understanding of the nature of time.

In any case, the Vaiśeṣika has made a commendable endeavour to prevent the possibility of the mistake of the understanding of time in terms of space, by a careful investigation of the distinctions between these two. Two of these distinctions, however, are of special importance. One of them consists in stating that, whereas spatial relations are changeable and reversible, temporal relations are unchangeable or constant and irreversible. It may be mentioned in this connection that Kant, despite the fact that he could not keep the distinction between space and time constantly present in his mind, drew this distinction and, what is more, emphasized its importance for the understanding of the nature of space and time respectively. Now the second of the two distinctions may be expressed by saying that the divisions of space are *relative*, contingent or changeable, whereas those of time are *fixed*. This may be explained as follows, on the understandiug that the divisions of time are the past, the present and the future. A point of space which is at one time to the east of a thing may be to the west of it at another time, but a moment of time which is either past or present or future in relation to a certain event will, on the other hand, always remain the same. As far as these two distinctions are concerned, the Vaiśeṣika is certainly above reproach in so far as it admits them and emphasizes their importance in the understanding of space and time. But it goes rather too far in holding the view that the past, the present, and the future are independent of each other and are individually and separately real. Even granted that this view is in itself faultless, it is certainly incompatible with the Vaiśeṣika conception of time as unitary and homogeneous.

As regards *manas*, although it is usually translated into the English word 'mind', it does not convey the sense of a spiritual substance as is done by the latter. On the contrary, it means the internal sense-organ (*antara-indriya*) as distinguished from the many and various external sense-organs (*bahirindriyas*). One of the differences between the internal sense (*manas*) and the external senses, according to the Nyāya-Vaiśeṣika, lies in that, whereas the latter are material, the former is *immaterial*, although Uddyotkara differs from Vātsyayana and Jayanta Bhatta in holding that it does not come under either of the two categories of materiality and immateriality. It seems, however, that the view of Uddyotkara is preferable to that of the latter on account of the fact that the Vaiśeṣikas regard *manas* as *corporeal* (*mūrta*), despite its being conceived to be immaterial. The reason which they have in conceiving *manas* to be corporeal derives from a view which is rather crude, namely, that it is capable of *movement*, and that nothing can move which is not corporeal. Be that as it may, another difference between the two, according to them, lies in that, whereas the external senses are capable of apprehending only specific objects, for example, colour or smell or the like, the internal sense-organ is gifted with the ability to apprehend all kinds of objects, irrespective of their specific differences. It may be of interest to note in this connection that, in the history of Western philosophy, Kant also came to draw a similar distinction between the inner sense and the outer sense.

Further, the *manas*, according to the Nyāya-Vaiśeṣika, is not only immaterial, corporeal and capable of movement, but, being a substance, is eternal and is, like the elementary material substances such as earth, water, etc., *atomic* in character. On account of its being atomic, *manas* is not perceptible, but is only inferable. The existence of *manas* may be inferred from the fact that even in the event of the intercourse of the self with the sense-organs and the intercourse of the latter with some external object or other, perception cannot take place if the *manas* does not come into contact with the self and the sense-organs. And this goes to show that even the perception of external objects is dependent upon the function of the internal sense-organ in addition to that of the external sense-organs. Moreover, the apprehension of subjective processes such as cognition, volition, pleasure, pain, etc. cannot be possible except in so far as there is an internal sense-organ in addition to the external sense-organs. Furthermore, the very fact that we can recollect colour, smell, etc in the absence of the function of our external sense-organs points towards the existence of such a thing as the internal sense-organ. But these arguments are of no avail unless the parallelism between the working of the external sense-organs and the internal sense-organ be satisfactorily established in detail. And this indicates the difficulty which, as far as one can see, stands in the way of the admission of the so-called internal sense-organ (*manas*).

As distinguished from the substances we have already investigated which are material, there is, in the view of the Nyāya-Vaiśeṣika, another, in fact, the only remaining one which is immaterial and is called the *ātman* (soul). According to some Nyāya-Vaiśeṣikas, the soul is directly and immediately known in virtue of a sort of internal awareness as is evident from one's statements such as 'I am', 'I am happy', etc. But the view that prevails among them is that the *ātman* is imperceptible or rather is recalcitrant to direct apprehension, and, consequently, that its existence is testified to by the scriptures and is also inferable from certain mental phenomena such as cognition, desire, aversion, pleasure, pain, etc. The main point about the inferability of the existence of the *ātman*, according to the Nyāya-Vaiśeṣika, lies in the consideration that the substrate which these mental phenomena must have cannot be the body, not to speak of any other material object, and so must needs be something immaterial called the *ātman*.

The argument which these philosophers have employed for the proof of the existence of the soul, is, however, important in another respect: it leads them to view the *ātman* as a qualitied being and enables them to determine its qualities. Accordingly, the Nyāya-Vaiśeṣika holds that mental phenomena such as cognition, desire, disposition, volition, pleasure, etc. are the qualities of the *ātman* in virtue of the latter's being the substrate of the former. But these are the *ātman's* special qualities in addition to the general qualities which it shares with other kinds of substances, namely, number, magnitude, etc. Of these general qualities of the soul, magnitude is of special importance in the understanding of the *ātman*. Curiously enough, the Nyāya-Vaiśeṣika not only attributes magnitude to the soul and thereby undermines its conception of it as immaterial,* but holds that its magnitude is the greatest, with the result that it comes to be conceived as ubiquitous (*vibhu*) in the sense that it is related to all corporeal substances. But this is not only fantastic in itself, but is incompatible with the Nyāya-Vaiśeṣika view which we shall mention below—the view, namely, that there are many souls.

No account of the Nyāya-Vaiśeṣika metaphysics of the *ātman* can, however, be complete without reference to the following points. In first place, the qualities of the *ātman*, according to the Nyāya-Vaiśeṣika, are not, as in the view of philosophers like Descartes they are, essential to it; they are its adventitious or accidental features, owing their origin to the occasional conjunction of the soul with the *manas* and external objects. That being so, the so-called qualities of the self must cease to exist on the termination of such conjunction in

* That the Nyāya-Vaiśeṣika is not free from the understanding of the soul on the analogy of material objects is evident from its attribution of magnitude to it. This is one of the reasons why we have held earlier that its conception of the relation between spirit and matter is not dualistic.

a state of dreamless sleep or of liberation. This shows that in its view of the soul, the Nyāya-Vaiśeṣika holds a position which is midway between two extremes, one consisting in holding that the soul is essentially a qualitied being and the other advocating, as the Advaita Vedānta advocates, the doctrine of *nirguṇa* (quality-less) soul, according to which the soul is essentially devoid of all qualities. Secondly, the Nyāya-Vaiśeṣika not only seeks to prove the existence of the soul, but also makes an attempt to prove the existence of *other selves*. In the latter respect it depends on analogical reasoning and infers the existence of other selves from their behaviour as understood on the analogy of one's own behaviour.

Thirdly, the belief in the existence of other selves on the part of the Nyāya-Vaiśeṣika naturally leads it to the belief in the existence of many selves. The argument which it has advanced in support of the latter belief is substantially the same as that which the Sāṁkhya has put forward for its admission of the plurality of souls. It is mainly based upon the consideration of the experiences and conditions of different individuals. That some are happy, while others are miserable; some are rich, while others are poor, etc. are facts which, according to the Nyāya-Vaiśeṣika as well as the Sāṁkhya, cannot be accounted for except on the understanding that the souls are essentially distinct from one another and, consequently, are many in number. But in this both the schools of philosophy are guilty of confusing the empirical and the transcendental self, the latter being above the distinction between happiness and misery, affluence and poverty, etc. Fourthly, while the earlier Vaiśeṣikas, including Kanāda, the founder of the Vaiśeṣika school of philosophy, made no reference to the Infinite Soul or God and thereby proved to be of an atheistic bent of mind, the later Vaiśeṣikas as well as the Naiyāyikas admitted the existence of the Infinite Soul called God and tried to prove His existence. But this presents a matter the consideration of which may be deferred till we reach the stage of the Indian philosophy of Religion.

Let us next enquire into the Nyāya-Vaiśeṣika concept of *guṇa* (quality) which is the second in its list of the categories. The Vaiśeṣikas define quality as that which is subsumed under the genus of quality (*guṇatva*) and inheres in a substance, but which is itself devoid of *quality* and also of *action* and at the same time differs from substance in not being an unconditional cause of conjunction and disjunction. This, among other things, implies that quality is not self-existent, but is dependent upon substance for its subsistence. Hence is evident the reason why substance, as previously observed, cannot be reduced to, or be understood in terms of, qualities. Besides, since substance alone can be said to have a quality or qualities, and since quality is not identifiable with substance, it necessarily follows that a quality cannot be spoken of as having a quality. And for a similar reason a quality cannot be held to be capable of *action.* But then, quality is not devoid of community (*sāmānya*). On the contrary, it is, by its very definition, subsumable under the genus *guṇatva.* And this accounts for the possibility of there being a diversity or multiplicity of qualities. And as regards the kinds of quality, different Vaiśeṣika philosophers present different lists of them, with the result that as many as twenty-four of them have come to be recognized. The enumeration and classification of the qualities and the treatment of them individually and separately with which the Vaiśeṣika has occupied itself may have some scientific importance. But they are of doubtful value from the strictly philosophical point of view.

It is of interest to note, however, that in India, as in the West, the category of substance and quality has sometimes been dismissed as spurious. Just as David Hume rejected this category and installed a stream of successive sense-impressions in its place, the Yogācāra Buddhists in India had earlier replaced this category by a series of momentary ideas. It is against this kind of phenomenalism and subjective idealism that the Nyāya-Vaiśeṣika emphasizes the all-importance of the category of substance and quality in the interpretation of the world of our ordinary experience.

An action (*karma*), according to the Vaiśeṣika, is a physical movement or motion, and it resembles a quality in being inherent in a substance and being devoid of quality. But it differs from a quality in being an *unconditional* cause of conjunction and disjunction and being not static but *dynamic* on the one hand, and being not permanent but *temporary* on the other. It is, then, evident that action is not self-existent, but is dependent upon some substance or other for its existence. How action is an unconditional cause of conjunction and disjunction may, however, be easily understood with reference to a concrete fact, namely, that the *motion* of a carriage is the material cause of its disjunction from one part of the ground and its conjunction with another. But then, the motion of the carriage is the non-inherent (*asamavāyī*) cause of conjunction and disjunction, whereas the carriage itself is their inherent cause in this case. This, of course, implies that an action, say, the movement of the carriage, is dependent upon a substance, for example, the carriage, for its production of conjunction and disjunction. But that, in the view of the Vaiśeṣika, is no reason why action should not be regarded as an unconditional cause of conjunction and disjunction.

The dependence of an action upon a substance is, however, conditional in that the substance concerned must be of limited dimension. For a substance like ether, space, time or the soul, which, in the view of the Vaiśeṣika, is ubiquitous and so is of unlimited dimension cannot, obviously, change its position and, consequently, is incapable of motion. Besides, an action suffers from another limitation in so far as it is, as mentioned above, only a temporary feature of a substance and so is non-eternal and thus is in a class apart from substances and qualities which are permanent or eternal. But then, this limitation of action is somewhat compensated for in virtue of its being subsumable under the genus *karmatva* which is eternal. And this opens up the possibility of the admission of a variety, diversity or multiplicity of actions. Accordingly, the Vaiśeṣika undertakes the scientific task of ascertaining the typical kinds of motion and, as a result, comes to recognize five of them respectively called upward motion (*utkṣepana*), downward motion (*avakṣepana*), contraction (*ākuncana*), expansion (*prasārana*) and locomotion (*gamana*). Now apart from the question whether this classification of motions is comprehensive or not, there is no denying the fact that it testifies to the praiseworthy display of scientific spirit on the part of the Vaiśeṣikas in their investigation of physical phenomena.

But judged from the philosophical point of view, the Vaiśeṣika view of motion as at least a temporary or non-eternal reality had to contend with the Buddhist view of it as unreal based on its doctrine of momentariness (*kṣanikavāda*). And thus was presented in ancient India a parallel to what happened in ancient Greece in the shape of Zeno's dismissal of the reality of motion in the face of the insistence on its reality by the realistically minded Greek thinkers. In any case, the Vaiśeṣika view of motion invites a problem, instead of conveying its solution.

We are now required to consider the Nyāya-Vaiśeṣika treatment of the category of community (*sāmānya*) which seems to be one of the most difficult concepts in the whole field of philosophy. According to the Vaiśeṣika, community is the essential and common character of all the individuals belonging to a class. Thus characterized, community corresponds to what is called 'universal' by Western philosophers. As is well known, the question of the nature and status of universals has given rise to a controversy which has led to the emergence of three major theories respectively called realism, conceptualism and nominalism. According to nominalism, the universal is but a word or a name which corresponds to nothing in the field of the mind or in the extra-mental world. But as far as the Nyāya-Vaiśeṣika is concerned, it, of course, admits that the universal is namable, but holds that its namability is accidental to its being and, consequently, that its being is not reducible to its name. Even so this combined school of Indian philosophy differs from conceptualism, according to which the universal is essentially a notion or a concept or an ideal construction. This school, of course, has no objection to raise against the view that we do have notions or ideas of the universals, but insists that the universals have a being of their own which is not identifiable with that of the notions corresponding to them. Thus it upholds a kind of realism of the Platonic type, according to which the universal, despite its namability and conceivability, is independently real. And it is on this account that the Nyāya-Vaiśeṣikas are in conflict with the Buddhists who advocate nominalism.

Now the foregoing characterization of *sāmānya* (community) as the essential common feature of all the individuals belonging to a class may serve as the basis of the determination of the peculiar characteristics of the *being* (*bhāva*) coming under this category. In the first place, the *sāmānya* is equally *inherent* in all the individuals coming under this category. Secondly, it is identically the same in the case of all the individuals in which it inheres. Thirdly, since it inheres in its identical form in many individuals, it produces the notion of the *inclusion* of the *many* within *one*. Fourthly, it is peculiar in that it is present entirely, simultaneously and ceaselessly in many individuals. And it is on this account that it can bring about the assimilative concept of their common character. Fifthly, the *sāmānya*, unlike the individuals in which it inheres, is eternal.

In this connection it may be of interest to note, however, that a common quality is not necessarily a *sāmānya*, and that in order for it to be a *sāmānya*, it must, according to the Vaiśeṣika, be free from at least six conditions, namely, oneness of the individual, co-extensiveness, cross division, infinite regress, self-contradiction and absence of relation. Thus no characteristic of *ether*, for example, can be called its community (*sāmānya*) for the simple reason that ether is only *one* of its kind or, in other words, that there is no class to which it may be said to belong as an individual member. Then neither physicality nor corporeality is fit to be recognized as a community in as much as they are partially *co-extensive* and involve *cross division* (*saṁkara*) as is evident from the consideration that the *bhutas*, that is, earth, water, fire and air, are both physical and corporeal, but ether is physical and yet not corporeal and *manas*, on the other hand, is corporeal and not physical. Infinite regress (*anavasthā*) as a deterrent of the possibility of community is illustrated in the arbitrary recognition of the class (*jāti*) of a class. The reason for this is that if a class should be brought under another class, the latter would in its turn be in need of being brought under a third class and so on *ad infinitum*. Now the typical instance of self-contradiction as the counteracting condition of the possibility of community is provided by the admission of the community or generality of particularity (*viśeṣa*). Since particularity is necessarily exclusive of generality, the recognition of the generality of particularity obviously involves self-contradiction (*rūpahāni*). Lastly, just as there can be no generality of particularity, there can be no generality of inherence either. The reason for this is that there can be no generality where there is no relation of inherence between generality and its substrate, and that there can be no relation of inherence between the generality of inherence and inherence itself.

It may also be mentioned that the the Vaiśeṣikas distinguish between two kinds of community (*sāmānya*), namely, the higher (*para*) and the lower (*apara*). Being (*sattā*), according to them, is the highest community or generality in as much as it subsists in the largest number of individuals, it being a fact that whatever exists comes under the concept of *being*. The generalities such as *dravyatva* (the genus of substance), *guṇatva* (the genus of quality) and *karmatva* (the genus of action), on the other hand, subsist in a limited number of objects and so may be called lower generalities. In fact, these generalities, unlike the generality of *being*, are the means of assimilation as well as discrimination and so are in a sense both *sāmānya* (generality) and *viśeṣa* (particularity). But very different is the case with the concept of *being*. It is devoid of *viśeṣa* (particularity) and is generality *par excellence*. It does not differ in different substrates, but remains identically the same in whatever may be its substrate.

We may bring our investigation of the category of *sāmānya* (community, generality or class) to a close, by making a brief reference to the controversy between the Nyāya-Vaiśeṣika and the Buddhists on this subject. The Buddhists seek to dismiss the reality of *sāmānya* or *jāti* (class) on two grounds, namely, (1) that we have no means of knowing any such thing as a community or class, and (2) that the individual alone is real, and that there is no community or class regarded as real in distinction from the individual. As regards the former point, the Buddhists contend that generality or genus cannot be known by means of indeterminate (*nirvikalpaka*) perception, because this kind of perception enables us to know an individual by itself alone and not in its relation to other individuals as is demanded by the apprehension of generality or genus. Nor can it, according to Buddhism, be known by means of determinate (*savikalpaka*) perception, because this kind of perception consists in the apprehension of an individual qualified by determinations (*vikalpa*) which are unreal ideal constructions. Inference and testimony, in the view of the Buddhists, are equally unable to provide the knowledge of generality and genus, because these two also involve determinations (*vikalpa*) and so cannot serve as the means of apprehending reality.

Moreover, there can be no generality or genus in distinction from the individual, because, as the Buddhists argue, the former cannot be perceived as different from the latter. As against this, the Nyāya-Vaiśeṣika may, however, reply that the perception of the individual is as good as the perception of the generality or genus, because the latter *subsists* in the former. But this proves unconvincing to the Buddhists. Their reason for this is that the generality may be said to subsist in an individual either *wholly* or *partly*, but that in the former case it cannot subsist in any other individual and so cannot be regarded as a generality and in the latter case it cannot also be called a generality, it being understood that generality, by its very definition, is required to subsist entirely in each individual. Apart from all this, the Buddhists are of the view that the relation of *inherence* in which the universal or generality is said to be held with the individual is unintelligible and, therefore, fictitious. The reason for this, according to them, is that the possibility of any relation between two things demands that they must be separate from each other; so that inherence which is said to be a relation between two inseparable entities such as the universal and the individual is no relation at all, it being understood that the two things, one of which is said to be inherent in the other, are really not two separate things held in relation to each other but are one and the same thing.

The reply of the Nyāya-Vaiśeṣika to the Buddhists' objection against its admission of the reality of generality may be briefly stated as follows. Since an individual may be apprehended as different from other individuals by means of indeterminate perception, it may equally well be apprehended as *similar* to other individuals by the same means. That being so, at least an implicit or rudimentary apprehension of generality may be said to be provided by indeterminate perception of the similarity of an individual to other individuals. And it is this implicit apprehension of generality which becomes explicit and articulate through the means of determinate perception. The Nyāya-Vaiśeṣika contends further that generality is not a mere name nor a mere ideal construction (*vikalpa*), because we can apprehend the common characteristics of objects without knowing their names and because the determinations (*vikalpas*) involved in determinate perception are not mere ideal constructions but are ontological realities. And arguing on this line, the Nyāya-Vaiśeṣika finds itself in a position to reaffirm its view of generality by stating that it subsists in individuals and yet is perceived as distinct from the latter. Of course, generality is not perceived as occupying a space different from that of the individuals. But that does not imply that it is not real, but only that it *subsists* in the individuals. Moreover, being partless, it cannot be said to subsist in part in many individuals. On the contrary, it subsists entirely in each individual.

Considering the nature of the controversy, a brief account of which has been given above, one cannot help feeling that the real significance of the admission of the categories has been altogether missed by the Nyāya-Vaiśesika in one way and by the Buddhists in another. Strictly speaking, the categories are mere tools for the use of those who seek to interpret the world of our day to day experience which is the only reality. That being so, the question that may be legitimately asked about the categories is whether they are useful for the purpose which they are intended to serve, namely, the interpretation of the world of experience. In any case, the question whether they are real or not is wholly irrelevant. But the Nyāya-Vaiśeṣika has asked the latter question, ignoring the former which is alone relevant.

And they have answered it in the affirmative. The Buddhists, having failed to realize that this question is irrelevant, have, on the other hand, answered it in the negative and have thereby demonstrated that they are united with their rivals by the tie of common ignorance of the real issue that was in need of decision.

Our next task is to enquire into the category of particularity (*viśeṣa*) which is diametrically opposed to that of generality (*sāmānya*) and is especially important in that it is the category from which the Vaiśeṣika derives its name. Be it mentioned at the outset, however, that the Sāṁkhya, the Yoga, the Mīmāṁsā and the Vedānta do not recognize particularity as an independent category, and it was left for Vātsyāyana to admit it and emphasize its importance. According to him, particularity represents the ultimate distinguishing feature of eternal substances such as space, time, soul, etc. This is exactly what is meant by the word 'viśeṣa'. But, for reasons best known to them, the Vaiśeṣikas hold that it would be unnecessary to assume the subsistence of many particularities in one eternal substance, and that it would be just right to regard each eternal substance as characterized by only one particularity. But even then, they have no escape from the awkward position marked by the admission of countless particularities in consequence of their view that eternal substances are infinite in number. It is, therefore, no wonder that quite a number of the schools of Indian philosophy should turn away in disgust from the untidy universe as conceived by the Vaiśeṣikas.

According to the Vaiśeṣikas, particularities do not, however, require other particularities to distinguish them from one another, lest there should ensue the fault of infinite regress; they serve to distinguish their substrates as well as themselves from one another. While the eternal substances themselves are in need of particularities for the determination of their distinctions from one another, their qualities do not stand in a similar need. For the particularities of the substances serve to distinguish the substances themselves as well as their qualities from one another. Since particularity is thus a distinguishing feature in itself, it cannot be said to have a community (*sāmānya*). For in the event of its having a community, the community itself might very well serve as the distinguishing feature, and, consequently, it would cease to be what it really is, namely, the distinguishing feature *par excellence*. But then, it is necessary to take notice of the fact that it is in the case of partless eternal substances alone that particularities are in demand for the determination of their distinctions from one another. Composite non-eternal substances, on the other hand, are immune from such demand in as much as they may very well be distinguished from one another by their parts, qualities, actions, conjunction with other substances and the like. Thus a brown horse is distinguished by the quality *brown* colour. A fast moving horse is distinguished by the action, namely, fast movement, and so on.

That particularities subsist in partless eternal substances is not, according to the Nyāya-Vaiśeṣika, ordinarily open to direct and immediate knowledge, but is known *inferentially*. Since all substances have some feature or other which distinguishes them from one another, eternal substances as substances, it may be argued, must have particularities or distinguishing features of their own. But then, in the view of the Nyāya-Vaiśeṣika, it is only the common folk who are solely dependent upon inference for their knowledge about the particularities of eternal substances. The Yogins, according to them, are, on the other hand, capable of direct and immediate perception of the particularities subsisting in eternal substances. But this view seems to be rather out of harmony with the scientific outlook which the Vaiśeṣikas undoubtedly bring to bear upon their attempt to interpret the universe.

As previously observed, the admission of the category of particularity leads to the presentation of the world as unnecessarily untidy. This is, perhaps, the reason why, not to speak of the schools of Indian philosophy other than the Nyāya-Vaiśeṣika, even a Naiyāyika of the stature of Raghunātha Śiromani dismissed this category as unnecessary. As far as the Buddhists are concerned, they find it easy to reject this category for the simple reason that there are, according to them, no such things as eternal substances. Moreover, they are quite justified in objecting that if the particularities, as the Nyāya-Vaiśeṣika holds, can distinguish themselves from one another without the help of further particularities, there is no reason why the atoms of the same kind, for example, should not be able to distinguish themselves from one another without the aid of particularities. Further, they argue that since production is a temporal phenomenon, the production, on the part of particularity, of discriminating cognition must be temporal, which must be out of the question in view of the fact that particularity, being according to the Nyāya-Vaiśeṣika, subsistent in an eternal substance, is itself eternal and hence incapable of producing anything in time.

It is now left for us to deal with the last of the six Vaiśeṣika categories of being (*bhāva*) called inherence (*samavāya*). According to the Vaiśeṣikas, inherence is the relation between two inseparable entities, one of which subsists *in* the other. Judged in this light, the relations between the whole and its parts, between a quality or an action and a substance, between the universal and the particulars and between particularity and an eternal substance are each an instance of inherence. For in each of these cases the former element is inseparably related to, and inheres in, the latter. The peculiarity of *samavāya* (inherence) can be best understood in contrast with another kind of relation between two entities which is called *saṁyoga*. The latter is a temporary relation between two entities which exist separately, whereas the former subsists between two inseparables and so is permanent or eternal. The permanence or eternity of the relation of inherence is matched by the incapacity of its relata for independent existence. But then, this incapacity is not one-sided but mutual. And this means that inherence as a relation, though it is eternal, is not internal but *external*. The eternity of the relation of inherence does not, however, imply that its relata are also eternal. On the contrary, they are transient. But, in the view of the Nyāya-Vaiśeṣika, there is no conflict between the eternity of the relation of inherence and the transiency of its relata.

Inherence, according to the Nyāya-Vaiśeṣika, is not, as in the view of the Buddhists it is, the same as identity. The reason for this according to the former is that the two entities held together by the relation of inherence produce the cognition of two things instead of one only. Hence is also evident the difference of the Nyāya-Vaiśeṣika from the Advaita Vedānta which construes inherence as non-difference or identity. If inherence thus is not the same as identity, it is not *svarūpasambandha* (the relation which is identified with either of its relata) either. For, according to the Nyāya-Vaiśeṣika, the relation of inherence, as previously mentioned, is external and not internal, and that being so, the question of the identifiability of this relation with either of its terms cannot arise at all. In this connection, the Vaiśeṣika observes that, in the case of the non-existence of a jar on the ground, the relation between the non-existence of the jar and the ground is not inherence but *svarūpasambandha*.

The special importance of the category of inherence, however, lies in that it lends support to the Nyāya-Vaiśeṣika theory of causality, according to which the effect is a new emergence (*ārambha*). As we may most conveniently discuss this theory later along with the alternatives to it, we may bring our investigation of the relation of inherence to a close with the following observations. The understanding of the relation between the cause and the effect in terms of inherence, as the Nyāya-Vaiśeṣika holds, makes room for the recognition of the distinctness of the effect from the cause on the one hand, and of the inseparability of the relation between the two on the other. In fact, the category of inherence has proved to be of great use in the case of the Nyāya-Vaiśeṣika in the vindication of its pluralistic realism in so far as it is with the help of this category that this combined school of Indian philosophy affirms the reality of substance and quality, action, generality, particularity, etc. The schools of philosophy which are opposed to this metaphysical doctrine of the Nyāya-Vaiśeṣika have, therefore, launched their attack, among other things, upon its concept of inherence.

B

THE BUDDHIST SCHOOLS OF REALISM

INTRODUCTION

That Buddhism has made room for realistic metaphysics is, perhaps, not so widely known, nor is easily intelligible, to those who are exclusively or even mainly interested in its later development called the Mahāyāna. The reason for this is that the two realistic schools of Buddhist metaphysics, namely, the Vaibhāsika and the Sautrāntika are affiliated to early Buddhism called Thera-vāda or Hīnayāna, and that later Buddhism called the Mahāyāna is well known for its two schools of metaphysics respectively known as the *Vijñānavāda* of the Yogācāras and the *Śūnyavāda* of the Mādhyamikas, both of which are far removed from realism. But apart from the question whether realism or else a metaphysical theory opposed to it should be the natural outcome of Buddha's own teaching, it seems probable that the *Vijñānavāda* and the *Śūnyavāda*, being highly sophisticated metaphysical doctrines, were at least partly the results of the impact of the already developed and diversified metaphysics of the Hindus upon the way of thinking initiated by Buddha which was more *practical* than *theoretical* in import and intent. In any case, it is not unnatural, but, on the contrary, may be in the fitness of things, that Buddhism, like Hinduism, should have room for one or more types of realistic metaphysics.

Now Buddhist realism owes its origin to the Sarvāstivādins, that is, the advocates of *Sarvāstivāda*, the doctrine according to which all things, no matter whether they belong to the past or the present or the future, exist. The most authoritative canonical work of these originators of realism is the *Jnāna-prasthāna* by Kātyāyanīputra. And the *Vibhāsa* (expounder) from which the Vaibhāsikas derive their name is the commentary on this very work. The Vaibhāsikas constitute one of the two most important schools of *Sarvāstivāda* and are known by the very name Sarvāstivādins, whereas the other school did not call itself Sarvāstivādin, but became known as Sautrāntika. The reason why the latter was called Sautrāntika is that it rejected the authority of the *śāstras*, namely, the *Abhidharmas* of the Sarvāstivādins and accepted the authority of that which is definitely ascertained from the *sūtras*, that is, *Sutrānta*. The Sautrāntika school of Buddhist realism is said to have been founded by Kumāralāta. But the original works of this school are not available. So the only source of information about the views of Sautrāntikas consists of the *Abhidharma-koṣa* of Vasubandhu and its Exposition (*Vyākhyā*).

Now the key to the understanding of any one of the diverse

metaphysical schools of Buddhism, including Vaibhāsika, the Sautrāntika, the Yogācāra and the Mādhyamika, lies in the realization of the fact that all of them are marked by a more or less complete departure from the Hindu way of thinking which is dominated by the idea of *substance* regarded as *permanent* and as logically *prior to causality.* It is this Hindu idea that Buddhism sets aside. And, negatively speaking, it entertains the ideas of substancelessness (*anātmatva*) and impermanence (*anityatva*). Positively speaking, it introduces the new idea of momentariness (*kṣanikatva*) and emphasizes the primacy of causality by advocating the doctrine of dependent origination (*pratitya-samutpāda*). Moreover, on the positive side, Buddhism naturally goes further in replacing the concept of substance by its novel concept of *dharmas* by which it means indivisible and unanalysable elements, each characterized by uniqueness (*svalakṣaṇa*), which are, ultimately, the ingredients of all concrete objects, whether physical or mental. All this together constitutes the background in which Buddhist metaphysics, whether realistic or idealistic or nihilistic, is certainly set. Let us then proceed to enquire how the Vaibhāsikas otherwise called the Sarvāstivādins have developed their metaphysical thinking in such a background,

(i) Vaibhāsika Realism

As previously mentioned, the Vaibhāsikas are in agreement with the Sarvāstivādins in holding that everything, no matter whether it belongs to the past or the present or the future, *exists.* This view is said to be supported by scriptural authority in as much as it is, as they hold, derivable from *Buddhavacana* (the sayings of Buddha). But no matter whether this is true or not, it is certain that they have not arrived at this view through any argument, but, on the contrary, have admitted it rather dogmatically in the name of having depended upon the deliverance of immediate intuition. However that may be, there arises, in this connection, the question as to how the Vaibhāsikas can hold as they do that a thing *continues* to exist through the past, the present and the future, in the face of the accredited Buddhist doctrine that everything is momentary and nothing *continues* to exist. As regards this question, it obviously raises a difficulty which, in spite of the many and various attempts which the Vaibhāsikas have made to resolve it, is *prima facie* irresolvable. Hence it is evident that it is by ignoring the inconsistency between *Sarvāstivāda* and the doctrine of momentariness that these philosophers admitted both these doctrines as constituents of their metaphysical theory.

In the view of the Vaibhāsikas, as in the view of the Vaiśeṣikas, the universe, then, is ultimately constituted by simple and unanalysable elements called *dharmas* by the former and *paramāṇus* (atoms) by the latter. So both these schools of philosophy are equally advocates of pluralism, but with at least two important differences. In the first place, whereas the *paramāṇus* of the Vaiśeṣikas are permanent or eternal, the *dharmas* of the Vaibhāsikas are impermanent or momentary (*kṣanika*). Socondly, whereas, according to the Vaiśeṣikas, concrete objects such as tables, chairs, etc constituted by a number of elements are wholes inhering in parts, in the view of the Vaibhāsikas, there is no such thing as a whole in distinction from the parts, so that concrete objects are mere aggregates (*skandhas*) of a number of *dharmas*. Of course, it might be objected against this position of the Vaibhāsikas by stating that the aggregation of the elements cannot come about of itself, but must be due to the operation of some principle or other. But it is precisely an objection of this nature which these philosophers seek to remove by falling back upon the principle of causality conveyed by the doctrine of *pratitya-samutpāda* and holding that the aggregation of the elements is due to the operation of this principle, instead of the principle of the inherence of the whole in the parts admitted by the Vaiśeṣikas.

Now the Vaibhāsikas are in agreement with commonsense in so far as they hold that both matter and mind are real. But these two, according to them, are real, not in the sense that they are substances characterized by permanence, but in the sense that they are aggregates of elements (*dharmas*) which, while being impermanent, are yet real in virtue of their simplicity, indivisibility and unanalysability. The Vaibhāsikas, however, have adopted a way of dealing with the universe which is a curious mixture of scienticism and anthropocentricism. They hold as scientists usually do that the universe is ultimately constituted by a fixed number of elements. But then, they seem to make a departure from the scientific standpoint of viewing the universe in so far as they hold the view that of the elements, which according to them are seventy-five in number, as many as seventy-two are conditioned (*saṁskṛta*) and the remaining three are unconditioned (*a-saṁskṛta*). What the Vaibhāsikas seem to have in view in their admission of the distinction between the conditioned and the unconditioned *dharmas* is the idea of showing that the universe is the field where human beings are thrown into a state of bondage, and it is also the field where it is given to them to win freedom or liberation. Accordingly, they hold that the elements (*dharmas*), conditioned by *avidyā* (ignorance) and the passion (*kleśas*) consequent upon it, cooperate with one another so as to present themselves as the stream (*sāsrava*) of phenomenal life (*saṁsāra*) marked by the presence of pain (*duḥkha*) or else the cause of pain (*samudāya*) and are thus held in a state of bondage. But this is not all about the universe so far as mankind is concerned with it. For the same elements, according to the Vaibhāsikas, are open to subjection to the counteracting process of their separation from one another and their suppression through the means of spiritual discipline (*mārga*), resulting in the emergence of *prajñā* (intuitive knowledge). In consequence, they are reduced to a state of quiescence, free from pain as well as the cause of pain which, in their view, is one of the three unconditioned elements called *nirvāṇa* or, to use the Vaibhāsika terminology, *pratisaṁkhyā-nirodha* (complete and everlasting liberation attainable through enlightenment).

To continue our enquiry into the Vaibhāsika account of the *dharmas* (elements), it is first necessary to mention that the remaining two unconditioned elements are: *a-pratisaṁkhyā-nirodha* and *ākāśa* (space). The former is cessation (*nirodha*) of a kind different from that which occurs in the case of *nirvāṇa* or *pratisaṁkhyā-nirodha*. And the difference lies in that the cessation in the latter case is absolute and permanent, being due to *prajñā* (intuitive knowledge), whereas in the latter case it is relative and temporary, being due to the absence of necessary conditions, instead of the presence of *prajñā*. As regards *ākāśa* (space), in the view of the Vaibhāsikas, it is ubiquitous and its essence consists in its freedom from obstruction, being incapable of obstructing and also being itself immune from obstruction. Be it noted, however, that the Sautrāntikas dismissed the so-called unconditioned elements as mere names without there being any reality corresponding to them.

An important feature of the Vaibhāsika analysis of the constituents of the universe is their classification of the *dharmas* (elements). In this connection we may be well advised in considering only that classification offered by them which is not determined by subjective considerations but is as far as possible objective or realistic. Objectively classified, the elements, according to them, come under five heads: (1) *rūpa* (matter), (2) *citta* (consciousness), (3) *cetasika* (states and characteristics of the mind), (4) *citta-viprayukta-saṁskāra* (powers that are neither mental nor material but common to both mind and matter) and (5) the unconditioned (*a-saṁskṛta*) *dharmas* which we have already considered. Now, as regards matter (*rūpa*), it is, according to the Vaibhāsikas, divisible into two kinds: the primary (*bhuta*) and the secondary (*bhautika*). The latter consists of innumerable material objects such as tables, mountains, houses, etc. and the former comprises earth, water, fire and air respectively characterized by solidity, moisture, heat and motion and having the respective functions of supporting, cohesion, ripening and expansion. But then, the Vaibhāsikas, being one of the schools of Buddhism, differ from the Nyāya-Vaiśeṣikas in holding that these material elements are not, as in the view of the latter they are, material *substances*, but are energies or forces. To this division of matter the Vaibhāsikas, however, add another, partly in accordance with their dismissal of the concept of material substance and partly in consideration of how matter presents itself to us. Thus matter, according to them, is divisible into the sensible qualities, namely, colour, smell, etc. and the five *indṛiyas* (sense-organs) regarded as a kind of subtle matter (*ṛūpa-prasāda*) and, lastly, unmanifest matter (*a-vijñapti-rūpa*) viewed to be the result, whether good or bad, of voluntary actions. This division of matter, as may be easily seen, is at least partly, if not wholly, anthropocentric.

Citta, in the view of the Vaibhāsikas, is contentless consciousness, and as such it is the only element of its kind. But then, it may be said to have as many *modes* as there are sense-organs to serve as the conditions of its arousal; so that there may be six modes of concious-ness, including five, corresponding to the five external sense-organs and only one invoked by the internal sense-organ. As regards the *cetasikas*, the Vaibhāsikas seem to have conducted a very subtle psychological analysis to discover them as is evidenced by the fact that their discovery includes *mahā-bhūmikas* (the characteristics which are common to all mental states), the general properties of *kuśala* (good) mental states, primary passions (*kleśas*), *a-kuśala* (evil) mental properties, *upa-kleśas* (subsidiary passions) and, lastly, the indetermi-nate (*a-niyata*) mental elements. As regards these psychological discoveries, their evaluation is not easy as it would depend upon arduous and painstaking researches in the field of psychology for which we have to wait for long. And the same is true about the powers that are said to be common to both mind and matter called *citta-viprayukta-saṁskāras*. In any case, it is doubtful whether they should be treated as elements (*dharmas*) at all, because they, as the Sautrāntikas came to realize, are ways of conceiving the behaviour of the elements rather than elements themselves, they being functions like attainment, continuation, decay, death, etc.

Now, given the conditioned (*saṁskṛta*) elements, concrete objects of our ordinary experience, as previously indicated, come into existence as a result of their combination in the form of *skandhas* (aggregates). According to the Vaibhāsikas, the *skandhas* are five in number: Rūpa (material factors), *Vedanā* (feeling), *Samjñā* (conceiving or generaliz-ing), *Saṁskāra* (volition and other mental forces) and Vijñāna (conscious-ness as such). From this list of the concrete objects it is evident, however, that the Vaibhāsikas, like other schools of Buddhism, are more interested in the world of mind than in the world of matter. And this is all the more evident from the consideration of the *āyatanas* and *dhātus* which the Vaibhāsikas in common with the majority of the adherents to Buddhism regard as coordinate with *skandhas*. For the *āyatanas* said to be twelve in number include the five external sense-organs and one internal sense-organ and the corresponding six kinds of sensible contents. And the *dhātus* include all the constituents of the *āyatana*, together with six kinds of awareness respectively invoked by the six kinds of sense-organs and having the six kinds of sensible contents as their respective objects.

Now it may be reiterated that the understanding of the nature of the universe, according to the Buddhists, including the Vaibhāsikas, presupposes the realization of the fact that it is ultimately constituted by simple and unanalysable elements, that these elements are combined together so as to form themselves into concrete objects, and that this combination is not due to chance or fate or the agency of God, but takes place in conformity with an inexorable law, the law of causality. That being so, our foregoing account of the metaphysics of the Vaibhāsikas has conformed to these requirements. But it may still be necessary to make a few observations about the Vaibhāsika treatment of the concept of causality, with reference to its application in the case of the human individual. In this regard, it is most important to observe that phenomenal life, the kind of life we ordinarily live, is the result of the aggregation of elements conditioned (*saṁskṛta*) by ignorance and passions and, what is more, is kept continuing from one birth to another and thus becomes a chain of existence (*pratitya-samutpāda*) attended with pain and suffering. That being so, the safety of the future of man, according to the Vaibhāsikas, would depend upon the undoing of the effect of *pratitya-samutpāda* (dependent origination) in the form of the elimination of pain and suffering, and the consequent emergence of the unconditioned or noumenal element called *prati-saṁkhyā-nirodha* or *nirvāṇa*. Thus, in the view of the Vaibhāsikas and indeed in the view of Buddhism in general, the future of the universe is bound up with the future of man and it consists in the overthrow of the might of causality by means of the practice of virtues (*śīla*), meditation (*samādhi*) and intuitive knowledge (*prajñā*) and the consequent replacement of the phenomenal order of the universe full of pain and misery by a noumenal order devoid of suffering as well as its potentiality.

We may bring the foregoing account of the metaphysics of the Vaibhāsikas to a close by observing that it is realistic not only because it treats both the realms of matter and mind as objectively real, but because it advocates the direct theory of knowledge, according to which both material and mental objects are known to us directly and immediately and not through any intermediary between ourselves as knowers and the objects of our knowledge. Nevertheless, it is necessary to bear in mind that the realism of the Vaibhāsikas, unlike this metaphysical doctrine as ordinarily understood, is subject to the limitation imposed upon it by the three ideas that are peculiar to Buddhism in general, namely, those of momentariness, substancelessness and particularity (sva-lakṣaṇa) as opposed to generality or universality (*sāmānya*).

(ii) Sautrāntika Realism

As previously mentioned, the Sautrāntikas started their programme of philosophical investigations in opposition to the

Sarvāstivādins and the authority of their *Abhidharmas* and with the idea of strictly adhering to the direct discourses (*Śāstra*) of Buddha. Accordingly, there was a distinctly negative side to their metaphysical position which consisted in the dismissal of whatever they considered to be objectionable about the views of the Sarvāstivādins and their collaborators, the Vaibhāsikas. In the first place, they rejected the main thesis of these two groups of philosophers, namely, that the elements exist in the past, the present and the future. Their reason for this was that this thesis amounts to stating that an element exists in the same sense in the past and the future as it does in the present and, consequently, that these temporal distinctions are meaningless and even unreal, which is absurd and, indeed, ruinous to the thesis itself. Moreover, the admission of the continued existence of things through the past, the present and the future is tantamount to the rehabilitation of a sort of *eternalism* which is an anathema in the estimation of Buddhism.

Furthermore, the thesis labours under the misleading view that whatever may be an object of thought *exists*. Of course, whatever exists admits of being thought of. But the converse is not necessarily true. It is precisely this which the Sarvāstivādins and the Vaibhāsikas completely ignored in their admission of the continued existence of the elements. And this brings us to the second point in the negative criticism of the Sarvāstivādins and the Vaibhāsikas by the Sautrāntikas. It consists in the condemnation of the former's tendency to hypostatize abstractions such as ideas or notions and even words. It is this tendency on the part of the Vaibhāsikas which, according to the Sautrāntikas, is responsible for their admission of a multitude of elements, some of which at least are fictitious. Accordingly, the latter rejected *ākāśa* (space), *nirvāṇa*, *citta-viprayukta* (non-mental powers) as well as the so-called past and future aspects of the *existence* of the elements, with the result that their list of the *dharmas* became much shorter than that of the Vaibhāsikas so as to conform to the law of parsimony. Thus in place of the long list of seventy-five elements admitted by the Vaibhāsikas, the Sautrāntikas offer a comparatively short list of forty-three elements classified under five heads: (1) *Rūpa* (matter), comprising four primary forms (*upādāna*) and four secondary or derivative forms (upādāya-rūpa), (2) *Vedanā* (feelings), including pleasure, pain and the neutral feeling, (3) *Saṁjñā* (signs; sense-organs), consisting of five external sense-organs and one internal sense-organ called *citta* or *manas*, (4) *Vijnāna* (consciousness) of six kinds corresponding to the six sense-organs, (5) *Saṁskāras* (powers or forces) numbering twenty in all, including ten good (*kuśala*) and ten bad (*a-kuśala*) ones.

But then, the background of the metaphysics of the Sautrāntikas and that of the metaphysics of the Vaibhāsikas are one and the same, both equally consisting in the ideas of momentariness, substancelessness and *sva-lakṣaṇa* taken together. So the difference between the two kinds of metaphysics may be said to consist in that, whereas the latter seeks to interpret the universe in terms of a larger number of elements, including some that are the results of the hypostatization of abstractions, the former seeks to do the same by making use of a smaller number of elements supposed to be unaffected by any manner of arbitrary manipulation and, consequently, to be objectively real. Even so, the metaphysics of the Sautrāntīkas, as is evident from a careful scrutiny of their list of the elements, is not altogether free from the fault from which the metaphysics of the Vaibhāsikas suffer, namely, the fault of depending upon a strange mixture of scienticism and anthropocentricism. And there was another tie to bind the two kinds of metaphysics together, which consisted in their being realistic on account of their common admission of the reality of the twofold world of matter and mind. Nevertheless, curious though it seems and yet it is true that the Vaibhāsikas and the Sautrāntikas were destined to remain in a state of mutual conflict as is shown by the fact that even on the common ground of realism they differed from each other, the former having held that our knowledge of objective reality is direct and immediate and is yielded by perception, and the latter having regarded this knowledge as indirect and mediate, that is, derivable from inference instead of from perception.

In fact, judged from the epistemological point of view, the metaphysics of the Sautrāntikas is based on representationism similar to that of the two well known Western philosophers René Descartes and John Locke. In holding that our knowledge of both mind and matter is indirect and mediate, the Sautrāntikas were in opposition to the direct theory of knowledge advanced by the Vaibhāsikas. And in holding at the same time that both mind and matter are objectively real, they were, on the other hand, opposed to the idealism of the Yogācāras according to which nothing is objectively real and everything is, ultimately, constituted by ideas (*vijnāna*). Their arguments in support of representationism are as follows. In the first place, they observe that external objects produce cognitions corresponding to them and, moreover, imprint their forms on these cognitions, but that the former cease to be when the latter come into existence. That being so, we have no means of knowing external objects directly and immediately and the only way in which we may be said to know them must be indirect and mediate, namely, by means of inference from the forms of our cognitions. What the Sautrāntikas mean by this may be stated thus. Cognitions are formless and homogeneous in themselves, but are diversified by their objects. In other words, different external objects produce different cognitions, by impressing their forms on them. In consequence, the forms inherent in cognitions resemble, or are representations of, the forms of external objects corresponding to them. And it is the forms of the cognitions themselves which we directly apprehend and it is from our apprehension of these that we infer the forms of external objects.

Secondly, there are, according to the Sautrāntikas, two kinds of cognitions respectively called *ālayavijñāna* which is of the nature of subject-cognitions (*ahamāspada*) and *pravṛttivijñāna* or object-cognition which is of the nature of 'this' (*idamāspada*). But then, the peculiarity of the former lies in that it is *uniformly* present, whereas the latter is peculiar in a different way on account of its appearance only on occasion. And this difference, according to the Sautrāntikas, points to the need for the *inference* of some external object or other as the cause of the latter kind of knowledge. But these arguments and others of their kind, however ingenious they may be, are vitiated by the failure to realize that once external objects are left out of the field of direct and immediate knowledge, they become impervious to all kinds of knowledge once and for all, and, consequently, that ground is prepared for the replacement of realism by subjective idealism through the intermediary of internal cognitions regarded as the spring-board for an inferential leap to the external object. Yet, curiously enough, the Sautrāntikas, as we shall see below, seek to refute the idealism of the Yogācāras, not knowing that they themselves had lent at least an indirect support to this metaphysical doctrine.

In the first place, the Yogācāra, like Berkeley, argues that since we have no means of knowing an external object except in virtue of our cognition of it, its existence is inseparable from and, indeed, is identical with, our cognition; so that its existence is purely mental and it cannot be said to be extra-mentally real. As against this argument, the Sautrāntika contends that it involves the arbitrary and unwarrantable identification of cognition and its content in as much as these two are really distinct from each other and so are recalcitrant to their identification with each other. But then, this contention might be appropriate in the case of the Vaibhāsikas and not in the case of the Sautrāntikas, according to whom the immediate content of cognition is something mental, namely, *vijñāna* (ideas). Secondly, the Sautrāntika disputes the identification of cognition and its object by stating that had the two been identical, my apprehension of an object, for example, the blue colour, would have been expressible in the proposition 'I am blue', instead of in the proposition 'this is blue' which is actually the case. But here again the Sautrāntika does not have a sound ground to stand upon. For, in spite of regarding the object of cognition as mental, the Yogācāra is free to hold that cognizing and the content of cognition are distinct, so that, on his view, one who perceives the blue colour is entitled to state that 'this is blue' instead of that 'one is oneself blue'. Thirdly, the objection raised by the Sautrāntika against the

Yogācāra consists in stating that it is absolutely improper to hold, as the latter holds, that the so-called external object is the result of the illusory externalization of what is really internal, namely, ideas. His reason for this is expressed by saying that even the illusion of externality cannot be produced except in so far as veridical cognition of externality is somehow and somewhere available. But then, this objection of the Sautrāntika is no less applicable in his own case than in the case of the Yogācāra, in as much as externality in his view is at best problematic, if not altogether illusory.

The point that stands out in this connection is, however, that subjective idealism is irrefutable from the point of view representationism such as that of the Sautrāntikas. The reason for this is that representationism as such is under the necessity of an inner dialectic to lead to subjective idealism and, consequently, that it is most ill-fitted to serve as the ground for any successful attack upon this obnoxious metaphysical doctrine. So the choice lies, not between Sautrāntikas and the Yogācāras, but between the Vaibhāsikas and the latter. But then, the claim which the Vaibhāsikas naturally have for their being preferred to the Yogācāras on account of their advocacy of uncompromising realism is more likely than not to be lost to them for no less a reason than that anthropocentricism plays a dominant role in their metaphysical pursuit so as to make their realism almost nugatory. Ours is not, however, a plea for the supremacy of realism, but against the arbitrary mixing up of scienticism and anthropocentricism together, with no other object in view than that of suggesting that, in the interest of science on the one hand and of metaphysics on the other, the two must be separated from each other and decision should be arrived at with regard to their respective applicability. And judged from this point of view, not to speak of the Vaibhāsikas and the Sautrāntikas alone, many a metaphysical venture, whether ancient or modern, has proved to be a sort of myth-making on account of its allegiance to both scienticism and anthropocentricism at the same time.

C

THE REALISTIC SCHOOLS OF MĪMĀMSĀ

Of the remaining kinds of Indian realism, the two schools of Mīmāṃsā respectively headed by Kumārila Bhatta and Prabhākara Miśra are nearest the realism of the Nyāya-Vaiśeṣika. The former, like the latter, are opposed to the *vijñānavāda* and the *śūnyavāda* of the Buddhists and insist on the objective reality of the external world by holding that it is as real as are the *ātmans* (souls). And, further, both the realistic schools of Mīmāṁsā follow the example of the Vaiśeṣika in making use of a number of ontological categories with a view to a planned investigation of the reality or reālities underlying the universe. But then, Kumārila and Prabhākara differ from each other as well as from the Vaiśeṣika with regard to the question as to how many and what these categories exactly are.

As we have previously seen, the Vaiśeṣika admits two broad kinds of categories respectively designated as *bhāva* (being; existence) and *abhāva* (non-existence). The latter, according to the Vaiśeṣika, stands for all kinds of non-existence, including prior non-existence (*pragabhāva*), posterior non-existence (*pradhvaṁsābhāva*), absolute non-existence (*atyantābhāva*) and mutual non-existence (*anyonyābhāva*). The former, on the other hand, is held to comprise six categories, namely, substance (*dravya*), quality (*guṇa*), action (*karma*), generality or community (sāmānya), particularity (viśeṣa) and inherence (samavāya). Now as far as Kumārila is concerned, he agrees with the Vaiśeṣikas in admitting the four kinds of *abhāva* (non-existence) and only four of the six categories of *bhāva* (existence), namely, substance, quality, action and generality, while rejecting particularity and inherence. His argument for the rejection of inherence as a separate category reminds one of the British philosopher F.H. Bradley's argument for the impossibility of such a thing as 'external relation'. It may be stated as follows.

Since inherence, according to the Nyāya-Vaiśeṣika, is the relation between two inseparables such as substance and quality, the whole and the parts, the universal and the particular, and the like, and since all kinds of relation, in its view, are *external*, the difficulty of the admission of inherence as a separate category may be expressed thus. The external relation of inherence between the substance and the quality or the like would necessarily require a second inherence to relate it to the substance on the one hand and to the quality on the other, and then a third inherence would be required to relate the second to the relata concerned and so on *ad indefinitum*. The infinite regress which thus presents itself must needs be avoided, and Kumārila holds that this would be possible only if inherence be separated from its ill-conceived relational character and is regarded as synonymous with 'identity in essence' (*tādātmya*). As regards particularity (*viśeṣa*), Kumārila, in agreement with Prabhākara on the one hand, and with the Sāṃkhya, the Yoga and the Vedānta on the other, rejects it in fulfilment of the need for the avoidance of another awkward situation consisting in the admissibility of innumerable particularities corresponding to the countless eternal substances held by the Nyāya-Vaiśeṣika to be real.

Prabhākara, on the other hand, dismisses the fourfold Nyāya-Vaiśeṣika category of *abhāva* on the understanding that it is not, as the Nyāya-Vaiśeṣika supposes that it is, separate from, but, on the contrary, is identical with, its locus (*adhikaraṇasvarūpa*), so that the non-existence of the jar on the ground, for example, is nothing but the ground concerned. But judged in the light of what we have previously observed, the ground on which Prabhākara thus rejects the category of *abhāva* seems to be unsatisfactory, although there is no doubt that this category is not a genuine one and in any case is out of place in any metaphysical investigation. Even so, it is creditable on the part of Prabhākara as well as on the part of Kumārila to have some regard for the law of parsimony so as to realize the need for the reduction of the number of ontological categories which have been already made current in the philosophical sphere. Nevertheless, Kumārila, despite his reduction of the number of the Nyāya-Vaiśeṣika categories of being or existence (*bhāva*) from six to four failed to observe the law of parsimony strictly, on account of his retention of the Vaiśeṣika category of *abhāva*, including the four kinds of non-existence. Prabhākara also failed to do the same in view of the fact that, while rejecting the category of *abhāva* altogether, he not only admitted five of the six Nyāya-Vaiśeṣika categories of *bhāva*, but contributed to the inflation of the number of the categories of this kind by the addition of three more respectively called *śakti* (potency), *sādṛsya* (similarity) and *saṁkhyā* (number).

But then, Kumārila seems to have been more serious about the strict observance of the law of parsimony than Prabhākara is found to be. For he, as mentioned above, rejected inherence and particularity as separate categories. And as against Prabhākara's additions to the list of the categories of *bhāva* (existence), he observes that these indeed point towards certain realities, but that they themselves cannot be regarded as separate categories of *bhāva* (existenee). Thus he agrees with Prabhākara in holding the view that *śakti* (potency) is precisely that in an object by virtue of which it is a cause and capable of producing an effect or effects. But that is no reason why *śakṭi* should be regarded, as Prabhākara regards it, as a separate kind of being. On the contrary, as Kumārila holds, it is an unperceived *quality* in a substance, which is inferable from the effect produced by it. Likewise, similarity (*sādṛsya*), according to Kumārila, is a quality, consisting in the possession, on the part of two or more substances, of the same arrangement of parts. Moreover, similarity admits of degrees. Therefore, it should not be regarded as a separate category of being. Lastly, as regards number (*saṁkhyā*), its significance may be said to lie in the numerability of substances. Consequently, as Kumārila holds, it should not be regarded as an independent category of being, but only as a *quality* of things or substances.

Now if we set aside all those categories which Kumārila and Prabhākara together have rejected, and take into account only those that they have accepted in common, we shall be left with four out of the Nyāya-Vaiśeṣika list of the categories of *bhāva* (existence), namely, substance, quality, action and generality or community. So it may well be held that the list of these four categories, being comparatively short, is in accord with the law of parsimony and, consequently, that it is just appropriate as a means to the interpretation of the universe. But it may still be asked why as many as four categories, instead of only one or two, should be required for the fulfilment of this end. And it may be pointed out that Jainism and the Sāṁkhya seek to interpret the universe in terms of two fundamental categories, namely, *jīva* and *ajīva* in the former case and *prakṛti* and *puruṣa* in the latter, and further, that the Advaita Vedānta is conspicuous for its attempt to understand the entire realm of existence in terms of only one fundamental category namely, Brahman, together with the subordinate category of Māyā (Cosmic Nescience). But then, it may be replied that the dualistic interpretation of the universe by Jainism and the Sāṁkhya and especially the absolutist metaphysics of the Advaita Vedānta are vitiated by the fault of oversimplification and that the removal of this fault which is obviously in demand cannot be brought about except by means of a more comprehensive interpretation of the universe than that which is provided by Jainism or the Sāṁkhya or the Advaita Vedānta. And this would, perhaps, be favourable to a hypothetical joint venture on the part of Kumārila and Prabhākara to investigate the domain of reality by the use of the list of four categories mentioned above, which conforms as far as possible to the requirement of the law of parasimony.

The question, then, arises whether the four categories of substance, quality, action and generality are all equally useful as the means of the investigation of the reality or realities in the universe, and, if so, whether they, taken together, can serve to provide a comprehensive understanding of the universe as it really is. The answer to this twofold question would, for obvious reasons, depend mainly upon the determination of how Kumārila and Prabhākara respectively understand these categories in detail. Let us, therefore, begin with the consideration of the detailed treatment of the category of substance by these two philosophers. Now, as regards the definition of substance, whereas Prabhākara agrees with the Vaiśeṣikas in defining it as the substrate of qualities, Kumārila differs from both the Vaiśeṣikas and Prabhākara in defining it as the substrate of dimension or size (*parimāna*) as well as qualities. Prabhākara is in further agreement with the Nyāya-Vaiśeṣika in admitting the same list of nine substances as is admitted by the latter, which comprises earth, water, fire, air, ether, self, mind, time and space. But Kumārila differs from both in admitting eleven substances in all, with the addition of darkness and sound to the list admitted by the Nyāya-Vaiśeṣika and Prabhākara in common. In admitting *darkness* as a substance, Kumārila bases himself on the consideration that it is a positive entity, being the substrate of the black colour, and not a mere negation, the negation of light, as it is in the view of the Nyāya-Vaiśeṣika and Prabhākara, and further, that it is directly apprehensible by means of the visual sense-organ. Sound, according to him, is, likewise, a direct object of apprehension by means of the auditory sense-organ and so is in need of being regarded as a substance in itself, and not as a quality of ether as it is conceived to be by the Nyāya-Vaiśeṣika and Prabhākara.

Apart from the difference between Kumārila and Prabhākara which has been noticed above, there are, as we shall immediately see, other differences between the two philosophers with regard to their detailed treatment of the categories admitted by them in common. The most important of these differences relates to the question as to how the substances admitted by both Kumārila and Prabhākara in common are *known*. Stated more precisely, the question is whether these are directly apprehended by means of perception or are indirectly known by means of inference. As regards this question, the two philosophers partly answer it in agreement with each other by holding that the four substances, namely, earth, water, fire and air are perceptible through the intermediary of some sense-organ or other.* But then, they partly answer it in opposition to each other in so far as Kumārila holds that ether, space and time are perceptible, whereas Prabhākara agrees with the Nyāya-Vaiśeṣika view that these are not perceptible, but can only be knowm indirectly by means of inference.

First as regards ether, Prabhākara, in agreement with the Nyāya-Vaiśeṣika, holds that ether is inferable on the ground of its being the substrate of sound regarded as a perceivable quality. But, as mentioned earlier, Kumārila rejects the view of sound as a quality and regards it as a substance itself. And, conceiving it to be eternal, indivisible and ubiquitous as he does, he comes to hold that the question of the possibility of its being inferred cannot arise, and, consequently, that it must be *perceptible*, lest its existence should remain unreeognized. As far as space and time are concerned, Kumārila emphasizes the importance of the fact that these are also eternal, indivisible, and ubiquitous and thereby arrives at the view that they, like ether, are recalcitrant to the possibility of their being inferred, and must be amenable to direct and immediate apprehension by means of perception. In this connection, Kumārila counters the view of space as inferable by affirming that the notions of east,

* Kumārila and his followers are of the view that composite substances are constituted by atoms, but that the atoms concerned are, like the particles of dust in the sun-beam, definitely perceptible. The atoms thus conceived are obviously in a class apart from the minutest primary atoms (aṇus) which, in the view of the Nyāya-Vaiśeṣikas, are the ultimate constituents of composite substances. But these philosophers hold that the atoms as conceived by the Nyāya-Vaiśeṣikas are non-existent in as much as we have no means of knowing them and the so-called yogic perception is spurious.

west, forward, backward, etc., which, according to the Nyāya-Vaiśeṣika, constitute the ground of the inference of space, are really the products of the visual sense-organ and have space as their content. In other words, the direct apprehension of east, west, etc., in Kumārila's view, is not the ground of the inference of space, but is *eo ipso* the perception of space itself.

Kumārila argues the *perceptibility* of time in a manner more or less similar to that in which he argues the perceptibility of space. His argument here is against the Nyāya-Vaiśeṣika view that it is the notions of simultaneity, succession and the like which constitute the ground of this inference of time. And it consists in countering this view by means of the statement that these notions are, as a matter of fact, yielded by perception and, what is more, have time as their content. Strictly speaking, these could not have been what they actually are, nor could they lead to the inference of time, had they originally been unrelated to time. That being so, these notions themselves, as Kumārila seems to have held, are the veritable bearers of the presence of time, instead of being the ground (*hetu*) of the inference of time. Now, as far as the mind (*manas*) is concerned, Kumārila accepts the view about it which is common to the major schools of Indian philosophy, namely, that it is the internal organ, as distinguished from the external sense-organs. But, curiously enough, he holds the fantastic view that the *manas* is eternal and all-pervasive and thus differs from the Nyāya-Vaiśeṣika view of it as *atomic*. The view of the *manas* as atomic in the Nyāya-Vaiśeṣika sense, of course, necessitates the view of it as imperceptible. But why Kumārila, while regarding the eternal, all-pervasive substances like ether, space and time as perceptible, should come to view the equally eternal and all-pervasive *manas* as imperceptible is unintelligible and indeed presents another curiosity.

Let us now consider how Kumārila and Prabhākara respectively deal with the *ātman* (self) which is the last of the nine substances admitted by them in common. It may be observed in the beginning that it was Sabarasvāmin who accorded a prominent place to the concept of the self in Mīmāṁsā philosophy, by holding that the *ātman* is distinct from the body, the vital forces, the sense-organs and also cognitions. According to him, the self is self-revealed or self-illumined (*ātmajyotiḥ*), that is, known by itself and not by others. But, curiously enough, he holds at the same time that the self is the *object* of I-consciousness (*ahaṁpratyaya*). Hence is evident the contradiction which vitiates Sabara's view of self-knowledge. It is this contradiction which Pārthasārathi Miśra and Prabhākara sought to resolve in their respective ways. The former denied the self-luminosity of the self on the ground of its absence during dreamless sleep, and agreed with the Naiyāikas in holding that the self is the object of I-consciousness or mental perception. Prabhākara, on the other hand, considered the self's knowledge of itself as an object to be an absurdity, and, consequently, held that there is no such thing as I-consciousness and that the self is known as the *subject* of all cognitions of objects. But as far as Kumārila is concerned, he allowed the contradiction of Sabara's view of self-knowledge to remain by holding that the self is at once self-illumined and the object of I-consciousness.

Kumārila, in further agreement with Sabara, holds that the self is distinct from the body, the vital forces, etc., and as such is eternal, immaterial, incorporeal and ubiquitous. Thus standing in contrast with whatever is material, the self, in his view, is the knower *(jñātā)*, enjoyer *(bhoktā)* and active agent *(kartā)*. In this Kumārila differs from the Sāṁkhya view of the self *(puruṣa)*, according to which it is the knower and the enjoyer, but not an active agent. In fact, he is nearer the Nyāya-Vaiśeṣikas than the Sāṁkhya in his view of the self, as is evident from the fact that he regards it as the substrate of the entire gamut of mental phenomena, including pleasure, pain, desire, merit, demerit, etc., although he holds, in disagreement with the Nyāya-Vaiśeṣikas, that these are the modifications of the self, in the face of his view that the self is eternal. Nevertheless, he is as insistent on the permanence or eternity of the self as are the Nyāya-Vaiśeṣikas. And, like the latter, he seeks to establish his view of the self as permanent by means of elaborate arguments against the Buddhist view of the self as a series of momentary ideas *(vijñānasantāna)*. But his performance in this respect consists in the reiteration of the Naiyāyika arguments against the Buddhist doctrine of the impermanence of the self.

Now, as far as Prabhākara is concerned, he is in agreement with Kumārila as well as the Nyāya-Vaiśeṣikas in holding the view that the self is distinct from the body, the sense-organs, etc. and as such is eternal and ubiquitous, and yet is numerically multiple, there being separate selves in separate bodies. But, as previously mentioned, he differs from Kumārila in denying the self-luminosity of the self. According to him, the self is the substrate of consciousness, but does not have consciousness as its essence. In holding this view, he seems to regard the self in itself as unconscious, although he, like the Nyāya-Vaiśeṣika, holds that consciousness is a quality of the self and not, as Kumārila holds, its modification. Consciousness as the quality of the self, according to Prabhākara, includes nine mental phenomena, namely, cognition, pleasure, pain, desire, aversion, volition, merit, demerit and impression, which are the products of the conjunction of the self with *manas*, the internal organ.

As mentioned above, Prabhākara upholds the doctrine of the multiplicity of the self. In this he is in agreement with Kumārila, the Sāṁkhya, and the Nyāya-Vaiśeṣika, and is opposed to the

Advaita Vedānta doctrine of the oneness of the self. His arguments in support of the former doctrine bear close resemblance to those which are advanced by the Sāṁkhya to prove that the *puruṣas* are many. Thus Prabhākara points to the facts that different individuals have different experiences, that they acquire different merits and demerits as a result of their different volitional actions, that some of them are miserable, whereas some others are happy and so on. And hence he concludes that there must be many selves and not one Absolute Self as the Advaita Vedānta holds. But, curiously enough, Prabhākara, like Kumārila, holds that the self is neither atomic nor coextensive with the body, but is *ubiquitous*. In holding this view he is obviously open to the difficulty of the incompatibility of his doctrine of the multiplicity of selves with his view of the self as ubiquitous. And, what is worse, this view cuts the ground from under the feet of his realism, although he is completely unaware of this fact. That Prabhākara, while being an advocate of realism, is not free from the idealistic proclivity is further evident from the fact that he brings anthropocentricism to bear upon his understanding of the universe. Thus he holds that the entire realm of reality is exhaustively covered by the following items taken together : the self as the enjoyer *(bhoktā)*, the body as the vehicle of enjoyment *(bhogāyatana)*, the sense-organs as the instruments of experience *(bhogasādhana)*; the external objects, together with pleasure, pain, etc. as the objects of experience *(bhogya)*, enjoyment and suffering respectively as the feelings *(vedanā)* of pleasure and pain.

It is not, however, necessary for our immediate purpose to go into further details of the metaphysical views of Kumārila and Prabhākara. From the little we have already come to know about these views it is evident that they differ from each other in fundamental respects and indeed so much so that their common membership of one and the same school of thought seems to be nominal rather than real. In any case, although they both profess to be realists, the interest of realism is not safe in their hands. This gives rise to the doubt whether realism can hold its own in freedom from the danger of being invaded by idealism, without being absorbed in some form of materialism or other, which is conspicuous for its veto on anthropocentricism. But then, even granted that materialism serves the interest of metaphysics better than idealism on account of its unimpeachable and inviolable realism, the question remains whether it suits the interest of the metaphysician as a human being. This is, however, far from suggesting that idealism is preferable to materialism in the interest of mankind. What is really meant is that the question just raised, although it is seldom asked, seems to be all-important in metaphysical investigations.

III

DUALISM

A

The Sāṁkhya Doctrine of Dualism

By dualism is meant that kind of metaphysical theory, according to which the entire universe comprises, and is explicable in terms of, two distinct and mutually exclusive principles usually regarded as material and spiritual respectively. Judged in this light, the Sāṁkhya system of Indian philosophy provides an outstanding example of dualism as a metaphysical theory. Although the Sāṁkhya, as we shall see later, admits an infinite number of spiritual beings, they may be regarded as coming under one and the same category of *spirit* in distinction from the category of matter. And, in consequence, the apparent difficulty of the treatment of the metaphysics of the Sāṁkhya as dualistic may be removed. Be it noted, however, that as far as dualism is concerned, the admission of a plurality of spiritual beings cannot be prejudicial to it provided that these are regarded, as the Sāṁkhya in India and Descartes and his followers in the West did regard them, as utterly disparate from matter. There is, therefore, no doubt that the Sāṁkhya is a typical representative of dualism in India just as Carteianism is in the West.

Now the two categories of being which the Sāṁkhya regards as disparate from each other are respectively called *prakṛti* and *puruṣa*, the former being conceived to be *single* and *material* and the latter *plural* and *spiritual*. For the understanding of the characterization of these two kinds of being by the Sāṁkhya, it is, however, necessary to note that this school of philosophy rejects the categories of substance, quality, action, generality, particularity and inherence which, as we have already seen, are made use of by the Nyāya-Vaiśeṣika in interpreting the universe. This indicates that the Sāṁkhya, like Buddhism which also rejects all these categories, has in view the idea of making a departure from the usual way of interpreting the universe and adopting a novel way to this end. How this is so will be evident from its characterization of *prakṛti* and *puruṣa*.

Let us first enquire into the Sāṁkhya view of *prakṛti*. In this regard it is necessary to note at the outset that the Sāṁkhya begins its metaphysical pursuit by admitting that the ultimate constituents of the universe are not open to direct and immediate apprehension and thereby avoids the dogmatic way of recognizing their existence which is usually adopted by philosophers and schools of philosophy. But to hold that these are not directly and immediately apprehensible, as the Sāṁkhya warns us, is not to imply that they do not exist, but only that they are too subtle *(sukṣma)* to enter into the field of perceptual experience. Their existence, then, is *inferable.* And as far as *prakṛti* is concerned, its existence is inferable from its products which constitute the material world of our day to day experience, consisting of a multiplicity of finite objects of diverse descriptions. Not only that; its characteristics are also determinable in contrast with those of its products. In the first place, since it is the ultimate cause of whatever is an effect, *prakṛti* must itself be uncaused. In other words, it must be the uncaused or, to use an Aristotelian phraseology, the first cause of the entire world of effects. Secondly, since individual things are transient or non-eternal, it would be absurd to conceive the ultimate cause to be non-eternal. That being so, *prakṛti* as the ultimate cause of the entire realm of effects must be *eternal.* Thirdly, since individual things which are the products of *prakṛti* are *finite,* limited in magnitude and indeed non-pervasive, *prakṛti* as the ultimate cause of whatever is an effect must be *infinite* and *all-pervasive (vibhu).* Lastly, since its products, that is, individual things, are manifold, conditioned, composed of parts and manifest *(vyakta), prakṛti* as their ultimate cause must be one, unconditioned, devoid of parts and unmanifest *(avyakta).* Thus matter *(prakṛti)* regarded as the ultimate cause of the universe as a whole is, in the view of the Sāṁkhya, one, eternal, unconditioned, infinite, ubiquitous, devoid of parts and unmanifest.

In its further characterization of *prakṛti*, the Sāṁkhya assumes that the world of fact, which is the product of this ultimate material stuff, bears no manifestation of intelligence within it and, consequently, arrives at the view that *prakṛti* itself as its cause must be unintelligent or rather *unconscious* with no prevision of end or purpose. In holding this view, the Sāṁkhya seems to be in agreement with philosophers like Schopenhauer on the one hand and with the materialists on the other. But then, it does not agree with the latter in advocating the mechanistic theory of evolution. This points towards an important feature of the metaphysical theory of the Sāṁkhya which may be explained as follows.

As previously mentioned, *prakṛti* is devoid of parts; and as such it is not an aggregate of parts, but a whole with three distinct aspects *(guṇas)* respectively called *sattva, rajas* and *tamas.* In this connection it is necessary to note, however, that the word *guṇa* in Sāṁkhya philosophy cannot and, in fact, does not mean 'quality' ascribable to *prakṛti* regarded as a substance. For, as we have already seen, the Sāṁkhya rejects the entire gamut of the Nyāya-Vaiśeṣika categories, including substance, quality, etc. So various suggestions have been made as to what this word could possibly mean in its use by the Sāṁkhya in connection with its characterization of *prakṛti.* But as far as we are concerned, the three *guṇas* may most suitably be taken to mean three distinct aspects of the ultimate material stuff called *prakṛti*. But then, since anthropocentricism, as we have previously indicated, seems to be an essential factor in the Indian way of interpreting the universe, the three *guṇas* have been understood in the light of this factor. Thus it has been held that the three *guṇas*, *sattva*, *rajas* and *tamas*, respectively correspond to the three kinds of feeling, namely, pleasure, pain and delusion or indifference. Nevertheless, it has also been held that *sattva* serves to manifest objects, *rajas* leads to *activities* and *tamas* is especially fitted to offer resistance.

The fact, in the view of the Sāṁkhya is, however, that *prakṛti*, in its primeval state, remains in a state of equipoise due to the suspension of the functions of its three aspects, with the result that in that circumstance there is only an indeterminate, undifferentiated and unmanifest whole of material stuff, but no manifest world with the wealth of colourful diversity and variety as is the world of our day to day experience. But then, the Sāṁkhya brings anthropocentricism to bear upon its understanding of the cosmic situation and, accordingly, argues that this situation cannot remain fixed in its primeval stage, but must change in the manner of the evolution of the universe into a determinate, differentiated and fully manifest world in the interest of the other half of the universe comprising human selves or *puruṣas* or, in other words, for the sake of their bondage through experience (*bhoga*) and their liberation (*kaivalya*) through wisdom or discriminative knowledge (*viveka*). This brings us to the Sāṁkhya theory of evolution which, as we shall see below, is a unique contribution of this school of Indian philosophy.

As previously mentioned, the primeval state of *prakṛti* is that of its equipoise or equilibrium. This means that its three aspects prevent one another from functioning in their respective ways, with the result that there prevails the absence of the necessary condition of its development or evolution. But then, since, as seen above, *prakṛti* must go through a process of development or evolve in fulfilment of a human demand, the initial state of its equipoise must come to an end, so that anyone of its aspects may preponderate over any other and, consequently, the process of the evolution of the universe may have a beginning. But how can this happen? As far as the Sāṁkhya is concerned, the answer must preclude reference to the agency of chance or fate or a divine being or beings. There is also nothing within *prakṛti* itself which, according to it, can put an end to its own state of equipoise. This process of elimination leaves the Sāṁkhya with no option but to regard the condition of the initiation of the process of the evolution of the universe as *transcendent* on the one hand and as *human* on the other. Accordingly, this school of philosophy comes to hold that the end of the state of equipoise of *prakṛti* and the consequent beginning of the process of the evolution of the universe are brought about by a kind of transcendental influence of the *puruṣa* upon *prakṛti*.

But this view calls into existence more serious difficulties than that which it seeks to resolve, namely, the difficulty with regard to the explanation of the world-process. In the first place, since *puruṣa*, according to the Sāṁkhya doctrine of dualism, is absolutely disparate from *prakṛti*, the exercise of any manner of influence, whether transcendental or otherwise, on the part of the former upon the latter is completely out of the question. So it is only by surrendering its dualism for the time being that the Sāṁkhya could entertain the view under consideration. Secondly, even granted that the possibility of the exercise of influence on the part of the *puruṣa* upon *prakṛti* is free from difficulty, it seems absurd to hold, as the Sāṁkhya holds, that the *puruṣa* who is but a part, and indeed a tiny and insignificant part, of the immeasurably vast universe, is competent to determine the beginning of the world-process in any manner whatsover. And no substantial difference would be made to this absurdity if the determining influence were ascribed to a corporation of *puruṣas*, instead of this individual *puruṣa* or that. In any case, whereas the attempt to account for the world-process with reference to the agency of chance or fate or God or gods is tantamount to taking "refuge in the asylum of ignorance", the attempt on the part of the Sāṁkhya to do that with reference to the influence of the *puruṣa* amounts to entering headlong into absurdity. It is this absurdity of the Sāṁkhya which the Yoga as well as Vijñānabhikṣu, one of the most outstanding champions of the cause of neo-Sāṁkhya, sought to overcome by foisting belief in the existence of God upon the orthodox Sāṁkhya.

It is curious, however, that the Sāṁkhya, which regards the actual process of evolution as founded upon the principle of causality as conceived by it, should at all differ from Buddhism in not relying solely upon this principle, but, on the contrary, should go beyond its province in accounting for the world-process. It is, perhaps, on account of its acceptance of the prevalent view of evolution as *periodic* or *cyclical* that it was confronted with the question of the beginning of the process of evolution. And, being antitheistic on the one hand, and being opposed to *yadṛchhāvāda* and fatalism on the other, it found no alternative but to fall back upon the idea of human agency with a view to answering this question. But this militates against the propriety of the periodic or cyclical view of the evolution of the universe and lends support to the view of the world-process as continuous and monolinear.

Now, once the primeval state of equipoise (*sāmyāvasthā*) of *prakṛti* is brought to an end by the transcendental influence of the *puruṣa* and some aspect of *prakṛti* or other comes to prevail over the rest so as to mark the beginning of the world-process, the evolution of the universe proceeds of itself in virtue of the operation of the principle of causality understood by the Sāṁkhya in terms of its *satkāryavāda* or *pariṇāmavāda* according to which the effect is pre-existent (*prag-sat*) in the cause and indeed is the modification (*pariṇāma*) of the latter. This calls for the following observations regarding the peculiarities of the Sāṁkhya theory of evolution. In the first place, *prakṛti* begins to evolve, not at its own initiative, nor at the initiative of anything regarded as superior to it such as God, but, curiously enough, at the initiative of that which is absolutely *foreign* to it, namely, the *puruṣa*. Secondly, the principle which, according to the Sāṁkhya, determines the evolution of the universe is, ultimately, non-mechanistic. For, in spite of the fact that the evolution, after it has once started, is governed by the principle of causality, the operation of this principle, according to the Sāṁkhya, is in unavoidable need of adjustment to the requirements of a transcendent purpose. Thus it is teleological. But then, the teleology in this case is not *immanent* as it is in the view of theism. It is indeed transcendent, but transcendent not in the deistic sense but in the humanistic sense in as much as the purpose which, according to the Sāṁkhya, governs the evolution of the universe is that of human selves (*puruṣas*), instead of that of a transcendent God or a *deus ex machina*.

Thirdly, the Sāṁkhya theory of evolution is divided from the theory of emergence or new creations in as much as that which comes into existence in the course of the evolution of the universe is, according to the former, but the modification of something which was already there. That being so, it seems that the idea of accounting for the qualitative variety and diversity in the world plays no important part in the Sāṁkhya theory of evolution. Fourthly, evolution, in the view of the Sāṁkhya, consists in the progression from the simple to the complex, from the homogeneous to the heterogeneous, from the undifferentiated to the differentiated, from the indeterminate to the determinate, or, in other words, from the unrevealed or unmanifest *(avyakta)* to the revealed or manifest *(vyakta)*. In holding this view, this school of philosophy displays unusual insight into one of the innermost secrets about evolution especially in the biological field. Lastly, whereas the majority of the theories of evolution hold that what comes later in the course of evolution is more refined than what comes earlier, the Sāṁkhya holds, on the contrary, that evolution is progression from the more refined to the less refined, from the refined to the gross as will be evident from the consideration of the succession of the evolutes of *prakṛti*. In the meanwhile it may be observed that in holding this view, the Sāṁkhya is obviously committed to the debatable assumption that the transition from the more developed to the less developed is more natural and more easily intelligible than the transition from the less developed to the more developed. In any case, it seems that the process of deterioration or degeneration which is noticeable in the world of human affairs seems to have made a profound impression upon the founders of the Sāṁkhya system of philosophy and, consequently, that they developed a rather pessimistic outlook which affected their philosophical views, including their view regarding the nature of evolution.

As previously seen, the Sāṁkhya admits *prakṛti* and *puruṣa* as the two fundamental categories in terms of which the universe, according to it, needs to be interpreted. But in addition to these two, this school of philosophy admits twenty-three more categories which are secondary or derivative, constituting as they do the entire gamut of the evolutes of *prakṛti*. Be it noted, however, that the word 'category' does not here signify what it does in its use in the case of the Vaiśeṣika. Now the first or rather the direct and immediate evolute of *prakṛti*, according to the Sāṁkhya, is *Mahat* (the Great) otherwise called *Buddhi (intellect)*. But it is not easy to ascertain why the first evolute should be given either of these two designations. So all that may be said in this regard is that this evolute, being the first in the order of succession, must, in conformity with the peculiarity of the Sāṁkhya theory of evolution which has been previously taken into consideration, be the most general and the most refined. Accordingly, the Sāṁkhya comes to hold rightly or wrongly that Intellect *(Buddhi)* is the most general *(mahat)* and the most refined of all that could possibly evolve out of *prakṛti*. And in view of this, *Buddhi* has been held to be characterized by the preponderance of the *sattva guṇa* which, being essentially luminous, is conspicuous for its refinement. Moreover, *Mahat*, being most general, represents cosmic intellect comprising all limited intellects and yet differing from the latter in having no felt reference to any object whatsoever.

The evolute of *prakṛti* next in order to *Mahat* is something less general and more specified than it, which has reference to the *self* and is called *Ahaṁkāra* (cosmic ego-consciousness or egoity) endowed with the capacity to have everything as its possible object, although there is no scope for the exercise of this capacity owing to the absence of the objective order of the universe. As regards *Ahaṁkāra*, it is important to note, however, that, unlike *Mahat* which is characterized by the preponderance of the *sattva*, it is dominated on the one hand by the *sattva* and on the other by the *tamas*, and that the *rajas* serves to reinforce the function of both. Another thing that deserves special notice in this connection is that, in the view of the Sāṁkhya, there is no cleavage between the *physical* and the *psychical*, both being regarded as belonging to the side of *prakṛti* as opposed to the spirit, that is, *puruṣa*. So the Sāṁkhya finds itself justified in holding as it actually does that *Ahaṁkāra*, in so far as it is dominated by the *sattva* as well as the *tamas*, is succeeded by two parallel series of evolutes—an internal or subjective series comprising five cognitive organs *(jñānendṛiyas)*, five conative organs *(karmendṛiyas)* and *manas* (mind), and an external or objective series consisting of five subtle elements *(tanmātras)*, namely, sound, touch, colour, taste and smell.

It is necessary to observe in this connection that the evolution of the subjective and the objective series in succession to the evolution of *Ahaṁkāra* is determined by the logic of anthropocentricism which, as previously mentioned, the Sāṁkhya has brought to bear upon its understanding of the nature of evolution. For once *Ahaṁkāra* (egoity) is manifest, there must be organs for the use of the ego and there must also be objects in order that it may have *experience* of the manifest world in fulfilment of its purpose. And it is this logic which further demands that the subtle objects, namely, sound, touch, colour, taste and smell should respectively evolve into the gross elements of ether, air, light, water and earth. This is, however, subject to the following *proviso*. The gross element (*bhuta*) of ether is generated solely from the subtle element (*tanmātra*) of sound; that of air comes out of the two *tanmātras* of touch and sound of which the former is primary; light is the outcome of three *tanmātras* taken together, namely, colour, touch and sound, among which the first is primary; water is the offspring of the four *tanmātras* of taste, colour, touch and sound, headed by the first; and lastly, earth is the product of all the *tanmātras* taken together, but under the lead of the *tanmātra* of smell.

Now, according to the Sāṁkhya, the process of evolution comes to an end with the emergence of the gross elements of ether, air, light, water and earth. But that does not mean that the fully manifest world is constituted by these five elements. The fact, on the contrary, according to the Sāṁkhya, is that this world is replete with concrete inorganic and organic objects which, unlike the gross elements, are objects of our experience. But, while this is true, it is also true at the same time that these objects are not *evolutes* of the gross elements. For the former are not new dimensions of reality (*tattvāntara*) given rise to by the latter, but are merely the results of different arrangements and collocations of all or some of the gross elements. This means that the five gross elements, according to the Sāṁkhya, are together sufficient as the means of the interpretation of the world consisting of inorganic and organic beings. But a most obvious drawback of this view is that it ignores the importance of space and time which, as the Vaiśeṣikas in particular realized, are essential to the understanding of the real nature of the world. In fact, the Sāṁkhya dismisses the independent reality of space and time on the one hand, and ignores the distinction between space and time on the other, by holding that space and time regarded as ubiquitous are indistinguishable from ether, and that finite or limited space and time are but modifications of ether as determined by its varying adjuncts. Thus does the Sāṁkhya take the arbitrary step of admitting the reality of the purely hypothetical entity called ether at the sacrifice of the empirically verifiable reality of space and time and thereby and in other ways also presents a distorted picture of the universe, no matter whether or not it is in demand for the fulfilment of the so-called spiritual purpose, that is, the purpose of the *puruṣa*. And this points towards the need for the consideration of the Sāṁkhya view of the nature and status of *puruṣa* which comes under one of the twenty-five categories admitted by this school of philosophy.

In the view of the Sāṁkhya, unlike in the view of many a philosopher or school of philosophy, our knowledge of *puruṣa* (self) is as indirect and mediate as is our knowledge of *prakṛti*, and both are equally derivable from *inference*. The arguments, on the basis of which this school of philosophy infers the existence of *puruṣa* are as follows. In the first place, the constituents of the world of nature are *aggregates* or *complexes* constituted by the three kinds of *guṇas: sattva, rajas* and *tamas*. That being so, they cannot be said to be sufficient in themselves, but must be subservient to some need or other just as beds, chairs, tables, etc., which are complexes, do not exist for themselves or on their own account, but for the fulfilment of the need of somebody or other. Hence it follows that that for whose sake the world of nature, consisting of aggregates, complexes or compounds, exists, must be said to be, ultimately, an uncompounded spiritual being, lest there would arise the difficulty of *regressus ad infinitum*. Secondly, as a corollary of the first argument, it may be further argued that since whatever is a compound is made of the three *guṇas*, that for the sake of which the compounds exist must be simple and, consequently, devoid of the *guṇas*. Thirdly, since that which is unconscious or non-intelligent is in need of being directed just as the non-intelligent chariot must be directed and guided by the charioteer, *prakṛti* and all its evolutes, being *ex hypothesi* unconscious and non-intelligent, must be dependent upon something intelligent for their direction and guidance, which something is the *puruṣa* in question.

Fourthly, since the objective world consists of an infinite variety of objects which are fit to be *experienced* and indeed are knowable (*bhogya*) and since these, being essentially unconscious, can have no experience of themselves as objects, there must be some subject of experience (*bhoktā*) or knower which may be suitably designated as *puruṣa*. Lastly, it is an unquestionable fact that there are at least some spiritually inclined persons who strive hard for the attainment of liberation, and that liberation is not an idle dream but a realizable possibility. But then, the realization of liberation on the part of anything belonging to the world of nature is out of the question in as much as pain and suffering, as the Sāṁkhya holds, are inalienable from its existence. That being so, there must be something utterly disparate from nature (*prakṛti*) in order that the realizability of liberation may be admitted and this something is none other than what is called *puruṣa*.

As regards the first four of these arguments, it may suffice to observe that they are far from being logical or objective and indeed suffer from the fault of being extralogically determined by anthropocentricism. And as far as the fifth and the last argument is concerned, it involves the logical fallacy of *petitio principii* or circular reasoning. For the realizability of liberation presupposes the very thing of which it is taken to be the ground of proof, namely, the existence of the self or spirit called *puruṣa*, as distinguished from *prakṛti* (Nature). The weakness of the Sāṁkhya arguments for the existence of the *puruṣa* which has thus come within sight is, however, noticeable, of course, in a different form, in the case of the arguments which this school of philosophy has put forward in support of its admission of the *plurality* of *puruṣas*. The latter arguments are as follows. In the first place, birth, death and the functions of the sense-organs vary from one individual to another. Thus when one individual is born or dies, all others are not born nor do they die. And if a particular sense-organ of one individual is defective, it is not necessarily the case that the same particular sense-organ of other individuals should also be defective. All this, according to the Sāṁkhya, leads to the conclusion that the *puruṣas* are many. But this argument is absolutely irrelevant to the purpose which it is intended to serve. The reason for this is that the self, the plurality of which it may be said to prove, is the *empirical* self and not the *pure* self or *puruṣa*, the plurality of which it seeks to prove, the question of birth, death, etc., being absolutely inapplicable in its case.

Secondly, it is an unquestionable fact that different individuals act differently, and not in the same way and at the same time as they would have done had there been only one self common to them all. That being so, argues the Sāṁkhya, there must be many selves, instead of one only. But this argument, like the former, is vitiated by the confusion of the empirical self with the pure self (*puruṣa*), because the question of *action* cannot arise in the case of the *puruṣa* in view of the fact that the Sāṁkhya itself conceives it to be inactive or actionless (*niṣkriya*). Thirdly, the intellectual and moral capacity and achievements are not the same in the case of all individuals as these would have been, had there been but one self. The fact, on the contrary, as the Sāṁkhya contends, is that the capacity and achievements in question vary from one individual to another. And this, according to this school of philosophy, suffices to prove the same thesis, namely, that there is a plurality of *puruṣas*.

But the difficulty of this argument is also the same as that of the others, and consists in the confusion of the empirical self and the pure self, because the intellectual and moral capacities and achievements, according to the Sāṁkhya itself, can only belong to the empirical self and not to the *puruṣa* whose concern is limited to the experience (*bhoga*) of the world and release from the bondage consequent upon it, that is, liberation (*kaivalya*).

As has been previously emphasized and as is also implied by the arguments which the Sāṁkhya has employed for the proof of the existence of the *puruṣa*, the metaphysics of this school of philosophy is the dualism of *prakṛti* (matter) and *puruṣa* (spirit). But this is particularly in evidence from the characterization of *puruṣa* by the Sāṁkhya, the key to the understanding of which lies in that it is conceived to be diametrically opposed to *prakṛti*. Thus, in the first place, whereas *parkṛti* is *complex*, being made up of the three *guṇas*, the *puruṣa* is *simple*, being free from differentiation by the *guṇas*, on account of its being altogether devoid of them. Secondly, *prakṛti*, together with all its evolutes, is just that which is *presented*. The *puruṣa*, on the contrary, is that *to* which it is presented and as such is the *sākṣī*. Thirdly, *prakṛti*, being constituted by the three *guṇas*, is inseparably bound up with pain and suffering, whereas the *puruṣa*, on account of its being absolutely devoid of the three *guṇas*, is free from pain and suffering (*kevala*) and as snch is eternally liberated. Fourthly, the *puruṣa* is absolutely untouched and unaffected by both attachment and aversion, which are the modes of the evolute of *prakṛti* called *Buddhi*, and as such it is *udāsīna* (unattached, indifferent). Fifthly, whereas *prakṛtī* and all its evolutes are merely objects (*viṣaya*), the *puruṣa* is just the opposite, being, negatively speaking, *a-viṣaya* (non-objective), and, positively speaking, the subject (*dṛṣṭā*) *par excellence*. Lastly, *prakṛti* is modifiable (*pariṇāmi*), and as such it is characterized by *agency* (*katṛtva*). The *puruṣa*, on the other hand, is recalcitrant to change or modification and as such it is devoid of agency, that is, is *a-kartā* (non-agent).

The above account of the characterization of the *puruṣa* by the Sāṁkhya calls for the following observations. In the first place, it is evident that this school of philosophy had worked out the doctrine of dualism in greater detail than Descartes did, and especially that the dualism of the former is more rigorous and uncompromising than that of the latter. Secondly, the Sāṁkhya, unlike Descartes, conceived the *puruṣa* more negatively than positively, so that the role of the *puruṣa* in the cosmic situation, unlike that of the Cartesian *cogito*, is almost negligible. That being so, the dualism of the Sāṁkhya is easily resolvable into a naturalistic and materialistic metaphysical doctrine by means of the elimination of the only obstacle to it, namely, anthropocentricism. Be it noted, however, that it is by having recourse to anthropocentricism that the Sāṁkhya, on the one hand, saves itself from absorption in naturalism and materialism and, on the other, falls in line with the orthodox tradition of Indian philosophy by admitting such things as bondage and liberation. We shall deal with the Sāṁkhya view of bondage and liberation along with the views held by other schools of Indian philosophy on the same subject, in Part Four of this work entitled Indian Philosophy of Religion. In the meantime it may be observed in conclusion that, consistently with its uncompromising dualism, the Sāṁkhya cannot admit any such thing as bondage and, consequently, is debarred from speaking of liberation, just as it cannot admit any such thing as our knowledge of material objects. The reason here is that in either case the *puruṣa* and *prakṛti* must be held in relation with each other, which *ex hypothesi* is out of the question.

B

THE DUALISTIC METAPHYSICS OF THE JAINAS

(i) Methodology of Metaphysics : The doctrine of Anekānta and Naya

We may begin here by observing that the Sāṁkhya, while it enjoys unquestionable recognition as an orthodox (*āstika*) school of Indian philosophy, the two heterodox (nāstika) schools of Buddhism and Jainism are allied with it on account of their being atheistic and pessimistic. But Jainism's alliance with the Sāṁkhya goes further in virtue of their common allegiance to the metaphysical doctrine of dualism. In fact, among the schools of philosophy in India, Jainism and the Sāṁkhya are together in a class apart, as advocates of dualism. But then, just as dualism in the case of the Sāṁkhya, as we have previously seen, is associated with a unique theory of evolution, that of the Jainas is set in the background of a unique conception of the methodology of metaphysical investigations which deserves careful consideration. We shall, therefore, make a brief enquiry into this conception before we proceed to the investigation of the Jain version of dualism.

The Jaina philosophers, like Kant long after them, were imbued with the idea of bringing about a revolution in the field of metaphysics, but in a way very different from that in which the latter sought to do the same. They held that everything in the world is *complex* in structure and as such has many aspects *(anekānta)*. That being so, it would be improper to view a thing in only one of its aspects and to hold, as philosophers often hold, that the knowledge of that thing derived thereby is *final*. On the contrary, as Jainism holds, it should be viewed in its many and various aspects in order that it may be properly comprehended. This constitutes the essence of the Jaina conception of the methodology of metaphysics which is known as *Anekāntavāda.* Judged from the standpoint of the doctrine of *anekānta,* the various schools of Indian philosophy, as Jainism contends, suffer from the fault of being partial on account of their viewing reality in one of its aspects only *(ekānta),* and thus being characterizable as *Ekāntavāda.*

Now the doctrine of *anekānta* naturally leads to another doctrine which is equally essential to the Jaina conception of the methodology of metaphysics and is known as the doctrine of *Nayas.* The word 'naya' means veridical cognition of one part, aspect, quality or mode of a multiform object *(ekadharmapratipatti). Naya,* then, differs from *pramā* in that, whereas the latter means comprehensive knowledge of things, the former is but partial knowledge of them. According to Jainism, *Nayas* in this sense are mainly of two kinds : *dṛavyanaya* consisting in the consideration of a thing as a *substance (dṛavya)* which unifies a number of qualities and relations, and *paryāyanaya* which views a thing as a mere assemblage of *qualities* and *modes.* Thus the latter ignores the substantial aspect of things and the former, on the other hand, ignores the qualitative and modal aspects of them. Each of these two kinds of *Nayas* again has several distinct forms. *Dṛavyanaya,* according to Jainism, has three forms respectively called *naigamanaya, saṁgrahanaya* and *vyavahāranaya.* All these three may, however, be given one common title, namely, *arthanaya* in as much as they refer to objects or meanings *(artha). Paryāyanaya,* on the other hand, has four different forms respectively designated as *ṛjusūtra, śabda, samabhiṛudha* and *evaṁbhuta.* All these four may, likewise, be given the common title of *śabdanaya* in as much as all of them refer to words *(śabda).*

It is not, however, necessary for us to enquire into all the forms of *dṛavyanaya* and *paryāyanaya.* We may consider only those among them which, according to Jainism, have been resorted to by the major schools of Indian philosophy, with the result that their metaphysical knowledge has become partial, instead of being complete or comprehensive as it ought to be. Let us, then, first take up *naigamanaya* for consideration. This form of the *dṛavyanaya* is that standpoint of viewing things which distinguishes between the *universal* and the *particular,* but regards the distinction between the two as *absolute,* instead of as being *relative,* and yet holds that things are made up of the universal and the particular. This standpoint, according to Jainism, is adopted by the Nyāya-Vaiśeṣikas, and as a result, this combined school of philosophy fails to realize that things may be said to be made up of both the *universal* and the *particular,* because the distinction between the two is not *absolute,* but relative and because the one apart from the other is, in consequence, a false abstraction.

We may consider another form of *dṛavyanaya* called *saṁgrahanaya.* As its very title indicates, it consists in viewing things from the most general standpoint without any reference whatsoever to their special features and, consequently, treating them as mere 'being'. But then, this kind of *naya* may assume either of two forms respectively called *parasaṁgrahanaya* and *aparasaṁgrahanaya*. The former consists in the consideration of things from the most general point of view as mere 'being', in complete disregard of their specific features. This standpoint, obviously misleading and mistaken, has, according to Jainism, been adopted by the Advaita Vedānta in so far as it denies the plurality of things and affirms the reality of an undifferentiated unity. As regards the other form of the *saṁgrahanaya,* namely, *aparasaṁgrahanaya,* it is, according to Jainism, the inferior kind of viewing things from the standpoint of generality. The generality in this case is not that of 'being', but of an intermediate kind such as that of matter. According to Jainism, the Sāṁkhya may be said to have had recourse to this standpoint of viewing things in so far as it holds that all material things, the living beings, the sense-organs, *manas,* etc., are equally the evolutes of *prakṛti,* in spite of their irreducible differences from one another.

The last form of the *dravyanaya* called *vyavahāranaya* consists in viewing things from the practical *(vyavahārika)* point of view and on the basis of sense-perception. As far as our perceptual experience is concerned, its objects are, on the one hand, *particular* and, on the other, *useful.* That being so, generalities as well as things that are not useful and yet are definitely real come to be ignored by the present standpoint of viewing things. Hence is evident the serious drawback of the *vyavahāranaya* which, in the view of Jainism, is the very foundation of the naturalistic and materialistic metaphysics of the Lokāyaṭa and Cārvākas.

Lastly, we may consider the first in the list of the different forms of *paryāyanaya* called *ṛjusūtranaya.* It is the standpoint of viewing things exclusively with reference to their momentary modes of the present and in complete disregard of their permanence or substantiality. Thus it ignores their past modes which no longer exist as well as the future modes which are yet to come into existence. The present standpoint of viewing things is diametrically opposed to the *saṁgrahanaya.* For whereas the latter denies all changes and differences, the former affirms the reality of changes and differences and denies the reality of permanence and identity. The *ṛjusūtra* standpoint, as Jainism points out, is, obviously, of fundamental importance to Buddhism in its different forms.

Now the twofold Jaina doctrine of *Anekānta* and *Naya* obviously implies that, no matter whether we deal with things or their qualities or relations, we cannot make any judgment about them which may be said to be *absolutely certain* or, in other worlds, to be of the form 'S is P'. On the contrary, any such judgment is unavoidably *conditional* or *hypothetical* in character so as to be in need of the addition of the word 'perhaps' or 'maybe' (*syāt*) to it. This brings to light the essence of *syādvāda* (the doctrine of maybe) which marks the culmination of the Jaina conception of the methodology of metaphysics. It, therefore, appears that the Jainas in ancient times had in view the idea of a philosophy of *maybe,* just as Vaihinger in modern times envisaged the possibility of a philosophy of *as if.* However that may be, Jainism did not rest content merely with the view that judgments about things and their qualities and relations must be *problemaitc,* instead of being absolutely certain. It went further in holding that such judgments may be made from seven different points of view (*saptabhanginaya*), and, accordingly, they may present themselves in seven different forms which may be stated as follows.

In the first place, the judgment in question may be affirmative (*vidhi*) and be of the form 'Maybe S is' (*syāt asti*). This kind of judgments, according to Jainism, is possible on the condition that a thing is viewed from the point of view of its own substance, nature place and time. Secondly, the judgment may be of the form 'Maybe, S is not' (*syāt nāsti*). This is a negative judgment (*niṣedha*) and may be made on the condition that judged from the point of view of its own substance, nature, etc., a thing is not the same as another thing. Thirdly, the judgment may be neither purely affirmative nor purely negative, but may be both at the same time on the condition that the thing concerned is viewed, on the one hand, from the standpoint of its own substance, nature, etc., and, on the other, from the standpoint of the substance, nature etc. of another thing. Thus it is of the form 'Maybe, S is, is not' (*syāt asti, nāsti*). In this connection it may be of interest to observe that both Śaṁkara and Rāmānuja have misunderstood Jainism in criticising it on the alleged ground that it has indulged in the absurdity of viewing a thing to be both existent and non-existent at the same time. For what Jainism has really in view in admitting judgments of this kind is that a thing *exists* as it is in itself, but cannot be said to exist when it is regarded as the same as another thing, which, obvionsly, does not involve contradiction.

Fourthly, judgments, as Jainism observes, may be of the form 'Maybe, S is indescribable (*syāt avaktavyaṁ*). This kind of judgment presupposes the distinction between that which is absolutely indescribable and that which is relatively (*syāt*) so, and is based on the admission of the latter and the rejection of the former. In this Jainism is of the view that what is absolutely indescribable such as the Māyā of the Advaita Vedānta is meaningless and indeed unreal and so is recalcitrant to any kind of judgment about it. That which is only relatively indescribable, on the other hand, is neither meaningless nor unreal, so that, as Jainism holds, judgment about it is possible. Fifthly, another kind of judgment which, according to

Jainism, is possible is of the form 'May be S is and indescribable' (*syāt asti avyaktavyam*). Judgments of this kind are, obviously, mixtures of the judgments of the first kind and those of the fourth kind, and, as such, they are, in the view of Jainism, quite legitimate. For there is no contradiction in holding that a thing, when judged from one point of view, exists, and, when judged from another point of view, is *relatively*, but not absolutely, indescribable. Sixthly, Jainism holds that just as mixtures of relative affirmative judgments about things and relative judgments of them as indescribable are thus justifiable, mixtures of relative negative judgments about things and relative judgments of them as indescribable are equally legitimate. Judgments of the latter kind are, obviously, of the form 'Maybe, S is not and indescribable'. Lastly, it may be argued that since relative affirmative judgments and relative negative judgments about the same thing may be legitimately combined so as to constitute mixed relative judgments of the form 'Maybe, S is, is not' and since a relative affirmative as well as a relative negative judgment about a thing is compatible with the relative judgment about the same thing as indescribable, the combination of a relative affirmative judgment and a relative negative judgment about a thing with a relative judgment of that very thing as indescribable is, in the view of Jainism, a legitimate possibility. The judgment resulting from such a combination will, obviously, be of the form 'Maybe S is, is not and indescribable'.

Now, of the seven kinds of judgments mentioned above, only the first and the second, that is, the relative affirmative judgments of the form 'Maybe, S is' and the relative negative judgments of the form 'Maybe, S is not' are, obviously, fundamental, and the remaining five are the results of their combination or else are derivatives from them. But apart from that, the fact that stands out is that the doctrine of the relativity of judgments (Syādvāda) and that of sevenfold judgment (*sapabhangīnaya*) are the corollaries of the relative pluralism (anekāntavāda) of Jainism. The question which arises, however, is whether the *anekāntavāda* and its corollaries are really of importance in metaphysical investigations as they are perhaps intended by the Jainas to be. As regards this question, it may be observed, in the first place, that the Syādvāda and the doctrine of sevenfold judgment, despite the objections that have been raised against them by the rivals of Jainism, are of outstanding logical significance, opening up a vista as they do to the reorientation of the outlook on the logic of propositions. But then, they are of little importance in the field of metaphysics in so far as this academic discipline is understood, as Jainism understands it in common with other schools of Indian philosophy, in the traditional sense in which metaphysics is the basis of logic and not *vice versa*.

Secondly, as far as the *Anekāntavāda* itself is concerned, its metaphysical significance is unquestionable in view of the fact that it draws the attention of metaphysicians to the inherent complexity and many-sidedness of things and thereby warns them against the fault of oversimplification to which they are usually prone. But that is far from conveying the suggestion that metaphysics has no escape from pluralism or that the view of ultimate reality as an undifferentiated unity is necessarily at fault. Even so, the warning in question is of considerable negative value in metaphysical investigations. But then, it is doubtful whether any metaphysician or school of metaphysics has obeyed the warning and, in particular, whether Jainism itself has conformed to it in its metaphysical investigations.

(ii) Jaina Metaphysics

Let us begin by mentioning that the topics which constitute the subject-matter of philosophy, in the view of Jainism, concern nine different items which are: (1) *jīva* (soul); (2) *a-jīva* (non-soul); (3) *punya* (merit); (4) *pāpa* (demerit); (5) *āsrava* (inflow); (6) *bandha* (bondage); (7) *samvara* (stoppage); (8) *nirjarā* (shedding of *karma*); (9) *mokṣa* (liberation). But, as is obvious, only the first and the second of these categories (*padārthas*), that is, *jīva* and *a-jīva* are metaphysically significant, whereas the rest concern morality or religion or both. That being so, we are at present required to enquire into the Jaina treatment of these two categories in particular. In this regard, Jainism is nearest the Nyāya-Vaiśeṣika in its employment of the concepts of substance, attribute and modification in the interpretation of the world of *jīvas* as well as the world of *a-jīvas*.

According to Jainism, the essence of a substance consists in its *existence*, so that whatever is a substance is real. A substance is *permanent* in the sense that its essence is characterized by indestructibility and continuity. But it is, as Jainism holds, also subject to generation (*utpāda*) and destruction (*vyaya*) in the sense that some new qualities may generate in it and some of its old qualities may suffer destruction. A substance, then, is permanent or eternal (*nitya*) in respect of its essential qualities (*sāmānya*) and impermanent or non-eternal (*anitya*) in regard to its changing qualities (*viśeṣa*).

As regards attributes and modifications, they, according to Jainism, belong to substance. But then, attributes belong to substance in the sense that the former and the latter are inseparable from each other and not, as the Vaiśeṣikas hold, in the sense that they are distinct from each other and that there is a relation of inherence (*samavāya*) between them. While attributes are thus essential to substance, *modes* (modifications) are due to *accidental* changes in the attributes of substance. Another difference between attributes and modes, in the view of Jainism, lies in that the former co-exist with one another in the substance, while the latter succeed one another in it. In other words, attributes are *simultaneous,* whereas the modes are *successive.*

In the light of what has been observed above, it is evident that the Jaina view of the nature of substance and attributes and their mutual relation is different from that of many other schools of Indian philosophy. Thus it is at variance with the Advaita Vedānta view which holds that substance alone is real and that its qualities are its false appearances; with the Buddhist view according to which substance is unreal, and the so-called substance is nothing but an aggregate (*skandha*) of qualities and lastly, as previously mentioned, with the Nyāya-Vaiśeṣika view that the substance and the attributes are absolutely distinct from each other, only with this difference that there subsists the relation of inherence between them.

We may now proceed to enquire into the essentials of Jaina metaphysics which lie in Jainism's treatment of the various substances recognized by it. These substances are six in number and are respectively called *jīva* (soul), *dharma* (the principle of motion), *adharma* (the principle of rest), *ākaśa* (space), *pudgala* (matter) and *kāla* (time). What deserves to be immediately noted about this list of substances is, however, that, whereas the first in it is called *jīva*, the remaining ones are together brought by Jainism under the single category of *a-jīva.* Hence it is evident that Jainism is an advocate of dualism in so far as it admits two kinds of reality, the *jīva* and the *a-jīva* which are obviously contradictorily related to each other. But then, it seems that the dualism of the Jainas is different from that of the Sāṁkhya or of Descartes and the Cartesians, in view of the fact that the dichotomy in the former case is not simply between spirit and matter as it is in the case of the latter, but between the soul and a fairly long list, including not only matter *(pudgala)* but other entities as well. Moreover, Jainism, while being an advocate of dualism, has, unlike the Sāṁkhya and Cartesianism, sought to overcome the natural shortcomings of the dualism of spirit and matter by including time and the principles of motion and rest along with matter and space within the category of *a-jīva.* Let us then try to ascertain whether, with these advantages at its disposal, Jaina dualism has succeeded in offering a better interpretation of the universe than that which is available from other forms of this doctrine.

The universe, according to Jainism, is thus divided into two halves, respectively consisting of the *jīvas* and the *a-jīvas.* First as regards the *jīvas,* they are spiritual substances. Negatively speaking, they are spiritual in the sense that they are immaterial, incorporeal or formless *(amūrta)* and distinct from the body and the sense-organs. But, curiously enough, Jainism conceives the *jīva* to be *svadehaparimāṇa,* that is, co-extensive with the body which it occupies. This shows that Jainism, unlike the Sāṁkhya and Cartesianism, finds it hard to overcome the ordinary tendency to understand the spiritual substance on the analogy of the body or the material substance. However that may be, the *jīva*, positively speaking, is endowed with the capacities to know, to feel and to act. Thus it is not only the *knower*, but, unlike the *puruṣa* of the Sāṁkhya and like the 'mind' of Descartes, is susceptible to the feelings of pleasure and pain and is also *active*. And as an *agent* or active being, the *jīva*, according to Jainism, is possessed of freedom of the will, so that it may choose to be tied up with the *karma*-matter and thereby enter into a state of bondage, and it may also voluntarily separate itself from the *karma*-matter so as to find itself placed in the state of liberation.

Jainism, however, distinguishes between the strictly ontological aspect and the phenomenal or practical aspect of the *jīva*. In its former aspect, it is eternal, being without beginning and without end. In the latter aspect in which it is united with .the *karmic* matter, it has both beginning and end, with the result that, while being really eternal, it undergoes birth and death. Be it noted in this connection that the idea of the eternity of the *jīva* is far from suggesting that it is absolutely one or the only one of its kind. On the contrary, Jainisim, like the Sāṁkhya, holds that the *jīvas* are many. Not only that; this school of philosophy distinguishes between two kinds of *jīvas*, each comprising innumerable individuals. One of these kinds consists of those individuals who are in a state of bondage *(saṁsārins)* and the other includes only those who are liberated *(mukta)*. The individuals of the former kind are limited by adjuncts *(sopādhi)*, are possessed of either gross bodies or subtle bodies, are impure, and have finite knowledge, owing to their being limited by the *karmic* matter. Those who are liberated, being free from bodily adjuncts (nirupādhi) as well as from the limitations caused by the *karmic* matter, are, on the other hand, pure and are possessed of unlimited or infinite knowledge or, in other words, are omniscient.

Now the ascription of consciousness and the capacity for knowledge to the spiritual substance and the denial of the same to whatever is material constitute the common feature of all kinds of metaphysical dualism, including that of the Jainas. But to go further and ascribe omniscience to the individual spiritual substance in its state of purity, as Jainism does, is tantamount to its elevation to a divine status, resulting in a travesty of the understanding of the spirit in contrast with non-spiritual beings, which is essential to dualism. This indicates that Jainism, while being an advocate of dualism, is lacking in steadfast allegiance to this metaphysical doctrine. Further indication about this is provided by the fact that the Jainas had long before Leibniz discovered traces of the presence of the spiritual principle in almost everything in the universe and indeed anticipated the metaphysical doctrine known as panpsychism which is definitely opposed to dualism. Accordingly, they held that all things in the universe, ranging between the material elements (that is, earth, water, fire and air) and human beings, are *jīvas*, but that they only differ from one another in the degree of perfection. Thus had Jainism arrived at a position which was later occupied by the monadism of Leibniz. But this only betrays the indecision that underlines the philosophical investigations of the Jainas.

It is now necessary to have a brief account of the Jaina conception of *karma* to which reference has been made above. As we have previously seen, the *jīva's* association with *karma* leads to the poverty of its spiritual quality in various ways, whereas its separation from the latter is tantamount to its being firmly established as a spiritual being in a state of purity and perfection. What, then, is *karma* which is thus a potent factor in the shaping of the density of man ? According to Jainism, *karmas* are infra-atomic particles of matter which are produced by the *actions* of mind, body and speech under the influence of desire, aversion and delusion. Despite the fact that these are, in the view of Jainism, material, they may still be called, as the Jainas call them, *karmas* on account of their being the products of *actions*. Even so, to conceive *karmas* to be material is to transcend the limits of propriety and to have recourse to a crude way of thinking. That the Jaina way of thinking in this regard is crude is further evident from the view held by Jainism, that the *karma*-matter flows into the soul and is made to stick to it by passions *(kaṣāya)*, with the result that it is thrown into a state of bondage. But this view, besides being crude, is flagrantly absurd in as much as the soul being immaterial as it is in the view of Jainism, the inflow of the *karma*-matter into it is inconceivable and, consequently, the bondage of the *jīva* should be out of the question. In any case, the admission of the association of the *karma*-matter with the *jīva* on the part of the Jainas is as incompatible with dualism as is the view of the pineal gland as the seat of the soul held by Descartes.

Although, as seen above, the Jainas regard the *karmas* as material, they have not brought them under the category of *a-jīvas* as opposed to the *jīvas*. This shows that they do not have in view a clear-cut distinction between spirit and matter. However that may be, the substances which come under the category of *a-jīva*, in their view, are : *pudgala* (matter), *dharma* (the principle of motion), *adharma* (the principle of rest), *ākāśa* (space) and *kāla* (time). But then, *kāla*, while being an *a-jīva*, is in a class apart from the remaining items coming under the same category, on account of its difference from the latter in being *unextended*. In other words, *kāla*, according to Jainism, is not *ajīvastikāya* (extended non-soul substance) as the remaining *a-jīvas* are. In this connection it may be of interest to note, however, that, whereas Cartesian dualism holds that whatever is non-spiritual is essentially *extended*, Jaina dualism is of the view that this is not so, the non-spiritual substance *kāla* being unextended. This is a pointer to the fact that Descartes ignored the importance of time in the interpretation of the universe, while Jainism saw the truth that space without time is unable to serve as a means to this end.

Let us first enquire into the Jaina view of *pudgala* (matter). As already indicated, *pudgala* is one of the non-spiritual substances which are *extended.* And as an extended substance, it has form or shape *(rūpa).* Besides being characterized by these primary qualities, *pudgala,* according to Jainism, is characterized by the so-called secondary qualities, namely, colour, touch, smell and taste. Further, it exists in either of two forms — in the form of *atoms (aṇus)* and in the form of aggregates *(skandhas)* of atoms. Thus Jainism, like the Nyāya-Vaiśeṣika, holds the atomic or granular view of matter. And, like the latter, it also holds that atoms are indivisible (*avibhāgin*), indestructible (*śāśvata*) or eternal (*nitya*) and corporeal (*mūrta*) elements of matter. Matter, in the other form, that is, in the form of *skandha,* is the result of the combination or integration (*saṁghāta*) of atmos. It is capable of modification (*pariṇāmaguṇa*) and so is subject to increase or decrease, growth or decay. And, unlike the atoms which have the unmanifest qualities of colour, touch, smell and taste only, aggregates of atoms have all these four qualities and sound in addition, as well as the qualities of hardness, softness, heaviness, etc. And this is a pointer towards the comprehensiveness of the Jaina concept of *pudgala* (matter). In fact, according to Jainism, not only the body, the sense-organs, the brain and the *karma* particles, but whatever is an object of sense-perception are material.

We next take up the Jaina view of *dharma* for consideration. It needs to be mentioned at the outset that, in the view of the Jainas, the word 'dharma' does not mean moral or religious merit (*puṇya*) as it does in the view of the Nyāya-Vaiśeṣika. Nor does it mean the Moral Ought as Prabhākara, the founder of one of the schools of Mīmāṁsā Philosophy, takes it to mean. On the contrary, Jainism uses this evaluative word in the most unusual sense of the imperceptible medium of the motion of matter as well as of the soul and regards it as an ontological reality and as a constituent of the physical universe. But apart from the question whether the word used here is suitable or not, the fact remains that, in virtue of its admission of *dharma,* Jainism succeeds in making room for the condition of the possibility of motion within the universe. In consequence, it avoids the difficulty of the Sāṁkhya and of Descartes due to their attempt to account for the possibility of motion in a supernatural way with reference to the transcendental influence of the *puruṣa* and the agency of a *deus ex machina* respectively.

Be it noted, however, that *dharma,* according to Jainism, does not make the spiritual and the material substances move. On the contrary, these move of themselves. *Dharma* is only the medium of their motion just as water is the medium of the movement of the fish. This implies that *dharma* itself is without motion. And it is not only devoid of motion, but is also lacking in all sensible qualities such as colour, smell, taste, etc. This is precisely the reason why *dharma* is imperceptible, although, as Jainism holds, liberated souls who are omniscient are capable of apprehending it. The lack of motion and the sensible qualities in its case is, however, amply compensated for, on account of its being characterized by *coextensiveness* with mundane space (*lokākāśa*) and the consequent *continuity*. Briefly stated, *dharma*, then, is the unitary, incorporeal, imperceptible, immobile, all-pervasive and continuous medium of motion.

Now, the word '*adharma*' which is the opposite of the word *dharma* is detached by Jainism from its usual moral or religious significance and is taken by it to mean the *support* or the helping condition of the *rest* of stationary things as well as of things in motion. It is, therefore, far from *adharma* to impel things to rest or to bring about the state of rest in anything. But then, without a proper support, things that are already in a state of rest cannot continue to remain in that state; nor can things that are in motion have any chance to have rest. The support which is thus in demand for the realization of the state of rest is, in the view of Jainism, exactly what is meant by the word '*adharma*'. But, despite the fact that it is the opposite of *dharma*, *adharma* has the same characteristics as the latter. Thus it is unitary, eternal *(nitya)*, formless (*amūrta*), immobile (*kriyāhīna*), coextensive with mundane space (*lokākāśa*), and hence all-pervasive. And, like *dharma*, it is also simple and non-atomic and is imperceptible, being devoid of sensible qualities. The only difference between *dharma* and *adharma*, then, consists in that, whereas the former is the auxiliary condition of motion, the latter is the similar condition of rest.

Next as regards *ākāśa*, it is important to note in the beginning that Jainism differs from most of the *āstika* schools of Indian philosophy, including the Nyāya-Vaiśeṣika, the Sāṁkhya, the Mīmāṁsā and the Vedānta, in that, whereas the latter mean ether by this word, the former understands it in the sense of *space*. In this Jainism displays the wisdom that lies in the preference of something empirically verifiable, namely, space, over something that is purely hypothetical, namely, ether. According to Jainism, space is similar to *dharma* and *adharma* in being unitary, eternal (*nitya*), all-pervasive (*vyāpaka*), incorporeal or formless (*amūrta*), devoid of sensible qualities and imperceptible. But the peculiarity of space, as Jainism holds, lies in that it provides accommodation to all kinds of substances, including even time. This is, however, objectionable, among other things, owing to its treatment of space as prior to, and more important than, time. In fact, Jainism, in common with many a philosopher or school of philosophy, is open to the charge of the arbitrary understanding of time on the analogy of space.

But Jainism creates further difficulties with regard to its conception of space by admitting two kinds of space, namely, mundane space *(lokākāśa)* and supermundane space *(alokākāśa)*. The former is held to accommodate all *jīvas*, all material objects, *dharma*, *adharma* and time, precisely the items which constitute the world. That being so, space is identical with the world. And yet, as Jainism holds, it is distinct from the world in so far as it is infinite and as such is the container of the world. As distinguished from the *lokākāśa*, there exists the *alokākāśa* (supermundane) space beyond the world. The latter, like the former, is held by Jainism to be infinite, eternal, formless, and imperceptible, being devoid of sensible qualities. But then, there is a fundamental difference between the supermundane space and mundane space in that the former, unlike the latter, is *pure* space or space *par excellence*, being completely devoid of any content. Thus there is no soul, no matter, neither *dharma* nor *adharma* and no time within the pure space.

Once the existence of space is admitted, it may, however, be contended that there is no need of postulating such things as *dharma* and *adharma* because it may well be held that space, besides providing accommodation to all and sundry substances, may serve as the auxiliary condition of both motion and rest. But the reply of Jainism would consist in stating that there is the supermundane space beyond the mundane space and the world, but that it is completely devoid of motion as well as rest. That being so, as the argument of Jainism would continue, space can have nothing to do with either motion or rest. But even then, it may be objected that the postulation of the supermundane space is a superfluity and, consequently, amounts to the violation of the law of parsimony in as much as it, even on the view of Jainism, has no part to play in the interpretation of the universe. So it seems that the attempt to interpret the universe on the part of Jainism and, for that matter, on the part of other schools of Indian philosophy, with the exception of the naturalists and materialists, is not strictly scientific nor even metaphysical but is by and large governed by some kind of supernaturalism or other and hence is indistinguishable from myth-making.

It now remains for us to enquire into the Jaina conception of time as one of the substances which constitute the world. Time, according to Jainism, is a substance. But, as previously mentioned, it is not an extended substance as are the remaining ones. Unlike other substances that are three-dimensional, time is one-dimensional and thus is at best a linear order in which moments do not coexist with, but succeed, one another. Thus far Jainism, in its attempt to understand the nature of time, seems to be above reproach except for its conception of time as a *substance*. But it creates a difficulty in its way by drawing the distinction between absolute time *(pāramārthika-kāla)* and relative or empirical time *(vyavahārika-kāla)* and holding the view that the former is the auxiliary condition of the continuance *(vartanā)* of substances, whereas the latter is the similar condition of their changes *(parivartana)* or modifications (pariṇāma). The difficulty in question is well indicated by the admissibility of other ways of explaining the continuance, changes and modifications of substances than that which has been adopted by Jainism. In the first place, it may be that substances continue to remain in the same state or else undergo changes and modifications of themselves without the help of any condition. Secondly, it may just as well be that the continuance, change and modifications of substances are conditioned by time, but time in one and the same sense in all the three cases. Thirdly, even granted the distinction of the two kinds of time which Jainism has drawn, it may be that the functions of these two are just the reverse of what this school of philosophy has taken them to be.

What we are trying to suggest is, however, that it may be just proper to distinguish the primary *modes* of time, namely, the past (before), the present (now) and the future (after), but that the very idea of the distinction of the *kinds* of time is tantamount to the ignoring of the peculiarity of time in the name of lifting the veil off the mystery of time. This is especially evident from the Jaina conception of absolute time as eternal in as much as eternity is just another name for timelessness. Even so, it needs to be mentioned in conclusion that Jainism has a distinct advantage over those philosophers or schools of philosophy who offer too simple an interpretation of the universe, say, in terms of the spirit alone or matter alone or both spirit and matter. And it has definitely served the cause of metaphysics better than many an ancient or modern system of philosophy by insisting that the interpretation of the universe demands the admission of the reality of the spirit and matter on the one hand and of several other items, including space and time and the media of motion and rest on the other. This may be construed as conveying the suggestion that metaphysics in India had a better fortune in the hands of the heterodox schools than in the hands of the orthodox ones.

IV

IDEALISM

INTRODUCTION

Idealism is usually held to be of two distinct kinds respectively called subjective idealism and objective idealism. But from the strictly metaphysical point of view, so-called objective idealism is really a form of Absolutism qualified by the adjective 'spiritualistic'. So idealism as a metaphysical doctrine should be none else than what is ordinarily called subjective idealism. But then, once objective idealism comes to be properly designated as spiritualistic absolutism, there would hardly remain any sense in speaking of any such thing as 'subjective' idealism. Yet there is no denying the fact that idealism is a genuine metaphysical doctrine. That being so, the qualifying word 'subjective' should also be dropped in order that idealism may come into its own as one independent metaphysical doctrine among many others of its kind.

Now idealism is a metaphysical doctrine which may be said to consist of a negative as well as a positive thesis. The former is expressed in the view that there is no such thing as an independently existing external world, and the latter consists in holding that the so-called external world is really internal, being constituted by the *ideas* of one's mind. Idealism in this sense was most prominently represented in the West by Malebranche and Berkeley, and in India by the school of Buddhism known as Yogācāra or *Vijñāna-vāda*. As far as Western idealism of the Berkeleyan type is concerned, it seems to be the immediate result of the operation of the inner dialectic of the metaphysical doctrine of dualism. For representationism, which is the inevitable epistemological counterpart of dualism, is, from its very nature, unable to hold its own, and, what is more, to save itself from absorption in *mentalism.* Hence is available the explanation of the transition from Locke to Berkeley and from Descartes to Malebranche.

A situation, similar to that which led to the emergence of the Berkeleyan idealism in the West had obtained in the history of Buddhism in India. As we have already seen, the commonsense realism of the Vaibhāsikas was followed by the representationism of the Sautrāntikas, but with the inevitable prospect of the transition from it to idealism—indeed the prospect which was fulfilled in the emergence of *Vijñāna-vāda* (the doctrine of ideas) in the hands of the Yogācāras. But then, there was a difference between the situation in question which was present in the West and that which presented itself in the history of Buddhism in India. The difference consisted in that the trend of Buddhist thought, unlike that of British thought and, for that matter, Western thought in general, had been subjectivist almost from its very beginning. Thus Buddhism denied the independent reality of at least some of the things such as substance, permanence, universality, etc., which, in the view of many a Hindu philosopher, is unquestionably real; and it regarded them as fabrications of the mind *(vikalpa)*. This position was reached even during the history of early Buddhism as is evident from the dismissal of the reality of these things on the part of the Sautrāntikas. And the vestiges of realism that survived the operation of the subjectivist trend of the Sautrāntika philosophy gradually disappeared until the arrival of a full-fledged idealism in the shape of the *Vijñāna-vāda*.

Now the *Vijñāna-vāda* of the Yogācāras and the *Śūnya-vāda* of the Mādhyamikas are allied together and yet are distinct from each other. And they are the two alternative metaphysical doctrines in which Buddhist thought may be said to have culminated. For the proper understanding of either of these two it would, however, be necessary to take special notice of two basic doctrines of the Mahāyāna school of Buddhism, namely, those of *Tathatā* (Suchness) and *Ālayavijñāna*. The former of these two doctrines was propounded by Asvaghosa in his book entitled *Mahāyānaśraddhotpādakaśāstra*. According to this doctrine, the ultimate reality or the immanent essence of the universe is *Suchness*, which is trans-empirical or noumenal and undifferentiated, being devoid of all kinds of distinction, whether between the subject and the object or between the discriminater and the discriminated. Suchness, then, is Void *(Śūnyatā)*. But then, it is further held that it has two aspects, in one of which it is unconditioned or immutable and in the other it is conditioned. In both these aspects *Tathatā* is mind or soul, so that in its unconditioned aspect it is the Transcendental Mind or the Absolute Soul, and in the conditioned aspect it is the empirical mind which is subject to all kinds of change, including birth and death. But why Suchness, which is essentially unconditioned and immutable, should at all be conditioned is, in the view of Asvaghosa, inexplicable. But he eventually sought to explain the relation between the former and the latter with reference to the principle of *avidyā*. It is as a result of the conditioning of the Absolute Suchness by *avidyā* (ignorance) that there emerges the multiplicity of empirical minds and empirical objects. But then, as Asvaghosa confessed, why there should be such a thing as *avidyā* is as inexplicable as is the question why there should be the unconditioned Suchness regarded as the Absolute Soul or the Transcendental Mind.

Asvaghosa did not, however, stop short at the inexplicability of the individuation of the Transcendental Mind. On the contrary, he held, as was also held by the author of the *Lankāvatārasūtra*, that the Transcendental Mind is the repository (Ālaya) of the dispositions *(vāsanā)* of actions accumulated during beginningless time which produce an infinite variety of object-cognitions *(vijñāna)*. Stated more clearly, this view consists in stating that the multiplicity and diversity of object-cognitions are not produced by external objects but are brought out by *Ālayavijñāna* from within itself, owing to the maturation of the dispositions lying dormant within it throughout the length of beginningless time. Thus did Asvaghosa lend support to idealism by bringing some aspects of the teaching of the Upaniṣads to bear upon the development of the Buddhist metaphysics on a new line which marks the departure of the Mahāyāna from the Hīnayāna. And his achievement in this respect was considerably strengthened by the doctrine of *Cittamātra* ('Mind only') propounded in the Laṇkāvatārasūtra, according to which the mind alone is real and external objects are as unreal as dreams *(māyāsvapna)*, mirage *(mṛgatṛṣnā)*, sky-flour *(khapuṣpa)*, an imaginary city in the clouds *(gandharvanagar)*, etc., But then, Asvaghosa served the cause of the Mādhyamika metaphysics no less than that of the idealistic metaphysics of the Yogācāras. For his concept of *Tathatā* (Suchness), on his own showing, is identical with the Mādhyamika concept of the Void *(Śūnya)*.

VIJÑĀNAVĀDA (IDEALISM)

As previously mentioned, it is the group of philosophers called Yogācāras who were the official architects of the metaphysical doctrine known as *Vijñānavāda* (the doctrine of ideas). The reason why these philosophers were so called is, perhaps, that they were in the habit of practising *Yoga.* The founder of the school to which these philosophers belonged was Maitreyanātha. But those who were mainly responsible for the development of *Vijñānavāda* were his pupil Asanga and Asanga's distinguished brother Vasubandhu. And those who continued the tradition of *Vijñānavāda* included Dinnāga, Iśvarasena, Dharmapāla and Dharmakīrti. But then, it should be noted that in the hands of these philosophers *Vijñānavāda* lost some of its original purity and got mixed up with some of the teachings of the Sautrāntikas. And the syncretic process thus set on foot proceeded further, resulting at last in the union of *Vijñānavāda* with certain aspects of the Mādhyamika doctrine of the Void, as may be ascertained from the works of Sāntirakṣita and Kamalasila, who represent the last phase of the development of *Vijñānavāda.*

As already indicated, the positive thesis of *Vijñānavāda,* (idealism) consists in holding that *vijñāna* (idea) is real and not otherwise, and, further, that it *alone* is real. That being so, the establishment of the metaphysical position expressed by these views would, on the one hand, demand the refutation of the view that *vijñāna*, strictly speaking, is not *real*, but only *apparent*, being characterized by *relativity*. And it would, on the other hand, demand the refutation of the view which, while not disputing the reality of *vijñāna*,, holds that external objects are realities *par excellence*, whereas *vijñāna* is only secondarily or derivatively real, being the product of the impact of external objects upon the mind through the sense-organs. Now as regards the former of these two views, it seems that no philosopher or school of philosophy has admitted it except the Mādhyamikas, according to whom *vijñāna* is not real simply for the reason that it turns out to be only apparent in the light thrown upon it by dialectical analysis. That being so, the *Vijñānavādins* are required to argue against this view of the Mādhyamikas. And as regards the latter of the two views, it is obviously the characteristic feature of realism in all its forms, including the direct realism of the Vaibhāsikas and the indirect or representationist realism of the Sautrāntikas. So the *Vijñānavādins* are, in their own interest, required to shoulder the additional burden of demonstrating the falsity of this view.

Now, as regards the Mādhyamika view that *vijñāna* is not real, but apparent or rather illusory, the *Vijñānavādin's* main argument against it lies in stating that, even granted that everything shows itself to be illusory when subjected to dialectical analysis, there is no denying the fact that illusion itself survives the onslaught of such analysis. But what else is illusion but a kind of cognition *(vijñāna)* ? So *vijñāna* cannot be exorcised by any manner of dialectical device. Moreover, admitting as they do such a thing as Śūnyatā in common with the Mādhyamikas, the *Vijñānavādins* hold that it is not a mere blank nor sheer emptiness, but is *pure* consciousness or cognition, that is, cognition devoid of the distinction between the knower and the known, between the subject and the object. And this, according to them, suffices to indicate that, whereas the object is not sufficient unto itself, but must have to depend upon consciousness or cognition, pure cognition is self-sufficient. Hence follows the reason why cognition may be infected by passions and undergo modifications, but is, on the other hand, capable of purifying itself through the elimination of its modification as well as the illusory duality of the subject and the object which may come to be superimposed upon it.

As regards the *Vijñānavādin's* arguments against the realist view of external objects as real, they vary from one prominent *Vijñānavādin* to another, so that taken together, they make up a long list which it is unnecessary for our immediate purpose to mention. We may therefore state only those that are especially important among them. In the first place, the *Vijñānavādin* argues that since cognition and its object are inseparable and since we cannot conceive or even speak of an object which is *unknown*, objects existing independently of cognition, that is, the so-called external objects are inadmissible. The main point in this argument, as is obvious, is identical with Berkeley's main thesis that *esse est percipi*. Secondly, it is argued that the possibility of cognition cannot be accounted for on the assumption of the independent reality of the object. The reason for this, according to the *Vijñānavādin*, is that, if the object is external, that is, outside cognition, as according to realism it is, then there can be no relation of its *identity (svārūpya)* with cognition which is demanded by the possibility of its being cognized. Thirdly, an important anti-realist argument was evoked by the Sautrāntika view that there must be independently existing external objects in as much as it is these which imprint their forms upon the cognitions produced by them and, consequently, there is similarity between the forms of the cognitions and the forms of the objects. The argument consisted in stating as follows. If there be complete agreement between the form of cognition and the form of the object, then there would arise the absurd situation that the cognition would resemble the object in being *unconscious*. If, on the other hand, the similarity between the two is partial, then that part of the cognition, the form of which is not similar to the form of the object, can alone be said to apprehend or be conscious of the object. But this would result in the absurd view that every cognition consists in the apprehension of everything. The *Vijñānavādin*, therefore, dismisses the Sautrāntika view in question, together with its main point consisting in the admission of the reality of extra-mental objects.

Fourthly, it is argued that the phenomena of illusion, hallucination and dream, which involve cognitions without there being any extramental objects corresponding to them, testify to the fact that cognition creates its own object, instead of being determined by objects existing independently of it. And what is thus true in the case of illusion, hallucination, etc., as the *Vijñānavādin* argument continues, must be equally true in the case of so-called veridical cognition. Hence, according to him, follows the conclusion that there are no such things as extramental objects. This argument resembles one of those which anti-realist philosophers in the West have employed in their criticism of the view which consists in the admission of the reality of independently existing objects. Fifthly, the *Vijñānavādin* observes that the dismissal of the reality of external objects does not, as it may be supposed that it does, create difficulties with regard to the explanation of the distinction between true and false cognition and the recognition of the undeniable facts concerning the commonness of the inter-subjective world, the durability of objects, etc. But, strictly speaking, these difficulties are insoluble consistently with the main thesis of idealism which consists in holding that successive ideas are the only reality.

If the idealist is, however, anxious, as were the Yogācāras in India and Berkeley in the West, to resolve them, he can do so only at a heavy cost, the cost of his main thesis, by falling back upon the concept of cosmic consciousness *(Ālayavijñāna)* and that of divine consciousness as the Yogācāras and Berkeley respectively did. But this not only amounts to making a departure from idealism strictly so called, but also to having recourse to a kind of super-idealism which is really the negation of that which is intended to be made perfect by means of it. That being so, the question naturally arises whether the negation of idealism, the need for which the idealist himself admits, not consciously, but only by implication, should be sought in the super-idealism of the *Vijñāna-*

vādin or of the Berkeleyan type or else in realism which contradicts the main thesis of idealism by insisting on the reality of extra-mental objects. The answer would depend upon the decision as to whether the aim of metaphysics should be the acquisition of grandiose sophistications for their own sake or the humble search for truth. If the decision is, as it should be, in favour of the latter alternative, then no doubt would be left about the necessity of the liquidation of idealism in the embrace of realism. And this would obviously amount to the need for the reversal of the process of transition from the Vaibhāsika to the Sautrāntika and from the latter to the Yogācāra.

Judged in the light of the above conclusion, the arguments of the *Vijñānavādin* against realism, some of which have been mentioned above, prove to be pointless. Besides, in a deeper analysis, at least some of them presuppose the very thing which they are intended to prove, namely, the unreality of extra-mental objects. Thus they may be said to be involved in the fallacy known as circular reasoning. The only escape from this difficulty in the case of the Yogācāras, as mentioned above, lay in their admission of the cosmic consciousness. And it is on the basis of this admission that they constructed a substitute for idealism properly so called, in the name of providing a supplement to the latter. We may, therefore, be well advised in bringing our enquiry into *Vijñānavāda* to a close with a brief account of the Yogācāra metaphysics of cosmic consciousness.

Let us begin by observing that it was Aśvaghoṣa who first introduced the idea of the Absolute into the Buddhist philosophy in terms of the concept of *Tathatā* (Suchness) and thereby determined the peculiarity of the trend of thought which pervaded the Mahāyāna school of Buddhism. *Tathatā* regarded as the Absolute was, however, open to a materialistic interpretation and, consequently, it might be held that the universe is ultimately reducible to, or deducible from, a primeval material stuff of unlimited dimension. But Buddha's opposition to the materialistic way of thinking that prevailed in his time proved to be the unfailing dissuasive of the materialistic interpretation of the Absolute. On the contrary, it was especially favourable to the subjectivist or idealist interpretation of reality. It was, therefore, quite natural for Aśvaghoṣa, as an adherent to Buddhism, and his associates and successors to conceive *Tathatā* to be *Vijñaptimātra* (pure consciousness), that is, consciousness characterized by immobility, unchangeability and unmodifiability. But then, this conception of the Absolute or Ultimate Reality was inconsistent with one of the basic tenets of Buddhism consisting in the doctrine of momentariness or ceaseless flux. On the other hand, it was absolutely devoid of the promise of bringing about the emergence of a world, consisting of finite minds and finite objects, on account of the Absolute's being conceived to be lacking in those characteristics that are needed for the fulfilment of this end.

The way out of the predicament which thus presented itself lay in either of two alternatives. One would consist the avoidance of the concept of the Absolute which really did not find a place in the teaching of Buddha. The other would call for a device which could serve to mitigate the twofold difficulty mentioned above. And as regards Mahāyāna Buddhism, it adopted the latter alternative in preference to the former. Accordingly, the Mahāyānists, including Aśvaghoṣa and the Yogācāras, came to hold that the immutable Absolute (*Tathatā*) comes, in an inscrutable manner, under the influence of the inexplicable principle of *avidyā,* and, in consequence, presents itself as the cosmic consciousness (Ālayavijñāna) characterized by dynamism and pregnant with a multitude and an infinite variety of dispositions. And, as they further hold, these dispositions, on their attainment of maturity, give rise to the world, consisting of an infinite number of finite minds and finite objects.

But then, judged in contrast with *Tathatā* (the Absolute Suchness) as it should be judged, the world, consisting of many minds and many objects, together with its repository, namely, *Ālayavijñāna,* must be *illusory*. And this brings out the crux of the situation, which may be briefly stated thus. The view that the so-called external world is not extra-mental, but really mental, being made of ideas or cognitions (*vijñāna*), is undoubtedly idealistic. But to hold this view and at the same time to declare, as the Yogācāras declare, that the world of ideas is illusory are, obviously, tantamount to the denial of idealism, together with the upholding of a metaphysical position, according to which the ultimate reality is indeterminate and indeterminable, precisely the position which is essential to the *Śūnyavāda* of the Mādhyamikas. Hence is evident the *reductio ad absurdum* of the metaphysics of cosmic consciousness (*Ālayavijñāna*) regarded as a part of, or as a supplement to, *Vijnañāvāda.*

V

ABSOLUTISM

INTRODUCTION

We have so far been concerned with the investigation of four types of Indian metaphysics respectively coming under the heads materialism, realism, dualism and idealism. These four cover almost all the schools of Indian metaphysics with the exception of the theistic schools of the Vedānta, the Advaita Vedānta and the Śūnyavāda of the Mādhyamikas. It is, therefore, left for us to enquire into these remaining kinds of metaphysics in completion of our task of investigating Indian metaphysics as a whole. Now, as we shall see in due course, the systems of metaphysics which we are about to start investigating differ from one another in fundamentals as well as in details. Nevertheless, they may be brought under a common doctrinal category called Absolutism. According to this metaphysical doctrine, the universe is, ultimately, unitary being analysable into, or traceable to, one fundamental principle which may be held to be characterizable in more than one way or else not to be characterizable at all, and which may be conceived to be related to the empirical world in a few alternative ways. Judged in the light of this definition, absolutism is likely to be non-materialistic rather than materialistic. The reason for this is that those who conceive matter to be ultimately real do not usually regard it as a unitary stuff, but as divisible into an infinite number of minutest particles called atoms, and, consequently, that they are unavoidably committed to the pluralistic view of the universe which is incompatible with Absolutism as defined here.

It, therefore, follows that, if such a thing as the Absolute must be admitted at all, it should be conceived to be either spiritual or neutral, being neither material nor spiritual or, if we may say so, nihilistic, being absolutely indeterminate and indeterminable.* Of these three possible ways of conceiving the Absolute, the second does not seem to have found a place in the sphere of Indian Metaphysics although it may be said to have been sometimes adopted by those in the West who are known as advocates of the so-called metaphysical doctrine of neutral monism. But then, the treatment of something as neutral, which is neither material nor spiritual is based on the arbitrary and indeed dogmatic assumption that the material and the spiritual are, in the present context, two such alternatives as cannot tolerate a third other than the neutral. In this connection it would be of importance to remind ourselves of Spinoza's view that Substance has an infinite number of attributes, only two of which, namely, extension and thought, are known to us. Judged in this light, the Absolute, which is said to be neither material nor spiritual should be regarded as indeterminate and indeterminable, instead of as neutral. Hence is evident the wisdom that underlies the nihilistic conception of the Absolute which presented itself in the field of Indian metaphysics as the foundation of the *Śūnyavāda* of the Mādhyamika Buddhists, and of which there is no parallel anywhere else in the world.

Now, as regards the spiritualistic conception of the Absolute, it is important to note at the outset that, not to speak of this conception, even the very idea of the Absolute is conspicuous for its

* Spinoza's conception of Substance as characterized by both thought and extension seems to suggest a way of viewing the Absolute in addition to the three mentioned here. But the difficulty about this is that the recognition of the Spinozistic way of conceiving the Absolute would amount to ignoring, as Spinoza himself ignored, the fact that matter (extension) is divisible and so is not ascribable to the Absolute.

absence in the majority of the schools of Indian philosophy—and this, despite the fact that the Upaniṣads, which are replete with discourses on the concept of the Absolute, constituted the background of metaphysical thinking in India. And, apart from the concept of the Absolute, even the concept of God, which is the nearest approximation to the concept of the Absolute, failed to attract as much notice of the metaphysicians in ancient India as was, perhaps, its due in that far-off age. This naturally leads to the assumption that, for some reason or other, the teachings of the Upaniṣads fell into disfavour to a considerable extent, and, consequently, that a meeting was brought about between the two opposite poles of orthodoxy and heterodoxy in metaphysical thinking. This accounts for the occurrence of several surprising phenomena in the philosophical sphere in India, including the atheism of the Sāṁkhya and the Mīmāṁsā, the close affinity between the Sāṁkhya and Buddhism and the determining influence of Buddhism upon Gauḍapāda, the originator of the Advaita Vedānta, which remains the most respected Indian metaphysical system till this day.

But then, the influence of the teachings of the Upaniṣads never came to an end. On the contrary, it always remained more or less active and was especially exercised upon those who were anxious to arrest the growth of heterodoxy even in the disguise of some form of orthodoxy or other. And this accounts for the emergence into prominence of the rather exceptional kind of absolutism which was familiarized by the Upaniṣads and which is common to all forms of the Vedānta. Thus, spiritualistic Absolutism found a prominent place in the metaphysical sphere in India alongside nihilistic Absolutism to which reference has been already made as well as several kinds of non-absolutistic systems of metaphysics which we have earlier brought under review.

As it would be convenient for us to begin here with the investigation of spiritualistic Absolutism, we may first try to indicate how this metaphysical doctrine has come to assume different forms, so that we may be able to deal with them separately and in a systematic manner. Now, the different forms of spiritualistic Absolutism, which have come to prevail in India are, of course, in agreement with one another in their view that the real is, ultimately, one and is the spiritual Absolute called Brahman. But they differ among themselves with regard to the question of the nature of Brahman and the allied question of the relation of Brahman to the empirical world, the world of our ordinary experience constituted by an infinite number and variety of spiritual, organic and inorganic existents. As regards this twofold question, it has been answered in two broad ways. One of them consists in holding that Brahman is the Absolute Identity and hence is devoid of all kinds of difference. That being so, it is further held, the empirical world characterized by multiplicity, variety and differences, which is ordinarily regarded as real, must, in an ultimate analysis, be the false appearance of Brahman, being the result of the concealment of the true nature of Brahman and the projection of an infinite variety of false appearances. Briefly stated, this amounts to holding that the empirical world is not the *realization*, but, on the contrary, the deprivation of reality and indeed is unreal *vis-a-vis* Brahman regarded as the Absolute or Ultimate Reality. This is precisely the view which is the corner-stone of Śaṁkara's *Advaitavāda* (the doctrine of the Non-dual) and, what is more, remains unprecedented in the history of metaphysical thought till today.

The other way of answering the twofold question under consideration is expressible in the view that Brahman is not a pure or absolute identity, but a concrete being and as such is identity in difference. And that being so, the empirical world, consisting of an infinite number and variety of finite existents, cannot be unreal but, as is further held, is precisely that which finds itself realized in the Absolute and at the same time is the medium in and through which the Absolute, that is, Brahman realizes itself. This view is held in common by a number of theistically oriented systems of absolutist metaphysics usually called the Vaiṣnava schools of the Vedānta. But, as we shall see in due course, these schools of the Vedānta view the mutual relation between Brahman and the empirical world, not in the same way, but appreciably differently. Keeping this in view, we may now proceed to investigate the different forms of spiritualistic Absolutism respectively propounded by the different Vaiṣnava schools of the Vedānta. If minor differences among the various Vaiṣnava metaphysicians be ignored, the different forms of their metaphysics may be brought under five distinct heads, namely, *Śuddhādvaitavāda* (the doctrine of the pure non-dual) propounded by Vallabha; *Dvaitādvaitavāda* (the doctrine of the dual-nondual) founded by Nimbārka; *Acintyabhedābhedavāda* (the doctrine of the inconceivable difference-nondifference) propounded by Caitanya; *Dvaitavāda* (the doctrine of the dual) founded by Madhva; and *Viśiṣṭādvaitavāda* (the doctrine of the qualified nondual) propounded by Rāmānuja. These metaphysical doctrines may then be dealt with separately and in the order in which they have been mentioned here.

A

THEISTIC ABSOLUTISM

(i) Pure Non-Dualism (Śuddhādvaitavāda)

It is necessary to observe at the outset that Vallava calls his metaphysical doctrine *Śuddhādvaitavāda* (pure non-dualism) with a view to distinguishing it from the *Advaitavāda* (the doctrine of non-dualism) of Śaṁkara. Thus, while Śaṁkara, as we shall see later, associates his non-dualism with the *māyāvāda* (the doctrine of Cosmic Ignorance) and correspondingly conceived Brahman to be affected by *māyā*, Vallabha rejects the *māyā-vāda* and, consequently, finds himself in a position to view Brahman to be unaffected by anything whatsoever, and, therefore, to be *pure (śuddha)*. Now once he rejects the doctrine of *māyā*, Vallabha is free to recognize the reality of the *jīvas* (selves) and the *jagat* (the world of nature). Even so, in order for him to establish his metaphysical theory of pure non-dualism, he, as an absolutist, is required to offer a satisfactory answer to the twofold question, respectively concerning the nature of Brahman and the origin of the *jīvas* and the *jagat* and their relation to Brahman.

As regards the first part of this question, his answer may be briefly stated as follows. In answering it he makes no secret of the fact that he is a Vaiṣnavite (adherent to the cult of Viṣṇu). Accordingly, he holds that that which is called the Brahman in the Upaniṣads is the same as that which is spoken of as Paramātman (the Supreme Self), the Puruṣottama (the Supreme Person) or the Lord Kṛṣṇa in the Bhāgavata. Having thus come to view Brahman theistically in the highest divine form, Vallabha proceeds to characterize Him, on the one hand, in the same manner as Brahman is characterized in the Upaniṣads and, on the other, in a manner as demanded by theism. Thus Brahman in the highest divine form as God, according to him, is only one without a 'second' (*ekaṁ eva advitīyaṁ*); is existence (*sat*), consciousness (*cit*) and bliss (*ānanda*); is eternal and omnipresent. He is also omniscient and omnipotent and is full of *rasa* (sweetness) and infinite joy. In particular, He is possessed of many powers, including evolution and involution, so that He can become anything at any time at will. This, if we may say so, provides the *rationale* of the emergence of the *jīvas* and *jagat* and indeed brings us to the second part of the question posed above.

Basing himself on scriptural authority, Vallabha holds that Brahman in the divine form, though He is sufficient in Himself, is lonely and so desires to be *many* in expression of His sportive spirit (*līlā*) and for the sake of mere pleasure. Accordingly, He creates the world, not out of nothing nor out of anything extraneous to Himself like the *māyā* as conceived by Śaṁkara, but out of His own essence (*svarūpa*). But then, since everything in the world, according to Vallabha, comes out of one and the same thing, namely, the *svarūpa* of Brahman in the divine form, he does not seem to have any means of accounting for the qualitative differences which exist among the constituents of the world and especially between spirit and matter. He, however, seeks to overcome this difficulty with reference to the two powers of God respectively called evolution (*āvirbhāva*) and involution (*tirobhāva*). Accordingly, he holds that it is in virtue of His former power that God manifests Himself in and through the world. But then, the exercise of this power goes hand in hand with the exercise of the latter power on His part. As a result, only one of His aspects, namely, existence (*sat*) is manifested in the *jagat* (the world of nature), whereas the other aspects of Him, namely, consciousness (*cit*) and bliss (*ānanda*) are suppressed in it. The *jīva*, on the other hand, bears the manifestation of the two divine aspects of existence (*sat*) and conciousness (*cit*), but is lacking in a share of the divine aspect of bliss (*ānanda*). Thus do the constituents of the world, in the view of Vallabha, differ qualitatively among themselves; and, naturally enough, they may be held to differ from one another in degree as well.

The fact that stands out in this connection is, however, that Brahman in the form of the Supreme Person or God is, in the view of Vallabha, the material cause as well as the efficient cause of the world. But this must not be construed too literally. For the conception of God as the material cause of the world does not, according to him, mean what it is ordinarily taken to mean, namely, that the world is the modification (*pariṇāma*) of God. Of course, Vallabha himself calls it the modification of God. Nevertheless, the modification in question, as he holds, is in need of being reinterpreted as immutable transformation (*avikṛtapariṇāma*). But in this he is obviously committed to a most glaring contradiction in as much as the modifiability of a thing is absolutely incompatible with its immutability. It is in view of this difficulty in which theistic Absolutism is apt to be involved that Śaṁkara brought in the doctrine of *māyā* and came to hold that it is not Brahman but *māyā* which is the material cause of the world, and that it is not Brahman either, but Īśvara (God as the appearance of Brahman under the influence of *māyā*) who is the efficient cause of the world. Thus did Śaṁkara try to remain faithful to Absolutism, whereas Vallabha tried unsuccessfully to serve the cause of theism and at the same time threw absolutism into jeopardy.

Even then, there remains a dilemma which lies between the affirmation of the reality of the Absolute and the affirmation of the reality of the world. That being so, there may be three possible ways of resolving it. One of them would lie in the affirmation of the reality of the world without the admission of any such thing as the Absolute as conceived in the Upaniṣads. This holds good in the case of the majority of the schools of Indian philosophy and seems to be most reasonable for the simple reason that the denial of the reality of the world is tantamount to an absurdity, he who denies being a part of the world, the reality of which is denied by him. The dismissal of the concept of the Absolute, on the other hand, would, for obvious reasons, involve no such difficulty. And this cuts the ground from under the feet of that alternative way of resolving the dilemma under consideration which is represented by the *Advaitavāda* of Śaṁkara and consists in the affirmation of the reality of the Absolute at the cost of the reality of the world. The third alternative would lie in the affirmation of the reality of the world, at least out of regard for commonsense, if not for any higher reason, whether moral or religious. And it would at the same time include the admission of the reality of the Absolute, lest exclusive regard for commonsense would lead to the undermining of moral and religious values and the consequent degeneration of mankind. This is precisely the alternative which has been adopted by the various schools of theistic Absolutism in India, including that of Vallabha which is under consideratian.

As far as Vallabha is concerned, he seeks to reconcile the reality of the world with the reality of the Absolute in the divine form not only by setting aside Śaṁkara's *māyāvāda* and the consequent view of the world as unreal, but by differing from other theistic absolutists such as Madhva who regards the relation between God and the world as *difference* (*bheda*) and Nimbārka, according to whom this relation is identity-in-difference (*bhedābheda*). Accordingly, he holds that the *jīvas* and the *jagat* are real for no less a reason than that their relation to the Absolute in the divine form is *identity* (*abheda*), they, as previously seen, being the manifestations of the *svarūpa* (essence) of God. There is, then, no *bheda* (difference) between God and the world. But this obviously amounts to upholding pantheism which is opposed to theism, the religious doctrine which Vallabha is most anxious to vindicate. He, however, tries to remove this difficulty by holding that, although the world is non-different from God, the two are still *distinguishable* in fulfilment of the demand of theism. And the distinction, he continues, lies in that the *jīvas* and the *jagat* are parts of a whole that is Brahman in the divine form as God. But this amounts to a vain indulgence in unnecessary use of words for removing a difficulty which is really irremovable. For the conception of the Supreme Person, namely, God as a *whole* made of *parts*, comprising the selves and the world of nature, is at best the height of crudity and at worst is ruinous to religion. Strictly speaking, there is no escape for Vallabha from pantheism in so far as he insists on the all-importance of the identity of the world with God and rules out the difference between them with a view to vindicating the reality of the world *vis-a-vis* the reality of the Brahman.

That Vallabha has landed himself in most of the difficulties of pantheism in the name of vindicating theism is especially evident from his treatment of the problem of the self. For understanding how this is so, it is first necessary to note that, according to him, Brahman has three distinct forms respectively designated as Para-Brahman or Puruṣottama, Antarayāmin and Akṣara-Brahman. Now as far as individual selves (*jīvas*) are concerned, they are inseparably bound up with, and indeed are helplessly dependent upon, Brahman in all these three forms. To the Para-Brahman they owe their love and worship. To the Akṣara-Brahman they owe their very existence in as much as they, according to Vallabha, spring out of Him as sparks come out of fire. And lastly—and this is especially noticeable—they have within themselves Brahman in the form of the Antarayāmin as their innermost being. In view of this, it may be said about the *jīvas* that it is not they who think, feel and act, but it is the Antarayāmin who thinks, feels and acts in and throught hem. In fact, Vallabha definitely holds that God is the ultimate directive cause (*kārayitṛ*) of all human actions and that human freedom is a part of God's freedom and sportive activity. And this speaks of the human predicament which is consequent upon the pantheistic conception of the relation between God and the world, including human selves.

The main point that emerges from the foregoing discussions is however, that the vindication of theism on rational grounds is one of the hardest tasks which metaphysics may choose to undertake. The truth of this is amply demonstrated by Vallabha's version of theistic Absolutism. But we have yet to see whether the other forms of this metaphysical doctrine also point in the same direction.

(ii) Dualistic non-dualism (Daitādvaitavāda)

As previously mentioned, the question which it is incumbent upon the advocates of theistic Absolutism to answer concerns the nature of the Absolute and the origin of the *jīvas* and the *jagat* as well as their relation to Brahman. So Nimbārka, the founder of the Dvaitādvaita school of the Vedānta, being an advocate of this metaphysical doctrine, is, like Vallabha, required to answer this twofold question satisfactorily in order for his metaphysical position to be placed on a sound foundation. But his procedure in this regard, though not exactly indentical with that of Vallabha, is not far removed from it either. For he, like Vallabha, accepts the Bhāgavata conception of Brahman as Puruṣottama (the Supreme Person), and ascribes to Him at least some of the characteristics that are ascribed to Brahman in the Upaniṣads as well as certain others which are held to befit Him as the Absolute of religion, as distinguished from the Absolute of metaphysics. Thus Brahman in the divine form as Puruṣottama, in the view of Nimbārka, is infinite, unconditioned, 'one without a second,' and the embodiment of existence (*sat*), consciousness (*cit*) and bliss (*ānanda*) *par excellence.*

Brahman in the divine form is also held by Nimbārka to be the creator, preserver and destroyer of the universe, consisting of spiritual, living and non-living beings. In particular, he, like

Vallabha, regards the Absolute of religion as the material as well as the efficient cause of the universe. And, like the latter, he holds that the Divine Being, being omniscient and omnipotent, transforms Himself into the world by His sheer power and will. Thus he comes to employ *pariṇāmavāda* (the doctrine of modification) in his understanding of the origin of the world out of God. Further, like Vallabha, he tries to remove the difficulty of the idea of the modifiability of the Divine Being by stating that He remains immutable in spite of His modification in as much as the modification relates to His inessential nature, while His essential nature remains absolutely unchanged and unaffected. But he cannot really mean what is conveyed by this statement, because, in his view, as in the view of Vallabha, the world comes out of His very essence (*svarūpa*). So there is no doubt that he lays himself exposed to the fault of self-contradiction—indeed the fault which, as we have already seen, has been committed by Vallabha.

But then, Nimbārka, it is important to note, differs from Vallabha in a more or less fundamental respect, namely, in that, whereas the latter lays special emphasis on the identity (*a-bheda*) of the *jīvas* and the *jagat* with the Divine Absolute, the former holds that their difference (*bheda*) from God is as important as their identity (*a-bheda*) with Him. This difference between the two philosophers may be explained as follows. As far as Vallabha is concerned, it is not that he is not interested in the vindication of religion. On the contrary, he yields to none in his enthusiasm in espousing the cause of theistic religion. But it seems that his special interest lay in the establishment of the reality of the world as against Śaṁkara's denial of the same, no matter whether or not this was essential to the defence of religion in any form. And it is on this account that he did not pay much heed to the idea of the difference of the world from Brahman, but emphasized the importance of its identity with the latter regarded as the paradigm of reality. This was the outcome of his conviction that once the identity of the world with Brahman thus regarded was realized, the reality of the former would be established beyond dispute.

Nimbārka, on the other hand, seems to have been especially interested in the vindication of religion which, as he came to realize, depended, among other things, upon the recognition of the importance of the *difference* (*bheda*) of the world and especially the *jīvas* from the Deity. This was obviously based on the assumption that, in the interest of religion, the vindication of the reality of the world is not so much in demand as is the certain recognition of the difference of the world from God. Hence follows the reason why Nimbārka, unlike Vallabha, attached special importance to the concept of difference (*bheda*) and thereby tried to suggest that the *transcendence* of God is as essential to religion as is His immanence signified by the identity of the world with the Deity. But this really brings out the crux of the whole situation, For, as Spinoza realized and, perhaps, rightly too, there is an inherent contradiction between the concepts of transcendence and immanence; and it was precisely for this reason that he dismissed the former and accepted the latter, with the result that religion, in his view, was unavoidably pantheistic.

Of course, there is another alternative, namely, that which would consist in the admission of the concept of transcendence and the rejection of that of immanence. And it is precisely that alternative which constitutes the foundation of that kind of religion usually characterized as deistic. But then, deism is uncompromisingly dualistic, and its metaphysical foundation lies in dualism, which is fundamentally different from the *Śuddhādvaitavāda* of Vallabha as well as the *Dvaitādvaitavāda* of Nimbārka, both of which, from the religious point of view, are attempts to reconcile the irreconcilables, namely, the concepts of trancendence and immanence. But strictly speaking, once the world is held to be identical with the Absolute and thus the immanence of the latter in the former is admitted, there seems to be no escape from pantheism or acosmism, no matter whether the idea of *bheda* (difference) is manipulated in the manner of Vallabha or in that of Nimbārka or in any other. So, no matter whatever else the religious significance of Absolutism may be, it seems certain that this metaphysical doctrine can yield neither theism nor even the less sophisticated form of religion which is said to come under the category of deism.

(iii) The Doctrine of Unthinkable Identity-in-difference (Acintyabhedābhedavāda)

We may begin by observing that Caitanya, to whom the metaphysical doctrine now under consideration owes its origin, himself declared that he was a follower of Madhva and adopted the dualistic standpoint of the latter in propounding his own metaphysical theory. But a careful scrutiny of his views would show that he was nearer Nimbārka than Madhva in view of the fact that he advocated a form of *Bhedābhedavāda* (the doctrine of identity-in-difference), as distinguished from the *Dvaitavāda* (the doctrine of duality) associated with the name of the latter. In fact, while agreeing with Madhva in his recognition of eternal distinction (*bheda*) between the Brahman in the divine form on the one hand and the *jīvas* and the *jagat* on the other, Caitanya was at one with Nimbārka in insisting on the identity or non-difference (*a-bheda*) of the latter with the former. The most important innovation which he introduced into the prevalent *Bhedābhedavāda*, however, consisted in his view that the coexistence of the two contraries in question, namely, *bheda* (difference) and *a-bheda* (non-difference; identity) is impervious to logical understanding (*acintya*), but is a matter of non-logical realization. Thus did Caitanya bring to light the inherent mystical aspect of the *Bhedābhedavāda* which was so long allowed to remain undisclosed.

Now, Caitanya, in common with other advocates of theistic Absolutism, was opposed to Śaṁkara's *māyāvāda* and the consequent doctrine of the unreality of the world (*jagatmithyātva*), and was insistent upon the reality of the world. One important consequence of this aspect of the *acintyabhedābhedavāda* of Caitanya was that the position of the indeterminate (*nirguṇa*) Brahman *vis-a-vis* the determinate (*saguṇa*) Brahman as conceived by Śaṁkara came to be altogether reversed. In the view of Śaṁkara, the *nirguṇa* (indeterminate) Brahman is the Ultimate and Absolute Reality, while the *saguṇa* (determinate) Brahman regarded as the creator, preserver and destroyer of the world, is, in contrast with the former, of an inferior status. Caitanya and his followers, on the other hand, held that the concept of the *nirguṇa* Brahman only marks a stage in the progression from a lower truth to a higher truth until the highest truth is reached in the realization of the *saguṇa* Brahman as the Lord of creation held in the relation of mutual love with his creatures. This is elaborated by Caitanya as follows.

It is on the authority of the Vedas that the Ultimate Reality, according to Caitanya and his followers, must be said to be none else than Hari regarded as the Lord (*Bhagavat*), that is, the Divine Being endowed with the six kinds of *bhaga* (characteristics of Lordship), namely, *aiśvarya* (majesty), *vīrya* (supreme strength), *yasas* (highest glory), *śrī* (perfect beauty), *jñāna* (perfect knowledge or intelligence) and *vairāgya* (perfect detachment). It is in relation to the Ultimate Reality thus conceived that the status of the indeterminate Brahman as conceived by Śaṁkara and that of the Paramātman regarded as the indwelling spirit of the created world need to be understood. Accordingly, the indeterminate Brahman and the Paramātman should, in the view of Caitanya, be viewed to be ancillary to Hari and be respectively regarded as the *angakānti* (personal halo) and a part (*aṁśa*) of the essence of Hari. Hence it is evident that the so-called Absolute Brahman as conceived by Śaṁkara is no independent reality, but is only a qualitative aspect of the Ultimate Reality regarded as Hari. And as regards the Paramātman (the Supreme Self), it is viewed to be that part of the essence of Hari which in the form of Viṣṇu enters into the world after its creation by Him.

In thus presenting Viṣṇu as subordinate to Hari, it is, however, far from Caitanya to regard Him as lacking in the plenitude which is an essential characteristic of divine existence. On the contrary, he holds that that which is a part may have a share in the infinitude of the whole of which it is a part. But, considering that the whole is *one*, whereas the parts are *many*, this view of Caitanya is obviously involved in the serious difficulty of the ignoring of the unquestionable distinction between the whole and the part, which is not resolvable except on some extra-logical ground or other. In any case, it follows that his attempt to vindicate theistic religion by means of his admission of the transcendence and immanence of God with reference to the distinction drawn by him between Hari regarded as the Lord of creation and Viṣṇu as the soul of the world, is a failure and a subterfuge. Hence it is once more evident how difficult it is to vindicate theistic religion. But it is yet too early for us to arrive at the final estimate in this regard in as much as we have still to consider a few more attempts to bring out the religious significance of Absolutism.

(iv) Dualistic Absolutism (Dvaitavāda)

It is first necessary to clarify the general nature of the metaphysical position of Madhva in view of the fact that the usual characterization of his metaphysical theory as Dvaitavāda (Dualism) is apt to lead and has sometimes actually led to a misunderstanding about his views. Be it mentioned at once that his metaphysical theory is not dualistic in the sense in which the Saṁkhya or Cartesianism, for example, is. For he is a Vedāntist, and as such he has no doubt in his mind about the ultimate reality of Brahman, so that he is not a stranger to absolutism or monism. And he, like other advocates of theistic absolutism, differs from Śaṁkara in dismissing the doctrine of *māyā* and in not regarding Brahman as *nirguṇa* (indeterminate) and devoid of differences or differentiations. On the contrary, he, like the latter, conceives Brahman to be *saguṇa* (determinate) and as the bearer of differences (*bheda*) within itself. But the question is whether the differences are *absolute* or *relative*, being set in the background of non-difference or identity (*a-bheda*).

The question raised above is indeed crucial in as much as on its answer would depend the future of theistic religion. As far as the majority of the advocates of spiritualistic absolutism are concerned, they are of the view that the 'differences' are relative and indeed are inseparable from the background of identity (*a-bheda*). But this view, as we have already realized to some extent and as Śaṁkara on the one hand and, maybe, also Madhva, on the other, realized, is untenable, *bheda* and *a-bheda* being contraries and, consequently, being incompatible with each other. Accordingly, Śaṁkara dismissed the idea of 'difference' (*bheda*) as supurious and regarded that of non-difference or identity (*a-bheda*) as the key to the understanding of the nature of the Ultimate Reality. Madhva, on the other hand, fell back upon his unshakable realistic tendency, and ruled out the idea of *a-bheda* and at the same time seems to have recognized the absoluteness of the idea of *bheda*. Not only that; he went further in holding finally that in the field of reality there are five eternal distinctions or differences, namely, between God and the individual soul, between God and matter, between the individual soul and matter, between one individual soul and another and between one material object and another. Thus does Madhva stand out as an advocate of an uncompromisingly pluralistic view of the universe. This view, considered in itself, may be all right or above reproach. But in the present context, it gives rise to the question whether it is compatible with Absolutism in any form and, in particular, whether it is conducive to religion of the theistic variety which Madhva seems to be trying to vindicate. It is in the light of his answer to this question that his metaphysical position needs to be judged.

Now, according to Madhva, Brahman in the divine form is Viṣṇu who is called the Supreme Self (*Parmātman*) and *Bhagavāna* (Lord) on account of His being endowed with the six characteristics of Lordship mentioned earlier. He is also to be held to be the Supreme Person (Puruṣottma) as well as the Inner Ruler or the World-Soul (*Antarayāmin*). In further characterization of Brahman in the divine form as Viṣṇu, Madhva regards Him as omniscient, omnipotent, perfect, eternal and immutable. And, what is more, He is conceived to be both immanent in the *jīvas* and the *jāgat* and transcendent from them. Thus no matter whether Brahman in the divine form is called Hari or Viṣṇu or be given any other designation, there is no doubt that Madhva is at one with other theistic absolutists in conceiving the Deity in such a way that His identity (*abheda*) with, and His difference (*bheda*) from, the world of souls and the world of nature are equally clearly admissible. It may be that he lays special emphasis on the difference of God from the world of souls and the world of nature. But, as we have already seen, Nimbārka also does the same. So it is not easily intelligible why Madhva's metaphysical theory should be called *Dvaitavāda* (Dualism), instead of a form of *Bhedābhedavāda* (the doctrine of identity-in-difference) similar to that of Nimbārka and Caitanya.

One important difference between Madhva and the other Vaisnavite metaphysicians whose views we have already investigated, however, lies in that, whereas the latter regard God as both the efficient and the material cause of the world, he regards *prakṛti*, instead of God, as its material cause and thereby saves himself from the difficulty of the application of the doctrine of modification (*pariṇāmavāda*) in the case of the existence of God. And it may be said that, on account of this difference between him and other theistic absolutists, Madhva is entitled to the view that God is different from the world without being at the same time identical with it, for the simple reason that it springs out of something other than God, namely, *prakṛti*, instead of the *svarūpa* (essence) of God. But this is not likely to hold good for the following reasons.

In the first place, if *prakṛti* be understood to be absolutely separate from, and independent of, God, Madhva would be presented to be what he really is not, namely, a dualist in the Cartesian or the Sāṁkhya sense. Secondly, on this understanding of *prakṛti*, the *jivas*, being spiritual existents, cannot be said to have been originated from *prakṛti* as their material cause. Thirdly, in spite of regarding *prakṛti* as the material cause of the world, Madhva, as we have previously seen, admits the omnipresence of God and especially His immanence in the world, besides His transcendence from it. Of course, he is in a class apart from other Vaiṣnavite metaphysicians in that he insists on not one, but as many as five distinctions as mentioned above. But the inflation of the number of 'distinctions' can hardly exorcise the 'identity' or 'non-difference' (a-bheda) which he has himself admitted overtly as well as by implication. The conclusion which, therefore, forces itself upon us is that Madhva's attempt to vindicate theistic religion is as ill-conceived, misleading and fruitless as are those of other theistic absolutists which we have already had the occasion to investigate.

(v) Qualified Non-dualism (Viśiṣṭādvaitavāda)

We may now proceed to enquire into the remaining form and, in fact, the earliest and the most outstanding form, of theistic Absolutism well known as *Viśistādvaitavāda* which was propounded by Rāmānuja, whose reputation as a Vedāntist metaphysician was only second to that of the great Śaṁkara. In the view of Rāmānuja, as in the view of other Vaiṣnavite metaphysicians, the Absolute of metaphysics is identical with the God of religion. Accordingly, he, like the latter, dismisses the distinction between the *saguṇa* Brahman and the *nirguṇa* Brahman which Śaṁkara admitted with a view to indicating that the Ultimate Reality is indeterminate (*nirguṇa*) and as such stands in contrast with whatever is determinate (*saguṇa*), whether God or *jīva* or *jagat*. Śaṁkara did not, however, admit, nor, consistently with his distinction between the two contraries, the *nirguṇa* and the *saguṇa*, could he admit, any such thing as *degrees of reality*. Since the *nirguṇa*, according to him, is ultimately real, its contrary, the *saguṇa* cannot be said to be more or less real; on the contrary, it must be regarded as ultimately unreal. But to be unreal is, in the view of Śaṁkara, the same as to be the product of *māyā*, the cosmic principle of illusion. The inevitable corollary of Śaṁkara's distinction between the *nirguṇa* and the *saguṇa* Brahman, then, is the doctrine of *māyā*, together with the consequent denial of the reality of the world. That being so, Rāmānuja, like other theistic absolutists, is under the necessity of dismissing this twofold doctrine of Śaṁkara.

Now, no matter whether or not the admission of the reality of the world is essential to religion as such, there is, perhaps, no doubt that the concept of *nirguṇa* Brahman cannot serve the purpose of theistic religion. For Brahman thus conceived, if not contrary to, is certainly far removed from, the concept of God or *Puruṣottama* (the Supreme Person), the centrality of whom to the theistic religion is unquestionable. Even so, the dismissal of the doctrine of *māyā* and the unreality of the world brings in its train a heavy burden for the theistic absolutists to bear—the burden of explaining the origin of the world regarded as real and, in particular, providing a satisfactory view of the relation between the *saguṇa* Brahman or God on the one hand and the *jīvas* and the *jagat* on the other. As far as Śaṁkara was concerned, he found it easy, no matter whether it was reasonable or not, to hold that the world has the *māyā* as its *material* cause. And thus he saved himself from the difficulty of conceiving Brahman to be subject to *pariṇāma* (modification), which, as we have already seen, the theistic absolutists have not succeeded in overcoming. Then as regards the question of the relation between the Brahman and the world, Śaṁkara, likewise, found it rather easy to answer it by holding that the latter is identical with, and as such is absorbed in, the former in demonstration of its unreality and the ultimate reality of Brahman. But as faras the theistic absolutists are concerned, no matter whether they emphasize the importance of 'difference' (*bheda*) or else of identity or 'non-difference' (*a-bheda*), they, as we have already seen, have really no option but to hold in common the logically absurd view that the relation in question is at once both *identity* and *difference* (*bheda-abheda*). In view of all this, it is necessary to enquire whether Rāmānuja's *Viśiṣṭādvaitavāda* conveys any suggestion towards the successful refutation of Śaṁkara's obnoxious doctrine of the unreality of the world and the resolution of the present difficulties of other Vaiṣnavite metaphysicians.

Now, Rāmānuja, like some other Vaiṣnavite metaphysicians, sought to refute Saṁkara's doctrine of *māyā* on which rests the latter's denial of the reality of the world. His arguments against this doctrine may be briefly stated as follows. In the first place, he urges that *māyā* is inadmissible on the ground that the possibility of its having a *locus* (*āśraya*) is ruled out in view of the consideration that the only two possible alternatives in this regard, namely, the individual self and Brahman are both out of the question, the former being the product of *māyā* and the latter being self-luminous and hence diametrically opposed to the same. Secondly, *māyā* cannot, as according to Śaṁkara it does, conceal Brahman because being self-luminous, there can be no end to its manifestation nor, consequently, the possibility of its concealment.

Thirdly, Śaṁkara holds that Brahman's association with the multiplicity and diversity of objects which constitute the world, while being a fact, is unreal. But Rāmānuja contends that it cannot be unreal in as much as it must have been permitted by Brahman Himself. Fourthly, Saṁkara holds that māyā cannot be either real or unreal. But Rāmānuja contends that that which is neither real nor unreal is absolutely beyond the scope of our apprehension, because, in the light of our apprehension, things are found to be either real or unreal. And to hold that *māyā* is *anirvacanīya* (indefinable), continues Rāmānuja, is to take shelter behind ignorance. Fifthly, Rāmānuja's objection consists in stating that we have no means of ascertaining the existence of *māyā*. Neither perception nor inference nor even scriptual revelation warrants its existence. In particular, *māyā*, to which reference is made in some of the scriptures, represents the creative power of God and not what Śaṁkara means by it, namely, the cosmic principle of illusion. Sixthly, the termination (*nivṛtti*) of *māyā*, objects Rāmanuja, cannot be brought about in the manner suggested by Śaṁkara, namely, by means of the knowledge of the identity of Brahman and the self. The reason for this is simply that such knowledge is not possible. Lastly, even granted that knowledge of this kind is possible, it cannot serve to put an end to *māyā* and its effect in the shape of human bondage. For human bondage consequent upon the influence of *māyā* is not a mere matter of ignorance but is the result of *karma* (action), so that its abolition cannot be brought about by means of abstract knowledge such as the knowledge of the identity of Brahman and the self, but would depend upon the faithful performance of determinate and indeterminate duties, meditation on God and the like.

The above objections of Rāmānuja against Śaṁkara's doctrine of *māyā* do not really have the sense of the refutation of this doctrine. The main reason for this is that they amount to the statement of some of the points in Rāmānuja's own metaphysical theory *vis-a-vis* the corresponding points in Śaṁkara's. In other words, in the name of refuting Śaṁkara's doctrine of *māyā* and *jagatmithyātva*, he has suggested the opposite of this doctrine as its extreme alternative. That being so, Rāmānuja, it may be reiterated, is placed under the obligation of undertaking the constructive task of accounting for the origin of the world regarded as real and offering a view of the relation between the world and Brahman in the divine form as God.

Now in order to have a clear idea of how Rāmānuja has performed this twofold metaphysical task, it would be necessary to ascertain his conception of Brahman in the divine form. Brahman in this form, in his view, is, of course, *determinate* (*saguṇa*) and not indeterminate (*nirguṇa*). And among the qualities he has ascribed to the *saguṇa* Brahman, some are those which have been mentioned in the Upaniṣads, but do not have the special significance of being the qualities of God, as distinguished from the Absolute of metaphysics. Thus the qualities of infinitude, eternity, unconditionedness, unboundedness, omnipresence and the like, which he attributes to God, are equally ascribable to the Absolute in the non-religious context. But then, he, on the other hand, attributes to the Absolute certain other qualities which have an unmistakable religious significance. This is evident from his conception of Brahman as possessed of knowledge (*jñāna*), or rather omniscience and infinite bliss (*ānanda*), as the creator, preserver and destroyer of the world, as the inner Self of the world, as the Lord (*Bhagavāna*) and so on.

But among the qualities ascribed to Brahman in the divine form by Rāmānuja and the other Vaiṣnavite metaphysicians, some are of special importance for our immediate purpose. One of the latter concerns God's creatorship of the world. This gives rise to several questions, only two of which may be considered in this connection. One of them refers to the motivation of divine creation and consists in asking why God created the world in the face of the fact that He is conceived to be self-sufficient. The answer which is usually offered to this question by Indian philosophers and has actually been offered by the theistic absolutists, including Rāmānuja, is that the only motive that led God to create the world is His sportive spirit (*līlā*), together with the idea of the atttainment of pleasure for its own sake. But this is not only vitiated by the fault of anthropomorphism but involves the curious understanding of God on the analogy of immature human beings such as children.

The second of the two questions relates to the material out of which God may be said to have created the world. In other words, it concerns the material cause (*upādāna-kāraṇa*) of the world. As far as Rāmānuja is concerned with this question, he, in agreement with the Sāṁkhya, holds that it is *prakṛti* which is the material cause of the world, and that it is, as a result of a succession of the modification (*pariṇāma*) of *prakṛti*, that the world, consisting of a multiplicity of selves and material objects, has come into existence. But this gives rise to a serious difficulty which may be stated thus. *Prakṛti* must be different from, or else a part or an aspect of Brahman. If the former alternative holds good, then Brahman, contrary to the view of Rāmānuja, ceases to be absolute. If, on the other hand, the latter materializes, there would be no escape from the conception of the Brahman as subject to modification (*pariṇāma*), which is obviously unacceptable to Rāmānuja. The only way out of this *impasse* seems to lie in holding that *prakṛti* is both different and non-different from the Brahman in the divine form. But this is tantamount to inviting a logical contradiction which may not meet with the approval of Rāmānuja.

It follows, then, that Rāmānuja failed in his attempt to explain the origin of the world. And this was bound to be so. For the existence of the world is one of the things which it is incumbent upon the metaphysician to accept as an ultimate datum, instead of trying to show off by making a vain attempt to explain it as Rāmānuja and many other metaphysicians have done. Judged from this point of view, Śaṁkara displayed unusual wisdom and insight in so far as he had recourse to the doctrine of *māyā* in the so-called explanation of the origin of the world. For this device on his part really amounted to admitting that the origin of the world is not amenable to an intelligible explanation, whether scientific or religious or metaphysical.

But even granted that Rāmānuja has succeeded in accounting for the origin of the world, his metaphysical theory entitled *Viśiṣṭādvaitavāda* (qualified non-dualism) should still be in need of being tested with reference to his view of the relation between Brahman in the divine form on the one hand and the *jīvas* and the *jagat* on the other. Now, as previously mentioned, religion in the ordinary sense not only insists on belief in God, but is equally insistent on difference (*bheda*) of the world from God, lest the practical side of religion consisting in the many and various religious practices should be out of the question and, in consequence, religion itself should prove to be inane. It is precisely for this reason that Rāmānuja, whose metaphysical theory, like that of other Vaiṣnavite metaphysicians, was religiously oriented, differed from Śaṁkara in his admission of the difference (*bheda*) between God and the world. But then, mere admission of difference between the two would at best lead to the acceptance of deism, according to which God is exclusively transcendent, that is, external to and so limited by, the world. But, no matter whether or not the deistic conception of God and His relation to the world is in tune with the genuine religious feelings, sentiments and active tendencies of man, there is no doubt that Rāmānuja and other Vaiṣnavite metaphysicians, who were *Brahma-vādins*, that is adherents to the doctrine of the reality of Brahman, could not rest content with deism, but sought after a religion with belief in a God who is not only *transcendent* from, but is also *immanent*, in the *jīvas* and the *jagat*.

So Rāmānuja, like other metaphysicians of his kind, undertook the task of vindicating that form of religion to which is essential the belief in a God who is both transcendent and immanent, that is, both different from, and identical with, the *jīvas* and the *jagat*. But then, he came to realize that the view of God in this light is vitiated by the fault of self-contradiction in as much as *difference* and *identity* or non-difference, being contradictories, are incompatible with each other. And yet, as Rāmānuja insists, God must be shown to be both transcendent and immanent in order that the truth of religion may be vindicated. Accordingly, he hit upon a new way of resolving the conflict between the transcendence and immanence of God. As is indicated by the very title of his metaphysical theory, namely, *Viśiṣṭādvaitavāda*, he holds that the *jīvas* and the *jagat* are the qualities (*viśeṣa*) or adjectives of God regarded as the Substance or Substantive. Since qualities or adjectives are inseparable from the substance or substantive concerned, the *jīvas* and the *jagat*, argues Rāmānuja, are inseparable from God regarded as their substance, so that God may well be held to be immanent in them. But then, the qualities of a thing are irreducible to, and so are different from, the thing itself. That being so, the *jīvas* and the *jagat* as the qualities of God are different from the latter, and, consequently, as Rāmānuja proclaimed, God is transcendent from them.

The fundamental difficulty of the above-mentioned attempt on the part of Rāmānuja to vindicate theistic religion lies on the surface. It consists in the arbitrary ontological interpretation of the logical relation between substance and quality as the relation between difference and non-difference. But even granted that God is *conceivable* as substance and the *jīva* as a quality, and that the relation between the two thus *conceived* is that of difference as well as non-difference, it does not necessarily follow that the relation between God and the *jīva* is, in *reality*, the same as that. So Rāmānuja's present position may be said to be vitiated by a fault similar to that which is involved in the ontological argument for the existence of God. Moreover, the treatment of the tangible world of selves and material objects as quality and the intangible God as substance bespeaks a kind of humility which is at best undignified and at worst uncalled for. Lastly, for the selves and material objects, and especially the former to be the qualities of God is for them to be devoid of any significance of their own. And that being so, Rāmānuja must be said to have tried in vain to rescue the world from the devastating effect of Śaṁkara's doctrine of *māyā*. So we are once more led to the conclusion that Absolutism does not lend itself to theistic interpretation, and that theistic religion is an outrage upon Absolutism. This points towards the Advaitavāda of Śaṁkara which we shall now proceed to investigate.

B

NON-DUALISM

(*Advaitavāda*)

We have already had many indications to the effect that the Advaitavāda of Śaṁkara is predominantly metaphysical, being devoted to the determination of the nature of the Ultimate Reality, which is usually regarded as the main task of metaphysics. But this is far from suggesting that the scope of his metaphysical theory is confined within the bounds of metaphysics. On the contrary, besides making an unusually penetrating and subtle enquiry into the nature of the Ultimate Reality, Śaṁkara has tried to work out the religious and ethical implications of his theory of Reality. And, what is more, he has tried to ascertain the destiny of man in the light of his metaphysical doctrine. Thus Śaṁkara's Advaitavāda is a complete and comprehensive philosophical system with its centre fixed at the view of the Ultimate Reality as 'One without a second.' As far as we are at present concerned with his Advaitavāda, we shall, however, confine ourselves to the understanding of his metaphysical theory, together with its religious implication, in order that his Absolutism may be presented in distinction from the various forms of theistic Absolutism on the one hand and from the Nihilistic Absolutism of the Mādhyamikas on the other.

Now, as regards the question as to what is ultimately real, the Upaniṣadic reply was that 'It is that by knowing which everything is known', and that the 'that' 'is Brahman'. So those among the Indian philosophers who drew inspiration from the Upaniṣads in their enquiry into the Ultimate Reality, were naturally dependent upon the characterization of Brahman which were available in the Upaniṣads. But then, the Upaniṣadic characterizations of Brahman are not always uniform, but, on the contrary, are sometimes mutually conflicting. That being so, the philosophers concerned were required to exercise their independent judgment in utilizing the Upaniṣadic characterizations of Brahman in their own enquiry into the nature of the Ultimate Reality. Now, one of the outstanding ways of the characterization of Brahman adopted in the Upaniṣads, was a negative one indicated by the cryptic statement '*Neti* (not this); *Neti* (not this)'. The importance of this negative statement lies in that it played the crucial role in the determination of the distinction of the absolutist metaphysics of Śaṁkara from the various forms of theistic Absolutism which we have already brought under review.

As far as Śaṁkara was concerned, he understood this statement in a straightforward way and in its strictly literal sense. Accordingly, he arrived at the view that Brahman regarded as the Ultimate Reality is indeterminate (*nirguṇa*). But, no matter whatever may be the advantage or disadvantage of this view, the Vaiṣnavite metaphysicians, on the other hand, held that the statement under consideration signifies the denial of only inauspicious or unseemly qualities to Brahman, implying thereby that Brahman is not indeterminate, but determinate (*saguṇa*), being characterized by the excellent qualities mentioned in the Upaniṣads and elsewhere. However that may be, the difficulty of Śaṁkara's view of the Ultimate Reality as indeterminate can hardly be exaggerated. It is indeed most devastating, cutting the ground as it would do from under the feet of the metaphysical enterprise. For the view of the Ultimate Reality as indeterminate should obviously be the beginning as well as the end of the metaphysical enquiry.

The predicament which thus presented itself could, however, be resolved in any one of three different ways. One of these would consist in holding that metaphysics regarded as the search after the so-called Ultimate Reality in spurious, but that it may still be genuine in the sense of an enquiry into something else that awaits determination. This is precisely the way which points towards the future of metaphysics, but which has so far been left ignored and neglected. The second way is indicated by the view that the conception of the Ultimate Reality as indeterminate is not the beginning, but the end of the metaphysical enquiry, which is reached through the dialectical analysis of the realm of the determinate (*saguṇa*). This is the way which was adopted by the Mādhyamikas, and which ushered into existence what we have called nihilistic Absolutism. But then, nihilistic Absolutism or Śūnyavāda has been left altogether barren, without the fulfilment of its promise of the future of metaphysics which it bears. The third and the last way is that of Śaṁkara which consists in the gradual regression from the indeterminate to the determinate as opposed to the process of gradual progression from the determinate to the indeterminate which constitutes the foundation of the *Śūnyavāda* of the Mādhyamikas. But this way is obviously ruinous to the future of metaphysics, the promise of which was initially held out through the view of the Ultimate reality as indeterminate.

But the question was how Śaṁkara could retrace his steps from the Indeterminate to the domain of the determinate which stood negatived and was thus beyond recognition. The answer was urgently needed, lest his metaphysical enterprise would, so to say, prove to be still-born. This situation of Śaṁkara, if one may say so, is similar to that in which Descartes was placed, as a result of his initial scepticism consisting in his refusal to admit anything determinate as real. And, despite the fundamental difference between the Advaitavāda of Śaṁkara and the Cartesian Dualism, there seems to a parallelism upto a certain point between the ways in which the two philosophers sought to recover the lost ground. If anything other than the *nirguṇa* Brahman must be held to possess at least a semblance of reality, Śaṁkara seems to have argued, it cannot be *alien* to oneself, but must be one's own self as warranted by I-consciousness (*ahaṁpratyaya*), corresponding to the Cartesian *cogito*.

But then, the I, the self or the ego, in the view of Śaṁkara, unlike in the view of Descartes, is, strictly speaking, *not real*; it only serves as the index to the peculiarity of the reality of Brahman. Brahman, then, is spiritual and indeed is possessed of the plenitude of spirituality. This shows how partly on the basis of scriptural authority and partly in virtue of his independent reasoning, Śaṁkara has regressed from the conception of Brahman as indeterminate to the conception of it as the Absolute Self, that is, the Atman. Not only that; the originally empty Ultimate Reality or the *nirguṇa* Brahman comes to be informed with *sat* (existence), *cit* (consciousness) and *ānanda* (bliss) regarded, not as its qualities (guṇa), but as the constituents of its essence. But what else is the Ātman thus conceived than the self or the ego expanded to the extent of infinity?* That being so, Śaṁkara's reinterpretation of the Indeterminate Absolute betrays the folly of anthropocentricism. Thus in his attempt to put the *nirguṇa* Brahman on the way to its determination, he lands himself in a difficulty which reminds us of Descartes' difficulty arising out of his employment of the ontological argument for the restoration of belief in the existence of God.

Śaṁkara's reinterpretation of Brahman as the Ātman did not, however, make any difference to his original view that it is devoid of all kinds of difference—its difference from anything of its own kind (*sajātīya-bheda*), its difference from anything of a different kind (*vijātīya-bheda*) and differences within itself (*svagata-bheda*). That being so, as far as he was concerned, the prospect of the restoration of the world of selves and the world of nature seems to have been out of the question. The theistic absolutists found no difficulty in affirming the reality of this twofold world on the ground of their view of Brahman as being essentially differentiated within itself. Descartes, likewise, found it rather easy to make the same assertion on the ground of the existence of God and with reference to His veracity. But Śaṁkara cound not and, perhaps, also did not avail himself of any such easy and humdrum device for the restoration of the world from the darkness of oblivion to the light of recognition. And yet bent upon the recovery of the lost ground as he was, he hit upon a device to this end which is as objectionable as it is characterized by a measure of novelty and ingenuity which seems to be unprecedented in the history of philosophy. This refers to Śaṁkara's doctrine of *māyā* and the allied concept of Iśvara (God) as well as his theory of causality known as the *vivartavāda* (the doctrine of appearances). These three together, in the view of Śaṁkara, serve a twofold purpose—the restoration of the world to whatever kind of reality may be considered its due, and the presentation of traditional religion in a new perspective—the perspective that may be regarded as just appropriate to it.

It would, however, be of little use to discuss, as it is sometimes discussed, whether Śaṁkara was justified in interpreting the Upaniṣadic concept of *māyā* in the sense of the cosmic principle of illusion as he actually did. Even granted that this concept was taken in the Upaniṣads to mean the creative power of the Brahman, Śaṁkara's

---

* *Vide* my *Glimpses of Indian Wisdom;* Munshiram Manoharlal; New Delhi; pp. 25–26.

reinterpretation of it does not matter in view of the consideration that, despite his being wedded to orthodoxy, he, as a philosopher, must have the freedom to make use of concepts in any manner that suits his philosophical purpose. And it seems that the predicament to which his philosophical position was initially reduced could not be resolved except by means of his new interpretation of the concept of *māyā* and his concept of Iśvara, as distinguished from the Vaiṣnavite concept of the Brahman itself in the divine form. Once Brahman regarded as the Ultimate Reality comes to be conceived, as Śaṁkara conceives it, as *nirguṇa* and untouched by any manner of difference or differentiation, the world characterized by variety and diversity cannot be held to be real in the same sense as Brahman. Nor can it be regarded as the effect produced by Brahman in any of the accredited ways in which effects are produced by causes, lest it should come to be viewed to be as real as the cause by which it is produced. And yet it must be, in a sense, real and, in a sense, also an effect of a cause or causes in order that a place may be assigned to it in the realm of existence. This is precisely the demand which, in the view of Śaṁkara, is fulfilled by means of thc doctrine of *māyā*, the concept of *Iśvara* and the unusual and unprecedented theory of causality known as *vivarta-vāda* (the doctrine of *appearances*).

According to Śaṁkara, *māyā* is the cosmic principle of illusion, but it is such that no explanation can be given about its origin nor can its status be definitely determined. So it may, as he holds, be regarded as beginningless (*anādi*). But then, it cannot be endless (*ananta*); on the contrary, it should be liable to be put an end to, lest the obscuration or concealment of the true nature of Brahman or the Ultimate Reality should, contrary to its inherent demand for its unobstructed self-revelation, come to be viciously perpetuated. The question of the status of *māyā* was, however, found by Śaṁkara to be the most difficult. Accordingly, he had no option but to hold that *māyā* is neither real nor unreal nor both nor neither or, in other words, that it is indefinable or unspeakable (*anirvacanīya*). In this Śaṁkara, obviously, violates the time-honoured 'laws of thought'. But there was for him no way out of this objectionable position, lest the view of *māyā* as real would adversely affect the absoluteness of Brahman and the view of it as unreal would, on the other hand, defeat the purpose of the explanation of the origin of the world, which it is intended to serve.

The most remarkable phenomenon which, in the view of Śaṁkara, presents itself in the background of *māyā* is, however, that *nirguṇa* Brahman *appears* as *saguṇa* Brahman or Iśvara endowed with *māyā* as His creative power and, consequently, the *rationale* of the existence of the world of selves and the world of nature comes within view. For Iśvara bound up with *Māyā* as His creative power is none else than the efficient as well as the material cause of this twofold world. *Māyā* is the source of the nuclei of whatever is due to exist. And Iśvara differentiates them into subtle elements, makes gross elements out of them and finally transforms them into the world. The world thus created by Iśvara is, of course, His modification (*pariṇāma*), but, strictly speaking, or, in other words, judged with reference to *nirguṇa* Brahman regarded as the Ultimate Reality, it is a body of (false) appearances (*vivarta*) as signified by Śaṁkara's doctrine of *jagat-mithyātva* (the unreality of the world).

Thus Śaṁkara, taking his start from the concept of *nirguṇa* Brahman in the background of complete nihilism, finally arrives at the determinate world of the *jīvas* and the *jagat* through the threefold unearthly and perilous path of the doctrine of *māyā*, the conception of Iśvara as the (false) appearance of Brahman and the unusual interpretation of causality in terms of the *vivarta-vāda*. It is therefore no wonder that he should have to entertain the curious view of the ontological status of the world, namely, that it is real and yet not really real. But he tries to avoid this difficulty—for he had no means of resolving it—in a most ingenious way, namely, by distinguishing three distinct dimensions or levels of reality. Thus he holds that the world may be regarded as real provided that its reality is viewed to be qualified as *vyavahārika* (empirical or pragmatic) and to be distinguishable, on the one hand, from the reality of Brahman qualified as *pāramārthika* (transcendental) and, on the other, from the so-called reality of illusory objects such as the snake-in-the-rope or the silver-in-the-nacre qualified as *prātibhāsika* (apparent). In this Śaṁkara comes to admit what the logic of Absolutism necessarily leads to, namely, distinctions of reality. And, whereas in the case of the doctrine of the Concrete Absolute such as that of the Vaiṣṇavites or Hegel, these distinctions are those of the *degree of* reality, in the case of the doctrine of the Abstract Absolute advocated by Śaṁkara, they should naturally be and they actually are distinctions of dimensions, levels or kinds, instead of degrees, of reality.

But then, for a thing to be the reality of a certain kind or a certain dimension and not of another is, obviously, for it to be both real and unreal at the same time. Similarly, for a thing to be real to a certain degree and not to be real to another degree is for it to be real and not to be real at the same time. Hence it is evident that the doctrine of the dimensions, levels or kinds of reality as well as the doctrine of degrees of reality leave the difficulty unresolved, which they are intended to remove—the difficulty involved in a thing's having to be viewed to be both real and unreal at the same time. The main point that deserves to be noted here is, however, that the concept of reality is *existential* and not *evaluative* and, consequently, that, whereas evaluative concepts admit of the distinctions of *kind* as well as *degree*, the concept of reality is recalcitrant to any such distinction, the only kind of distinction that is relevant in connection with it being the distinction between reality and unreality. In fact, reality and unreality, being contraries, are separated by disjunction; so that the admission of kinds or else degrees of reality is, in either case, tantamount to the arbitrary elimination of the ineliminable relation of disjunction between reality and unreality. And this suffices to indicate that Absolutism, in either of the two forms distinguished above, is a failure as a metaphysical theory and, consequently, that the enquiry into the Ultimate Reality is futile.

The anomaly of the status of the world, which, as seen above, is consequent upon its being conceived to be the product of the so-called divine power of *māyā*, should naturally have an important bearing upon the nature of science which is devoted to the investigation of all that happens in the world. Accordingly, science should be in need of being treated as an enquiry set in the background of *nescience* and, consequently, as the bearer of the demand for its transcendence in *wisdom*, consisting in the realization of the identity of the world with the non-dual or undifferentiated Brahman. Since traditional religion, that is, the religion of God conceived to be the creator, preserver and destroyer of the world is, in Śaṁkara's view, set in the same background of nescience as science, it is equally in need of being transcended in the manner of the religious aspirant's rising above the limits of rituals, prayer and worship and his realization of his identity with the 'One without a second', which, according to Śaṁkara, is the goal of the religion of man.

Thus the irrational demand of the doctrine of the abstract Absolute for the appearance of the world of selves and nature in the care of science on the one hand and the religion of God on the other comes to be met with its equally irrational counter-demand for the disappearance of this world with its twin care-takers. And this should happen on no other account than that the impression may be created that as if there were an awakening from a dream, as if nothing were really the matter, as if the world never existed—precisely the impression which is called for by the view of the Ultimate Reality as the unobjective and undifferentiated Absolute. This, it is necessary to note, is of inestimable worth in so far as it conveys the suggestion of the legitimate need for the restraint of this-worldliness and for the recognition of the limitations of science and the religion of God with regard to the fulfilment of the destiny of man. But then, the irony of the situation lies in that Śaṁkara's Absolutism is inseparable from the tragic consequence that human destiny is, as it were, due to be left unfulfilled for ever in as much as man himself has no escape from his disappearance, along with the world, into the abysmal void of the undifferentiated Absolute.

C

NIHILISTIC ABSOLUTISM

(*Śūnya-vāda*)

For the completion of our programme of investigation of the Indian metaphysical theories we are at *last* required to deal with the Śūnya-vāda of the Mādhyamikas which we have previously characterized as nihilistic Absolutism. Against this characterization of the Śūnya-vāda it may, however, be objected that the culmination of this metaphysical doctrine lies, not in nihilism consisting in the denial of all determinate existence, but in a sort of *gnosis*, that is, the intuitive knowledge of the real regarded as the Absolute. But this objection betrays the failure to realize that, unlike the Hegelian dialectical method which consists in the gradual transition from the conflict between an affirmation and a negation to a higher affirmation until the highest affirmation in the shape of the Absolute Idea is arrived at, the Mādhyamika dialectical method is the gradual progression from the conflict between an affirmation and a negation to a higher or more comprehensive negation until the highest or the most comprehensive negation in the form of cosmic negation (*sarva-śūnyatā*) is reached. But even granted that the dialectical method, which is the vehicle of thought, comes to an end with its delivery of the cosmic negation, and that intuition, as distinguished from thought, shoulders the *onus* of further procedure, it is difficult to understand how that which thought has found to be the cosmic negation may, in the light of intuition, present itself to be just its opposite, namely, the cosmic affirmation in the form of the Absolute Reality. It, therefore, seems that the objection under consideration is but the expression of the biased opinion that the protestantism or heterodoxy of Buddhism is only nominal, and that the Buddhist philosophy in its highest development is allied with the teaching of the Upaniṣads and is not far removed from the Vadānta.

That the Śūnya-vāda is nihilistic may be more or less conclusively established as follows. As is well known, the ultimate aim of philosophical investigations, according to the majority of the non-materialistic schools of Indian philosophy, is to determine how man can live in a state of freedom or, in other words, can live a liberated life. But to this end it is first necessary to ascertain what, ultimately, is the hindrance to human freedom or brings about the bondage of man. As far as Buddha was concerned, he was of the view that uncontrolled desire is the root cause of human bondage and the most potent obstacle to man's attainment of real freedom. Accordingly, he came to realize that the control of desires must be the necessary condition of the elimination of human bondage and the surest remedy for the prevailing want of human freedom. Now the control of desires is, of course, a matter of *practice*. But then, practice without a sound theoretical basis for it to stand upon, as he thought, is more likely than not to be fruitless and even misleading. In view of this, Buddha arrived at the conclusion that it would be necessary to accept certain fundamental principles and to meditate upon them in order that desires might be successfully controlled in practice. These are the well known principles of *duḥkha* (suffering), *anitya* (impermanence) and *anātman* (non-self). Since the last two of these principles are of a predominantly metaphysical character, the two Mahāyāna schools of Buddhism, namely, the Yogācāra and the Mādhyamika, which were conspicuous for their extraordinary interest in metaphysical pursuits, sought to develop them as far as possible with special reference to the idea of the control of desires.

The discovery was made by the Yogācāras as well as the Mādhyamikas that desire, like knowledge, is a bipolar phenomenon, involving the *subject* of desire on the one hand and the *object* of desire on the other. So both these schools of metaphysics came to realize that the elimination of desires would depend upon the contemplation of the unsubstantiality of the self (*pudgalanairātma*) as well as of the elements of existence which constitute the object (*dharma-nairātma*). Thus the Yogācāras, the advocates of *Vijñāna-vāda* as they were, sought to demonstrate that the self as well as the object are spurious, and that there is only *vijñāna* (consciousness), so that the possibility of there being any desire at all should be completely ruled out. But the Mādhyamikas went further in getting rid of the last vestige of determinate existence, namely, consciousness, and demonstrating that everything is *śūnya* (void; indeterminate), being devoid of what may be called the 'innate state' (*svabhāva*). In consequence, they found themselves in a position to affirm with perfect certainty that desires are out of place in the entire realm of existence.

Now if the main object of Buddhist philosophy be regarded, as it should certainly be regarded, as the determination of the metaphysical prerequisite of the elimination of desires regarded as the root-cause of human bondage, then the metaphysical doctrine which would be appropriate to this end should naturally be negative in form as well as import. The reason for this is that the demand here is not for the affirmation of anything, but for the negation of a negation, it being understood that human bondage is a deprivation and indeed the worst deprivation that it may be given to man to suffer. Of course, it may be questioned whether the *Vijñāna-vāda* of the Yogācāras or the *Śūnya-vāda* of the Mādhyamikas can really provide the metaphysical foundation of human freedom. But this question, in spite of its relevance, is not of immediate concern in the present connection. The immediate demand of the situation, as already mentioned, is not for the affirmation of anything, but for the negation of a negation; and it is met by the *Śūnya-vāda* of the Mādhyamikas. What may positively follow from the negation of the negation as an accomplished fact is, however, a highly controversial question towards which the attitude of Buddha and Buddhism is that of unmitigated aversion. The point which we are driving at here is really that the distrust in, and the dislike of, nihilism, which seems to be responsible for the ascription of a positive significance to the *Śunya-vāda,* is irrational and uncalled for, especially in view of the fact that hardly any positive doctrine formulated in the philosophical sphere can hold its own or remain unchallenged for long. It is in defiance of this irrational distrust and dislike that the Mādhyamikas have emboldened themselves to declare the Ultimate Reality to be absolutely indeterminate or void (*niḥsvabhāva*), against the remaining schools of Indian philosophy, according to which the ultimate reality or realities, as the case may be, are either really determinate or are at least apparently so.

It is, however, difficult to ascertain whether or not the realistic theory of the Vaibhāsikas had anything either directly or indirectly to do with the development of the *Vijñāna-vāda* and the *Śūnya-vāda.* But there is no doubt that the critical realism of the Sautrāntikas prepared the ground for the emergence of both these metaphysical doctrines of the Mahāyāna section of Buddhism. As we have previously seen, the critical realism of the Sautrāntikas is a form of representationism which consists in holding that the *immediate* object of our knowledge is an idea (*vijñāna*), but that the scope of our knowledge extends further and includes the thing in itself of which the idea concerned is a copy or representation. The question, however, arises as to what the thing in itself is. The reply of the Sautrāntikas is that it is the product of the objectification of the idea which is the immediate content of knowledge. But what else can this mean except that the thing in itself is no objective reality, but is a conceptual construction (*vikalpa*)? So it was easy for the Yogācāras to bring about the transition from critical realism to *Vijñāna-vāda* by holding that there is no such thing as the non-mental object. And further, the object, as distinguished from consciousness, being thus eliminated, the subject, which is nothing but the correlative of the object, is, of necessity, thrown overboard, with the result that the entire realm of existence comes to be conceived as co-extensive with the field of consciousness (*vijñāna-mātra*).

The dialectic of the movement of thought from the critical realism of the Sautrāntikas to the *Vijñāna-vāda* of the Yogācāras, a brief account of which has been given above, was, however, such that it could not reach its culmination without a critical enquiry into consciousness which the Yogācāras came to regard as the Ultimate Reality, in virtue of their resolution of the conflict between the subject and the object. As far as consciousness is concerned, the question arises whether there is any conflict centering round it which proves troublesome and so is in need of resolution. It is precisely this question which exercised the Mādhyamikas, and their reply was in the affirmative. Now the view of consciousness as the Ultimate Reality is not peculiar to the Yogācāras but has also been held by the influential school of the Vedānta in so far as it regards consciousness (*cit*) as an essential constituent of the essence of the Brahman conceived to be the Ultimate Reality. But then, the Vedānta holds that consciousness is essentially permanent, and that differences and changes are falsely superimposed upon it. The Yogācāras, on the other hand, are of the view that consciousness consists of momentary and ever-changing ideas, and that permanence and identity are but conceptual constructions (*vikalpa*) superimposed upon it. So, the Mādhyamikas point out, there arises, in connection with consciousness, a conflict between permanence and momentariness, between identity and difference, which is indeed troublesome and so needs to be resolved by means of the selection or rejection of either the Yogācāra or the Vedānta doctrine of consciousness in as much as the one is as plausible or else as objectionable as the other. Hence follows the Mādhyamika conclusion that both the metaphysical points of view (*dṛṣṭi*) are in need of being dismissed with a view to the apprehension of the Ultimate Reality.

It would be of interest to note, however, that the dialectical method which the Mādhyamikas have employed in the development of their metaphysical theory called *Śūnya-vāda*, and some idea about which has been given above, is essentially the *middle path* which Buddha himself followed and exhorted his disciples also to follow in deciding problems which admit of mutually conflicting solutions. And to follow the middle path, according to Buddha, is to reject both the mutually conflicting alternatives such as 'this is *sat* (existent)' and 'this is *asat* (non-existent)', precisely the step which the Śūnya-vāda recommends for adoption. That the Śūnya-vāda, resulting from the employment of the Mādhyamika dialectic, owes its origin to the teaching of Buddha is also evident from the fact that the law of dependent origination (*pratitya-samutpāda*) which is the central element in the teaching of Buddha, constitutes the very foundation of this metaphysical doctrine of the Mādhyamikas. According to this law, which, in the view of Buddha, is of universal application, nothing can be original (*a-kṛtṛima*) or to be independent of others for its existence or again to come into existence without having a prior existence. That being so, nothing can be said to possess a state of *its own*, that is, 'an innate state' (*svabhāva*); so that statements such as 'this *is* or *is not* in itself such and such' are inadmissible. And this obviously brings out the essential feature of the *Śūnya-vāda*.

It would, therefore, be wrong to hold, as is sometimes held by the students of Buddhism, that Buddha was exclusively concerned with the practical problems of human life and had hardly any interest in metaphysical speculations. Of course, there is no doubt that the practice of metaphysics was not his *forte*. But there is no denying the fact either that his practical teaching was based upon a theoretical foundation which was the result of what may be called the critique of extant metaphysical doctrines. The peculiarity of this critique, which may otherwise be called the dialectic, consists in that it rejects the mutually conflicting metaphysical doctrines without leaving any remainder. And it is this critique which in its further development presented itself as the Mādhyamika dialectic. Now the ordinary speculative tendency is towards judicious acceptance, that is, the acceptance of a number of views as possible alternatives as typified by the *Anekānta-vāda* of Jainism or else the acceptance of the *synthesis* of a number of differing viewpoints which constitutes the Hegelian dialectic. As against either of these two ways of acceptance, there stands the way of total rejection which was suggested by Buddha for the first time in the history of philosophy, and which received its final shape in the hands of the foremost among the Buddhist philosophers like Nāgārjuna, Āryadeva and others.

It is necessary to mention, however, that it is difficult, if not impossible, for the human mind to rest content with a state of pure negation. So there was the inevitable demand for a shift from the position of negation to that of affirmation. But then, the required position of affirmation should on no account be one of those which have already been left behind, lest the carefully planned and well conceived process of negation should prove to be utterly futile. So the demand of the situation really was the complete reorientation of the outlook of metaphysics with regard to its method as well as its subject-matter. But this demand which really conveys the message of Buddha and bears the promise of Buddhism remains unfulfilled till this day. Nevertheless, the need for the replacement of negation by affirmation naturally remained in force, and kept on pressing for its fulfilment. It was, therefore, no wonder that even some of the foremost advocates of the *Śūnya-vāda* should eventually succumb to the influence of the Vedānta and, further, deviate from the spirit of this metaphysical doctrine by way of rehabilitating a form of theism in terms of the view of the Tathāgata (Buddha) as Bhagavat (personal God) endowed with perfection and power. Thus was enacted the tragedy of an unprecedented line of thought which, if it were allowed to bear fruit, could not only bring about a revolution in the realm of philosophy, but, to use a terminology of Karl Marx, change the world.

VI

CONCLUDING REMARKS

The foregoing review of the Indian metaphysical theories may now be brought to a close with a few concluding remarks. In the first place, it needs to be observed that India, like Greece, gave birth to materialsim, but that materialism, as we have previously seen, could not, due to its own folly, prove to be visibly influential in the philosophical sphere in this country. Nevertheless, it left its indelible mark on those schools of Indian philosophy which did not advocate Absolutism as a metaphysical doctrine. This is evident from the fact that the dualistic and the realistic schools of Indian philosophy recognized the independent reality of matter alongside that of spirit without making the least suggestion that matter in any way suffers by comparison with spirit. And this brings us to our second point which consists in stating that it is, perhaps, the implicit influence of materialism which, despite the prevalence of the Upaniṣadic teaching, prevented the large-scale growth of Absolutism which, as mentioned earlier, is more likely to be spiritualistic than materialistic. Thirdly, Absolutism, though it never became the predominant feature of Indian philosophy in general, did come into existence in the shape of the assertion of the central point in the teaching of the Upaniṣads. But curious though it seems, and yet it is true, that Absolutism, which retained its spiritualistic character in the hands of the various kinds of Vedāntists and even the Yogācāras, had eventually to shed it as a result of the Mādhyamikas' view of the Absolute as purely indeterminate. In view of all this, it is no doubt a travesty of fact to hold, as many Western and Indian scholars have held, that Indian philosophy is predominantly spiritualistic.

Fourthly, as has been previously mentioned, the main object of philosophical investigations, according to the majority of the orthodox as well as the heterodox schools of Indian philosophy, is to determine the metaphysical foundation of human freedom or the liberation of mankind. This is especially evident from the emphasis which both Buddhism and the Sāṁkhya laid upon the practical need for metaphysics with respect to the fulfilment of human destiny. Thus the Sāṁkhya declares that it is the knowledge of the fundamental principles underlying the world which alone is the means of the elimination of all kinds of human suffering consequent upon the bondage of man. But even granted that human freedom rests upon a metaphysical foundation, and that the intimate knowledge of it is one of the prerequisites, if not the only prerequisite, of the attainment of freedom, there would arise a serious difficulty which may be stated thus. Since the metaphysical doctrines admitted by the different schools of Indian philosophy are not only different from one another, but are, in some cases, mutually conflicting, it is extremely doubtful whether there can be any such thing as the metaphysical foundation of human freedom and whether it can be definitely ascertained, even if its possibility be taken for granted. Moreover, if the standpoint of the Mādhyamika dialectic is brought to bear upon the present situation, it would inevitably follow that none of the conflicting metaphysical doctrines can provide the metaphysical foundation of human freedom even if it is supposed to have one.

The view of the aim of Indian philosophy as practical in the sense mentioned above, although it is widely prevalent and is usually entertained with enthusiasm, cannot, then, be said to carry conviction. Strictly speaking, the non-materialistic schools of Indian philosophy, like the school or schools of Indian materialism, are devoted to the search after the Ultimate Reality or realities for its own sake and not with a view to the fulfilment of an ulterior end. But this is far from suggesting that the question of the metaphysical foundation of human freedom is illegitimate or uncalled for. Even so the point is whether the metaphysical foundation in question consists in the fundamental principles underlying the world as held by the prominent schools of Indian philosophy or else in the fundamental principles of human conduct. Of course, it may be argued that since man, after all, is a part of the world and, consequently, that his destiny is related to his place in it, the fundamental principles of human conduct cannot be determined without reference to the fundamental principles underlying the world. But this argument, besides being platitudinous, is wide of the mark. The reason for this is that the problem of freedom or liberation arises, not in spite of, but because of, man's place in the world and, consequently, that the fundamental principles of conduct, which may be said to constitute the metaphysical foundation of human freedom, needs to be determined, not with reference to man's relation to the world as such, but with reference to what is really *wrong* about this relation. And what is wrong in this respect needs to be determined, not with reference to the non-human phenomena in the world, but with reference to human affairs. That being so, neither science nor metaphysics in the sense of an enquiry into the reality of the world as a whole can, for obvious reasons, be of any special help in the discovery of the metaphysical foundation of human freedom. This conclusion may be taken to convey the suggestion that ethics and religion, which are primarily concerned with human affairs, may succeed in performing the task of discovering the fundamental prerequisite or prerequisites of the attainment of freedom or liberation, which it is not given to either science or metaphysics in the ordinary sense to perform. How far or whether at all this suggestion is meaningful, it will be a part of our task to determine in the next two parts of this work respectively entitled Indian Ethics and Indian Philosophy of Religion.

VII

INDIAN THEORIES OF CAUSATION

Although reference has been already made to some of the Indian theories of causation at different places in this work, a separate treatment of all of them together may be considered necessary for at least two reasons. In the first place, every metaphysical theory is associated with an appropriate theory of causation. That being so, the various metaphysical theories which have been previously investigated are likely to appear in a clearer perspective in the light thrown upon them by the theories of causation respectively corresponding to them. Secondly, and this is especially important, the novelty of the Indian speculations on the nature of causation seems to be quite impressive so that the theories of causation resulting from them deserve a special investigation.

The principle of causation may be provisionally expressed by stating that nothing happens accidentally, and that all happenings or events are individually due to something which is called their cause. The causal principle thus stated would, of course, present itself to be a commonplace to any adult member of a somewhat civilized society of today. But the human race must have had to wait for centuries before it became mature enough to envisage this principle. Its earliest attitude towards happenings or events coming within the field of its experience, perhaps, manifested itself in the belief that all events are accidental, which is known as *yadṛcchāvāda* in Indian philosophical literature. But not to speak of primitive people with almost no capacity for serious thinking, even advanced people with a pronounced philosophical bent of mind such as the Cārvākas threw the causal principle overboard and had recourse to the doctrine of accidental happenings (*yadṛcchāvāda*). Of course, their admission of this doctrine was not a matter of naïve belief, but was the outcome of their dismissal of the causal principle on the ground that the relation of invariable concomitance between the cause and the effect, which is essential to this principle, is not warranted by experience and so is inadmissible.

But the inadmissibility of the relation of concomitance between the cause and the effect, as seems to have been realized by a later generation of the Cārvākas, need not necessarily lead to the doctrine of accidental happenings, but may well call for another and perhaps a better alternative which, too, might be raised to the status of a doctrine under the title of *svabhāva-vāda* (naturalism). This doctrine, like the earlier one, does not recognize the notion of cause, but regards the so-called effect as *self-existent*, instead of as *accidental*. The attitude towards the phenomena of nature expressible in either *yadṛcchāvāda* or *svabhāvavāda* could not, however, be maintained for all time to come. The orderliness of natural phenomena as exhibited in the inexorable regularity of sunrise and sunset, the changes of seasons, etc. did, in course of time, impress itself upon the Indian mind as it did upon the mind of the ancient Greeks. And already in the Vedic age, the concept of *ṛta*, literally standing for the "course" (of things), but taken to signify immutable and inviolable order, was made use of in the understanding of all events in the domain of nature and, what is more, was regarded as applicable to moral and religious fields as well. Hence followed the inevitability of the recognition of the causal principle in consideration of the fact that this principle is a way of the unfolding of the cosmic order. And there was hardly any school of philosophy in India which did not devote itself to the task of bringing out its implications and thereby construct a theory of causation.

Now, what is required to be done for bringing out the implications of the causal relation is primarily to determine the logical relation between the cause and the effect on the one hand, and the metaphysical relation between the two on the other. As regards the former aspect of the task, it would consist in the decision of the issue as to whether the relation between the cause and the effect is *necessary* or *contingent*. And as far as its latter aspect is concerned, it is a demand for the determination of the existential status of the two in relation to each other. In this connection, it is important to note, however, that philosophy in the West has confined itself to the discussion of the logical question as to whether the causal relation is necessary or contingent, and seems to have been unconcerned with the question concerning the relative existential status of the cause and the effect. Philosophy in India, on the other hand, has preferred to deal with the latter question, not being sure whether the former is legitimate or not. Even so, it should be borne in mind that Indian philosophy, while it was indifferent to the question as to whether the causal relation is *a priori*, that is, universal and necessary or merely probable, recognized—of course, in an indirect manner—the question whether this relation is invariable concomitance or not. In fact, philosophers in India discussed the question of invariable concomitance (*vyāpti*) in connection with their enquiry into the nature of inference with special referencc to the relation between the major term and the middle term in the major premise in a syllogism. And those who admitted the possibility of the relation of invariable concomitance between the two, came to admit the possibility of inference as a legitimate source of cognition. Those, including the Cārvākas and their materialist allies who, on the other hand, denied the possibilty of this relation, dismissed the claim of inference to be a source of cognition at all. However that may be, in its treatment of the problem of causation, Indian philosophy has confined itself to the discussion of what we have characterized as the metaphysical issue, and the various Indian theories of causation are primarily the ways of deciding the same.

As previously mentioned, the Cārvākas and their materialist allies were the only philosophers who did not admit any such thing as *cause* and, consequently, regarded the so-called effect as *accidental* or else *self-existent*. So they cannot be said to have constructed a theory of causation in the sense indicated above. As far as the Buddhists are concerned, their doctrine of *pratitya-samutpāda* (dependent origination) is, of course, diametrically opposed to the Cārvākas' rejection of the causal principle in so far as it consists in holding that nothing is uncaused and that everything is dependent upon something else for its origination. Thus, whereas according to the Cārvākas, the world consists of accidental happenings or self-existent events, the Buddhists are of the view that it is governed by the inexorable law of dependent origination, there being no room within it for any accidental happening or anything that may be called self-existent. But then, the doctrine of dependent origination is not a theory of causation in the sense under consideration because it is, obviously, unconcerned with the question regarding the existential status of the cause and the effect in relation to each other. Even so, as we shall see later, the Mādhyamikas, in course of their pursuit of the dialectical method, dealt with this question and, as a result, arrived at a theory of causation intended to be an alternative to the others of its kind.

Let us now begin by mentioning the chief Indian theories of causation which are three in number and are respectively known as follows:

A. Satkārya-vāda (the doctrine of the pre-existence of the effect) or *Pariṇāma-vāda* (the doctrine of the modifiability of the cause).

B. *Asatkārya-vāda* (the doctrine of the prior non-existence of the effect) or *Ārambha-vāda* (the doctrine of the effect as a new beginning).

C. *Vivarta-vāda* (the doctrine of the effect as *appearance*).

To these three may be added a fourth which, like the third, is unique in the history of philosophy, and may be designated as *Asatkāraṇa-vāda* (the doctrine of non-existence (*asat: śūnya*) as the cause). Now the first among these theories was propounded by the Sāṁkhya and proved to be the most popular in the philosophical atmosphere in India, as is evident from the fact that it was admitted by the Yoga, the Bhagavad Gītā and the Vaiṣnavite schools of the Vedānta founded by Rāmānuja, Nimbārka and Vallabha. The second theory of causation in this list was constructed by the Nyāya-

Vaiśeṣikas and remained confined within the circle of the philosophers belonging to their school of thought. The third was propounded by Śaṁkara and has remained the official theory of causation of the school of Advaita Vedānta. The fourth was the contribution of the Mādhyamikas and indeed is the Buddhist theory of causation *par excellence*. It needs to be added, however, that Jainism cannot be said to have propounded a distinct theory of causation of its own. It held a view of the causal relation which was partly in agreement with Sāṁkhya's *pariṇāma-vāda* and partly at variance with it as well as the Nyāya-Vaiśeṣikas' *asatkārya-vāda*.

The understanding of these theories of causation and, in particular, their difference from one another would, however, be greatly facilitated, if the questions in the answers to which they really consist be first taken into account. The first and the foremost of these questions is whether both the cause and the effect are real or, only one of them is real or, let us say, existent, and the other unreal or non-existent. Secondly, if both of them are real or existent, the question may be asked whether they are so in the same sense or in different senses. Thirdly, the question may arise as to whether or not there is a time-gap between the cause and the effect or, in other words, whether the latter *succeeds* the former or is *simultaneous* with it. Now as regards the first question, the Sāṁkhya-Yoga and the Nyāya-Vaiśeṣika agree in holding that both the cause and the effect are real. The Advaita Vedānta and the Mādhyamikas, on the other hand, offer a negative answer to it, but in two different and indeed diametrically opposite ways. Thus the Advaita Vedānta headed by Śaṁkara regards the cause as real and the effect as of the nature of *appearance* (*prapañca*) and, in a sense, unreal, while the Mādhyamikas conceive the cause as unreal or non-existent and the effect as real or existent.

As regards the second question, the answer of the Saṁkhya-Yoga consists in holding that the effect is a modification (*pariṇāma*) or, let us say, a mode of the cause and, consequently, that the cause is real in a *primary* sense, while the effect is so in a *secondary* sense, the relation between the two being expressible in terms of the category of substance-mode. The Nyāya-Vaiśeṣikas, on the other hand, do not understand the relation between the cause and the effect in terms of this category and, in fact, regard the effect as a new creation (*ārambha*) out of the destruction of the cause. In consequence, they find themselves in a position to hold that the cause and the effect are both real and in one and the same sense, despite the difference of their respective nomenclature. As far as the Advaita Vedānta and the Mādhyamikas are concerned, it seems at first sight that, in view of their answer to the first question, the question under consideration does not arise in their case. But while this is true, there may still arise the question of the ontological distinction between the *absolute* and the *relative*, instead of the similar kind of distinction between independent reals or between substance and mode. And judged from this point of view, the cause, according to the Advaita Vedānta, is *absolutely* real, while the effect is only *relatively* (that is, empirically or pragmatically) so, it being understood, however, that Brahman is the cause *par excellence* and everything else is an effect. The Mādhyamikas, likewise, are of the view that the reality of the effect is only *relative*, but that the absolute is not reality, being or existence, as in the view of the Advaita Vedānta, but unreality, non-being or non-existence called *Śūnya*, which, strictly speaking, is the all-pervasive cause.

It needs to be noted, however, that the Advaita Vedānta, an adherent of *ātma-vāda* (the doctrine of substance) as it is, is of the view that the cause, that is, Brahman, is substance and, consequently, that the effect is transformation (*pariṇāma*) of the cause—but transformation which in this case is really distortion or falsification. The Buddhists in general and the Mādhyamikas in particular are, on the other hand, opposed to *ātma-vāda* and, consequently, are precluded from regarding the effect as the transformation (*pariṇāma*) of the cause in any sense whatsoever. In fact, they replace the *ātma-vāda* of the orthodox schools of Indian philosophy by their *kṣanika-vāda* (the doctrine of momentariness) or the concept of *substance* by that of temporal series. That being so, the relation between the cause and the effect, on their view, cannot be construed in terms of the category of the substance-mode, but must be the same as the relation between the antecedent and the consequent. This brings us to the last of the three questions raised above which calls for the decision as to whether or not there is a time-gap between the cause and the effect.

As far as this question is concerned, Buddhism's answer, as seen above, is in the affirmative for the simple reason that it substitutes the concept of temporal series for that of substance which presupposes the denial of the ultimate reality of time, and, consequently, is recalcitrant to the temporality of the causal relation. But this is far from suggesting that the understanding of the relation of the cause and the effect as that of the antecedent and the consequent instead of as substance and mode, must go hand in hand with the view, as held by the Mādhyamikas, that the cause is non-being or *Śūnya*. As we shall see later, this view of the Mādhyamikas is untenable. But their recognition of the essential temporality of the causal relation is an unmistakable testimony of their exceptional philosophical insight. It is precisely this insight which remained outside the reach of the Sāṁkhya and its followers on the one hand and the Advaita Vedānta on the other, on account of their adherence to *ātma-vāda* and the consequent view of the cause as *substance*. In fact, both these schools of Indian philosophy missed the truth that something is a cause not in itself, but only in relation to something else called its effect. This means that the concept of cause is *relative* and, consequently, that it cannot be represented by the concept of substance which is absolute. The attempt on the part of the Sāṁkhya and the different schools of the Vedānta, including the Advaita Vedānta, to remove this difficulty by regarding the effect as the mode (*pariṇāma*) of the cause regarded as substance is at best a subterfuge. The category of substance and mode, it would be of interest to note, is the metaphysical counterpart of the logical category of ground and consequence. And this would suffice to indicate that the understanding of the relation between the cause and the effect in terms of the former category is as arbitrary and unwarranted as is the understanding of it in terms of the latter category by the rationalist philosophers in the West most prominently represented by Spinoza.

Now it was sufficiently demonstrated in the West especially by David Hume that the recognition of the inherent temporarlity of the causal relation and the consequent understanding of the relation of the cause and the effect as that of the antecedent and the consequent presuppose the dismissal of the way of interpreting things in terms of the category of substance. But, curiously enough, the Nyāya-Vaiśeṣikas, on the contrary, held that *ātma-vāda* (the doctrine of substance) is not incompatible with the temporality of the causal relation, and that one may admit this doctrine and yet affirm, without contradicting oneself, that the effect is divided from the cause by a time-gap and as such is related to the latter as its consequent instead of as its mode (*pariṇāma*). Their reason for this is that the effect cannot come into existence so long as the cause retains its self-identity and does not cease to exist, and that its coming into existence *follows upon* the destruction of the cause. But this admission of the destructibility of the cause on their part amounts to the surrender of the concept of substance which is basic to their understanding of things, including those that are said to be causes. Hence it is evident that the Nyāya-Vaiśeṣikas, unlike other advocates of the doctrine of substance, proved faithful to *fact*—the fact of the temporality of the causal relation in this case—at the sacrifice of *consistency* of thought by means of ascribing destructibility to substance which is, according to them and by definition, indestructible.

As seen above, the Nyāya-Vaiśeṣikas, on the one hand, conceive the effect to be *non-existent* in the cause as is signified by the designation of their theory of causation as *asatkārya-vāda*. On the other hand, they hold that it *begins* to exist subsequently to the destruction of the cause as is implied by the alternative designation of their theory of causation as *ārambhavāda*. But both these ways of characterizing the effect and the consequent way of conceiving the relation between the cause and the effect as that of succession, instead of co-existence, are, in the view of the Sāṁkhya, tantamount to a gross misunderstanding of the causal principle. Its reasons for this, which in fact constitute the main thesis of its theory of causation called *satkārya-vāda*, are as follows.

In the first place, the effect must be pre-existent in the cause, because if it is not so, it would be a sheer non-entity and because a non-entity cannot be said to be brought into existence. Secondly, only certain things are chosen as causes for the production of certain effects, which implies that the effect is pre-existent in the cause. Thus oil-seeds, and not pieces of wood, are chosen for the production of oil, because oil is potentially present in them. Thirdly, since it is not a fact that everything can be produced everywhere or by anything and everything, it follows that the cause and the effect are inseparably bound up together or, in other words, are co-existent. Fourthly, since the cause must be such that it has the requisite power to produce, and the effect, on the other hand, must be such that it is fit to be produced, it follows that the effect must exist before it is produced, for, otherwise, it cannot be a fit effect to be produced. Lastly, the effect must be homogeneous with the cause just as the cloth which is made of yarns is homogeneous with the latter, which implies that the effect exists in the cause.

Now the above arguments advanced by the Sāṁkhya in support of its own *satkārya-vāda* and against the *asatkārya-vāda* of the Nyāya-Vaiśeṣikas are, obviously, not independent of one another, but are, in the final analysis, different ways of expressing the main thesis of *pariṇāma-vāda* which consists in stating that the cause and the effect are consubstantial, the difference between the two lying in that the former is *substance* and the latter its *mode*. But the question is whether the view of the effect as the mode of the cause regarded as substance is a faithful representation of the real nature of the causal relation.

The decision of this question, it is important to note, would depend upon the consideration of the apparent anomaly involved in the causal relation which consists in that the effect, for example, smoke is, in a sense, *inseparable* from the cause, namely, fire, and yet exists separately from the latter. It is on this anomaly that the majority of the theories of causation, whether Indian or Western, have foundered. As regards the Indian theories of this kind, the *pariṇāma-vāda* or *satkārya-vāda* of the Sāṁkhya has obviously emphasized the importance of the inseparability of the effect from the cause to the utter neglect of the separateness of the former from the latter. The *asatkārya-vāda* or *ārambhavāda* of the Nyāya-Vaiśeṣikas, on the other hand, attached undue importance to the separateness of the effect from the cause, ignoring altogether the inseparability of the former from the latter. Hence it is evident that the Sāṃkhya and its followers on the one hand and the Nyāya-Vaiśeṣikas on the other produced a travesty of the causal relation on account of their failure to view the causal relation in its entire perspective.

It may be worthwhile to note in this connection that the conflict between the Sāṁkhya and its followers on the one hand and the Nyāya-Vaiśeṣikas on the other is comparable to the conflict between the Western rationalists who understood the causal relation in terms of the relation between ground and consequence and the empiricists headed by Hume who interpreted the relation between the cause and the effect as the relation between the antecedent and the consequent. The difference between the two kinds of conflict, be it noted, lies in that the former is *metaphysically* oriented, whereas the latter is set in a *logical* background. However that may be, there was the need in India as well as in the West for the realization that the proper understanding of the causal relation is dependent upon the recognition of the inseparability of the effect from the cause and its separateness from the latter at the same time. But the fact in this regard is that it is not in India, but in the West that this realization came about in the shape of Kant's unique and unprecedented suggestion that propositions concerning the causal relation should be *a priori* as held by the rationalists and *synthetic* as held by the empiricists led by Hume.

It is far from us to suggest, however, that Kant has succeeded in showing that propositions concerning the causal relation are *a priori* and synthetic. On the contrary, he seems to have failed to do that. And the reason for this, perhaps, is that the question of the nature of the causal relation falls outside the sphere of logic (or epistemology) as well as metaphysics, and that it may be most suitably investigated within the field of theoretical physics. Even so Kant's realization of the need for the understanding of the causal relation with reference to the effect's inseparability as well as its separateness from the cause stands as a landmark in the history of philosophy and a perpetual warning to those whose mind is too slothful to make an attempt to see the whole truth about the causal relation. In contrast with this, stand the performances of the Mādhyamika school of Buddhism and the Advaita Vedānta. Far from even recognizing the need for the vindication of the twofold relation of the effect to the cause, both these schools of Indian philosophy made short work of the apparent anomaly of the causal relation: the former did this by treating the cause as non-existent (nothing or Śūnya) and the latter by denying the reality of the effect, as a testimony to the abuse of metaphysics in either case. The conclusion that forces itself upon us is, then, that the net result of philosophical investigations of the causal relation in India is no less disappointing than that which the philosophers in the West have produced by means of their investigation of the same phenomenon through the centuries.

PART 3

Indian Ethics

INTRODUCTION

As previously mentioned, the aim of philosophical investigations, according to the majority of the schools of philosophy in India, is not purely *theoretical*, but predominantly *practical*. That being so, it is presumable that ethics should have an important role to play in philosophical enquires in India. And as a matter of fact, most of the major schools of Indian philosophy have taken great pains to answer the question as to how life can be best lived, no matter whether their answers are satisfactory or not. But then, it has often been held especially by Western scholars of Indian philosophy and culture that philosophy in India is conspicuous for its indifference to, and even escapism from, the problems of morality strictly so called. As regards this view, it seems to be the outcome of a mistaken view of the nature of Indian philosophy *in general* which is derived from a superficial understanding of *some* of the Indian philosophical doctrines such as the so-called pessimism of Buddhism and the Sāṁkhya, the doctrine of the illusoriness of the world (*jagatmithyātva*) advocated by the Advaita Vedānta, the *Śūnyavāda* (the doctrine of the Void) of the Mādhyamikas and the like.

Of course, these doctrines seem at first sight to be antithetical to the moral aspirations of man in as much as they may be said to be, in one way or another, tantamount to the denial of the future of man which is but another name for the negation of the possibility of the realization of any ideal, whether moral or other, which he may be said to cherish. But then, it is seldom realized that behind their superficial interpretation there lies their deeper significance which consists in their conveying the demand for the restraint of the excess of this-worldliness which is the *conditio sine qua non* of the realization of the ideal or ideals of human life.

Apart from this, it is certainly arbitrary and unwarranted to attempt, as many Western scholars of Indian philosophy have from time to time attempted, to fit the diverse philosophical systems of India into a Procrustean bed and thereby argue that the outlook of Indian philosophy in general is non-moral or even anti-moral. But if an impartial and unprejudiced enquiry be made into the treatment of the problems of human life by the different schools of philosophy in India, it will be found that most of the problems which are usually discussed by Western writers on ethics have received due consideration in the field of Indian philosophy.

True, problems like that of the nature of ethical propositions, which have been recently raised by Western writers on ethics under the influence of the so-called 'revolution' in philosophy marked by he emergence of linguistic philosophy, did not naturally have any chance of being treated by Indian ethics. But that does not really matter. For it is a highly debatable question whether problems of this kind, which obviously pertain to the logic of language, should have a place in the field of moral philosophy, and, in particular, whether the treatment of them would in any way contribute to the determination of the criterion of the distinction between good and evil, right and wrong, or the understanding of the nature of the moral ideal which seems to be the main task of ethics. Another point that deserves notice in this connection is that in the West, ethics in its developed form presented itself in the beginning as a part or an aspect of politics. This is particularly evident from the conception of this academic discipline entertained by Plato and Aristotle. But it was due to the advent of the Christian outlook on life in Europe that Western ethics, sometimes, though not always, succeeded in extricating itself from the influence of politics. Even so it has, perhaps, never been strictly autonomous, being sometimes dependent upon metaphysics and at other times upon some of the positive sciences and especially psychology and biology. As regards Indian ethics, it does not seem to have ever been allied with politics. But being predominantly practical in outlook and thus being characterizable as applied ethics, its beginning, on the other hand, was *ritualistic*. Due to a subsequent rise of a revolt against ritualism, Indian ethics, however, came to acquire an anti-ritualistic trend, although ritualism does not seem to have ever lost its importance altogether in the Indian view of the realizability of the moral ideal. In any case, in spite of its relative freedom from ritualism, Indian ethics, like its counterpart in the West, was never completely autonomous, but was dependent upon metaphysics on the one hand and psychology on the other.

Besides the points of agreement and difference between Indian and Western ethics, some of which have been indicated above, the former possesses at least one characteristic which serves to bring out its most outstanding difference from the latter and indeed place it in a class apart from ethics as it is usually understood to be. The characteristic in question consists in the recognition of the all-importance of the ethico-spiritual ideal of *mukti*, *mokṣa*, *kaivalya* or *nirvāṇa* in human life and the attempt to determine the way to the realization of this ideal.

Now, Indian ethics, it is important to note, has passed through a gradual process of development from one stage to another, corresponding to the development of morality itself from a lower stage of customary or objective morality to a higher stage of reflective or, let us say, subjective morality and from the latter to the highest or the absolutist stage, marked by the emergence of the most highly developed consciousness of the ethico-spiritual ideal of *mokṣa* or any one of its equivalents, attended with the most earnest feeling of the need for its realization. But in course of its development in this manner, Indian ethics has, on the one hand, dealt with the usual question concerning the standard of morality and has, on the other, insisted on the excellence of the notion of *ahiṁsā* (non-violence) as a guide to the conduct of moral life. In view of all this, the salient features of the scope of Indian ethics may be stated as follows :

(i) Objective Morality : Classification of duties
(ii) Reflective Morality :
  A. The psychological basis of Ethics
  B. Virtues and their classification
(iii) The Moral Standards
(iv) The Ethics of Non-Violence
(v) The Ethico-spiritual Ideal of *Mukti, Mokṣa, Kaivalya* or *Nirvāṇa* and the Way to its Realization.

But then, the last of these topics, as we have previously indicated time and time again and shall explain in due course, falls outside the scope of ethics as it is ordinarily understood, and is just fit for inclusion within what in the Indian context should be called Philosophy of Religion. So in this part of the work we shall be required to deal with the first four topics in the above list. Let us then proceed to the treatment of them separately and in the order in which they have been mentioned here.

I

OBJECTIVE MORALITY : CLASSIFICATION OF DUTIES

It is necessary to observe at the outset that morality, although it has much to do with *outward* actions, is a predominantly inward phenomenon, concerning as it mainly does the motive of the agent, his freedom of the will, allied with his sense of responsibility and obligation. Understood in this sense morality is reflective or subjective. But then, reflective morality is not *sui generis*. On the contrary, it is a development from a lower form of morality characterizable as customary or objective which is embodied in a code of external acts and bears the demand for outward conformity to the same. The claim of the so-called objective morality to be recognized as a form of morality is, however, justifiable on the ground that it is a means of the establishment as well as the maintenance of social order, and especially that it marks an early stage in the evolution of morality and indeed is the groundwork of morality strictly so called. It is with objective morality thus understood that we are immediately concerned.

The code of external acts in which objective morality is embodied is held by Indian ethics to comprise two kinds of *dharmas** (duties), respectively called *varṇāśrama-dharmas* (duties pertaining to one's social class and one's specific stage in life) and *sādhāraṇa-dharmas* (common duties, that is, duties which are equally binding on all the members of the community). Now, as is well known, the *varṇas* recognized by Indian sociology are four in number, namely, the *Brāhmanas* (those who are devoted to learning and intellectual and spiritual pursuits), the *Kṣatriyas* (the warrior class which is responsible for the protection of the community against internal as well as external dangers), the *Vaiśyas* (those who are devoted to agriculture, industry and trade) and, lastly, the *Śudras* (those who are required to devote themselves to the service of all). The basis of this division of the community into the four *varṇas* is obviously *functional*. And it is on this account that the sociologists in ancient India, like Plato in ancient Greece, thought that the division of the community into functionally distinct classes is the best means of the promotion of its welfare. Like the concept of *varṇa*, the concept of the *āśramas* (stages of life), according to those who were interested in social organization in ancient India, represents a principle of the regulation of social life. And the *āśramas* recognized by them were also four in number, namely, the *Brahmacārin* (the student), the *Gṛhastha* (the house-holder), the *Vānaprasṭhī* (the forest-dweller) and, lastly, the *Sanyāsin* (the ascetic). It would be of interest to note in this connection that, despite the influence which the two regulative principles of social life wielded in the early history of India, departures were sometimes made from their strict observance in practice. However that may be, the fact remains that Indian ethics, in its formative period, built up a moral code by including within it the *varṇāśrama-dharmas* (the duties relating to the four social classes and the four specific stages of the life of the individual).

As regards the *varṇāśrama-dharmas*, it is important to note that they are of a *relative* character, being applicable to a certain social class and not to another and to a certain stage in an individual's life and not to another. And judged in this light, the duties relating to specific social classes and specific stages in individual life may be said to constitute the sphere of what Kant called 'hypothetical imperatives'. But then, they are not hypothetical in the

* Although the word 'dharma' is used in the sense of virtue as well as in the sense of religious merit, here it means 'duty'.

Kantian sense in as much as they are not conditioned by the subjective choice of the individual on whom they are binding. On the contrary, they are *unconditionally* or *categorically* obligatory in the spheres to which they are respectively applicable. Thus the duties prescribed for the observance of *Kṣatriyas* are unconditionally binding upon any and every *Kṣatriya,* although they have nothing to do with another social class, say, *Brāhmana,* or *Vaiśya* or *Śudra.* The same is true *mutatis mutandis* in the case of the duties relating to the different specific stages in individual life. The fact that stands out, however, is that, on account of its recognition of the duties relating to specific stages in individual life, in addition to those which relate to specific social classes. Indian ethics is at once both individual and social and as such is more comprehensive than that of Plato which is predominantly, if not exclusively, social.

Lest a code constituted merely by relative duties should be inadequate as a guide to the conduct of moral life, Indian ethics has admitted a code of common duties (*sādhāraṇa-dharmas*) which it is incumbent upon every man to observe, irrespective of his position in society or his individual capacity. The idea underlying the recognition of the *sādhāraṇa-dharmas* is that every man is born with a number of debts (*ṛṇas*) to be paid off, including those which he respectively owes to the society into which he is born and to mankind in general with which he is united by the tie of common humanity. As regards the former of these two debts, he can pay it off by means of the observance of the *varṇāśrama-dharmas.* And in order to make it possible for him to pay off the latter, Indian ethics found it necessary to admit *sādhāraṇa-dharmas.* The admission of these *dharmas* is intended to put a check upon individual and social egoism which the scheme of *varṇāṣrama-dharmas* is apt to beget and thereby bring about a just and fair adjustment of the interests of individuals and societies to the wider interests of humanity at large.

CLASSIFICATION OF DUTIES

As we have seen above, objective morality, which Indian ethics admits in distinction from other forms of morality, including subjective morality, is held by it to be constituted by *dharmas* (duties). And as regards the *dharmas,* they are regarded by it as external acts to which outward conformity is due. We have already mentioned two kinds of duties understood in this sense, namely, the *varṇāśrama-dharmas* and the *sādhāraṇa-dharmas,* and have thus presented a classification of them which was, perhaps, made for the first time by Manu. But then, the difficulty of Manu's classification of duties consisted in that the duties which he brought under the head *sādhāraṇa-dharma** aim at the attainment of the individual's moral perfection, but are devoid of any *positive social significance* and, consequently, that the ethics of sociality came to be sacrificed at the altar of extreme individualism. This was, however, due to the fact that in his understanding of the duties of the moral aspirant, Manu was under the overwhelming influence of the Hindu view of individual self-sufficiency as the ideal of human life. According to this view, every man is a law unto himself and the arbiter of his own destiny; so that social duty is of no avail and social service is a contradiction in terms. The truth, on the contrary, is that it is not the concept of sociality, but that of individual self-sufficiency which is at fault. And it is the failure on the part of Manu to realize this truth which has vitiated his understanding of the *sādhāraṇa-dharmas*.

But then, it is far from suggesting that the ethics of Manu is egoistic. On the contrary, the fact is that the Manusaṁhitā, like the Epics, the Mahābhārata and the Rāmāyana, advocates altruism in so far as it insists on the importance of the observance of *ahiṁsā* (non-injury; non-aggression) in the conduct of the practical affairs of the individual and society. But the drawback here is that *ahiṁsā*, even granted that it has a positive significance, is more likely than not to be ineffective on account of its indefiniteness consequent upon its negative formulation. So in order that the inadequacy of the ethics of individual self-sufficiency could find its remedy in the ethics of sociality, the concept of *ahiṁsā* was in need of being supplemented by a concept or concepts which would present its positive significance in the clearest perspective. An attempt has been made in this direction by some of the schools of Indian philosophy, including the Nyāya as represented by Praśastapāda.

Like Manu, Praśastapāda classifies the duties under two broad heads which he respectively calls *sāmānya-dharmas* (common or generic duties) corresponding to the former's *sādhāraṇa-dharmas*, and *viśeṣa-dharmas* (specific or relative duties) which Manu designated as as *varṇāśrama-dharmas*. As regards the second class of duties, it is, according to Praśastapāda, of two kinds, namely, those which respectively concern the different social classes (*varṇas*) and the different stages of life (*āśramas*). It would, however, be unnecessary for our immediate purpose to go into the details of Praśastpāda's classification and enumeration of the various duties coming under the head *viśeṣa-dharma*. What is especially important about his

* These are the duties which, according to Manu, constitute the sādhāraṇa-dharmas : dhṛti (steadfastness); kṣamā (forgiveness); dama (application); cauryābhāva (non-appropriation; avoidance of stealing); śauca (cleanliness); indṛiya-nigraha (control of the sensibilities and sensuous appetites); dhi (wisdom); vidyā (learning); satya (truthfulness) and akṛodha (restraint of anger).

view of objective morality in the present connection is the improvement he has made upon Manu's treatment of the common duties of men, irrespective of the differences of their *varṇa* and *āśrama*. And the improvement lies in his recognition of the negative duty of *ahiṁsā* (non-injury), together its definitely positive counterpart consisting in *bhutahitatva* (good-will to all creatures). Thus does Praśastapāda present a more comprehensive and indeed humanitarian ideal of life in the realization of which the individual could conquer his illusory self-sufficiency and enter into communion with his fellows, and thereby pay off the debt he owes to mankind. Hence it is evident that the promise of the ethics of humanity, which is borne by the recognition of common duties in distinction from specific duties and which remained unfulfilled in the case of Manu, is directed towards its fulfilment by Praśastapāda.

Another way of the classification of duties, which is different from that of Manu as well as the Naiyāyikas, has been adopted by the Mīmāṁsā school of Indian philosophy. The two main classes here are not the *generic* and the *specific,* but the *laukika* (secular) and the *pāramārthika* or *śāstrika* (transcendental or scriptural). The *laukika* duties concern the natural life of man and so are derived from experience as to what is beneficial or else harmful to him. That being so, the authority that is attached to them is only relative and problematic and by no means infallible or absolute. So ethics, in so far as it is merely concerned with the *laukika* duties, is purely relativistic and does not deserve to be called ethics in the strict sense of the term. It is precisely in view of this difficulty that the Mīmāṁsakas admit such things as the *pāramārthika* duties. Even so, they are careful enough to note that the *pāramārthika* duties include *kāmyakarmas* (duties conditional upon individual desires) in addition to the *nityanaimittikakarmas* which are duties characterized by unconditional authority, and, consequently, that in its concern with the *kāmyakarmas*, ethics is open to the limitation of relativism, and so is far removed from what it ought to be. As regards the *nityakarmas* and the *naimittikakarmas*, the former are unconditionally obligatory for all time, whereas the latter are equally unconditionally obligatory but only when their *nimittas* or special occasions arise. But since both of them are unconditionally obligatory, ethics, in so far as it is concerned with them, is, at least in theory, the universal ethics of humanity, as distinguished from relativistic ethics, whether individualistic or socialistic or rather communalistic. Thus the admission, on the part of the Mīmāṁsakas, of the *pāramārthikakarmas* in distinction from the *laukikakarmas* serves more or less the same purpose as is served by the admission, on the part of the Naiyāyikas, of the *sāmānya-dharmas* in distinction from the *viśeṣa-dharmas*.

Besides the three types of classification of duties which we have already considered, there is a fourth which may be called a *deduction* rather than a classification of duties. It has been offered by Rāmānuja, the founder of the *Viśiṣṭādvaita* school of Vedānta philosophy. According to him, God is the Moral Ideal and as such is endowed with moral perfection. That being so, the duties of man, as Rāmānuja seems to have thought, are easily and conveniently determinable with reference to the various moral charateristics with which God is endowed. So just as the secular duties of man, in the view of the Mīmāṁsakas, are inductively deducible from the experience of what actions are beneficial and what are harmful to him, so all common duties of man, according to Rāmānuja, are deductively deducible from the consideration of the various aspects of divine perfection.

Now the conception of God as the moral ideal involves the attribution of certain excellent or auspicious qualities (*kalyāna-guṇa*) to Him. Thus God as Lord (*Bhagavāna*) is conceived to be invested with the responsibility for the removal of whatever is evil and imperfect in finite beings even as light is singularly fitted to dispel darkness. This, in other words, means that the absolute knowledge that is in God is but the active enlightening of His creatures who are held in incessant and inseparable relations to Him, but are ignorant of their own good and evil. Secondly, God is conceived to be Almighty. But since His might is an aspect of His moral perfection, He uses it for the noble purpose of enabling His weak and helpless creatures to avoid whatever is evil and pursue all that is good. Thirdly, allied with His might thus understood, is His *forgiveness* for those who are guilty of moral slips, but are brought to the consciousness of the error of their ways of behaviour and are really penitent. Lastly, to crown His moral perfection, He is endowed with the quality of *compassion* for His suffering creatures. These being the different aspects of divine perfection, it is, in the view of Rāmānuja, incumbent upon human individuals to mould their lives after the pattern of the Life Divine. Accordingly, the primary duties of man should be (a) to use his knowledge for the achievement of the highest end, consisting in the enlightenment of his ignorant fellows, (b) to employ his power for no other purpose than that of enabling his helpless fellows to realize their own good; (c) to forgive those who are morally guilty, but are penitent; (d) to cultivate the attitude of compassion for the suffering humanity, so that the burden of suffering it has to bear may be lightened.

This classification or rather deduction of duties, unlike those of Manu, the Naiyāyikas and the Mīmāṁsakas, is ethico-theological, they being held to be ontologically implied in the different aspects of the perfection of the Divine Being. The idea underlying it is that man, strictly speaking, is a veritable image of God, and, consequently, that his ultimate destiny lies in the vindication, by his way of life, of the truth that he is that. However that may be, there is no doubt that the duties deducted by Rāmānuja are common (*sādhāraṇa* or *sāmānya dharmas*), as distinguished from the duties aiming at self-culture or else communal welfare. That being so, he, like the Naiyāyikas and the Mīmāṁsakas, may be said to have a universal ethics of humanity in view. And this is due to the prevalence, among the orthodox schools of Indian philosophy, of the view that of the various debts which it is incumbent upon man to pay off, the most important is that which he owes to mankind in general (*manuṣya-ṛṇa; ṛṣi-ṛṇa*) and that he can pay it off only by dedicating himself to the service of humanity.

It would be of interest to note in this connection that the types of classification of duties, which we have so far considered, agree in admitting common duties in distinction from specific duties. It is on this account that they envisage the possibility of the universal ethics of humanity in distinction from the ethics of individual self-culture and the ethics of communal welfare. But there is another classification of duties—if it may be so called at all—which amounts to the admission of specific duties (*varṇāśrma-dharmas*) on the one hand and of the absence or negation of duties on the other. This is precisely the classification which may be said to have been offered by Śaṁkara, the foremost protagonist of the Advaita Vedānta. According to him, the observance of the *varṇāśrama-dharmas* constitutes the external discipline which is the necessary preliminary step towards the attainment of the ideal of human life, consisting in the realization of the identity of the individual self with the Absolute self that is Brahman. And in order that this external discipline may serve a useful purpose there arises the need for an internal discipline which, in the view of Śaṁkara, is consequent upon the awareness of the distinction between the eternal and the non-eternal, the cultivation of the feeling of detachment from all selfish desires for earthly and even heavenly good, the development of the qualities of tranquillity (*śama*), restraint (*dama*), resignation (*titikṣā*), renunciation (*uparati*), concentration (*samādhi*) and steadfastness of mind (*śṛaddhā*) and lastly, an intense desire for liberation (*mokṣa*). The accomplishment of this internal discipline on the part of the aspirant for liberation (*mumukṣu*), in the view of Śaṁkara, is followed by his realization (*anubhava*) of his identity with Brahman and, consequently, his admission into a sphere which is beyond good and evil and where duties *eo ipso* are out of place and actions performed are invariably spontaneous. So, as Śaṁkara may be said to have held, there can be no such thing as the universal ethics of humanity; there is only a religion instead—not the religion of God, but the religion of salvation.

Now, as previously seen, the common duties are unconditional, being obligatory on every man, irrespective of his *varṇa* (social class) and his *āśrama* (specific stage in life). The specific duties, on the other hand, are hypothetical or conditional, being relative to one's *varṇa* and *āśrama*. That being so, the heterodox schools of Indian philosophy, whether Lokāyata or Jaina or Bauddha, which do not recognize such things as *varṇa* and *āśrama*, cannot speak of common duties in distinction from specific duties. In their view, duties, if there should be any, must needs be unconditional and common to all men. But that does not mean that they are all equally advocates of the possibility of the universal ethics of humanity. On the contrary, those who belong to the Lokāyata school hold that the highest and most fundamental duty of every man is to attain for himself the greatest pleasure with the least admixture of pain. Theirs then is the egoistic ethics of the hedonistic type which is diametrically opposed to the universal ethics of humanity under consideration.

As far as Jainism is concerned, the duties recognized by it such as vows (*vrata*), restraints (*gupti*), meditations (*anuprekṣā*), right conduct (cāritra), etc., primarily aim at the purification of the individual soul in the manner of its being separated from the various kinds of *karma*-matter which have been superimposed upon it in the course of its intercourse with the world (*saṁsāra*). And the purification of the soul in this manner, according to Jainism, amounts to the fulfilment of its ultimate destiny in the realization of liberation (*kaivalya*). This, perhaps, suffices to indicate that Jaina ethics is in a class apart from the egoistic-hedonistic ethics of the Laukāyatikas. In fact, it is the ethics of individual self-culture extended to its absurd limit marked by the abstract purity of the soul. Moreover, it is, in the view of Jainism, the same as religion, the religion of individual salvation. But it is obviously far removed from the universal ethics of humanity.

Allied with, but different from, the ethics of the Jainas thus understood, is the ethics of the Buddhists of the Hīnayāna school. According to them, the common duties of man lie in the pursuit of the Eightfold Path consisting of right views (*samyak dṛsti*), right resolve (*samyak saṁkalpa*), right speech (*samyak vāk*), right conduct (*samyak cāritra*), right livelihood (*samyak ājīvaka*), right effort (*samyak vyāyāma*), right mindfulness (*samyak smṛti*) and, lastly, right concentration (*samyak samādhi*). A careful scrutiny of the detailed account of these duties will show, however, that their aim, like that of the duties prescribed by Jainism, is to promote individual self-culture directed towards the final attainment of *arhatship*. And since an *arhat*, according to Hīnayāna Buddhism, is an individual who is completely sanctified and thus is free on account of the destruction of all his *āsavas* (taints), namely, sensuality (*kāmāsava*), desire for rebirth (*bhāvāsava*), ignorance of the four noble truths (*avijjāsava*) and acceptance of heretical views (*ditthāsava*), he, as an individual, resembles the liberated individual conceived by Jainism to be *kevala.** Hence it is evident that the ethics of Hīnayāna Buddhism, like that of Jainism, is the ethics of individual self-culture regarded as synonymous with the religion of individual salvation.

But the situation with which we have so far been concerned completely changes in consequence of the Mahāyānist idea that the spiritual progress of man should not come to an end even when it reaches the highest point in individual self-culture and that there remains the need for the development of the consciousness of humanity within each and every individual in order for him to realize the truth that his destiny is inseparably bound up with those of his fellows. And it is with this idea in view that Mahāyāna Buddhism insisted on the supreme importance of the four sublime duties, namely, benevolence towards all creation (*maitrī*), compassion towards the distressed (*karuṇā*), joy at others' happiness (*muditā*) and indifference towards others' faults (*upekṣā*). These are the duties which, according to this school of Buddhism, it is incumbent upon each and every man to observe so that the ideal of *arhatship* may be transmuted into that of *Bodhisattvahood* or *Buddhahood* and individual self-culture may be sublimated into the universal liberation of mankind. Thus does Mahāyāna Buddhism envisage the possibility of the universal ethics of humanity in the true sense of the term, which is but another name for the religion of universal liberation.

II

REFLECTIVE MORALITY

Although the generic duties, like the specific ones, form part of objective morality, yet some of them and especially most of those that are admitted by the Jainas and the Bauddhas are different from the latter in having a subjective or psychological significance. This is evident from the fact that they are concerned with *cittaśuddhi* (purification of the mind) and the inner excellence of the will which are of inestimable value in moral life. What we are trying to suggest here is, however, that there, perhaps, is no hard and fast line of demarcation between objective and subjective morality and, correspondingly, between duties and virtues. Nevertheless, there is need for the investigation of reflective or subjective morality with a view to the understanding of the nature of the purificatory or sanctifying process through which the moral

*The difference between Buddhism and Jainism in this regard lies in that whereas, according to Jainism, the individual is a permanent soul, in the view of Buddhism, he is but an ever-changing aggregate of elements.

aspirant may pass after a period of his discipline brought about by his outward conformity to a set of external acts regarded as duties, and may, in consequence, be elevated to a higher level of moral life. This raises the whole question of the psychological basis of ethics and points to the need for the determination of the constituents of the inward excellence of moral life called *virtues*. Let us then begin with the investigation of the Indian treatment of the psychological basis of ethics.

A

THE PSYCHOLOGICAL BASIS OF ETHICS

The main requirement here is twofold, being the analysis of volition and the analysis of consciousness of duty. As regards the former requirement, it involves the understanding of the distinction between voluntary and non-voluntary activities and, more particularly, the analysis of volition as such, together with the analysis of consciousness of freedom in willing which is essential to the ethical treatment of responsibility and obligation.

(a) Analysis of Volition : Voluntary and Non-voluntary activities

According to the Naiyāyikas and especially Prasaśtapāda to whom reference has been already made, the distinction between voluntary and non-voluntary activities mainly lies in that the cause or the antecedent condition in the latter case is the life of the organism (*jīvana*), whereas in the latter it is desire (*icchā*) or else aversion (*dveṣa*). Thus non-voluntary activities, including the reflex and automatic actions, are held to be organic functions, while voluntary activities are regarded as determined by foresight and choice. But then, both the kinds of activities are viewed to be *teleological* in character, non-voluntary actions being regarded as subserving the ends of organic life and voluntary actions as the means to the subservance of ends consciously aimed at and chosen. It is important to note, however, that the scope of voluntary actions has been rather unusually restricted by the Naiyāyika Dinakara Bhatta in terms of his view that these actions not only exclude the organic actions, namely, the reflex and the automatic actions, but also the actions performed under the urge of blind impulses. Voluntary actions, according to him, are, then, those actions which are not only consciously chosen but are also determined by one's own will, that is to say, are such that their choice is *free*.

Analysis of Volition and Consciousness of Freedom

According to Prabhākara, the founder of one of the two rival schools of Mīmāṁsā philosophy, volition involves the following factors:—

(1) The idea of something to be done (*kāryatājñāna*)
(2) The desire to do it (*cikīrṣā*), of course, involving the consciousness that it is capable of being done (*kṛtisādhyatājñāna*)
(3) The act of volition itself (*pravṛtti; kṛti*)
(4) The conative impulse in the organism (*ceṣṭā*)
(5) The overt act (*kṛiyā*)

It needs to be noted in this connection that the first factor in this process can gradually lead to the successive ones provided that the idea of the act in which it consists is not a bare idea, but is one which has been appropriated by the self, or with which the self has identified itself. The point here is that the mere idea of an act, that is, an idea with which the self has not identified itself may only generate the knowledge that the act concerned is capable of being performed, but not the knowledge that *it must be performed*, which is really the antecedent condition of the desire as well as the will or volition to act. Judged in this light, *kāryatājñāna*, in Prabhākara's analysis of volition, should be taken to mean the consciousness that something *must be done*. As regards the second factor in the above analysis of volition, namely, the *desire* to do something (*cikīrṣā*), the question may arise as to what its antecedent condition exactly is. According to Prabhākara, it is the simple consciousness that something is to be done, and that it can be done by the will. But the Naiyāyika brings the utilitarian consideration to bear upon his understanding of the condition of desire and, consequently, holds that it is the consciousness that that which is to be done is conducive to one's own good (*iṣṭasādhanatājñāna*). The difference between Prabhākara and the Naiyāyika in this respect may then be expressed by stating that whereas the real motive of voluntary actions, according to the latter, is something *external*, in the view of the former, it is the self itself as identified with the idea of something to be done.

It would be of interest to note in this connection that Prabhākara's conception of the motive of volitional actions as the identification of the self with the idea of the performance of them serves to render the ethics of rigorism more perfect than it was in the hands of Kant. While holding that feelings or inclinations as such are *pathological*, Kant entertained the view that love of duty and reverence for the Moral Law, despite the fact that they are feelings, are exceptions to the rule. And in this he obviously sacrificed the purity of the ethics of rigorism. It is this drawback of Kantian rigoristic ethics which was removed by Prabhākara by eschewing all reference to pathological mental phenomena, and admitting the centrality of the self, in his understanding of the motive of voluntary actions. There is another respect in which Prabhākara differs from, and indeed goes further than, Kant. It relates to the question of freedom. Kant found no trace of freedom in the field of the human mind except in man's consciousness of duty. Accordingly, he came to hold that freedom is a purely ethical phenomenon, being the implicate of our consciousness of the Moral Law. Prabhākara, on the other hand, held that consciousness of freedom is invariably involved in all acts of volition and as such is generically psychological.

But Prabhākara's analysis of volition without any reference whatsoever to pathological feelings resulted in the ignoring of the fact that volitional acts, besides being due to desires (*icchā*), are, on the other hand, sometimes conditioned by aversion (*dveṣa*) with a view to the avoidance of some evil or other. And this is one of the inadequacies of Prabhākara's analysis of volition which the Naiyāyikas especially noticed. The difference between Prabhākara's and the Naiyāyika's views with regard to the analysis of volition may then be stated as follows. In the first place, according to Prabhākara and his followers, the primary motive of volitional acts has hardly anything to do with the consciousness of good or evil, but consists in the identification of the self with the idea of the act to be performed. In the view of the Naiyāyikas, on the other hand, it is, positively, the idea of good without any outweighing evil and, negatively, the idea of evil without any outweighing good. Secondly, as regards the relation between the motive of volitional acts and the consciousness of duty, Prabhākara holds that the former, being the identification of the self with the idea of the act to be performed, is related to the latter as *ground* is to *conseqennce*. In other words, he is of the view that the consciousness which constitutes the motive and the consciousness of duty are two distinct psychological phenomena, and that the latter logically follows from the former just as the conclusion follows from the premises. The Naiyāyikas, on the other hand, hold that the two mental phenomena, namely, the consciousness of good (*iṣtasādhanatājñāna*) and the consciousness of duty (*kārya tājñāna*) are not separate from each other, but are held together into a unitary complex, it being the case that the object of the two forms of consciousness is one and the same.

We may now direct our special attention to the question as to what constitutes the desirability (*iṣtatva*) of the object of desire. The view of Prabhākara and those who are in agreement with him does not come in for consideration in the present context in as much as the idea of good, according to them, is not essential to the volitional process. We are, therefore, required for the present to confine ourselves to the enquiry into the Naiyāyikas' answer to the question just now before us. The Naiyāyikas, be it noted at the outset, may be said to agree with the Cārvākas in holding that the desirability of the object of desire consists in its productivity of happiness or else its capacity to ward off suffering. But then, they distinguish between happiness and sensual pleasure and insist on the recognition of the qualitative difference of happiness or pleasure* and thereby reject gross the hedonism of the latter. And in this they resemble the utilitarian moral philosophers like Bentham and Mill. Not only that; they recognize the qualitative distinction between ordinary or empirical actions prompted by attraction (*rāga*) towards happiness or by aversion (*dveṣa*) to suffering and the non-empirical or transcendental impulse towards *mokṣa* (liberation) regarded as the highest good. And they hold that the former, being under the sway of the two forces of attraction and aversion, are not *free* actions in themselves, nor can serve as the condition of the realization of the highest good that is the freedom of *mokṣa*. Hence it is evident that, in the view of the Naiyāyikas, there are two kinds of objects of desire : (a) *sukhaprāpti* (attainment of happiness) or *duḥkhaparihāra* (avoidance of suffering) or both, and (b) the realization of absolute freedom *(mokṣa)* the desire for which is, of course, pure or non-empirical and not pathological or empirical. This suffices to indicate that the Nyāya school of Indian philosophy and the others that are in agreement with it admit a two-tiered ethics—the lower ethics of refined hedonism on the one hand and the higher ethics of liberation on the other. But the latter may well be designated as a form of religion rather than a form of ethics. According to Prabhākara and his followers, on the other hand, the lower tier of ethics is out of the question in as much as the idea of the object of desire *(iṣta)* is uncalled for. Since ethics, in their view, should then be non-empirical or transcendental, its status may be said to be religious rather than ethical.

Let us now have a brief discussion of the views regarding the nature of the object of desire and freedom of the will held by the three heterodox schools of Indian philosophy—the Cārvāka, the Jaina and the Bauddha. As regards the Cārvākas, they, as has been already indicated, hold that the highest and indeed the only object of desire is pleasure, without recognizing any qualitative difference among pleasures as such. Desire, in their view, then is

---

*** Both Gangeśa and Mathurānātha, the two outstanding members of the Navya-Nyāya school of Indian philosophy speak of the vaijātīya (specific) difference of quality among the various kinds of svargasukha (happiness in heaven). And in this they are obviously opposed to the usual view that these sukhas differ among themselves only in quantity or degree.**

purely and exclusively empirical or pathological, the possibility of any non-empirical or transcendental desire being out of the question. That being so, the Cārvākas, as Prabhākara, Kant and even the Naiyāyikas would contend, has no means of recognizing any such thing as freedom of the will. The reason for this, according to them, would be that the desire for pleasure and, for that matter, for any other empirical object, is characteristic of the bondman and indeed is foreign to the freeman. If the desire for pleasure is, then, devoid of freedom, it can find no place in ethics in as much as ethics without freedom of the will, it may well be urged, were, as it were, the play of Hamlet without the Prince of Denmark. Hence arises the curious situation, namely, that hedonistic ethics or any of its empirical alternatives is no ethics at all, and that the non-empirical or transcendental ethics, namely, the ethics of liberation, as we have previously observed, is a form of religion, instead of ethics.

However that may be, as far as the Jainas are concerned, they, like Prabhākara, admit no such thing as empirical ethics with its preoccupation with happiness or any other empirical object regarded as the object of desire. According to them, the desire for empirical objects owes its origin to the obscuration of the innate perfection of the self due to wrong belief, attachment, aversion, delusion and passions. So the demand of morality, in their view, is not the empirical demand for indulgence in desires for such objects, but the transcendental demand for the removal of the obscuration of the perfection of the self by means of right belief, right knowledge, vows, penances, meditation, passionlessness and perfect tranquillity. The transcendental moral demand thus characterized is, in fact, the Moral Law *(niyoga)* which, according to Jainism, is the command, not of God—for the Jainas do not believe in God—but of a perfect, omniscient person *(arhat)* who has realized his innate perfection. Even so Jainism goes further in holding that the Moral Law, though it appears at first sight to be externally imposed, is really self-imposed, is imposed by the self upon itself. Thus Jainism, like Kant, admits freedom of the will in the sense of self-determination and regards it as the ethical implicate of the Moral Law, instead of as a mere psychological phenomenon. It is then evident that the ethics of the Jainas is rigoristic and may be said to be the ethics of perfectionism, as distinguished from the ethics of hedonism. But then, the moral ideal as conceived by them represents the fulfilment of the ultimate destiny of man independently of the religion of God. That being so, their ethics, strictly speaking, is the substitute for religion in the ordinary sense and so is, in a sense, another name for religion itself.

Now Buddhism, like Jainism, regards the purification or sanctification of the inner life as a moral demand of supreme importance, on the understanding that it is the indispensable means to the realization of the highest good conceived to be *nirvāṇa* (elimination of egoity). The fulfilment of this demand, according to Buddhism, would consist in the removal of ignorance (*avidyā*), passions (*kleśa*) and uncontrolled desires (*tṛṣnā*), together with the entire gamut of the sordid affections of the human mind consequent upon them. And the means to this end, as Buddha himself held, lies in the pursuit of the *middle path* of moderation which steers clear of the two extremes of self-indulgence and self-mortification regarded as equally unprofitable and ignoble. The middle path in question, as we have previously seen, is the well known Eightfold Path, the pursuit of which would amount to the performance of *pure* acts, as distinguished from *impure* acts.

Pure acts, according to Buddhism, are those acts that are free from the depravity (*āsava*), involving ignorance and desire as well as from passions (*kleśa*). They are then acts of freedom, as opposed to impure acts which are the outcome of human bondage. And it is, as Buddhism holds, the pure acts which lead to the realization of the highest good that is *nirvāṇa*. Hence it is evident that Buddhism is at one with Jainism in holding that human freedom is not a mere psychological phenomenon, but a necessary implicate of the moral demand for the realization of the highest good. But then, since the highest good is held by Buddhism, in common with Jainism, to be the fulfilment of the ultimate destiny of man, it follows that the so-called moral ideal is religious rather than moral, and that human freedom, ultimately, transcends from the lower level of morality to the higher level of religion—of course, religion, not in the traditional sense, but in a sense which is yet to be brought to light. Even so, human freedom leaves its impact upon the moral level. And this accounts for the Buddhist ethics of altruism founded upon *ahiṁsā*, together with its definitely positive counterpart consisting of *maitrī* (benevolence towards all creation), *karuṇā* (compassion towards the distressed) *muditā* (joy at others' happiness) and *upekṣā* (indifference towards others' faults). Thus does Buddhism admit a second order of human freedom which yields the ethics of altruism and regard this ethics as the necessary harbinger of the religion of *nirvāṇa*.

(*b*) *Analysis of Consciousness of Duty*

The consciousness of duty, according to Indian ethics, is not merely the consciousness of the act that is morally binding, but involves the cognizance of the merit of righteousness (*dharma*) which is consequent upon the proper performance of the duty. So in the analysis of consciousness of duty, it is necessary, as a preliminary step, to ascertain the meaning of *dharma* and the relation of *dharma* to *karma* or prescribed duties. But then, the difficulty in this regard is that the word *dharma* has been understood differently by the different schools of Indian philosophy. Thus, according to the Sāṁkhya, *dharma* is a function of the mind which is a product of the evolution of *prakṛti*. That being so, the self (*puruṣa*), being, in the view of the Sāṁkhya, disparate from *prakṛti* and its evolutes, is absolutely unaffected by *dharma* (merit) as well as its opposite *adharma* (demerit). These two are only significant in the empirical life of the self but cannot be said to belong to the self in any manner whatsoever.

But the Nyāya-Vaiśeṣikas distinguish between the empirical aspect of the self, that is, the aspect in which it is a participant in worldly life (*saṁsāra*) on the one hand and the transcendental aspect of it on the other. Accordingly, they hold that *dharma* and *adharma*, although they cannot affect the transcendental self in any manner whatsoever, belong, not to the mind, but to the self itself in its empirical aspect. Thus, while the self in its transcendental life is situated in a supermoral plane and so is free from both *dharma* and *adharma*, in its empirical life it forms part of the moral order and is determined by righteousness and unrighteousness. Even so these determinations of the self, as the Nyāya-Vaiśeṣikas further hold, are only temporary modifications of it which are amenable to removal by means of spiritual discipline, resulting in the realization of its transcendental purity.

Now since *dharma* and *adharma* are, in the view of the Nyāya-Vaiśeṣikas, the qualities of the self in its empirical aspect, they cannot be said to have any objective implication, but must be only subjectively significant. Hence it follows that acts as such, being objective, cannot, according to these philosophers, be themselves righteous or unrighteous. Merit and demerit must then belong, not to acts themselves, but to their intention (*abhisandhi*). That is why the actions which are the outcome of pure intentions (*viśuddhābhisandhijātaḥ*) are ordinarily called meritorious and those that owe their origin to impure intentions (*duṣtābhisandhijātaḥ*) are popularly spoken of as unrighteous. It is important to note, however, that the Sāṁkhya is in agreement with the Nyāya-Vaiśeṣikas in holding the view that *dharma* and *adharma* are purely subjectively significant, but with this difference that, while according to the latter these two belong to the self in its empirical aspect, in the view of the former, they are exclusively the function of the mind.

The Buddhists also advocate the subjectivist view of *dharma* and *adharma* by stating that these are but the dispositions (*vāsanā*) of the mental continuum (*citta*) which are subject to elimination on the transcendental level. But then, since they are *dispositions* of the mind, they are not, as according to the Sāṁkhya they are, temporary functions of the mind. On the contrary, they are enduring traits or tendencies of the mind. However that may be, the Sāṁkhya, the Nyāya-Vaiśeṣikas and the Buddhists agree among themselves in holding the view that righteousness and unrighteousness are subjective concepts and have only an empirical significance, their employment being confined within the limits of empirical life. But to this view is opposed that of the Mīmāṁsakas, according to which *dharma* and *adharma* are *objective* and *external*. The latter view is based on the understanding that *dharma* is not a quality or a function or a disposition, but is an *object* (*artha*) worthy of being aimed at. Not only that; it is an *artha* that is sanctioned by scriptural prescriptions (*codanā*).

But even granted that *dharma* is objective, being a desirable object in the sense of some *sāstrika* (scriptural) act or other, it may still be asked whether the act concerned is an *artha* on its own account or else on account of something which it serves to reveal. As regards this question, the school of Mimāṁsā philosophy headed by Kumārila Bhatta answers it by accepting the former alternative, while the school founded by Prabhākara Miśra answers it in terms of the latter. According to Prabhākara, *dharma* is not identifiable with the act (*kriyā*) prescribed by the scripture; it is non-empirical or supersensuous, being revealed by the authoritative suggestion (*preraṇā*) to the will conveyed by the imperative (*niyoga*) involved in a scriptural prescription. It is important to note, however, that scriptural prescriptions, according to Prabhākara, may not only involve *arthas* (good), but also *anarthas* (evils). So only those prescriptions which involve *arthas* can, in his view, give rise to *dharma* in and through their supersensuous effects (*apūrva*).

Kumārila Bhatta and his followers, on the other hand, hold that the ceremonial and sacrificial acts (*yāgādi*) prescribed by the scripture are in themselves the constituents of *dharma* or moral good. So, in their view, *dharma* is not, as according to Prabhākara and his followers it is, a certain supersensuous potency (*apūrva*) with which Vedic prescriptions are supposed to be endued, but consists of the acts prescribed by the scripture. A necessary corollary of this view is that no scriptural prescription can lead to any *anartha* (evil), and that as far as evils are concerned, they come within the scope of the prohibitory or negative prescriptions (*niṣedha-codanā*) of the Vedas which are obviously intended to lead to *arthas* (good) and not to *anarthas* (evils). It is then, plain that as against the Sāṁkhya, the Nyāya-Vaiśeṣika and the Bauddha who regard *dharma* as subjective in one sense or another, the Mīmāṁsakas treat it as an objective category consisting, according to Prabhākara, in a sort of supersensuous potency (*apūrva*) with which the scriptural prescriptions are imbued or, as in the view of Kumārila, in the acts prescribed by the scripture. But the Mīmāṁsakas do not stand alone in their advocacy of the objectivist view of *dharma*. The Jainas share this view with them as is evident from the fact that *dharma*, according to them, consists of subtle forces contained in atoms capable of producing specific effects. It remains to be mentioned, however, that, on account of their rejection of the authority of the scripture as well as their uncompromisingly this-worldly outlook on life, the Cārvākas do not recognize such things as *dharma* and *adharma* but rest content with the view of one's own greatest pleasure as the highest good.

Our next task is to enquire into the typical Indian views regarding the moral value of external acts of duty or, in other words, the relation of *dharma* to *karma*. We may conveniently begin here with the consideration of the Buddhist view on this subject. From what we have already observed about the view held by the Bauddhas concerning the nature of *dharma*, it is obvious that external acts of duty (*karmas*), according to them, have no intrinsic moral worth or, in other words, cannot be spoken of as being inherently characterized by *dharma*. The utmost that may be said about the *karmas* from the moral point of view is that they may have an instrumental value, consisting in their serving as a means of the purification of the mind. In substantial agreement with this view of the Buddhists, the Sāṁkhya points out that most of the *karmas* prescribed by the Vedas involve *hiṁsā* (injury to sentient creatures) and, consequently, are devoid of any positive moral value. And what is thus true about the *karmas* prescribed by the scripture is, in the view of the Sāṁkhya, *mutatis mutandis* true about empirical actions prompted by motives of gain or expediency. It is not the case, however, that, *karmas* are of no significance in the moral life of man. On the contrary, they are of importance to him in the conduct of his moral affairs, but subject to the proviso that they may contribute to the purification of his mind. But then, the Sāṁkhya, while condemning ceremonialism in common with the Buddhists, differ from the latter by admitting what they deny, namely, that the ceremonials possess a certain power or potency (*apūrva*) to produce certain specific effects such as happiness in heaven. And yet it is fully alive to the consideration that happiness in heaven (*svarga*) is, after all, perishable and so is in a class apart from the highest good (*paramārtha*) which is *mokṣa*.

As regards the Nyāya-Vaiśeṣikas, although they, like the Sāṁkhya and the Bauddhas, advocate the subjectivist view of *dharma*, they do not go so far as the latter in condemning ceremonialism. On the contrary, they hold that *dharma*, despite the fact that it is a quality of the self, is in need of being acquired through the proper discharge of an objective code of duties, which consists of the *sādhāraṇadharmas* and the *varṇāśramadharmas* to which reference has been already made. These duties, according to the

Nyāya-Vaiśeṣikas, are morally significant in that they are conducive to *dharma* (righteousness) and so are morally obligatory. As regards ceremonials, since they are included among these duties, they are, of course, morally obligatory. But, in the view of these philosophers, they are so, not because they, as Prabhākara and his followers hold, possess a certain supernatural potency (*apūrva*), but because they are conducive to the moral perfection of those who perform them. One of the corollaries of this view, however, is what is most emphatically condemned by the Bauddhas, the Jainas and the Sāṁkhya, namely, that the *hiṁsā* (aggression, violence or injury to sentient creatures) sanctioned by the Vedas is morally justifiable.

Even so the Nyāya-Vaiśeṣikas admit that ceremonials are subordinate to morality and not the latter to the former. But it is this relative position of morality and ceremonials which is reversed by the Mīmāṁsakas and especially Kumārila Bhatta and his followers, in terms of the view that the moral or the ethical is subordinate to, and what is more, is resolvable into, ceremonials. Thus is presented the extreme externalistic conception of morality in the history of Indian ethics. Be it noted, however, that Prabhākara and the members of the school of Mīmāṁsā philosophy founded by him do not share the extreme externalistic conception of morality entertained by the Bhātta school. According to the former, the ceremonials or external acts of duty are morally obligatory, not because, as held by the latter, they are prescribed by the Vedas, but because they are possessed of intrinsic validity as duties or constituents of the moral order (*apūrva*) revealed through the experience of the self. Thus Prabhākara's doctrine of the *apūrva* serves to mitigate the extremism of Kumārila's externalistic conception of morality and thereby rescue morality from its resolution into ceremonials.

Two more views about the moral value of external acts of duty respectively held by the Advaita and the Viśiṣtādvaita schools of the Vedānta deserve special consideration. According to Śaṁkara, the foremost protagonist of the Advaita school of the Vedānta, there are two distinct levels of morality, the lower morality of desire (*pravṛtti*) and the higher morality of cessation of desire (*nivṛtti*). The former of these two levels of morality concerns the satisfaction of desires and so it naturally holds good in the case of the majority of human beings who are participants in the ordinary day to day life and are governed by the two forces of attraction (*rāga*) and aversion (*dveṣa*). That being so, lower morality comprises the duties, the performance of which would lead to the fulfilment of desired ends. These ends, according to Śaṁkara, may be empirical (*dṛṣta*) as well as non-empirical (*adṛṣta*). Accordingly, the morality of *pravṛtti* should consist of two kinds of duties—

duties of an empirical nature (*dṛṣṭārthaka-karma*) and duties of a non-empirical nature (*adṛṣṭārthaka-karma*). The former of these two kinds, as Śaṁkara holds, comprises customs and traditional rules of conduct as well as certain others derivable from the sciences of medicine, politics, etc. The latter consists of those duties which are prescribed by the *karma-kānda* of the Vedas, that is, that part of the Vedas which is exclusively concerned with the prescription of duties.

These two kinds of duties do, of course, have a moral significance in as much as they are productive of *dharma* (merit). But then, the merit produced by them is transitory and perishable, which indicates that they constitute the morality of the bondman and not that of the freeman. So their moral value would, in the view of Śaṁkara, ultimately depend upon their capacity to prepare the individual for his journey along the path of cessation of desires (*nivṛtti-mārga*) with a view to the realization of the highest good (*paramārtha*). The higher morality, negatively speaking, would, then, consist in cessation (*nivṛtti*) from desires and, consequently, from duties directed towards the satisfaction of desires. And, positively speaking, it would, according to Śaṁkara, consist in the cultivation of disinterested virtues without reference to any empirical end and the practice of spiritual discipline such as the development of the qualities of tranquillity (*sama*), restraint (*dama*), etc. And it would, in consequence, reach its culmination in the intuitive knowledge of the identity of the individual with Brahman, amounting to *jīvanmukti* (liberation during life-time on earth) which constitutes the fulfilment of the ultimate destiny of the individual. But higher morality thus understood, as we have been suggesting time and time again, is but another name for a kind of religion—the religion of human liberation.

It is important to note, however, that, in addition to the two kinds of morality recognized by Śaṁkara, namely, the morality of desire and that of cessation of desire, a third kind called the morality of disinterested duties *(nivṛttikāmanā-karma)* has been admitted especially by Manu and the Bhagavad Gītā. And as far as Rāmānuja, the founder of the Viśiṣṭādvaita school of the Vedānta is concerned, he disagrees with Śaṁkara's view of the higher morality as freedom from duty *(karmasanyāsa)* and, like Manu and the Gīta, holds that morality reaches its highest perfection in the performance of duties without any desire for the consequence. But then, Rāmānuja, like the majority of Indian philosophers, looks upon morality as ancillary to religion—of course, theistic religion in his case. Accordingly, he holds that duties are valuable, not in themselves, but as means to divine knowledge. So only those duties need to be performed which are conducive to divine knowledge and those that are obstacles to this knowledge must needs be abjured. But this is far from suggesting that there is a supermoral plane of life free from the need for the performance of duties *(karmasanyāsa)*. On the contrary, Rāmānuja holds that even in the highest stage of his spiritual development, the individual is required to perform his unconditional duties without any desire for the consequence in order that his divine knowledge and spiritual enlightenment may be an ever-increasing process.

As previously indicated, the consciousness of duty, according to Indian ethics, is a complex psychological process, involving the consciousness of the act that is morally binding, together with the righteousness or merit *(dharma)* which is due to accrue from its proper performance and, in particular, the consciousness of the *authority* with which the duty presents itself to the moral agent. We have already tried to ascertain the meaning of righteousness *(dharma)* and the relation of righteousness to acts of duty as understood by the different schools of Indian philosophy. So for the completion of our account of the analysis of the consciousness of duty offered by Indian ethics, it is still left for us to enquire into its analysis of the consciousness of the authority which attaches to acts of duty.

It is necessary to bear in mind, however, that as far as the orthodox schools of Indian philosophy are concerned, the ethical code, according to most of them,* comprises a strictly moral code and a ceremonial code of scriptural or rather Vedic injunctions *(vidhis)* and prohibitions *(niṣedhas)*. That being so, it would be necessary for us to enquire into the attempts made by the different orthodox schools of Indian philosophy to account for the consciousness of the authority with which the two kinds of acts of duty are invested. But our task would be much simpler in our dealings with the heterodox schools of Indian philosophy in the present context. The reason for this is that they do not admit such things as scriptural injunctions and prohibitions and, consequently, that the ethical code, in their view, is strictly and exclusively ethical, having no place for ceremonial acts. We may then begin with the consideration of the typical explanations of the consciousness of the authoritativeness of scriptural imperatives, which have emerged from the orthodox circles of Indian philosophy.

Let us first consider how the Mīmāṁsakas try to account for the consciousness of the authoritativeness of the Vedic imperatives which, in their view, are of supreme importance in moral life. It needs to be noted, however, that the Mīmāṁsakas are not agreed

*The Sāṁkhya, despite the fact that it is an orthodox school of Indian philosophy, is an exception in this respect in as much as it condemns the so-called ceremonial duties on account of the perishable character of their effects as well as their involvement in ahiṁsā such as animal slaughter, etc. Even so, the Sāṁkhya admits that the scriptural imperatives are capable of producing effects such as happiness.

among themselves in this regard. On the contrary, the two schools of the Mīmāṁsā respectively headed by Kumārila and Prabhākara differ from each other in their explanation of the authority with which scriptural imperatives present themselves to the moral agent. Of course, both the schools are of the view that there is a moral order which includes the scriptural imperatives as its essential constituents. But the Bhātta school indulges in crude thinking in so far as it holds that these imperatives are a sort of *causes,* analogous to physical causes, and, like the latter, are productive of effects, one of which is their authority over the mind of the moral agent. The causal explanation of the consciousness of the authority of scriptural imperatives is, however, regarded by Prabhākara and his followers as improper in view of the consideration that scriptural imperatives are inherently authoritative and, consequently, that he who is conscious of them is, on that very account, conscious of their authority over him. And that being so, the causal explanation of the consciousness of their authoritativeness, according to Prabhākara, is vitiated by the failure to understand their true nature.

The difference between the two scchools of the Mīmāṁsā in the present regard may then be expressed by stating that, whereas, according to the Bhāttas, the consciousness of the authority of the scriptural imperatives results from their impersonal *operation* or *process (bhāvanā),* in the view of the Prābhākaras, it is no result of a process or operation, but is a unique (uncaused) feeling of impulsion *(preraṇā)* on the part of the moral agent. Even then, the two schools are in agreement with each other in that neither of them brings any extraneous consideration to bear upon the explanation of the consciousness of scriptural authority. And this indicates the point from which the Nyāya-Vaiśeṣikas make a departure in their attempt to account for the exercise of authority on the part of Vedic injunctions and prohibitions over the mind of the moral agent. According to these philosophers, scriptural imperatives are not, as in the view of the Mīmāṁsakas in general they are, *impersonal;* they are unquestionably *personal,* being commands of the divine person or God. But that alone is not sufficient for the explanation of the matter under consideration. In order that divine commands in the form of scriptural imperatives may exercise their authority in an appropriate manner, as the Nyāya-Vaiśeṣikas seem to have argued, there must be something on the side of the moral agent which would serve as the condition of his consciousness of their authority. This something, according to them, is none else than *phalecchā,* that is, the desire *(icchā)* for the consequence *(phala)* which is due to accrue from obedience to scriptural injunctions *(vidhis).* Thus the Nyāya-Vaiśeṣikas' explanation of the consciousness of the authority of scriptural imperatives consists in holding that these are not impersonal, but are the commands of the Divine

Person and that they compel the moral agent to be conscious of their authority, not directly and immediately, but through the intermediary of his *phalecchā* (desire for the consequence).

It appears, then, that in the field of Indian ethics of the orthodox variety there prevailed two radically divergent explanations of the consciousness of the authority which scriptural injunctions *(vidhis)* are apt to exercise over the mind of the moral agent. One of these consists in holding that this consciousness is not determined by any extraneous condition and so is unconditional, categorical or rather self-determined or spontaneous. The foremost representatives of this view are the Mīmāṁsakas, including the Bhāttas as well as the Prābhākaras, it being understood that these two schools of the Mīmāṁsā differ from each other only with respect to the understanding of the exact nature of the spontaneity of that consciousness. The other explanation, on the other hand, amounts to stating that the consciousness in question is determined or mediated by something or other and as such is lacking in spontaneity and indeed is conditional or hypothetical (of course, not in the Kantian sense).

The conditionality of the consciousness of the authority of scriptural imperatives is, of course, due to its being determined by the desire for the consequence. But then, the consequence as well as the desire for it may be empirical or else non-empirical or transcendental. So the conditionality of this consciousness may also be either empirical or transcendental. Now as far as the Nyāya-Vaiśeṣikas are concerned, this conditionality is empirical in as much as the desire for the consequence, which is supposed to determine the consciousness of the authority of scriptural imperatives, according to them, is the desire for the *happiness* which is due to accrue from obedience to these imperatives. And as regards the Sāṁkhya, although, as previously observed it condemns the scriptural imperatives, yet it holds that these are capable of producing human happiness. So it may be said to be in agreement with the Nyāya-Vaiśeṣika in admitting the empirical conditionality of the consciousness of the authority of scriptural imperatives. But the case is different with the Viśiṣtādvaita and the Advaita schools of the Vedānta. According to Rāmānuja, the founder of the former school, the consciousness of the authority of scriptural imperatives is not spontaneous, but conditional on account of its being motivated or determined by the non-empirical desire for divine knowledge. And in holding this view he obviously assumes that obedience to these imperatives is one of the means to the attainment of divine knowledge which is the highest good.

In this connection it would be worthwhile to note that the Mīmāṁsakas, not being believers in religion, found it rather easy to regard the consciousness of the authority of duty as spontaneous, instead of as being determined or motivated by the idea of an end supposed to be higher than the performance of duty for its own sake. But this is far from suggesting that belief in religion is incompatible with the doctrine of duty for duty's sake. For this doctrine insists on the freedom of the sense of duty from empirical ends such as health, wealth, happiness and the like, but not from non-empirical ends like divine knowledge, *mokṣa* or liberation. So it is quite understandable why Rāmānuja, while insisting on the supreme importance of the performance of duty for its own sake, found it possible to regard the consciousness of the authority of scriptural imperatives as ultimately determined by the religious idea of the attainment of divine knowledge. Śaṁkara, the foremost Advaita-Vedāntist, also viewed this consciousness as conditional, instead of as spontaneous, on the understanding that obedience to scriptural imperatives is significant only in that it is but a preliminary step in the process of spiritual realization which culminates in the direct and immediate experience of the identity of the individual with Brahman. But then, in the view of Śaṁkara, unlike in the view of Rāmānuja, the consciousness of the authority of scriptural imperatives as well as the need for obedience to them, as previously indicated, completely disappear when the culmination of the spiritual realization is reached.

It now remains for us to enquire into the views held by the orthodox as well as the heterodox schools of Indian philosophy regarding the nature of the consciousness of the authority of the duties other than the scriptural imperatives. Let us first deal with the views of the heterodox schools on this subject. As far as the Cārvākas are concerned, the consciousness of the authority of duty, in their view, is *conditional* in as much as the authority is exercised over the mind of the moral agent, not directly and immediately, but through the intermediary of his desire for a balance of pleasure over pain or suffering. And this means that the obligatoriness of the moral imperative is none but the causal operation of a foreseen or anticipated pleasure on the agent's will. Then, as regards the Bauddhas and the Jainas, they insist on the all-importance of the purity of the motives of actions and regard their visible or empirical consequences as unimportant in the ethical scheme of life. This would at first sight seem to indicate that the consciousness of the authority of duty, in their view, is unconditional or spontaneous. But the fact is really different. For ethics, which is primarily concerned with duties, is, according to them, subordinate to religion, not the religion of God, but the religion of liberation without belief in God. That being so, the consciousness of the authority of duty, while being empirically unconditioned or spontaneous, is transcendentally conditioned, being, in their view, motivated by the non-empirical desire for liberation.

Among the orthodox schools of Indian philosophy, the Nyāya-Vaiśeṣikas, however, present a curious situation in so far as they seem to put ethics into two water-tight compartments which may be respectively designated as the ethics of bondage and the ethics of liberation. As regards the former, its peculiarity lies in that the consciousness of the authority of duty in its case is *empirically* conditioned, being determined by the idea of the realization of some empirical good or other (*iṣtasādhanatājñāna*). In this the Nyāya-Vaiśeṣikas are definitely in alliance with the Cārvākas, but with this difference that, whereas, according to the latter, the good (*iṣta*) is pleasure, in the view of the former, it may be pleasure or something else, say, freedom from suffering as the case may be. But then, their difference from the Cārvākas goes further and indeed is more profound than the present one. Thus, whereas the Cārvākas recognize no such thing as the ethics of liberation in distinction from the ethics of bondage, the Nyāya-Vaiśeṣikas admit the ethics of liberation regarded as unconnected with, and distinct from, the ethics of bondage. Nevertheless, the consciousness of the authority of duty in the case of the ethics of liberation, in their view, is not spontaneous, but conditioned—of course, conditioned transcendentally by the non-empirical desire for liberation.

It would be of interest to note the profound significance of the distinction drawn by the Nyāya-Vaiśeṣikas between the ethics of bondage and the ethics of liberation. It consists in that the ethics of liberation is really no ethics, but a feature of religion—of course, the religion of God in this case. And that being so, ethics, strictly speaking, is the ethics of bondage which is empirical, being primarily concerned with the good (*iṣta*), and as such is an attempt to determine how life can be lived best and in the most suitable manner in a state of bondage. This points towards a truth which the Mīmāṁsakas have missed in so far as they hold that the consciousness of duty is spontaneous and is absolutely uninfluenced by the idea of the good (*iṣta*). This view, in an ultimate analysis, is tantamount to the surrender of ethics on the one hand and of religion on the other. But what is thus true in the case of the Mīmāṁsakas proves to be true in a different manner in the case of a few other orthodox schools of Indian philosophy and especially the Advaita and the Viśiṣṭādvaita schools of the Vedānta. As previously observed, both these schools of the Vedānta rule out the empirical determination of the consciousness of the authority of duty and admit its transcendental determination by the non-empirical desire for liberation. And thereby they, in effect, liquidate empirical ethics, the ethics of bondage which, as we have been suggesting, is ethics *par excellence*. But how religion is affected in the process will be considered later.

As already seen, Buddhism and Jainism, on the one hand, and

the Advaita and the Viśiṣṭādvaita schools of the Vedānta, on the other, discount empirical ethics which may be otherwise called objective ethics on account of its preoccupation with the *good* (*iṣta*). But in this they, while insisting on the all-importance of the religion of liberation with or without belief in God as the case may be, are quite alive to the importance of subjective or reflective ethics with regard to spiritual realization. This is due to their belief that the purification of the mind or the self (*cittaśuddhi*) is the *conditio sine qua non* of the culmination of the process of spiritual realization in liberation, and that *cittaśuddhi* is not so much a matter of the performance of duties as it is a matter of the cultivation of virtues. This suffices to indicate that the task of subjective ethics, as distinguished from objective ethics, is to ascertain and classify the virtues, the cultivation of which is the way to liberation. This brings us to the next topic for our investigation, entitled "Virtues and their Classification."

B

VIRTUES AND THEIR CLASSIFICATION

We may begin by reiterating that there, perhaps, is no hard and fast line of demarcation between duty and virtue or at least that it is rather difficult to draw a clear line of distinction between the two. This may be evident from a careful scrutiny of the attempts that have been made by moral philosophers in the West as well as in India to understand the nature of duty and virtue in distinction from each other. But apart from this, the principle on the basis of which virtues have been classified is sometimes such that its acceptance betrays the failure to understand their characteristic peculiarity. This is well illustrated in the classification of virtues offered by Vātsyāyana in his commentary (*Bhāsya*) on the Nyāya-Sūtra of Gautama. He adopts the *source* of virtues (*dharma*) as the principle of their classification and holds that their sources are three in number, namely, *śarīra* (body), *vāk* (speech; vocal utterances) and *manas* (mind). In this Vātsyāyana is obviously guilty of the misunderstanding of the nature of virtues. For neither the body nor speech nor even mind in the Indian sense can be regarded as the source of any virtue, virtues really being the essential features of the inner excellence of the self, as distinguished from the body and speech and mind which may at best be the vehicles of the expression of virtues. Judged in this light, it seems strange that Vātsyāyana should regard charity or munificence (*dāna*), succouring the distressed (*paritrāṇa*) and social service (*paricaraṇa*) as bodily (*śārīra*) virtues. Moreover, the characterization of them as virtues, instead of as duties, seems to be open to dispute.*

Similar difficulties may arise with regard to Vātsyāyana's admission of *satya* (veracity), *hitavacana* (beneficial speech), *priyavacana* (agreeable speech) and *svaddhyāya* (the reciting of the Vedas) as virtues with *vāk* (speech) as their source of origin. In this connection it may be observed, in the first place, that the reciting of the Vedas is certainly not a virtue, and even granted that it is a duty, instead of a virtue, it is not, for obvious reasons, a duty of universal application (*sādhāraṇa-dharma*). Secondly, the uttering of beneficial words, agreeable speech and veracity, although they relate to speech, owe their origin to a certain excellent quality of the self, instead of speech itself.

The case, however, is different with the virtues which Vātsyāyana regards as originating from the mind. The three virtues which he brings under this category, namely, *dayā* (kindness, benevolence or tenderness), *aspṛhā* (unworldliness or indifference to material advantages) and *śṛaddhā* (reverence; piety), deserve to be regarded as essential features of the inner excellence of the self and, consequently, as virtues in the strict sense of the term. In this connection it may be of interest to observe that the negative virtue of *aspṛhā* (unworldliness) points to the Indian conception of the spiritual ideal as a life of complete detachment, signifying the absolute autonomy of the self. Nevertheless, the negative attitude towards the world which is undoubtedly expressed by this virtue is considerably mitigated by some of the virtues of a definitely positive import such as benevolence, charity, social service, etc., which are recognized by Vātsyāyana. Even so, as observed before, Vātsyāyana is not always able to view virtue in distinction from duty and, in particular, he fails to realize the peculiarity of virtues, as is evidenced by his classification of them under the three heads *śārira* (bodily), vācika (linguistic) and *mānasa* (mental). But, as we shall see below, attempts have been made by Patañjali, the founder of the Yoga school of orthodox Indian philosophy as well as the heterodox Bauddhas and the Jainas to remove some of these difficulties of Vātsyāyana.

It needs to be observed at the outset that Patañjali's interest in the understanding of the nature of virtues and their classification is mainly determined by his idea that the cultivation of certain virtues is the necessary prerequisite of the practice of Yoga. Accordingly, they are, in his view, of the nature of restraint (*yama*) and are intended to eliminate evil passions from the mind and thereby purify it. Judged in this light, the virtues, according

---

* It seems that the difficulty of the understanding of duty and virtue in distinction from each other is at least partly, if not wholly, due to the ambiguity of the word 'dharma' on account of its being used in the sense of duty as well as virtue.

to him, are as follows.

(a) *Ahiṁsā* (lit. abstention from injury to living creatures). Although its literal meaning is thus negative, *ahiṁsā*, according to Patañjali, is positively significant, implying as it does good will and amity with all creatures. A special feature of Patañjali's treatment of the virtue of *ahiṁsā*, however, lies in his holding the view that there must be no exception to the cultivation of this virtue, and that animal sacrifices enjoined by the Vedas should be completely abjured. While it may thus prove to be the means of the removal of an evil that enjoys the sanction of the scripture, *ahiṁsā* is also important in that it implies, and indeed holds within its ambit, quite a few excellent virtues. Thus it implies the virtue of restraint of the feelings of aversion or hate which are possible determining conditions of cruelty (*hiṁsā*). It also implies abstention from the use of harsh words as well as intimidation which may be counted as forms of cruelty. Hence it is evident that *ahiṁsā* is in itself the highest virtue and, in fact, is the basis of many others.

The next in Patañjali's list of virtues is *satya* (veracity or truthfulness), which consists in the correspondence of one's thought and speech with the objective fact or event as evidenced by perception or any other reliable source of cognition. Veracity, then, implies, in the first place, that the speaker should apprehend *correctly* the object about which he is required to speak in order that his apprehension may be free from error or illusion *(bhṛānti)*. Secondly, the implication is that he should *faithfully* describe in words what he has already apprehended correctly, so that he may be free from the guilt of having recourse to intentional deceit (*pravañcanā*) or indulgence in meaningless words (*pratipatti-bandhyā*). But then, Patañjali sets a limit to the observance of veracity in view of the consideration that even the most truthful speech may sometimes hurt or harm somebody or other. Accordingly, he holds that veracity is not strictly so called except in so far as it is directed towards the good of the people concerned.

Asteya (lit. abstention from stealing), according to Patañjali, is another virtue which is as much in demand as any other with a view to the purification of the mind. For the understanding of the true significance of *asteya*, it is, however, necessary to note the meaning of its opposite *steya*. The word '*steya*' not only means stealing or unlawful appropriation of another's property but also unlawful greed (*spṛahā*). That being so, *asteya*, the opposite of *steya*, should mean not only outward abstention from unlawful appropriation of another's property, but also inward freedom from greed. In this connection it is worthwhile to mention that, despite the fact that in Indian legal literature certain appropriations of property (*pratigrahas*) are regarded as lawful, it has sometimes been held that appropriation or ownership of property as such is unlawful, so that *asteya* should be construed as *asp̣rhārūpa*, that is, unworldliness or total indifference to material advantages of life.

Now, be it noted that among the major schools of Indian philosophy, both orthodox and heterodox, there prevailed the view that the sex instinct is one of the most potent factors to contribute to the contamination of the mind or the self and thereby prove to be an obstacle to the spiritual realization of the individual. Sharing this view with many other Indian philosophers as he did, Patañjali came to regard *brahmacarya* (restraint of the desire for sexual enjoyment) as one of the important virtues. But he understood this virtue in a comprehensive sense and accordingly held that *brahmacarya* not only means the restraint or control of the organs which are directly concerned with sexual enjoyment, but also the control of the very thought of this kind of enjoyment.

The last in Patañjali's list of virtues is *aparigraha* (renunciation), signifying the attitude of indifference to material prosperity *(abhyudaya)* in view of the consideration that it involves all sorts of disvalue, including cruelty (*hiṁsā*). Thus it is held that the accumulation of riches is not possible without having recourse to deceit (*a-satya*) and many other reprehensible means. *Aparigraha* understood in this sense should, however, be distinguished from *aspṛhā* or *asteya* to which reference has been already made. The former arises out of the consciousness that material prosperity is tarnished by moral faults like deceit, cruelty, etc. The latter, on the other hand, arises as a reaction against the ignoble feelings of pride (*dambha*), attachment (*āsakti*), etc. which are held to be invariable concomitants of the sense of ownership of property.

The foregoing account of Patañjali's treatment of the virtues may be brought to a close with the following remarks. In the first place, he is of the view that these virtues should be cultivated universally by all individuals, irrespective of their social position, station in life, occupation and individual capacity. Secondly, his insistence on the necessity of the universal cultivation of the virtues formulated by him seems to be the outcome of his idea that the different and indeed mutually conflicting ethical codes which are in ordinary use among individuals and societies should be replaced by a universal ethical code in order that humanity may be brought together. Thirdly, Patañjali's recognition of the virtues of *asteya* (unworldliness) and *aparigrha* (renunciation) on the one hand and that of *ahiṁsā* in the positive sense of goodwill to all creatures on the other is significant in that it envisages the synthesis of the ideal of individual freedom of the ascetic type with that of the active altruistic concern with the good of all living beings. Such a synthesis, it is important to note, would undoubtedly serve to relieve the former ideal of its individualistic rigorism. And it would, on the other hand, bring out the true significance of altruism by suggesting that the pursuit of the good of others is a sheer vanity without a prior training in self-restraint and control of worldliness.

Let us now have a brief account of the Buddhist treatment of virtues. The virtues, according to Chandrakīrti, one of the foremost members of the Mādhyamika school of Buddhism, may be classified under four heads, namely, *vijñapati-samutthāpikā* (morality that is overt), *avijñaptayaḥ* (moral traits that are unmanifested or are without outward expression), *paribhāgānvayam karma* (morality arising from communal responsibility) and, lastly, *cittābhisaṁskāra-manas karma* (morality arising from the self-determination of the mind.)

First, as regards the moral traits which express themselves in overt action, they are either *kuśala* (beneficial) or *akuśala* (harmful or injurious) and the medium of their expression may be either *vāk* (speech) or *śarīraceṣtā* (bodily action). Thus under this class there may be two kinds of virtues, the virtues of speech and the virtues of physical action. And to these two kinds of virtues, according to Chandrakīrti, there respectively correspond the vices of speech and those of physical action.

As regards the virtues coming under the second class, they are really subconscious determinations of a beneficial nature *(kuśala-svabhāva)* which result from a pious resolution or else from the outward performance of a meritorious act even for the first time. Thus a person may firmly resolve not to follow the path of evil and his resolution may produce a subconscious modification of his personality, in consequence of which, he may, without any effort on his part, invariably eschew the path of evil and follow that of righteousness. It may also happen that a person, who performs an act of merit for the first time, may, from the very moment he does it, be subconsciously determined to direct his life towards righteousness. Not only that; the determination may be a part and parcel of his personality. It remains to be added, however, that what is due to happen in the case of subjective dispositions of a harmful nature *(akuśalasvabhāva)* must be exactly the opposite of what is thus found to happen in the case of the subjective dispositions of a beneficial nature *(kuśalasvabhāva)*.

One of the peculiarities of the Buddhist treatment of virtues lies in that it is allied with the view that morality may accrue from communal or institutional responsibility just as it does arise out of individual responsibility. And it is on this account that Buddhism recognizes a third category of virtues called *paribhāgānv-ayam-karma*. Accordingly, it holds that virtue may accrue to us from the righteous acts of the society to which we belong or the institution which we have established. And just the opposite may happen if the acts of our society or our institution are unrighteous. The fact that stands out in this connection is, however, that Buddhism has added an altogether new dimension to ethics by recognizing such a thing as social or institutional morality in distinction from individual morality, the idea of which usually dominates ethical investigations.

Lastly, as regards virtues and vices resulting from conscious resolve or the self-determination of the mind, the most important point to notice is that this category of virtues and vices differ from the first and the second categories of them. For while the first consists of virtues and vices arising from *overt acts* and the second comprises only those virtues and vices which accrue from *subconscious modifications* of the mind, the virtues and vices coming under the present category arise neither from overt acts nor from subconscious determinations of the mind, but from the conscious self-determination of the mind (*mānaskarma*). This conscious self-determination of the mind or the self may, however, be of three different forms, namely, the conscious resolve of self-restraint (*ātmasaṁyamakam*) or its opposite (*viparyyayaḥ*), the conscious resolve to cultivate benevolence (*parānugrahakam cetaḥ*) or its opposite *viparyyayaḥ*) and the conscious resolve to establish the bond of amity and peace with all creatures (*maitram cetaḥ*) or the opposite (*viparyyayaḥ*). Now it would be worthwhile to note in this connection that the recognition, on the part of Buddhism, of morality resulting from the conscious self-determination of the self does not seem to have any originality about it. Nor does its recognition of morality accruing from overt acts entitles it to any originality in its ethical investigations. But there is no doubt about the novelty of its approach to ethical problems in so far as it comes to recognize social or institutional morality on the one hand, and unconscious and subconscious morality on the other.

It is now left for us to enquire into the Jaina view of the nature of virtues and their classification. We may begin here by observing that Jainism does not seem to be so much interested in the classification of virtues as in the understanding of their nature and in their enumeration. As we have previously seen, according to Jainism, the soul, in the course of its earthly life, is covered over with *karma*-matter and is thereby rendered impure. That being so, it is incumbent upon the individual to bring about the *saṁvara* or *nirodha* (arrest) of the influx of *karma*-matter into the soul (āsrava). Virtue or righteousness (*dharma*), in the view of Jainism, is then a way (*upāya*) of the arrest of *karma*. It is, moreover, the manifestation of the highest excellence of the self. Judged in this light, the virtues, according to Jainism, are as follows: forgiveness (*kṣamā*), humility (*mārdava; mṛdutā*); sincerity or straightforwardness (*ārjava* or *ṛjutā*); cleanliness (*śauca*); veracity (*satya*); practice of physical hardship and privation (*tapas*); renunciation (*tyāga*); strenuousness (*ākiñcanya*) and continence (*brahmacaryya*).

It is evident from the list given above that Jainism does not recognize other-regarding virtues such as benevolence and social service. This shows that Jaina ethics is primarily governed by the idea of individual self-culture, instead of the idea of goodwill to others. That this is so is further corroborated by the fact that forgiveness which is not usually included in the orthodox Hindu list of virtues is recognized by Jainism as an important virtue, and that forgiveness, after all, amounts to the moral elevation of the forgiver at the cost of the forgiven.

We may next take into account a rather new way of the classification of virtues—if, of course, it may be so called at all,—which has emanated from a Jaina source. This classification seems at first sight to be subjectivist in so far as it is based on the understanding of virtue and vice, righteousness and unrighteousness not merely with reference to the consequences of happiness or suffering (*sukhaduḥkhaphala*) but with reference to subjective *intention* (*abhisandhi*). And as regards *abhisandhi*, Jainism holds that it may be either *pure* (*viśuddhyānga*) as in the case of virtue or righteousness and impure (*saṁkleśānga*) as in the case of vice or unrighteousness.

Now impure intention, according to Jainism, may be of two kinds: *ārta* (distressing or afflicting in nature) and *raudṛa* (aggressive or violent). And each of these two kinds of impure intention gives rise to four vices. Thus the impure intention of the *ārta* kind manifests itself in the attempt to escape from unpleasant situations; the attempt to be in contact with the pleasant, when alienated from it; mental engrossment in misery or suffering (*vedanā*) and the desire for the acquisition of power (*aiśvarya*) which is not yet attained. The impure intention of the *raudṛa* kind, likewise, gives rise to four vices, namely, cruelty (*himsā*), untruthfulness or mendacity (*anṛta*), stealing or wrongful possession (*steya*) and aggressiveness in the maintenance of the ownership of property (*viṣayasaṁrakṣana*). Pure intention, according to Jainism, may, likewise, be of two kinds, namely, that which is devoted to the contemplation of the ideal of duty (*dharmadhyānasvabhāva*), and that which is devoted to the contemplation of the ideal of perfection (*śukladhyānasvabhāva*).

It is then evident that the above classification is more concerned with the determination of vices than with the determination of the virtues. The underlying idea here seems to be that virtues are more likely than not to be cultivated, if the vices are thoroughly known and if, in consequence, serious attempts be made to steer clear of them. This is probably the reason why most of the classifications of virtues in Indian ethics go hand in hand with classifications of vices. The point that needs to be taken into account in this connection is, however, that the acquisition of knowledge, the performance of duty and the cultivation of virtue, perhaps, amount, in an ultimate analysis, to the negation of the negations, which are respectively ignorance, dereliction and vice. That being so, a thorough investigation of these negations seems to be a necessary prerequisite of their negation in order that the corresponding affirmations in the shape of unblemished acquisition of knowledge, unflinching performance of duties and unfaltering cultivation of virtues may come within one's easy reach. This points to one of the essential features of the methodology of philosophical investigations in India which has been seldom taken notice of.

Another point that deserves to be mentioned in conclusion is that if the list of virtues recognized by the Indians be compared with the list of the cardinal virtues recognized by the Greeks, it will be found that there is no room, in the Greek list, for the virtues of detachment (*asp̣rhā*), compassion (*dayā*) and reverence or faith (*śṛaddhā*), which according to the Indians, are of supreme importance. Of course, the Indians do not include in their list of virtues those that are of fundamental importance in the estimation of the Greeks, namely, justice and friendship which are definitely characterized by worldliness. But this seems to be due to their proneness to underestimate the value of worldliness. Hence it is evident that the Greek ethical outlook, which has prevailed in the West till this day, is predominantly worldly, whereas that of the Indians is indicative of the restraint of worldliness by its opposite. This may serve to distinguish the Indian ethical outlook from that of Christianity. Of course, Christianity is at one with Indian ethics in recognizing compassion (*dayā*) and faith (*śṛaddhā*) as of inestimable moral value. But then, according to the Indians, these virtues need to be cultivated with a view to the realization of detachment (*asp̣rhā*) which does not seem to be essential to the Christian ideal of life.

III

THE MORAL STANDARDS

It was at one time quite usual with Western writers on ethics to devote considerable attention to the question of the standard of morality and discuss the typical views with regard to it. But the situation seems to have changed in recent times on account of the inroad of linguistic analysis into the various branches of philosophy, including ethics. As regards Indian ethics, the discussion of this question separately or on its own account, perhaps, was never one of its special features. Nevertheless, its treatment of the fundamental practical problem of human life in various ways has made room for various theories of the moral standard. It is, however, beyond the scope of the present work to deal with all of them. We may, therefore, try to provide brief accounts of some of the typical ones, and to this end we may begin with the Indian theory of the moral standard as custom or tradition (*lokopadeśa*).

A

THE THEORY OF THE MORAL STANDARD AS CUSTOM OR TRADITION

As we have previously seen, some of the schools of Indian philosophy, including even the Advaita Vedānta, have held that the field of duty is constituted, among other things, by customary or traditional practices. Not only that; it has sometimes been affirmed that customs or traditions is one of the standards of morality. But even granted that the question of the moral worth of customs and traditions does, for some reason or other, come to be ignored, it may be rather easy to realize that both of these vary from a preceding age to a succeeding one and, what is more, may sometimes be mutually conflicting and thus be lacking in universality. That being so, it would be natural to hold that, strictly speaking, custom or tradition as such cannot be a moral standard so as to serve as the criterion of the distinction between the good and the evil, the right and the wrong. In view of this it may be suggested that the criterion in question should be some *lokaprasiddhi* (universally accepted opinion or consensus) or other, if there be any. This suggestien is not necessarily opposed to the view of custom or tradition as a moral standard. It only conveys the idea that nothing can be a moral standard which is not universally accepted or does not admit of universal application. So custom or tradition may be regarded as a moral standard provided that it conforms to the requirement of this idea. But this obviously throws both of them into the background and amounts to the virtual recognition of consensus (*lokaprasiddhi*) as the standard of morality.

Even so the question may arise—and, in fact, it has actually arisen in the field of Indian ethics—whether consensus (*lokaprasiddhi)* should be treated as a moral standard on its own account or on account of something else to which it may be conducive. And as regards this question, its answer has assumed two broadly different forms. One of these consists in holding that consensus is self-sufficient as a moral standard. This view, it would be of interest to note, may meet with the approval of those among the recent moral philosophers in the West who regard public opinion as the most suitable means of the resolution of moral disputes. But according to the latter of the two views, the moral significance of consensus is not intrinsic but *extrinsic*. And in this regard, it has been suggested, in the first place, that consensus owes its positive moral significance to the well-being *(upakāra)* to which it may be conducive. Secondly, it has been pointed out that the well-being in question should not be regarded as confined to the psychological feeling of *happiness* but as inclusive of organic well-being in the sense of the increase of life. This seems to be an approximation to the view of the biologically-minded moral philosophers in the West like Herbert Spencer and Leslie Stephen who regard the increase of life as a characteristic feature of the evolution of morality. Thirdly, it has been held that the moral singificance of consensus lies, not in its being conducive to anything, but in its being the medium or vehicle of the revelation of the Moral Law as embodied in the scripture. According to this view, consensus then derives its moral authority from the *Śāstra* (scriptures).

B

THEORIES OF LAW AS THE MORAL STANDARD

The above reference to Moral Law brings us to the consideration of the theories of Law as the moral standard. These theories ordinarily refer to the laws of nature, tribal laws, social laws and divine laws. As regards the first of these four kinds of laws, the Greeks regarded them as most suitable guide to the proper conduct of the affairs of human life. But then, human behaviour being radically different in nature from natural events, the view of the laws of Nature as the moral standard seems to be ill-conceived. It is, perhaps, for this reason that this view has found no place in Indian ethics. And as far as thé tribal and social laws are concerned, they may be said to be included within customs and traditions and so there arises no need for the admission of separate theories of tribal and social laws as the moral standards in addition to that of custom or tradition regarded as the standard of morality. It is, perhaps, in view of this that Indian ethics has attached great significance to *personal* laws, as distinguished from natural, tribal and social laws, and regarded them as reasonable standards of morality.

Now personal laws may be divine; and, as a matter of fact, those schools of Indian philosophy and especially the Nyāya-Vaiśeṣikas, who believe in God, regard personal laws as divine and hold that the laws or commands which have emanated from God constitute the standard of morality. Those Indian philosophers, on the other hand, who do not believe in God, namely, the Cārvākas, the Bauddhas and the Jainas, regard the personal laws as non-divine and attach some importance to them as the standard of morality. But an altogether different aspect of the situation is presented by the Mīmāṁsakas, who, like these heterodox philosophers, do not believe in God, and yet differ from them as well as from the Nyāya-Vaiśeṣikas and their confréres in dismissing the idea of personal law, whether conceived to be divine or non-divine. And in further difference from both, they hold that the standard of morality is an impersonal *(apauruṣeya)* law, or a set of such laws, comprising the injunctions *(vidhis)* and prohibitions *(niṣedhas)* emanating from the Vedas. Thus, according to the Mīmāṁsakas, the Moral Law with reference to which the distinction between the good and the evil, the right and the wrong needs to be drawn, is a constituent of an objective or independently existing moral order and as such is authoritative in itself and is in no need of deriving its authority from any *personal* source, whether divine or otherwise.

Let us now briefly refer to the heterodox theories of non-divine law as the moral standard. First as regards the Cārvākas, they hold that the king is the highest earthly authority *(lokasiddho rājā parameśvaraḥ)* and, consequently, that his injunctions and prohibitions respectively determine the right and the wrong. Of course, they, as hedonists, hold that the individual's pleasure determines the right and his pain determines the wrong. But then, the distinction between these two is, ultimately, determined by the authority of the king in as much as he, in the view of the Cārvākas, is the dispenser of all happiness and suffering. But this seems to be incompatible with the progressive outlook of the Cārvākas to which reference has been already made.

According to the Jainas and the Bauddhas, on the other hand, temporal authority is of no consequence with regard to the determination of the distinction between the right and the wrong. The reason for this is that the earthly sovereign is as imperfect as the common herd and that obedience to his authority is governed by the hope of reward or the fear of punishment and so would be prudential but by no means moral. That being so, the only person whose authority can play a suitable and effective role in the sphere of morality, in the view of the Jainas and the Bauddhas, are the Arhats and the Buddhas who are conspicuous for their spiritual perfection. So it is not the commands of the earthly sovereign, but the injunctions and prohibitions prescribed by spiritual experts that would determine what is morally right and what is its opposite. But then, lest the Arhats and the Buddhas should, in consequence, come to be regarded as eternally perfect and thus resemble God as conceived by the theists, both the Jainas and the Buddhists hold that there is an unending succession of Arhats and Buddhas and, consequently, that their perfection is not eternally realized, but is subject to a ceaseless process of development.

We may next consider the views of the Indian theists who hold that God is the moral governor of the world and, consequently, that the moral standard is the law of righteousness as enjoined by Him. According to some of them, rightness and wrongness are not objective categories, but are determined respectively by the injunctions and prohibitions prescribed by God. Even so, such injunctions and prohibitions do not, in their view, constitute the moral law, but only reveal it. But the Nyāya-Vaiśeṣikas differ from them in holding that the commands of God, which are embodied in the scripture, do not merely reveal this law, but constitute it. As distinguished from these two theistic views of the divine law as the moral standard, there, however, is a third, according to which the moral law is neither revealed nor constituted by the commands of God, but is God Himself in the form of Brahman. This view is held by a certain section of the Vedāntists and the argument advanced by them in its support may be explained as follows.

The essence of injunctions (*vidhis*) presenting themselves as the moral law consists in their *obligatoriness.* This must be due to their being characterized by a kind of self-evident authority. But nothing can be said to be possessed of self-evident authority which is not self-validated. And to be self-validated is to be a self-establishing experience, that is, an experience which is self-accomplished or, in other words, is accomplished (*siddha*) from eternity. It follows, then, that injunctions (*vidhis*), in virtue of their inherent obligatoriness, are, in an ultimate analysis, an eternally self-accomplished experience which is *eo ipso* absolute and as such is but another name for Brahman. But then, such is the moral situation that they present themselves to the individual agent, not as something eternally accomplished, but as the moral law to be obeyed as something to be accomplished (*sādhya*) in time.

Thus we are presented with a theory of law (*vidhi*) as the moral standard according to which *vidhi* is neither *personal* in the sense of being prescribed by a personal God nor is *impersonal* in the sense of being without a personal law-giver. It is indeed unique. And its unprecedented novelty consists in identifying the moral law with Brahman regarded as the eternally self-accomplished superpersonal absolute experience and in holding that the moral law owes its authority to the self-fulfilled reality of the Absolute thus conceived. This, while being divergent from what Śaṁkara would himself hold, conveys the suggestion towards his transcendental theory of the ideal life which may be briefly stated below.

According to Śaṁkara, the moral law as presented by the Vedic injunctions and prohibitions is impersonal in the sense that it is only brought to light by the communicator (*vaktā*) of the Vedas, but is not created by him. The communicator is, of course, *Īśvara* (God or the Lord) and not, as the Jainas and the Bauddhas hold, a spiritual expert (*āptapuruṣa*). But, surprisingly enough, Śaṁkara holds that the Vedas, after all, are of an empirical character and as such are true in a relative or pragmatic (*vyavahārika*) sense but untrue in the absolute (*pāramārthika*) sense. That being so, the value of the prescriptions of the Vedas is at best pragmatic and consists in their usability for the overcoming of grosser untruths. But, strictly speaking, life governed by them is empirical and is tarnished by the ill-effects of bondage and so is in need of being transcended by the realization of the identity of the individual and Brahman in and through *karmasanyāsa* (freedom from the bond of duty). Thus, while according to the above theory, moral life, despite its empirical character, reflects, at least partially, if not completely, the nature of the Absolute (Brahman), in the view of Śaṁkara, the moral life, being incorrigibly empirical, is the total negation of the ideal life which is not only the conquest over grosser untruths, but also over the untruths which make up morality.

C

THE THEORY OF THE MORAL STANDARD AS SOCIAL STABILITY OR SOCIAL GOOD

The theories of the moral standard which we have so far considered do not involve direct reference to anything that is of a social quality and cannot, therefore, be said to have raised the question as to whether anything concerning society may have a part to play in the determination of what is right and what is wrong. But it is precisely this question which has occupied the serious attention of some of the philosophers in India. Accordingly, they have come to conceive the moral standard in either of two distinct ways, namely, as *lokasthiti* (maintenance of the stability of society) and as *lokasiddhi* (fulfilment of the demand for social good).

As regards *lokasthiti*, it may be of interest to note that the Mahābhārata refers to it, but understands it, not in the sense of social stability, but in the sense of the preservation of living beings (*lokapālana*). But here we are concerned with the former sense of this word and not with its latter sense. Now the theory of the moral standard as social stability—even supposing that it has a genuinely moral significance—obviously has the idea of *moral order* particularly in view to the neglect of the idea of *moral progress*. But these two ideas are not mutually incompatible as seems to be implied by the theory of the moral standard under consideration. On the contrary, the two are essential to each other and, what is more, the one without the other is a false abstraction and indeed is lacking in moral quality. So the theory of the moral standard as social stability hardly deserves to be so called. In any case, it is vitiated by the fault of conservatism. Moreover, there is no such thing as a single society. On the contrary, there are many and various societies. They differ from one people to another and from one geographical region to another. That being so, the factors which may contribute to the stability of a certain society may render another society unstable. Hence it is plain that the present theory of the moral standard is unavoidably relativistic and, consequently, that it is unable to provide an objective or universal criterion of the distinction between right and wrong as it is, in virtue of its very designation, incumbent upon it to do.

It is, therefore, no wonder that there should be no dearth of thinkers in India to reject the theory of the moral standard as social stability and yet to insist on the view of this standard as something that is characteristically social. In consequence, there arose the opportunity of the introduction into Indian ethics the concept of good which has proved to be of far-reaching consequence in the history of ethics in India as well as in the West. Thus having this concept at their disposal and at the same time viewing it in the social perspective, some Indian philosophers have come to conceive the moral standard as social good (*loka-śreyaḥ*). This conception of the moral standard may easily make room for moral progress and thus overcome the conservatism alongside the limitation of regional and communal morality to which the theory of the moral standard as social stability, as seen above, lays itself open. Even so, its real worth would depend upon how the concept of good is understood, no matter whether it is viewed to be individual or social. And this brings us to the theories of the moral standard as end.

D

THEORIES OF THE MORAL STANDARD AS END

As we shall gradually see, the theory of the moral standard as *end* has assumed quite a few distinct forms in Indian ethics. But the most outstanding and the most widely discussed among them is the theory of the moral standard as pleasure, well known for its advocacy by those members of the Lokāyata movement who are known as the Cārvākas. Now since no philosophical literature of the Cārvākas themselves has come down to us, our knowledge of their philosophical views, including those on morality, is derived from the writings of their adversaries and critics. So, no matter whatever might have been their real ethical position, the Cārvākas have been presented to us as the advocates of the grossest form of egoistic hedonism which draws no distinction between sensual and refined pleasures and holds that one's own greatest and most intense pleasure with the least admixture of pain is the highest good. Nevertheless, as we have mentioned earlier, information is also available about the refined *(suśikṣita)* Cārvākas who, like Bentham and Mill in the West, introduced various grades of refinement into hedonism so as to relieve this ethical doctrine of the stigma of egoism and sensualism. Even so, the majority of the schools of Indian philosophy have found fault with their ethical doctrine and brought out the difficulties of hedonism which it may be worthwhile to take notice of.

(a) Criticism of Hedonism by some of the Anti-hedonistic Schools of Indian Thought

One of the most cogent criticisms of hedonism is offered by the Mahābhārata by stating that the desire for pleasure is insatiable in as much as it grows as a result of indulgence in it and, consequently, that the pursuit of pleasure is attended with strife and pain and disappointment. The Mīmāṁsaka Kumārila seeks to expose the absurdity of the gross form of hedonism by observing that the pleasure derivable from virtuous acts is comparatively feeble, whereas that which is yielded by wicked acts is more likely than not to be strong and, consequently, that, from the hedonistic point of view, wicked acts must be preferable to virtuous ones.

Vijñānabhikṣu, one of the leading members of the theistic school of the Sāṁkhya, has put forward several objections against hedonism. He observes, in the first place, that ceaseless and indiscriminate search after pleasure is unable to yield lasting satisfaction to the individual. For wealth and other material objects, the possession of which yields pleasure, are liable to come to an end or to be lost and their loss is inevitably attended with pain and suffering. Secondly, the pleasure that is derivable from the possession of material advantages is, after all, transient, it being certain that it either ceases to be felt or is followed by pain. Thirdly, the kind of pleasure that is derivable from the satisfaction of the desire for material advantages, as Vijñānabhikṣu points out, is not essentially different from pain or suffering. The reason for this, according to him, is as follows. The acquisition of material advantages undoubtedly involves a strenuous effort which is unavoidably attended with pain. Moreover, this acquisition, despite the fact that it gives rise to pleasure, cannot put an end to all kinds of suffering. Furthermore, the attainment of one's individual pleasure is tantamount to the denial of others' claim to the same and so is sinful.

One of the most incisive criticisms of hedonism is that which has been offered by the Naiyāyikas. According to them, the highest good and indeed the supreme ideal of life is not the attainment of pleasure or happiness, but absolute freedom from pain and misery and suffering. The realization of this ideal, in their view, demands the avoidance of pleasure as well as pain. This view of the Naiyāyikas is based on their understanding of the relation between pleasure and pain. Their own view about this relation differs from two other views, one of which is held by the Buddhists. According to the Buddhists, whatever exists is of the nature of pain, and pleasure as a positive experience does not exist (*sarvaṁ svarūpataḥ duḥkhaṁ, sukhaṁ svarūpataḥ nāsti*). But the Naiyāyikas reject this view on the ground that it is contradictory to actual experience in this regard.

Another view about the relation between pleasure and pain consists in stating that pleasure, despite the fact that it presents itself to be a positive experience, is not really so, being a subtle form of pain (*duḥkhavikalpa*). But this view is also rejected by the Naiyāyikas on two grounds, one psychological and the other moral. The former consists in stating that the will (*pravṛtti*) functions not only with a view to the avoidance of the evil attended with suffering, but also with a view to the attainment of the good which is capable of yielding pleasure or happiness. And this, according to the Naiyāyikas, goes to show that pleasure is as positive an experience as is pain or suffering. The moral ground, in the view of the Naiyāyikas, is that pleasure or happiness is the appropriate reward of righteousness (*dharma*) and, consequently, that it must be a positive experience, instead of being pain or suffering in disguise, lest the purpose of righteousness should be defeated.

The third view about the relation between pleasure and pain, which is, in fact, the view of the Naiyāyikas themselves, consists in holding that both of these are positive experiences, but that the two are always and in every case inseparably bound up together and, consequently, that neither of the two can be attained or avoided without the attainment or avoidance of the other at the same time. That being so, if absolute freedom from pain or suffering be, as according to the Naiyāyikas it must be, the ideal of life, then the realization of this ideal should be in need of the total abandonment of the search after pleasure or happiness. And this cuts the ground from under the feet of hedonism.

(b) Departures from Hedonism

Let us begin here by adverting to the curious situation of hedonism. It consists in that this ethical doctrine has received more disapprobation than approbation through the ages, and yet that most of the non-hedonistic theories of the moral standard which have found place in the history of ethics in India or elsewhere have centred round it and indeed have figured as departures from it. This is testified to by the number and variety of criticisms to which hedonism has been subjected by the different schools of philosophy in India, and some of which have been mentioned above. Not only that; as will be immediately evident, the theories of the moral standard as end which we shall now bring under review are primarily attempts to remove what is considered to be hedonism's inadequacy or else to make an improvement upon this doctrine in one way or another.

One of the ethical theories which may be regarded as a departure from hedonism is most suitably represented by Buddha's doctrine of the *middle path*. According to this doctrine, the moral standard or the ideal of life consists in the mean between two extremes—one consisting in a life exclusively devoted to the pursuit of pleasure or happiness as hedonism would have it, and the other amounting to a life exclusively dedicated to the practice of austerities as recommended by the antithesis of hedonism, namely, ascesticism. But this does not signify the surrender of hedonism any more than it may be taken to mean the surrender of asceticism. On the contrary, it is tantamount to the acceptance of both hedonism and asceticism as transformed in the crucible of their mutual influence.

Another departure from hedonism is represented by the Jaina theory of the moral standard as purity of motive *(viśudhdāngābhisandhi)* to which reference has been already made. This theory, it is necessary to note at the outset, does not dismiss pleasure or happiness as unimportant, useless or undesirable. On the contrary, it admits the concept of happiness in the individualistic sense of one's own happiness as well as in the altruistic sense of other's happiness. But then, it does not find any intrinsic moral significance in happiness as such and, in consequeuce, goes beyond both individual and general happiness in search of something which is not unconnected with happiness and yet is the determinant of what is right and what is wrong. And it discovers this something in pure motive or intention (*viśuddhāngābhisandhi*). Thus does Jainism seek to make an improvement upon hedonism by shifting the moral standard from the consequence of actions in the form of happiness to the purity of their motive.

Another way of departure from hedonism lies in the conception of the moral standard or the ideal of life as something on the transcendental level which corresponds to that which is happiness on the empirical level. The typical representations of this something are to be found in the Greek concept of *eudaemonia* and, more appropriately, in the Upaniṣadic concept of *ānanda* (transcendental bliss) which the Advaita Vedānta, in particular, regards as the highest good and the supreme ideal of life.

Now, as we have previously indicated, it is not difficult to realize that pleasure or happiness in the empirical sense cannot be the highest ideal of life as hedonism conceives it to be. The question then arises as to what that ideal should be. One answer to this question is derivable from asceticism, according to which the elimination of the desire for happiness is the highest good for mankind to aim at. But this view, being purely negative, is really no departure from hedonism and indeed leaves this ethical doctrine with its influence unimpaired. It is precisely for this reason that the distinction has been drawn in the Upaniṣads between two definitely positive concepts, those of the *śreyaḥ* (the intrinically good) and the *preyaḥ* (the merely pleasant). So the situation now concerns the choice between the ideal ot *śreyaḥ* and the ideal of *preyaḥ*, instead of the indiscriminate choice of the ideal of *preyaḥ* or even the choice of the renunciation of the ideal of *preyaḥ* in preference to the acceptance of this ideal. And the Kathopaniṣad holds that to choose the ideal of *preyaḥ* is to be deprived of the highest good, whereas to choose the ideal of *śreyaḥ* is to attain the highest good.

But then, to call the hedonistic ideal of life *preyaḥ* and to distinguish it from the ideal of life alternatively regarded as *śreyaḥ* does not seem to be enough to bring out the reason why the latter ideal of life should be preferable to the former. This inadequacy of the Upaniṣadic attempt to make a departure from hedonism seems to have been brought home to Śaṁkara. Accordingly, the ethical distinction between the *preyaḥ* and the *śreyaḥ* was construed by him as, ultimately, the metaphysical distinction between two contraries, namely, the principle of *avidyā* (nescience) pointing towards unreality and that of *vidyā* (knowledge) with its capacity for leading to reality. In consequence, Śaṁkara found himself in a position to hold that to choose the *preyaḥ* would amount to choosing to follow the path of *avidyā* in pursuit of unreality, whereas to choose the *śreyaḥ* would be the same as to choose to follow the path of *vidyā* in pursuit of reality. And this, as may easily be seen, would suffice to explain why the *śreyaḥ*, as the Upaniṣadic recommendation goes, should be preferable to the *preyaḥ* and be regarded as the highest good (*summum bonum*). Nevertheless, this attempt on the part of Śaṁkara to make out a clear case for a departure from hedonism betrays his intellectualistic bias resulting in the arbitrary imposition of metaphysical significance upon ethical concepts.

Śaṁkara did not, however, stop at the metaphysical interpretation of the concepts of the *preyaḥ* and the *śreyaḥ*, but went further to draw the distinction between the consequences which, according to him, would respectively follow from the pursuit of the ideal of *preyaḥ* and the ideal of *śreyaḥ*. Thus, he came to hold that the pursuit of the ideal of the *preyaḥ* would result in empirical pleasure consequent upon the possession of some external object or other. The pursuit of the ideal of the *śreyaḥ*, in his view, would, on the other hand, give rise to transcendental satisfaction of the nature of self-satisfaction or self-contentment (*ātmasantosa*) consequent upon self-realization (*ātmalābha*).

Now self-realization, according to Śaṁkara, is the realization, on the part of the individual, of his identity with the Absolute, that is, Brahman. That being so, the transcendental satisfaction regarded as self-contentment (*ātmasantosa*) or *ānanda* (bliss), which is consequent upon self-realization in this sense, should naturally be, and Śaṁkara holds that it is, imperishable or eternal, autonomous or self-dependent (*svayāṁlabdha*) and pure. In contrast with transcendental satisfaction thus characterized, empirical pleasure, dependent upon the possession of external objects as it is, would, in the view of Śaṁkara, be perishable or transient, heteronomous (*anyāpekṣa*) and impure. This obviously reinforces the reason for the preferability of the ideal of the *śreyaḥ* to that of the *preyaḥ* and, consequently, for a departure from hedonism.

But then, the advantage which Śaṁkara's transcendentalism thus has over the empiricism of hedonism should really be regarded as spurious. The reason for this is quite simple and consists in that the self-realization of the individual, on which transcendental satisfaction is held to be consequent, is tantamount to his annihilation in the manner of his absorption in Brahman and, consequently, that transcendental satisfaction, whether called *ātmasantosa* (self-contentment) or *ānanda* (bliss), even supposing that it can somehow come into existence, should in vain try to find its enjoyer or the experiencing subject. Hence it is evident that the moral ideal or, let us say, the moral standard, which is really recalcitrant to pleasure as conceived by the hedonists, loses its significance as well as its identity in the transcendental self-satisfaction as understood by Śaṁkara. Śaṁkara's achievement in this regard may at best be said to consist in bringing out the *reductio ad absurdum* of hedonism, but not in making a successful departure from this doctrine. This points towards the difficulty of combating hedonism and finding out an alternative that would prove to be its corrective.

IV

THE ETHICS OF NON-VIOLENCE (*AHIMSĀ*)

Reference has been already made to the concept of *ahiṁsā* at various places in this work. But in view of the most serious consideration that this concept has received in the treatment of the problems of morality in India, it would, perhaps, be worthwhile to elaborate what we have only casually observed about the ethical significance of *ahiṁsā*. Now, no matter whether or not the word 'non-violence' is the appropriate English equivalent of the Sanskrit word '*ahiṁsā*', we are, for our present purpose, treating these two words as synonymous in consideration of the acceptance of their synonymity in recent ethico-political deliberations in India.

Be it noted at the outset that Western ethics, mainly governed by the traditional Greek view of morality as it has been through the centuries, has hardly any room for such a virtue as *ahiṁsā*. For *justice* which is the social virtue in Plato's list of the cardinal virtues, however important it may be with regard to the establishment of social order, cannot reach the moral and spiritual height of *ahiṁsā*. Of course, the religion of Jesus as revealed in his Sermon on the Mount remained and perhaps still remains unsurpassed in its emphasis of the supreme importance of non-violence amounting to self-effacement as the means of spiritual realization or the fulfilment of human destiny. But then, the religion which the West was in need of having, and actually had, from the East, was not that of Jesus, but Christianity which, on account of its being contaminated by the imperialism of Rome was, and still is, far from being a religion of peace with the concept of non-violence as its basic principle. It is, therefore, no wonder that the Graeco-Roman tradition should continue to pervade the ethical thought of the West, resulting in the neglect of the cause of peace through the ages.

It is far from us to suggest, however, that the Indian attitude is absolutely non-violent or that indulgence in violence is foreign to the Indian mind. On the contrary, the truth seems to be that in the world of ours which has been and still is full of violence, it is not easy for any people, the Indians not excepted, to maintain a non-violent attitude, however it may try to do that. Even then, there stands out the unparalleled fact that it was in India that an attempt was, for the first time, made with great success to build up a huge political organization upon the foundation of the principle of non-violence during the reign of Asoka the Great and under the influence of Buddhism. This was undoubtedly due, among other things, to the strong and all-pervasive authority which the idea of *ahiṁsā* wielded in the mental atmosphere in India.

How the idea of *ahiṁsā* first originated before it became widespread and was almost universally accepted by the thinking people in India, is, however, difficult, if not impossible, to determine. But then, it is a fact that at least some of the ideas which have proved to be of profound significance and of far-reaching importance to mankind had a simple or, let us say, humble beginning. Thus the concept of *ṛta* (law), for example, which was at first used by Indian thinkers for the explanation of the orderliness of natural phenomena, subsequently acquired deeper significance and found wider scope in so far as it was brought to bear upon the determination of the moral worth of human conduct. Keeping this in view, we may refer to Manu's use of the concept of *ahiṁsā* in connection with the relation between the teacher and his pupils. Thus he states that one who instructs others with a view to their welfare should observe the rule of *ahiṁsā* (not causing pain) and speak sweet and gentle words to them.* This may lead one to guess that the recommendation of the adoption of the rule of *ahiṁsā* on the part of the teachers was made by Manu and, perhaps, also by his predecessors as a remedy for the harsh treatment which teachers are usually in the habit of meting out to their pupils. And once the concept of *ahiṁsā* was thus introduced, it not only came to stay, but, it may be further guessed, gained wider and wider scope until it was construed as the governing principle of the relation between man and all living beings.

But even granted that the above hypothesis regarding the origin of the concept of *ahiṁsā* is untenable, the fact that remains indisputable is that this concept has been almost universally accepted from one period of Indian history to another and has found a prominent place in various kinds of Indian literature, whether Vedic, Paurāṇic, philosophical, religious or the like. But before we go into the question of the prevalence of the concept of *ahiṁsā* in these ways, we may just mention two points—one relating to the alleged antiquity of this concept and the other concerning its conflict with another concept opposed to it. As regards the former point, some writers on Jainism hold that Ṛṣabha was the first among the *tīrthankaras*, and that it is he who first revealed the *ahiṁsā-dharma* (the religion of non-violence) long before the advent of the Aryans in India. But this view cannot be borne out by historical evidence. The reason for this is that Mahāvira, the historical founder of Jainism was contemporaneous with Buddha and both of them flourished after the arrival of the Aryans in India, and that they were equally insistent on the supreme importance of the practice of *ahiṁsā* as the way to salvation. Even so, there is no doubt that Jainism is especially conspicuous for its admission of *ahiṁsā* as the fundamental ethico-religious idea just as it is well known for its recognition of *anekānta-vāda* (the doctrine of the multi-point-of-view of reality) as the philosophical ideal.

As regards the latter point it needs to be observed that the ancient ethico-religious situation in India, as revealed in the light

---

*Vide Manusaṁhitā II, 159.

of the testimony provided by Vedic literature, was marked by the conflict between two parallel developments of thought—one emphasizing the all-importance of the practice of *ahiṁsā* in the sphere of human affairs and the other insisting on the obligatoriness of the performance of rituals involving animal sacrifice prescribed by the scripture. In this connection, it may be surprising to note, and yet it seems true, that the supporters of the doctrine of *ahiṁsā* were mainly kings or princes belonging to the Kṣatriya class, whereas the champions of the cause of ritualism were mostly *Brāhmana* 'priests. It was, therefore, no wonder that it should have devolved upon the *Kṣatriya* prince Siddhārta to preach and practise the religion of *ahiṁsā* and thereby attain Buddhahood, and that it should have been left for the *Kṣatriya* king Asoka to set, before the humanity afflicted with age-old suffering from the tyranny of autocracy, the unique example of empire-building upon the foundation of the humanistic principle of non-violence. And it was also not surprising that the Cārvākas and their followers should have condemned the Brāhmanas for their exploitation of the laity with a view to the fulfilment of their selfish ends. But this is far from suggesting that the Cārvākas were supporters of the doctrine of *ahiṁsā*. On the contrary, they, being advocates of the grossly egoistic form of hedonism, would not mind the performance of wicked acts, including acts of violence, provided that it would be conducive to sensual pleasure. Even so, they were justified in condemning all kinds of ritualism, not because ritualism might involve the killing of animals, but because it was regarded as religious and they themselves were no believers in religion.

Now, as regards the prevalence of the idea of *ahiṁsā* among the Indian people and in the successive periods of Indian history, we may begin by observing that the Vedas and especially the Ṛgveda, which contain the earliest record of at least some of the details of the Indian way of life, condemn injury to life (*hiṁsā*) as one of the worst sins and are conspicuous for their praise of non-violence (*ahiṁsā*) as one of the most commendable virtues. And yet the fact remains that it is the Vedas which were responsible for the prescription of rituals involving animal sacrifice. Hence it is evident that the Vedas arrived at a strange settlement of the conflict between the two mutually opposed ideas of *hiṁsā* and *ahiṁsā* by having recourse to a sort of makebelieve, namely, that ritualistic animal sacrifice did not, as it were, involve any injury to life (*hiṁsā*). Thus there came into existence, at a comparatively early stage in the history of India, a way of thinking which made room for the admission of the doctrine of *ahiṁsā* alongside the approval of ritualistic animal sacrifice.

This way of thinking, it is of interest to note, has, through the centuries, influenced the minds of the Hindus, comprising the orthodox (*āstika*) section of the Indian people, and has produced an impact upon their literature, including not only the Vedas, but also the Upaniṣads, the Epics, the Purāṇas and philosophical writings. Thus Manu held that the desire for the good of all creatures ultimately leads to supreme happiness. Not only that; he went so far as to state that one who permits another person to kill a creature or buys or sells flesh or even cooks it, is guilty of *hiṁsā* (injury to life). And yet he was of the view that animal sacrifice prescribed by the Vedas should be treated as a case of non-killing. The Mahābhārata also falls in line with the way of thinking under consideration. Accordingly, it regards *ahiṁsā* as one of the two highest virtues, the other being truthfulness. But, curiously enough, it at the same time approves of the practice of a moderate measure of violence (*hiṁsā*) for the sake of livelihood and holds that the capital punishment of dangerous criminals is no sin. Even the orthodox schools of Indian philosophy were no exception in this regard. Most of them, either tacitly or overtly, approved of ritualistic animal sacrifice on the pretence that it was no injury to life. Of course, the Sāṁkhya and the Yoga, despite their affiliation to the orthodox circle of Indian philosophy, got rid of this false pretence which came into vogue since the Ṛgvedic age, and came to regard injury to life (*hiṁsā*) as sinful, no matter whether or not it was prescribed by the scripture. But then, the effect of this view was, to all intents and purposes, undermined by the Sāṁkhya itself in so far as it expressed the opinion that the sin (*pāpa*) accruing from ritualistic animal sacrifice is outweighed by the righteousness (*puṇya*) yielded by it.

But very different was the case with the serious heterodox way of thinking as represented by Jainism and Buddhism. Both these schools of thought refused to be misled by the false pretence in question and whole-heartedly espoused the cause of peace based on the sole foundation of the principle of non-violence. As previously mentioned, *ahiṁsā*, according to Jainism, is the very essence of religion and the way to the achievement of the ultimate goal of human life or the fulfilment of human destiny. But then, Jainism carried the idea of *ahiṁsā* to an absurd limit so as to make it yield the recommendation of the observance of all kinds of austerities, including self-mortification. The point that needs to be borne in mind in this connection is, however, that once the idea of *ahiṁsā* is misdirected and carried to an extreme in the manner of the recognition of the all-importance of self-mortification, its real purpose, which would consist in its being brought to bear upon the establishment of inter-personal relations between oneself and one's fellows, is more likely than not to be defeated. For the field of human interests is, after all, subject to the operation of the principle of economy; so that if a man is led by the idea of *ahiṁsā* to be unduly interested in self-discipline through such rigorous means as self-mortification, then he would naturally, if not necessarily, lose interest in making use of this idea in the establishment of strictly human relations between himself and others of his kind. But then, the result need not be confined to such a state of negation. On the contrary, there may ensue a positive compensation for it which would consist in following the path of least resistance by way of merely observing the formality of catering to the needs of insects and birds in the name of practising *ahiṁsā*. That this conveys a true picture of an aspect of the situation of Jainism will, perhaps, be brought home to any discerning student of this religion which rose contemporaneously with Buddhism, and which, like the latter, dedicated itself to the task of introducing a new religious outlook in place of the one brought into existence by the Vedas and fostered by Brāhmanism.

Buddhism, on the other hand, refrained from indulging in any manner of extravagance in making use of the idea of *ahiṁsā* and tried to appreciate its true spirit, lest its inherently humanistic significance should be lost in the ferment of fanaticism. This is evident from Buddha's preference for, and his own pursuit of, the middle path. But then, as we have previously observed, the concept of *ahiṁsā*, despite its unquestionable importance as a means of the establishment of the relation of mutual amity between man and man, is, after all, negative and conveys no definitely positive suggestion as to how this relation may be brought into existence. As regards this difficulty, it may be said to have been resolved by both Jainism and Buddhism in virtue of their view that this concept, though negative in form, is positive in import. Thus love and kindness, as Jainism holds, constitute the basis as well as the positive significance of the idea of *ahiṁsā*. And, as has been already mentioned, Buddhism presents the positive aspect of *ahiṁsā* in the form of an entire gamut of excellent virtues of unsurpassable humanistic quality, namely, *maitrī* (benevolence towards all creation), *karuṇā* (compassion towards the distressed), *muditā* (joy at others' happiness) and *upekṣā* (indifference towards others' faults).

Now, in view of what has been observed above, there is no doubt that Jainism and Buddhism admitted the concept of *ahiṁsā*, not in the sense of a pure negation, but in the sense of certain positive virtues. But it seems that even then there remain indefiniteness as well as uncertainty as to the way of practising *ahiṁsā*. Of course, it may be said that to practise *ahiṁsā* positively is to love, and be kind to, others, to feel compassion for the distressed and so on. But then, the fact remains that people do not always or in all circumstances 'love their neighbour', despite the fact that they are instructed by men of religion to do that. Hence it is evident that there is something in or about the individual which is a hindrance to his invariable and unconditional practice of *ahiṁsā* in a positive way. To this end it would not, therefore, be enough for him to be instructed by a Mahāvīra or a Buddha or a Jesus to love his neighbour. What, then, is needed is a sort of therapy, consisting of the diagnosis of the hindrance in question and the prescription of the remedy for it. The remedy in demand, it is most important to note, should steer clear of *precepts* to which mankind has been unnecessarily subjected through the ages, and consist of the principles of conduct, conformity to which is the *sine qua non* of the invariable and unconditional practice of *ahiṁsā*. And it is the discovery of these principles which is all-important with respect to the achievement of the ultimate goal of human life and indeed is the hitherto unfulfilled task of the religion of man.

PART 4

Indian Philosophy of Religion

INTRODUCTION

It is necessary to observe at the outset that 'religion' is a European word and means a fixed and determinate relationship between the human individual and some super-human being called the Supernatural, the Self-existent, the Absolute or, simply, God. But religion in this sense or, as we should rather say, in a sense similar to it, is not altogether out of place in the Indian scheme of spiritual life. On the contrary, the theistic or Vaiṣnavite schools of the Vedānta, the Nyāya-Vaiśeṣika and even the Advaita Vedānta make room for the religion of God. But then, this religion does not always and in every case have the same importance from the Indian point of view, as it invariably has in the estimation of the Europeans. For, according to the strictly Indian way of thinking, it is but a casual and by no means an essential element in the process which is the way to the fulfilment of human destiny and which may be simply called the Way or religion as the Way, as distinguished from the religion of God. Strictly speaking, the Way thus characterized is to the Indian thinking what the religion of God is to that of the Europeans. And judged in this light, the religion of God, signifying as it does a fixed relationship between the human self and the Divine Self, does not seem to be compatible with its Indian counterpart which is essentially a movement or a dynamic process. It is, therefore, not surprising that the Sāṁkhya and the Mīmāṁsā among the orthodox schools of Indian philosophy on the one hand and the two heterodox schools of Jainism and Buddhism on the other should as they actually did dismiss the religion of God as spurious and conceive religion as the Way to be the sole spiritual concern of mankind.

It is then evident that atheism, amounting to the rejection of belief in God, does not, from the Indian point of view, necessarily involve the surrender of the idea of spiritual realization but may make room for this idea as signified by religion as the Way. But then, the rejection of the religion of God as well as religion as the Way, no matter whether or not it is desirable, is not an impossibility, but, on the contrary, well may come within the scope of the human freedom of choice. This is clearly demonstrated by the

Cārvākas who not only do not believe in God, but do not also recognize any ideal for mankind to pursue except that of the greatest sensual pleasure of the individual. Diametrically opposed to the Cārvākas, however, are the Nyāya-Vaiśeṣikas and the Vaiṣnavites who admit both the religion of God and religion as the Way. But then, there is an important differnce between the Nyāya-Vaiśeṣikas and the Vaṣinavites with regard to the question of the relation between these two forms of religion. According to the latter, the two are inseparable from each other and, together, constitute an integral whole; so that the one apart from the other is a false abstraction. This amounts to holding that belief in God, together with its practical implications, constitutes the Way, that is, the way to salvation *(mukti)*. The Nyāya-Vaiśeṣikas, on the other hand, hold that the religion of God and religion as the Way, while not being incompatible with each other and, positively speaking, being equally admissible, do not form themselves into an integral whole, but have separate roles to play in the life of man, the role of the latter, unlike that of the former, being concerned with his liberation. Hence it is evident that the religion of God does not, according to the Nyāya-Vaiśeṣikas, play as important a part in the life of man as it does in the view of the Vaiṣnavites. That this must be so was initially indicated by the fact that Kanāda, the founder of the Vaiśeṣika school of philosophy, made no definite reference to God or the Divine Soul in the *Vaiśeṣika-Sūtra* in connection with his view of the origin of the authority of the Vedas.*

There is still another view of the relation between the religion of God and religion as the Way which is held by Śaṁkara, the foremost protagonist of the Advaita school of the Vedānta. He, like the Nyāya-Vaiśeṣikas and the Vaiṣnavites, admits both these forms of religion. But he differs from them in holding that the religion of God holds good within the limit of a certain level of spiritual development, and that that level is a lower one beyond which there is a higher level where this religion is unavoidably reduced to non-existence, yielding place to a kind of religion as the Way. So, according to Śaṁkara, there arises neither the question of the integration of the two forms of religion into a whole nor that of the co-existence of the two with separate roles to play in the life of man. The religion of God, in the view of Śaṁkara, were, as it were, a ladder which one may use in order to climb higher, and when this end is achieved, it inevitably falls to the ground, conveying the message that there is no return from the apex of spiritual

*Kanāda's own words are : "The authority of the Vedas is due to the utterance of him or them"; Vaiśesika-Sūtra, i, 1.3; x, ii, 9. Thus he leaves the question absolutely uncertain whether the authority of the Vedas is due to the utterance of God or the seers (ṛṣis).

development after it is once reached. It is important to note, however, that this view of Śaṁkara is in agreement with the corresponding view of the Jainas and the Bauddhas except in that, whereas the former avoids extremism by viewing the religion of God to be at best an aid to the spiritual realization vouchsafed by religion as the Way, the latter follow the path of religious radicalism, equipped with the view that one must steer clear of the Scylla of the religion of God and the Charybdis of Cārvāka hedonism on the way to spiritual realization.

The foregoing observations suffice to indicate the principal topics which need to be discussed in connection with the treatment of the Indian philosophy of religion. These may be listed as follows:—

I. Indian Atheism.
II. Indian Religion of God.
III. Indian Religion as the Way.

Let us then proceed to deal with these topics separately and in the order mentioned here.

I

INDIAN ATHEISM

One of the views about the Indian people which ordinarily prevails in India itself as well as abroad is that they are conspicuous for their religious outlook on life. But this view may only hold good if the word 'religion' is arbitrarily taken to mean a mass of superstitious beliefs born of ignorance, and it is equally arbitrarily held that religion goes hand in hand with political and economic backwardness. Of course, there is no doubt that the bulk of the Indian population has remained and still does remain steeped in the darkness of ignorance and, consequently, are held in the grip of irrationality, and that they, for this reason as well as others, are still far off from the extent of the material prosperity which they are really in need of. But that should no more be a reason for the growth and propagation of religion than for the overthrow of the religion that be. And, as a matter of fact, the history of India is interspersed with movements of religious reform on the one hand and successful attempts to eliminate the religion of God and put atheism in its place on the other. As regards the latter aspect of Indian history with which we are at present especially concerned, it may, among other things, be pointed out that all the major schools of heterodox (*nāsitika*) thought, including the Cārvāka, the Jaina and the Bauddha, and two out of the six major systems of orthodox (*āstika*) philosophy, namely, the Sāṁkhya and the Mīmāṁsā, rejected the religion of God and had recourse to atheism.

Now, as regards the Cārvākas, it needs to be especially noted that they have not advanced elaborate arguments, as other atheistic schools of Indian philosophy have done, against the religion of God and in support of atheism. As a matter of fact, their atheism is consequent upon their dogmatic procedure—for what else could it be?—comprising, among other things, the following steps. The first and the foremost of these is their rejection of the authority of the Vedas, together with belief in Soul, pre-existence and future life, which is the outstanding feature of the teaching of the Vedas and the Upaniṣads, and, indeed, is essential to the religion of God. Next comes their treatment of the world as the sole reality, together with their view of it as ultimately and irreducibly material. This view, it is hardly necessary to mention, leaves no room for anything supernatural or spiritual and, consequently, is recalcitrant to the religion of God. The last of these steps is epistemological, consisting in their view of perception as the only source of cognition. Since perception—of course, in the ordinary (*laukika*) sense—is confined to the apprehension of those things only which present themselves through the intermediary of the sense-organs, supersensible beings such as God, it may well be held, cannot be apprehended and so must be regarded as fictitious. And this amounts to the employment of extreme empiricism in the elimination of the religion of God, which bears a resemblance to the employment of the same epistemological doctrine by the logical positivists in recent times in the elimination of metaphysics.

Of course, atheism is contrary to the spirit of the teachings of the Upaniṣads, which are summed up in the insistence on the ultimate reality of the Absolute Spirit called Brahman. This is precisely the reason why the Cārvākas, atheistically inclined as they were, started by overthrowing the authority of the scriptures, including the Vedas and the Upaniṣads. And this example of the Cārvākas has been followed by the Jainas and the Bauddhas in their attempt to establish the claim of atheism as against that of the religion of God. But then, their rejection of the authority of the scriptures is only a preliminary step towards, but is, on no account, a means to the fulfilment of, this end. In fact, the Jainas and the Bauddhas and especially the former engaged themselves in polemics with a view to establishing the superiority of atheism to the religion of God.

Let us then begin with Jainism and have a brief account of its antitheistic arguments. These arguments are mainly directed against the Naiyāyikas who depend, among other things, upon what is usually called the causal argument with a view to proving the existence of God. This argument is based on the presupposition that the world is of the nature of an *effect*, and consists in stating that it must, therefore, have an efficient cause (*nimitta-*

kāraṇa), and that the cause in demand is God. As regards this presupposition, the Naiyāyikas try to justify it on the understanding that whatever is made up of parts is an effect, and that the world consists of parts. But Jainism's main contention in this regard is that the conception of the world as constituted by parts cannot be rendered intelligible in a manner which is unobjectionable or else does not adversely affect the Naiyāyikas' own philosophical position in some respect or other. Accordingly, Jainism finds itself in a position to conclude that the world does not admit of being conceived to be of the nature of an effect, but should, on the contrary, be regarded as self-existent, and, consequently, that the question of its being created by God as its efficient cause does not arise.

But even granted that the world is of the nature of an effect, it does not necessarily follow, as Jainism further contends, that its cause must be only one, namely, God. In this connection, Jainism disapproves of the Naiyāyika view that the existence of many gods would lead to a state of conflict among them, with no better prospect than the emergence of a chaos, instead of a cosmos. And as against this view, Jainism observes that if such a wonderful thing as the beehive needs a society of bees for its creation, the world which is far more wonderful than a beehive, must have depended for its creation upon a society of gods, instead of a single God without any assistance. This observation on the part of Jainism is obviously opposed to the theistic belief.

Another point in the Naiyāyikas' theistic argument consists in stating that the *variety* which characterizes the world of human beings cannot be accounted for except on the admission of the existence of God. But this has been objected to by Jainism as follows. The variety, as illustrated in the world of human beings, in the happiness of some of them and the unhappiness of some others, supposed to have been created by God, must have been created by Him either in accordance with their merits and demerits or independently of these. If the former alternative be admitted, it would follow that God really is not what the theist conceives Him to be, namely, the independent Lord (*Bhagavāna*). If, on the other hand, the latter alternative be accepted, the consequence would be equally unsatisfactory from the theistic point of view in as much as it would amount to stating that God makes some of His creatures happy and others unhappy in an arbitrary manner and, therefore, is guilty of partiality so as to cease to be himself (*anīśvara*). In view of this, Jainism arrives at the conclusion that the Law of *karma* alone is sufficient to account for the variety which is manifested in the world as a whole, and that the Naiyāyika conception of God as the Lord of *karma* (*karmādhyakṣa*) is redundant and so needs to be dismissed.

Lastly, Jainism raises the most pertinent question as to the motive which let God to create the world. Since the activities of intelligent beings are usually motivated by either self-interest or compassion for others and since God is *ex hypothesi* a supremely intelligent being, His motive in the creation of the world, as Jainism argues, must have been either some interest of His own or His compassion for His creatures. But the former alternative, as Jainism contends, is inadmissible in as much as God, being an eternally fufilled being, can have no unfulfilled desire and, consequently, cannot be said to have any interest of His own. And as regards the latter alternative, it is equally without any bearing upon the present situation. The reason for this is that compassion is the desire to remove the suffering of others, but that before creation there is none to suffer nor is there any suffering, standing in need of being removed. Since God cannot, then, be spoken of as having any motive to create the world, it would, according to Jainism, be utterly futile to try to prove His existence on the supposition that He is the creator of the world. If it is held, however, the God has created the world, not out of any motive, but in sport (*krīḍā* or *līlā*), it would follow that His creative act is as purposeless as the play of a child which, obviously, would not become Him. But there may be still another difficulty of the causal argument for the existence of God, if the idea of creation be given up and, consequently, God comes to be regarded as the cause of the world in the sense that the latter follows from His nature (*svabhāva*). And the difficulty, according to Jainism, would be that, on this view of causation, all effects should be regarded as the outcome of the *nature* of their causes, with the result that the hypothesis of the existence of God would be uncalled for.

Now a careful consideration of the nature and quality of the theistic and the anti-theistic arguments, some of which have been briefly mentioned above, will, perhaps, lead to the discovery of the truth that it is as futile to try to prove the existence of God as it is to make an attempt to disprove the same. This is precisely the truth which was realized for the first time in the history of mankind by Gautama the Buddha, as is evident from his silence on the questions concerning supersensibles such as the Absolute, God or the like. This silence on his part should not, however, be construed as implying his belief in the reality of the supersensible. On the contrary, the uncertainty about his real attitude towards the supersensible, which has been left behind by his silence under consideration, can be easily removed in the light of the implications of some of his basic doctrines, and it can be definitely established that his teaching is opposed to absolutism as well as theism.

Among the doctrines, that which may be said to constitute the foundation of the Buddhist philosophy as a whole, and which is especially relevant in the present context, concerns Buddha's new conception of causation as dependent origination *(pratitya-samutpāda)*. And what is particularly important about the doctrine of dependent origination is the admission of its universal applicability by Buddha himself and his followers. What this means, according to them, is that nothing can be said to exist in itself and by itself or, in other words, be a *substance* and, positively, that everything originates in time as an effect of some cause which in its turn must have originated as an effect of some other cause and so on *ad indefinitum*. The entire field of reality or the universe as a whole, in the view of Buddhism, then, is essentially a causal nexus so as to preclude the possibility of there being any such thing as the First Cause, that is, the cause which is not an effect in its turn. This view is obviously opposed to the conception of God as the uncaused cause of the world which is essential to theism. It is, therefore, not surprising that Buddha, as a report in the Pali Canon goes, should ridicule the conception of God as the creator of the world (Brahmā) by stating that it is a delusion on the part of Brahmā to think that he is the omniscient and omnipotent creator of the world, past, present and future, while the fact, on the contrary, must be that he is as subject to origin and destruction as any other thing.*

It may be argued, however, that since the doctrine of dependent origination is a law, the law of the inter-relation of the phenomena of the world, there must be someone who is related to it as the law-giver, and who is also responsible for the supervision of its operation. But this argument is obviously based on the understanding of the law governing the universe as a whole, namely, the law of dependent origination, on the analogy of man-made laws such as social or political laws, and so is anthromorphic. It is precisely for this reason that Buddhism holds the view that the law of dependent origination cannot be said to have been created or designed by God, nor can its operation be regarded as being in need of divine supervision. This law, according to Buddhism, is simply there, and it operates of itself and without the guidance of anyone's purpose. Thus are set aside the teleological as well as the causal arguments which the theists usually employ with a view to reinforcing belief in the existence of God.

As is well known, the concept of morality, in addition to those of causality and teleology, is sometimes brought to bear upon the theistic argument for the existence of God. In view of this, Buddhism is circumspect enough to observe that the hypothesis of God regarded as the creator of the world and as a perfect being is untenable. The reason for this, as Buddha himself is reported in

*Vide Dhighanikāya; Pāthikasūtta, iii, 1.

Aśvaghoṣa's *Buddhacarita* to have mentioned in connection with his conversation with Anāthapindika, is that the joy and sorrow, the love and hate which spring up in conscious individuals should, on the theistic hypothesis, be creations of God, and, consequently, that God Himself must be capable of having these mental phenomena so as to lose His claim to perfection. Moreover, since God, according to theism, is the maker of all that happens in the world, all deeds said to be performed by human individuals should, after all, be regarded as His performances, with the result that the distinction between right and wrong would lose its sense, and the practice of virtue would serve no purpose whatsoever.

Lastly, mention may be made of an unusually ingenious objection against the causal arguments for the existence of God which was raised by Yaśomitra from the point of view of the Buddhist doctrine of flux. Since the cause being given, all its effects must be given at one and the same time, the effects, supposed to be produced by God and to constitute the world as a whole, should be *simultaneously* present. But the fact, on the contrary, is that the effects concerned present themselves successively, instead of simultaneously. That being so, it may well be objected that God cannot be the cause of the world which is in a state of ceaseless flux, and where effects are produced in succession and not all at once. Of course, it may be replied that the effects are produced by God with the help of certain conditions, and that the fulfilment of these conditions is a temporal process, with the result that the production of effects must needs be successive and not simultaneous. But it may still be objected that the conditions concerned may be said to be sufficient to produce the effects so as to leave no room for the hypothesis of the divine causation of the world. And it would not do to rule out this objection on the basis of the assumption that God is the First Cause, and the conditions in question are the second causes. The reason for this is that, judged as it should be from the point of view of the doctrine of dependent origination, the concept of the First Cause, that is, the cause which is not an effect in its turn, is spurious.

It now remains for us to provide brief accounts of the antitheistic arguments advanced by the Sāṁkhya and the Mīmāṁsā, both of which belong to the orthodox *(āstika)* circle of Indian philosophy. First, as regards the Sāṁkhya, its arguments against the religion of God are mainly as follows. Since the hypothesis of God is usually admitted with a view to the explanation of the existence of the world, the Sāṁkhya's main contention is that this hypothesis is absolutely unnecessary in as much as neither of the two kinds of causes, namely, the material cause and the efficient cause, to which the world may be said to owe its existence, is identifiable with God. The reason for this, according to the Sāṁkhya, is that the material cause of the world is *prakṛti* regarded as the primeval material stuff, and its efficient cause consists of the merits and demerits of the individual souls *(puruṣas)*. As we have previously seen, the original state of equilibrium of *prakṛti,* in the view of the Sāṁkhya, is disturbed by the transcendental influence of the *puruṣas* and, as a result, *prakṛti* evolves and brings into existence all things ranging between the Mahat and the gross elements, namely, earth, water, fire, air and ether, of which the world is made. And the Sāṁkhya further holds that *prakṛti* evolves in this manner for the sake of the experience *(bahoga)* of the *puruṣas* and that its subsequent dissolution is intended to bring about their liberation *(kaivalya)*. Thus is presented by the Sāṁkhya a picture of the world-process which has no room for either divine creativity or divine purpose, but may be said to be solely concerned with man and nature and the intercourse between them.

Of course, it may be be contended that *prakṛti,* being *ex hypothesi,* unintelligent, its evolution must be in need of intelligent guidance and supervision and, consequently, that there must be an omniscient being in order for this need to be fulfilled. But the Sāṁkhya replies that *prakṛti,* despite the fact that it is unintelligent, can serve to fulfil the ends of the *puruṣas* by way of bringing into existence their experience and their liberation, even as the unintelligent milk from the udder of the cow can contribute to the nourishment of the calf. This reply, being based on an analogy, is obviously lacking in cogency. But the Sāṁkhya tries to make up for this defect by turning the table against the theist by bringing to his notice the old difficulty which is due to arise out of the question as to the motive of God in His creation of the world. Mention may be made in this connection of the objection of the Sāṁkhya to the Naiyāyikas' arguments for the existence of God on the ground that the Vedas must have a creator, and that, they being repositories of eternal truths, their creator cannot be any human being or beings, but must be an infinite and omniscient being, namely, God. The objection of the Sāṁkhya simply consists in stating that the question of the creation of the Vedas does not arise in as such as they, being embodiments of eternal truths, are impersonal *(apauruṣeya)*, that is, cannot be said to have been created by a person, whether human or divine.

It may be observed in conclusion that whereas authorities on the Sāṁkhya, like Vācaspati and Aniruddha, hold that this school of Indian philosophy is avowedly atheistic, Vijñānabhikṣu, the famous author of the *Sāṁkhyapravacanabhāsya*, is of the view that the Sāṁkhya does not deny the existence of God, but only holds that His existence cannot be proved, as is evident from the statement in the Sāṁkhya-sūtra, namely, that 'there is no proof for the existence of God *(Īśvarāsiddhe)*. But then, this view can by no stretch of logic or imagination be said to amount to affirming the existence of God. Not only that; if the Sāṁkhya-Kārikā of Iśvarakṛiṣna be regarded, as it should be regarded, as providing an authentic account of the philosophical position of the Sāṁkhya, then, as we have seen above, there would be no getting away from the fact that the outlook of this school of philosophy is unquestionably atheistic. It seems, then, that Vijñānabikṣu sought to reinterpret the teaching of the Sāṁkhya from the standpoint of the theistically oriented philosophies of the Yoga and the Vedānta, instead of trying to consider it on its own account.

Lastly, we are required to make an enquiry into the attempt made by the Mimāṁsā school of philosophy to make out a case for atheism as against some of the prevailing theistic arguments. The first thing to be noted in this connection is that the Mīmāṁsā is primarily concerned with ritualistic morality and that, on this account, it enjoins the performance of sacrifices to many gods. This is apt to create the impression that this school of philosophy advocates polytheism or the religion of many gods. But, strictly speaking, this cannot be so. The reason for this is that the gods to whom sacrifices are offered, according to the Mīmāṁsā, are not objects of worship, nor are they viewed to be responsible for the grant of rewards for the offerings made to them. On the contrary, the Mīmāṁsā holds that it is the unseen potency *(apūrva)* generated in the individual performer of sacrifices which, in independence of the gods, bears fruit in the shape of the reward for his sacrificial offerings. So the gods have no function to perform on account of which there could be a religion centering round them. It is precisely for this reason that later Mīmāṁsā denies the existence of the gods, and regards the reference to them in the *mantras* (hymns) as a mere way of praising, or emphasizing the importance of, the sacrifices.

In any case, the fact remains that the Mīmāṁsā eschews all reference to God, as distinguished from the gods. Jaiminī, the founder of this school of philosophy, makes no mention of God. And Kumārila and Prabhākara, the respective heads of the two rival schools of the Mīmāṁsā, go further in advancing arguments against theism which make no secret of their pronounced atheistic tendency. In fact, their atheism is a necessary corollary of their realistic attitude towards the world and especially their naturalistic view of the world-process based on the theory of causation known as *pariṇāma-vāda* or *satkārya-vāda* which they advocate in common with the Sāṁkhya. According to this view, whatever comes into existence is but the modification of something that already exists; so that there can, strictly speaking, be no such thing as *creation*. That being so, theism loses its ground in so far as it is at least partly dependent upon the causal argument for the existence of God.

But then, an element of crudity is noticeable in Indian atheism in so far as it seeks to refute the causal argument for the existence of God by contending that the cause must be *bodily*, but that the conception of God as having a body cannot be justified, nor can it be rendered intelligible. And Kumārila and Pārthasārathi Miśra have an equal share of this crudity in their rejection of the hypothesis of God as the cause of the world. Moreover, Kumārila is opposed to the Nyāya-Vaiśeṣika view that God creates the world out of the atoms, but with the help of the merits and demerits of finite souls. But his opposition applies to the former part of this view and not to the latter. Thus he agrees that the diversity in the world is due to the diversity of the merits and demerits of finite souls, but he denies that God is the creator of the world. But Pārthasārathi Miśra goes further than Kumārila in holding that not only God is not the cause of the world, but also that the diversity of the merits and demerits of finite souls is not sufficient to account for the diversity in the world. According to him, the diversity in the world is due to the diversity of physical causes, together with the diversity of the merits and demerits in question.

Kumārila further argues that in order that one can believe that God has created the world, there must be someone to testify to this fact, but that this demand does not admit of fulfilment. The reason for this that the creatures who came into existence for the first time did not obviously know how they were born, and that God's own assertion of His having created the world, even supposing that it is somehow available, may be lacking in veracity, it being presumable that He makes that assertion merely to show off. Hence Kumārila arrives at the conclusion that the creation of the world by God is not amenable to proof. And this conclusion is reinforced by him with reference to the old difficulty which, in his view as in the view of the Sāṁkhya, arises in connection with the question as to God's motive in His supposed creation of the world. And in this Pārthasārathi Miśra is at one with Kumārila. But he adds that there is an additional reason why God cannot be regarded as the creator of the world. The reason is that He is viewed to be the creator as well as the destroyer of the world, but that creation and destruction being contraries, one and the same cause, namely, God cannot be said to be both a creator and a destroyer.

Prabhākara is, however, more explicit than other Mīmāṁsakas in his attempt to eliminate the hypothesis of God as the creator of the world. Thus he observes that all effects are produced by their *natural* causes and without the intervention of any imaginary supernatural cause. Animals and human beings are born of their parents, and, similarly, all things in the world are produced by their appropriate causes, independently of any intervention whatsoever on the part of God. And he, like Kumārila, is opposed to the Nyāya-Vaiśeṣika view that God has created the world out of atoms with the aid of the merits and demerits of finite souls. His reason for this opposition is, however, very subtle and consists in stating thus. God being a substance and the merits and demerits of finite souls being qualities that are foreign to Him, there can be no contact between the former and the latter. On the other hand, the atoms being material and God being spiritual, the contact between the two must be equally out of the question. That being so, the Nyāya-Vaiśeṣika view under consideration is untenable.

Lastly, it may be mentioned that all the Mīmāṁsakas, including Kumārila and Prabhākara, are equally opposed to the Nyāya-Vaiśeṣika argument for the existence of God on the alleged ground that the Vedas must have had a creator and that the creator in question could be none else than God. The Mīmāṁsakas, like the Sāṁkhya, dispose of this argument by observing that the Vedas being embodiments of eternal verities, the question of their having been created cannot arise at all, it being understood that creation is a temporal phenomenon, whereas eternity is the negation of temporality.

II

INDIAN RELIGION OF GOD

We are using here the expression 'religion of God', instead of "theism", in view of the consideration that the religion of God need not necessarily be theistic, but may also be deistic as it is in the case of the Nyāya-Vaiśeṣikas. As previously mentioned, the chief protagonists of this kind of religion are the Nyāya-Vaiśeṣika, the Vaiṣnavite Vedānta and the Advaita Vedānta. But to this list must be added the Yoga which, despite the fact that it is allied with the Sāṁkhya in many ways, does not accept the latter's atheism, but is conspicuous for its belief in God. The fact that these schools of philosophy make room for the religion of God is, however, significant in that theology has a place in the field of Indian thought, but indeed one which is precarious, being exposed to the challenge of atheism on the one hand, and that of religion as the Way on the other.

But then, theology in India is unconcerned with such a thing as the sole human Incarnation of God as well as with a Prophet or Prophets entrusted with the communication of God's will to the rest of mankind. That being so, Indian or, as we should in this connection rather say, Hindu theology should naturally be and indeed is different from Christian theology, whether Catholic or Protestant, as well as from Judaic and Islamic theologies. And if the eschatologies and the codes of religious practices, with which the religions of the Hindus are associated, are, as they can very well be, left out of account, without prejudice to these religions, then Hindu theology may have a legitimate claim to be regarded as a kind of philosophy of the religion of God. And in that event, Hindu theology, rechristened as the Hindu philosophy of religion may be said to have to deal with three main questions respectively concerned with the proofs of the existence of God, the nature of God and His relation to the world *(jagat)* and human individuals *(jīvas)*. We may then proceed to enquire into the treatment of these questions by the Hindu philosophy of religion, and begin our enquiry with its treatment of the question concerning the proofs of the existence of God.

A

PROOFS OF THE EXISTENCE OF GOD

We may first observe here that those schools of philosophy which start with an unshakable belief in God and accordingly treat this belief as the *rationale* of the enquiry into the human as well as the non-human situation of the world are obviously in no need of any proof of the existence of God and, consequently, would not undertake the unnecesssary, nay, sacrilegious task of proving His existence. These are really the schools of philosophy which start from the concept of the Absolute theistically interpreted as God or, in other words, are advocates of theistic absolutism, and are identifiable with the Vaiṣnavite schools of the Vedānta in India. But then, those who start from the concept of the Absolute, interpreted only spiritualistically and not theistically at the same time, and yet, for some reason or other, feel, as Śaṁkara did feel, the need for the admission of the religion of God, are, from the very nature of the case, under the necessity of vindicating the existence of God. This provides one indication of how there arises the need for the proof of God's existence. And another indication of this kind is to be found in the case of those schools of philosophy which are no advocates of absolutism, but, on the contrary, are realistically and pluralistically oriented, and yet, curiously enough, feel the need for the admission of the religion of God. The reason for this is that since their main philosophical position is inherently indifferent to the question of the existence of God, they are required to undertake to prove His existence in order for their admission of the religion of God to have at least a semblance of justification. The Indian schools of philosophy answering to this description are obviously the Nyāya-Vaiśeṣika and the Yoga. Thus we see why the Vaiṣnavite schools of the Vedānta are under no obligation to undertake to prove the existence of God, and why, on the other hand, it is incumbent upon the Advaita Vedānta of Śaṁkara, the Nyāya-Vaiśeṣika and the Yoga to undertake this task.

Now as previously indicated, the Vaiśeṣika school of Indian philosophy, being primarily interested in the enquiry into the phenomena of Nature and thus having a predominantly scientific outlook, was originally indifferent to the question of religion, even supposing that it was not definitely committed to atheism. It, therefore, seems that its association with the Nyāya was one of the circumstances, if not the only circumstance, which was responsible for its being subsequently drawn towards religion, resulting in the demonstration of the realizability of the union of science with belief in God. But then, it is rather difficult to understand why the Nyāya, being primarily interested in logic and epistemology, should develop an interest in religion as it actually did. The difficulty increases further in view of the fact that it is the Nyāya school of philosophy which argued most forcefully and elaborately in support of belief in God, and, what is more, spared no pains to refute antitheistic arguments. However that may be, it would be of interest to observe that the Indian theistic arguments and especially those that are advanced by the Nyāya-Vaiśeṣikas, as we shall immediately see, bear some sort of resemblance to those which form part of the philosophy of religion in the West.

Let us first have an account of the causal or cosmological argument which is common to the Nyāya-Vaiśeṣikas and their confréres in India as well as in the West. Just an Western philosophy of religion insists on the *contingency* of the world and therefrom argues its dependence upon God for its creation, so do the Nyāya-Vaiśeṣikas, as we have previously seen, start from the view of the world as of the nature of an *effect* and regard this view as sufficient to warrant the conclusion that the world is created by God. But then, the causal or cosmological argument as elaborated by the Nyāya-Vaiśeṣikas has certain peculiarities which it would be worthwhile to note. In the first place, God, according to these philosophers, is only the *efficient* cause, and is by no means the material cause of the world. The material cause, in their view, consists of the atoms which are *given* in order that God can create the world out of them. Be it noted in this connection that the Yoga also admits a kind of cosmological argument and accordingly holds that the material cause of the world which, according to it, is *prakṛti*, is *given* and not created by God, and that God is only the efficient cause of the world, while being inactive, instead of being active as

He, in the view of the Nyāya-Vaiśeṣikas, indeed is.* It is then evident that God's creativity, in the view of the Nyāya-Vaiśeṣikas as well as the Yoga, is subject to a limitation and, consequently, that He is not all-perfect as He should be and as He is ordinarily conceived to be.

Secondly, the cosmological argument of the Nyāya-Vaiśeṣikas differs from its Western counterpart in pointing towards another limitation of God's creativity and, consequently, of His perfection. This is due to its embodying the view that the merits and demerits of finite souls, like the atoms, are also *given*, and that it is with the help of these that God has created the world with a view to introducing *variety* into it. Hence it is evident that the cosmological argument as formulated by the Nyāya-Vaiśeṣikas not only suffers from the fault of adding to the limitation of God's creativity as well as His perfection, but is also vitiated by anthropocentricism which, for obvious reasons, is incompatible with the object of the cosmological argument for the existence of God. It is, therefore, no wonder that the atheistic schools of Indian philosophy such as the Sāṁkhya should and indeed did dismiss this argument as futile.

Thirdly, the Nyāya-Vaiśeṣikas, while holding rather unreasonably that the atoms regarded as the material cause of the world are not created by God, use the cosmological argument for widening the scope of divine creativity in a fantastic manner. Thus, according to the earlier Naiyāyikas such as Udayana, God is the creator of the moral law *(vidhi)*, arts, including carpentry, smithy, etc., language, comprising speaking and writing, and the Vedas regarded as replete with the knowledge of supersensibles which is beyond the reach of human individuals. Moreover, the cosmological argument has been employed by the Nyāya-Vaiśeṣikas not only to prove that God is the creator of the world, but also that He is its preserver and destroyer. In this, it would be of interest to note, these philosophers have only conformed to the requirement of the classical theory of the world-process, that is, the cyclical theory, which is common to the Indians and the Greeks, and according to which this process consists of an endless succession of cycles and each cycle comprises the three phases of creation *(sṛisṭi)*, preservation *(sthiti)* and destruction *(pralaya)*. But the Western version of the cosmological argument is free from this complication, being primarily intended to prove the existence of God as the creator of the world.

It needs to be noted in this connection that, of the theistic arguments which are well known in the West, it is the causal or cosmological argument which has been treated as the most impor-

*This modification of the cosmological argument has been made by the Yoga under the influence of the Sāṁkhya, according to which prakṛti is the material cause of the world, and spirit, as distinguished from matter, is inactive (niskṛiya).

tant by those schools of Indian philosophy which seek to vindicate belief in God. But even then, they have not failed to recognize the value of the moral and the teleological arguments as means of proving the existence of God. First as regards the moral argument, both Gautama, the author of the Nyāya-Sūtra and the founder of the Nyāya school of philosophy, and Vātsyāyana the well-known commentator on the Nyāya-Sūtra have made a suggestion towards it in terms of the view that the free volitions of finite souls which, if left alone, would have remained fruitless, are rewarded with success as a result of the favourable intervention of God. This view certainly does not answer to any well formulated moral argument for the existence of God such as that of Kant. But it undoubtedly implies that the success of actions springing from human freedom needs to be accounted for by the hypothesis of God as the supreme moral authority. And judged in this light, it is an approximation to the moral argument for the existence of God. Moreover, the recognition of the connection of the creativity of God with the merits and demerits of finte souls, which is an essential element in the cosmological argument of the Nyāya-Vaiśeṣikas, seems to be an indication of the awareness on their part of the moral aspect of the demand for the admission of the existence of God.

Now, while the majority of the Nyāya-Vaiśeṣikas are especially interested in the cosmological argument for the existence of God, Jayanta Bhatta is one of the few among them who have realized the importance of the teleogical argument as a means of the vindication of belief in God. Accordingly, he argues that, since things characterized by order, design or arrangement *(sanniveśa)* such as buildings, roads, garments, etc. are invariably the products of the agency of intelligent human beings, the world, consisting of mountains, trees, rivers, etc., which is likewise characterized by these very qualities, cannot be said to have accidentally come into existence, but must be held to have been designed and produced by an omniscient and omnipotent being called God. Of course, it may be objected that the arrangement or design in the world, even supposing that it really exists, is very different from that which is to be found in the products of human agency, and, consequently, that the so-called evidence of design in the world of nature does not warrant the hypothesis of God as the creator of this world. But Jayanta replies by falling back upon the logic of inference and accordingly holding that there exists the relation of invariable concomitance *(vyāpti)* between design in *general* and the existence of an intelligent creator just as there is between smoke and fire. The presence of smoke in the kitchen, he continues, is, of course, different from the presence of smoke in the forest. But that cannot prevent the inference of the existence of fire in the forest from the presence of smoke in it. So, for a similar reason, concludes, Jayanta, the inference of the existence of God from the presence of design in nature is above reproach. But then, Jayanta fails to realize that his reasoning here, being analogical, must be far from being conclusive.

It would be worthwhile to note, however, that among the theistic arguments which form part of the traditional Western philosophy of religion, that which has no counterpart in the Hindu philosophy of the religion of God is the ontological argument as formulated for the first time by Anselm and later modified by Descartes. The reason for this seems to lie in the realization, on the part of the Hindu philosophers, of the truth that the *existence* of a thing is prior to the *idea* of it, and, consequently, that the transition from the latter to the former, which is essential to the ontological argument for the existence of God from the idea of Him, is not logically permissible. This, it is hardly necessary to mention, brings out the main point in the objections which have been raised from time to time against the Western version of the ontological argument. But then, it does not follow that the only form of the ontological argument is that which came into vogue in the West, and that the ontological way of arguing the existence of God was absolutely unknown to the Hindus. On the contrary, the fact is that Patañjali, the founder of the Yoga school of Indian philosophy, not only employed the cosmological argument in a modified form to which reference has been already made, but, as we shall see below, made use of a kind of argument for the existence of God which had nothing to do with the transition from the idea of God to His existence and yet deserves to be called *ontological.*

In this connection, Patañjali starts from the consideration of the fact that the qualities of things admit of variations of degree, so that one thing may have a certain degree of a certain quality, whereas another may have a lesser or greater degree of the same quality as the case may be. And then he brings the principle of *continuity* to bear upon this consideration and, accordingly, comes to hold that the variation of the degree of qualities is a *continuous* process which can only come to an end at a point marked by the realization of their highest degree. This view amounts to stating that thought is governed by an inevitable dialectical process which proceeds from a lower degree of the quality of a thing to its higher degree and from there to its still higher degree and so on until its highest degree is reached. It is in the light of the dialectical process of thought thus characterized, that Patañjali argues that the capacity to know, which is a quality and obviously admits of variations of degree, must reach the highest degree of its development in omniscience, that omniscience must not remain a more possibility, but must find its realization is actuality, and, consequently, that God as the omniscient being must exist. Now, while Patañjali thus makes use of a new brand of ontological argument for proving the existence of God as the Omiscient Being, Vyāsa, in his *Yogabhāsya* (Commentary on the Yoga-Sūtra of Patañjali, employs the same argument to prove the existence of God as the embodiment of great power, unequalled and unsurpassed (*sāmyātiśayavinirmukta*) or, in other words, as the highest Lord (*Īśvara*).

It now remains for us to enquire into Śaṁkara's arguments for the existence of God. But to this end it is first necessary to observe that from the point of view of his conception of the Ultimate Reality, the world is unreal or illusory and, consequently, that the question that really arises in connection with the world is not that of its *creation*, but that of the origin of the illusion that it is. In fact, in the view of Śaṁkara, the concepts of God, creation, etc., with which religion is ordinarily concerned, are, in the final analysis, mere figments of imagination. But it seems that, with a view to making a concession to popular opinion, Śaṁkara allowed the relaxation of the rigour of his devastating metaphysical position for the time being, and came to hold that these concepts which are really meaningless show themselves to be pregnant with significance in the context of our day to day experience, as distinguished from the transempirical encounter with the Ultimate Reality. Thus does Śaṁkara restore to philosophy the view of the world as real—of course, real in the empirical sense. And, in consequence, he finds himself confronted with the entire gamut of the questions which it is the wont of the philosophy of the religion of God to deal with—the questions concerning the proofs of the existence of God, the nature of God and His relation to the world and finite selves.

As regards the proofs of the existence of God, Śaṁkara admits all the three of them which were in vogue in the field of Indian philosophy, namely, the cosmological, the teleological and the moral. As far as the cosmological argument is concerned, his approach to it lies in his rejection of the atheistic view of the world as self-existent and his acceptance, in agreement with the Nyāya-Vaiśeṣikas and Patañjali, of the view of it as of the nature of an *effect*. But then, while holding, in common with the latter, that God is the efficient cause (*nimitta-kāraṇa*) of the world, he differs from them in affirming that its material cause (*upādāna-kāraṇa*) is neither the atoms as held by the Nyāya-Vaiśeṣikas nor *prakṛti*, as in the view of the Yoga, but God Himself, of course, in association with *Māyā*. Saṁkara's reason for his regarding God in this sense as the material cause of the world seems to lie in his realization of the need for the removal of the limitation of God's creativity and the consequent deprivation of His perfection, resulting from the view that independently existing atoms or else *prakṛti* is the material cause in question. But then, Śaṁkara's position becomes extremely difficult in consequence of his view of God Himself as the material cause of the world. The difficulty consists in that, God being *ex hypothesi* spiritual and the world being at least partly non-spiritual or material, the former, granted that He can well be held to be the efficient cause of the world, can by no stretch of logic or even imagination be regarded as its material cause and this, despite his view that God is not Brahman as such, but Brahman falsely appearing as *Īśvara* (God) through the intermediary of the cosmic principle of nescience called *Māyā*. In view of this, it would, perhaps, be advisable not only to steer clear of the sacrilege of allowing the limitation of the perfection of God, but also to keep off the other sacrilege of conceiving God to be at least partly material, and to rest content with the view of the world as self-existent so as to leave God undisturbed wherever He is.

But then, Śaṁkara, like the Nyāya-Vaiśeṣikas, persists in his attempt to vindicate the religion of God, and to this end he takes refuge in the teleological argument on the alleged ground that there are unmistakable evidences for the presence of design, arrangement and adaptation in the world as a whole. Just as clay is made by the potter into such a well-designed thing as a pot, so the undifferentiated material stuff constituting *Māyā*, argues Śaṁkara, is fashioned by God into the well-planned, well-arranged and well-designed world as it is actually found to be.* But in this Śaṁkara, like many a theist in India as well as in the West, not only ignores the evidences for the lack of design and adaptation which is amply provided by the world, but also fails to realize that analogical reasoning, on which he is mainly depending here, is unable to yield any definitive conclusion.

But even the cosmological and the teleological arguments together, as Śaṁkara seems to have realized, are not adequate to provide the assurance that God really exists. So he resorts to the time-honoured moral argument, presumably on the understanding that this argument, being primarily concerned with human affairs to which the others are more or less indifferent, is likely to add a new dimension to the attempted proof for the existence of God and thereby reinforce it. Accordingly, he admits the prevailing Hindu view that the law of *karma* is not suffiicient unto itself, but is in need of depending upon God for its proper operation and, consequently, that it is necessary to admit the existence of God as the Lord of the law of *karma (karma-adhyakṣa)*. According to this

* Vide Śārīraka-bhāṣya on Brahma-sūtra, II. 2, 1.2; also Śaṁkara-bhāṣya on Aitareya Upaniṣad, i. 3.

view, it is God who is responsible for the assessment of the moral worth of human actions by way of rewarding the righteous ones among them with happiness and the unrighteous ones with suffering. But this not only implies the sacrilegious admission of the inability of God to prevent moral evil, but also militates against the usual conception of God as the embodiment of unbounded mercy. Hence is evident the wisdom of the Mīmāṁsā view that it is not any person, whether human or divine, but an impersonal, unseen force or power, (*apūrva*) resulting from human actions, which produces, in due course, human happiness or human suffering as the case may be.

But then, this view of the Mīmāṁsakas is as mysterious and unverifiable as is that to which it is intended to be an alternative, and so is hardly preferable to the latter. This suffices to indicate the difficulty of the situation concerned which, perhaps, none realized so clearly as Śaṁkara seems to have done. This is evident from his final admission that the existence of God is, after all, opaque and recalcitrant to *proof*, and that it is the *Śruti* (scripture) alone which can provide the assurance of the existence of God.* But then, there may be at least two more alternatives, besides the one which Śaṁkara thus suggests. One of these would consist in the total overthrow of the authority of the scripture and the consequent rejection of the religion of God as in the case of the heterodox schools of the Cārvākas, the Jainas and the Bauddhas. The other would amount to the rejection of that aspect of the scriptural authority which pertains to the affirmation of the existence of God, resulting in the admission of atheism as in the case of the Sāṁkhya and the Mīmāṁsā.

B

THE NATURE OF GOD AND HIS RELATION TO THE WORLD AND FINITE SELVES

No apology is, perhaps, needed for our mixing up the question of the nature of God with that of His relation to the world and finite selves. These two questions are obviously interdependent, so that the treatment of the one in separation from the other, as has been rightly understood by the philosophers concerned, is not only not feasible, but is almost impossible. In order to ascertain how the different schools of Indian philosophy, which have made room for the religion of God, have dealt with this twofold question, it is, however, necessary first of all to have a clear understand-

* Vide Sārīraka-bhāsva on Brahma-sūtra, 1, 1, 3.

ing of the place they have assigned to the concept of God in their respective schemes of reality.

First as regards the Vaiśeṣikas and the Naiyāyikas, the former, as we have previously observed, started with an attitude of supreme indifference to the question of the existence of God which is almost indistinguishable from that of the atheist. And Gautama, the founder of the Nyāya school, devoted only three cryptic aphorisms to the concept of God which have been interpreted by his commentators like Vācaspati as signifying the decisive rejection of the view of God as the material cause of the world alongside the admission of the view of Him as its efficient cause. This suffices to indicate that the atoms, which, in the view of the Vaiśeṣikas as well as the Naiyāyikas, constitute the material cause of the world, are at least as important as, if not more important than, God as its efficient cause. In any case, God, according to them, is out of place in, and is by no means integrated with, the world, on account of His not being its material cause.* He is then, as they actually hold, a mere architect of the world, a *deus ex machina,* having no living interest in, but, on the contrary, being indifferent to, the affairs of the world. This is deism which is an attempt and indeed a vain attempt to avoid atheism, being a stranger to the enthusiasm, fervour and the sense of dedication which constitute the essence of the religion of God in the strict sense of the term.

Now, no matter whether or not belief in God is an integral part of the Nyāya-Vaiśeṣikas, philosophical outlook, the fact remains that they made room for this belief within it and attempted to formulate their view of the nature of God and of His relation to the world and finite selves as they were required to do. Since God, as the cosmological argument serves to show, is the creator of the world, He, as these philosophers argued, must be *omniscient.* The reason for this, according to them, is that He could not create the world, had he not been in possession of the knowledge of whatever there is. And since He must, then, be omniscient, He, as they argued further, must, on that very account, be *one* or, in other words, there must not be many gods. For, if gods are many, they would naturally be finite souls like us and be lacking in omniscience and, consequently, in the capacity to create the world.

What is especially important to note about the Nyāya-Vaiśeṣika view of the nature of God is, however, that, according to it, He is an *individual* soul or rather a *person* endued with certain excellent or auspicious qualities and absolutely devoid of the sordid

* The Nyāya-Vaiśeṣikas, of course, regard God also as the preserver of the world. But that does not convey any special significance in as much as it merely amounts to their conformity to the traditional Indian belief that God is not only the creator, but also the preserver and, what is more, the destroyer of the world.

ones. Of course, the Naiyāyikas differ among themselves as to the nature and number of the qualities which may be said to belong to God. But they agree in holding that God, besides being *omniscient* and *one* as the creator of the world, is endued with omnipotence, sovereignty or Lordship (*aiśvarya*), merit or righteousness, desire and volition both untainted by affliction (*kleśas*) and unrestricted with regard to their objects, intuition, that is, the capacity to know things directly and without the aid of sense-organs, eternal happiness, freedom, subject to the self-imposed limitation of the law of *karma* and, lastly, moral perfection conjoined with eternal liberation. Negatively speaking, God, according to the Nyāya-Vaiśeṣikas, is devoid of demerit or unrighteousness, ignorance or want of knowledge, pain, aversion, delusion and indeed all the qualities which ordinarily present themselves to be reprehensible in human estimation. From all this it is evident that these philosophers have viewed God in terms of the refined version of religious anthropomorphism which consists in the ascription to God of only those qualities which are of an ideal character from the human point of view, as distinguished from the crude form of this doctrine which permits the attribution to Him of human foibles as well as human merits, and which was grotesquely represented by Xenophanes of ancient Greece by the observation that buffalos would have conceived God to be horny had they been able to think of Him at all.

As regards the Nyāya-Vaiśeṣikas' view of the relation of God to the world and finite selves, it is obviously determined by their deistic conception of Him. God must, in their view, be externally related to the physical world in consequence of their hypothesis that the atoms, space, time and ether, which are the material constituents of this world, are not created by Him, but, on the contrary, are as eternal as He Himself is. And the finite selves being, in their view, likewise coeternal with God, the relation between the latter and the former should naturally be that of mutual externality. That both the world of nature and the world of finite selves are, according to the Nyāya-Vaiśeṣikas, external to, and independent of, God is particularly evident from their view that the former is governed by the Laws of Nature and the latter by the Law of *Karma*. And this would obviously imply that God's sovereignty or Lordship *(aiśvarya)* is limited by the independent operation of these two kinds of law.

But, despite the incompatibility of deism and its implications with the admission of the unrestricted Lordship of God, the Nyāya-Vaiśeṣikas take the arbitrary step of viewing this limitation of His Lordship to be self-imposed, thereby implying that the Laws of Nature and the Law of Karma are *willed* by God and, consequently, that His Lordship remains absolutely unaffected. It is by means of this device that these philosophers not only find themselves in a position to conceive God as *Karmādhyakṣa* (Lord of the Law of *Karma*) but also to secure justification for their admission of the traditional Hindu view that He possesses absolute sovereignty over the world, being responsible for its preservation and destruction, besides being its creator. Even so there remains an irresolvable difficulty with regard to their recognition of the absolute sovereignty of God in so far as they, as previously observed, hold that He creates the world with the help of the merits and demerits of finite selves with a view to introducing *variety* into it.

As seen above, the Nyāya-Vaiśeṣikas resorted to an arbitrary device with a view to vindicating the absolute sovereignty of God over the world of nature. And, according to them, God exercises this sovereignty not only in a general way in His capacity as the creator, preserver and destroyer of the world. They regard Him as doing the same in a specific way as well. Thus, in the view of the Nyāya-Vaiśeṣikas, it is to God that the physical world owes the laws by which it is governed and, what is more, He imparts motion *(spanda)* to the atoms by a fiat of His will, combines them into dyads and finally produces concrete physical objects out of them. Thus God, according to these philosophers, wields absolute controlling authority over the physical world, subject to the only limitation that the material constituents of this world are *given* to, and not *created* by, Him.

God's sovereignty over finite selves, in the view of the Nyāya-Vaiśeṣikas, is likewise subject to limitation, owing to their being conceived to be coeternal with Him. But then, His relation to finite selves, according to them, is different from His relation to the world of nature as it should be due to the difference that naturally exists between selves and physical objects. Accordingly, the Nyāya-Vaiśeṣikas hold that God is related to the finite selves as the father is to his children. He teaches them the Moral Law and rewards them for their virtue and punishes them for their vice. And it is for their sake that He has created the world, on the understanding that it is in the world that they can be happy or be subject to suffering according as they practise virtue or indulge in vice. This implies that, whereas God is possessed of absolute freedom and is the embodiment of moral perfection, finite selves are endued with limited freedom, with the result that it is open to them to obey or else to disobey the Moral Law. And this, in the view of the Nyāya-Vaiśeṣikas, points to the two aspects of the responsibility of God *vis-a-vis* finite selves, one of which is positive and the other negative. The former aspect of His responsibility, according to these philosophers, consists in His supervision of the merits and demerits of finite selves with a view to the determination of their respective rewards and punishments. And the latter lies in His non-interference with their ultimate destiny. This only testifies to the blind conformity on the part of the Nyāya-Vaiśeṣikas to the traditional Hindu conception of the individual as the sole arbiter of his own destiny—indeed the conception which, despite whatever merit it may be said to have, is, from the religious point of view, most unattractive conveying as it does the suggestion that God is a passive spectator of the tragic drama of human life and so is unworthy of the adoration which is supposed to be His due.

We may now proceed to enquire into the Yoga view of the nature of God and His relation to the world and finite selves. In this connection it is necessary to begin by observing that the Yoga system of Patañjali, while being in substantial agreement with the philosophical doctrines of the Sāṁkhya, differs from the latter in admitting the existence of God. But Patañjali's introduction of belief in God into the philosophical system constructed by the Sāṁkhya does not seem to be due to his idea of the fulfilment of any unavoidable religious demand. For, while he views worshipful meditation on God as a means of the freedom of the self from bondage, he does not regard it as the only means to this end. On the contrary, he, like the Sāṁkhya, is of the view that the knowledge of the distinction between the self and the not-self, which has hardly anything to do with religion in the ordinary sense, is the adequate and indeed the sole means of liberation.

The reason for Patañjali's admission of the existence of God, then, seems to be mainly theoretical and may be said to consist in his idea of removing the difficulty of the Sāṁkhya view of the initiation of the evolutionary process of the world as due to the transcendental influence of finite selves *(puruṣas)*. God's transcendental influence, as he seems to have thought, may suitably serve the purpose which, as the Sāṁkhya erroneously held, could be served by the same kind of influence of finite selves. But in this Patañjali fails to realize that God, being in his view as disparate from *prakṛti* as are the *puruṣas* in the view of the Sāṁkhya, should be as unable to initiate the evolutionary process of the world as the *puruṣas*, according to him, must be. Hence it is evident that belief in God is an arbitrary imposition upon the scheme of reality which is common between the Sāṁkhya and the Yoga and, consequently, that it is out of place in the Yoga system of philosophy in a stricter sense than it is in that of the Nyāya-Vaiśeṣikas.

In view of the conclusion reached above, it can hardly be expected that the Yoga can offer a satisfactory view of the nature of God and of His relation to the world and finite selves. Although the Yoga may be said to view God to be the efficient cause of the world, this view is, to all intents and purposes, rendered nugatory in so far as it holds that God is as *inactive (niskṛya)* as are the *puruṣas* in its view as well as in the view of the Sāṁkhya. In fact,

Patañjali himself does not definitely mention God as the efficient cause of the world. And Vyāsa, the commentator on the Yoga-Sūtra of Patañjali, goes further in holding that it is not God but the merits and demerits of the finite selves *(puruṣas)* which are the efficient cause of the world. But it is Vācaspati who represents the Yoga as an advocate of the view of God as the efficient cause of the evolution of the world. Vijñābhikṣu, one of the foremost protagonists of the theistic *(seśvara)* Sāṁkhya, is in agreement with Vācaspati in holding the view that God disturbs the equilibrium of the three *guṇas, sattva, rajas* and *tamas,* removes all obstacles to their redistribution into various forms, and guides their evolution for the enjoyment or rather experience *(bhoga)* as well as the liberation *(kaivalya)* of the *puruṣas* (finite selves).

It is, then, evident that God, in the view of the Yoga as in the view of the Nyāya-Vaiśeṣikas, is externally related to the world and finite selves. Thus He is the *deus ex machina,* whose relation to the world of nature is confined to His removal of the obstacles to its evolutionary process from outside and in an inexplicable manner. In any case, the world of nature, according to the Yoga, is eternal, uncaused and indestructible, so that God, in its view, is not, as He, in the view of the Nyāya-Vaiseṣikas is, the creator, preserver and destroyer of this world. And it is equally far from the Yoga to hold that God is the creator, preserver and destroyer of the world of finite selves, they being, according to it, as eternal, uncaused and indestructible as is the world of nature. This indicates that the same looseness, lack of integration and externality are characteristics of God's relation to finite selves as are inseparable from His relation to the world of nature.

But then, there is, according to the Yoga, an important difference between the positive aspect of God's relation to the world of nature and that of His relation to finite selves—indeed the difference which is consequent upon the difference that there must be between physical objects and selves. The former, as previously mentioned, consists in His indirect and inactive contribution to the evolution of *prakṛti* into a well-ordered world of nature by means of His removing the obstacle to this process. The latter, on the other hand, lies in His equally indirect and inactive contribution to finite selves' acquisition of experience *(bhoga)* as well as their realization of liberation *(kaivalya)* in so as their worshipful meditation on Him is at least one of the means to this end. It is curious to note, however, that, in spite of the limitation of God's capability thus indicated, the Yoga chooses to ascribe to God all the qualities which are expressive of the highest degree of majesty or Lordship *(aiśvarya)* and moral perfection such as omniscience, omnipotence, eternal knowledge, veracity, compassion and the like. And this serves to bring out the simple fact that religion flourishes on faith at the expense of logic and reason.

Our next task is to make an enquiry into Śaṁkara's view of the nature of God and His relation to the world *(jagat)* and finite selves *(jīvas)*. To this end it is first necessary to ascertain the place of the concept of God in his philosophical system. In this regard, we have the following observations to make. Śaṁkara, like many an absolutist in India as well as in the West, began his philosophical investigations with the admission of the concept of the Absolute as basic. But then, he realized, as many other absolutists also seem to have done, that, strictly speaking, the Absolute is amenable to treatment only from the standpoint of the Absolute itself, and consequently, that the concept of the Absolute cannot be admitted as the basic principle in any philosophical enquiry that one may undertake. Thus is presented a predicament, the way out of which, as Śaṁkara and presumably other absolutists have been misled to think, lies in bringing the human point of view, that is, the point of view of finite selves to bear upon the enquiry *(jijñāsā)* into the Absolute. The question then is as to how this can be carried out.

As far as Śaṁkara is concerned, his answer may be stated thus. He recognizes three distinct divisions of human experience respectively associated with dreams, waking life and dreamless sleep. And he holds that the Absolute, which he, following the teaching of the Upaniṣads, calls Brahman, needs to be viewed from the standpoints of the second and the third forms of human experience and, moreover, that the relation between Brahman viewed from the former standpoint and Brahman viewed from the latter should be understood in terms of the relation between things respectively viewed from the standpoints of the first and the second forms of human experience. Now since human experience during waking life presents a world, consisting of a diversity of material objects with diverse names *(nāma)* and forms *(rūpa)*, the Absolute might well be viewed materialistically in the light of the deliverance of this kind of experience. But then, the Upaniṣadic conception of the Absolute as Brahman being almost invariably spiritualistic and, moreover, having at least occasional affiliation to religion, Śaṁkara could not even visualize the possibility of interpreting the Absolute materialistically, and followed the path of religious tradition so as to arrive at the conception of Brahman as God. Brahman thus conceived, in the view of Śaṁkara, then, is the substrate of the world characterized by multiplicity, variety and temporality. But he, unlike philosophers such as Spinoza, succumbs to the influence of traditional religion and, accordingly, comes to conceive God as the *cause* of the world, instead of as *identical with* it. Thus he avoids pantheism, and with a view to avoiding deism at the same time, he regards God not only as the efficient cause of the world, but, in a sense, also as its material cause. As a result, he reaches the theistic conception of God as being beyond the world in His capacity as its cause and yet as being within it in the form of its material cause.

But then, the picture so far portrayed completely alters when Brahman comes to be viewed from the standpoint of human experience as it is in a state of dreamless sleep. According to Śaṁkara, what is presented by this kind of experience is devoid of multiplicity, variety, etc., precisely the characteristics of the world presented by human experience during waking life. That being so, he might, like the Mādhyamika Buddhists, hold that the content of human experience during dreamless sleep is a mere Void or Vacuity *(Śūnyatā)*. But, instead of doing that, he held that this content is not a mere negation, but something positive, being the I *(ahaṁ)* with existence *(sat)*, consciousness *(chit)* and bliss *(ānanda)* as its threefold essence. This enables Śaṁkara to reach the conception of Brahman as the unchanging, non-objective and undifferentiated Absolute Identity of the Self *(Ātman)* with existence, consciousness and bliss as its essential features.

Thus the Absolute viewed from the human standpoint presents itself, on the one hand, to be God held in an inalienable relationship with the world characterized by multiplicity, variety, etc. and, on the other, to be the Absolute Identity of the Self which posits itself upon the negation of this world, together with its divine dispensation. These are, then, two contradictory conceptions of the Absolute, one of which only may be admitted to the exclusion of the other, for the simple reason that two contradictories cannot be admitted together, although both of them can be rejected at the same time. Hence there arises a fresh predicament. But as far as Śaṁkara is concerned, he seeks to resolve it by means of holding, for reasons best known to himself alone, that the latter conception of Brahman needs to be admitted in as much as it cancels the former even as the deliverance of our experience during our waking life may cancel that of our experience is the case of our dreams and, for that matter, our illusory and hallucinatory experiences.

Thus it is evident that the concept of God has a curious position in Śaṁkara's philosophical system, being in a sense essential to it and being, on the other hand, out of place in it—indeed a position which is very different from that which it has in the philosophical system of the Nyāya-Vaiśeṣikas or in the Yoga system of Patañjali. Śaṁkara's meaning here, however, seems to be this. The religion of God is a step—of course, a provisional and by no means the final step—towards the human individual's spiritual realization. It should, therefore, be admitted and practised by him in order that he may be put on the way to spiritual realization and may eventually be brought to the consciousness of its futility as well as of the need for its replacement by religion as the Way. But more of this anon. In the meanwhile we may just have a brief account of Śaṁkara's view of the nature of God and His relation to the world and finite selves in the light of what we have observed about the place of the concept of God in his system of philosophy.

It should be noted at the outset that in the view of Śaṁkara, God *(Īśvara)*, the world *(jagat)* and finite selves *(jīvas)* are of the same existential status in so far as they all are equally empirically real, but transcendentally unreal, being false appearances of indeterminate *(nirguṇa)* Brahman. But within the empirical domain they may be held to differ from one another with regard to their nature as well as the relations among themselves. Thus Śaṁkara, in agreement with the traditional view of God as a unique being, holds that He is the creator, preserver and destroyer of the world. And as such, He is One, there being none superior or even equal to Him. Since the pure Absolute, that is, indeterminate *(nirguṇa)* Brahman, in Śaṁkara's view, is alone unconditioned, *Īśvara* who is determinate *(saguṇa)* Brahman, is regarded by him as *conditioned*—but conditioned by the *sāttvika* (excellent) aspect of *Māyā*. Nevertheless, God *(Īśvara)*, according to him, is self-subsistent, not having to depend upon any other substratum for its subsistence. God, being the material cause of the world, is, of course, immanent in it. But that only means that He is the substratum of the world and not *vice versa*. This is precisely the reason why Śaṁkara, in agreement with one of the prevailing religious beliefs, views God to be the inner essence as well as the inner ruler *(antaryāmin)* of the world. And yet God, according to him, is no participant in the joys and sorrows, enjoyments and sufferings in the world; He is only the Eternal Witness of all that happens in the world of nature and the world of finite selves.

The above observations are only an indication of Śaṁkara's view of the nature of God and His relation to the world and finite selves. But as far as his view of God's relation to finite selves in particular is concerned, his conception of God as Person is of special significance. The Divine Person is regarded by Śaṁkara as being imbued with excellent empirical qualities *(saguṇa)* in order that the purpose of religion understood in the ordinary sense may be served by way of the finite selves' offering of prayer to Him. And this points towards the many and various aspects of the contrast between the status of God and that of the finite selves *(jīvas)* which Śaṁkara admits in common with the believers in God. As previously mentioned, God, according to him, is conditioned by the excellent aspect of *Māyā*, whereas the finite selves are regarded by him as subject to determination by its impure aspect. Hence follows the reason—if reason it may at all be called—

why the relation between *Iśvara* and the *jīvas* should be—and as Śaṁkara holds that it is—the same as the relation between the ruler and the ruled, between the master and the servant. Of course, he holds that God shows favour and does good *(upakāra)* to the finite selves. But that hardly produces any substantial change in the obnoxious ruler-ruled or master-servant relation between God and the finite selves admitted by him.

Moreover, despite his view of God and the finite selves as alike false appearances of Brahman, Śaṁkara reduces the latter to a derogatory status in other ways also. Thus he holds that, while both God and the finite selves are alike conditioned by *Māyā*, the former is not, but the latter are, deluded by it. In consequence, the finite selves, as he further holds, get involved in empirical life *(saṁsāra)* and, as a result, have to undergo suffering, whereas God is absolutely free from such involvement and so is above the reach of suffering. This means that God is inherently free and eternally liberated *(mukta)*, whereas the finite selves are unavoidably held in a state of bondage and so are condemned to a life of struggle for liberation with no certain prospect of its achievement. Not only that; whereas God is conceived to be absolutely free in the sense of being morally perfect and thus being beyond merits and demerits, virtue and vice, good and evil, the finite selves are regarded as having limited freedom by which is meant the freedom to practise vices as well as virtues and thereby acquire demerits and merits and entitle themselves to the award of punishment as well as reward from God regarded as the Lord of the Moral Law.

Thus we have, in brief, an account of the device by means of which Śaṁkara installs one false appearance of indeterminate *(nirguṇa)* Brahman, namely, God far above another kind of the false appearances of the same Brahman, namely, the finite selves, in the name of vindicating the religion of God. But then, his fault here, however great it may be, is excusable on the ground that God and the world and the finite selves, together with the religion of God, in his view, are, after all, illusory, and, consequently, that mankind has a sigh of relief to heave on its being assured that it is really not morally and spiritually so fallen as the religion of God conceives it to be.

Lastly, it is incumbent upon us to investigate the views about the nature of God and His relation to the world and the finite selves, which have been held by the theistic absolutists or the Vaiṣnavites as they may be otherwise called. Much of what we are required to observe in this regard has, however, been already mentioned in connection with our earlier treatment of theistic Absolutism in its chief forms. We may, therefore, confine ourselves to the statement of the most important pionts on the subject before us. It needs to be noted at the outset that the Upaniṣads presented several distinct trends of thought, of which at least two were particularty noticeable. One of these two emphasized the *identity* of Brahman, the *jīvas* (finite selves) and the *jagat* (world), and the other insisted on *differences* among the three. The former was developed by Śaṁkara into *Advaitavāda* which, as we have already seen, admits the religion of God, but reduces it to a precarious position. The latter, on the other hand, has been reinforced, in the hands of the Vaiṣnavites, by the teaching of the *Āgamas* so as to result in the replacement of Śaṁkara's *Advaitavāda* by theistic philosophy of one kind or another.

In fact, all the schools of theistic absolutism are agreed among themselves in dismissing Śaṁkara's distinction between *nirguṇa* (indeterminate) Brahman and *saguṇa* (determinate) Brahman, together with his doctrine of *Māyā,* precisely the devices which Śaṁkara made use of in denying the ultimate reality of the world and finite selves as well as obliterating the difference *(bheda)* between Brahman on the one hand and the finite selves on the other. Now no matter whether or not the recognition of the *reality* of the *jagat* and the *jīvas* is essential to the religion of God, the admission of their *difference* from God is an imperative demand of this brand of religion. The reason for this is that observances such as prayer, worship, meditation, etc, which are essential to the religion of God, presuppose the difference of the *jīvas* and, for that matter, of the *jagat*, from God. That being so, the *jīvas* and the *jagat* must be held to be real, because if they are not real the question of their difference from God would be altogether meaningless.

But then, as a result of their dismissal of Śaṁkara's distinction between *nirguṇa* Brahman and *saguṇa* Brahman, together with his doctrine of *Māyā,* and their consequent admission of the reality of the *jagat* (world) and the *jīvas* (finite selves), the theistic absolutists were required to shoulder the burden of explaining the origin of these two kinds of reality as well as their relation to *saguṇa* Brahman. As far as Śaṁkara was concerned, he found no difficulty in accounting for the origin of the *jagat* and the *jīvas* in so far as he could conveniently hold, as he actually did hold, that God as associated with *Māyā* is the efficient cause of the world, and that God held in the same association or, let us say, *Māyā* itself is its material cause. In consequence, the Absolute as such, that is, *nirguṇa* Brahman was left absolutely unaffected as it should be. On the other hand, Śaṁkara was in a position to explain with equal ease the relation of the *jagat* and the *jīvas* to Brahman by holding that the former are, ultimately, absorbed in, or disappear into, Brahman in demonstration of their own unreality and the absolute reality of the latter.

No such easy way of the explanations in demand was, however, possible in the case of the theistic absolutists on account of their view of the Absolute, that is, Brahman as essentially determinate *(saguṇa)*. Since Brahman conceived to be determinate is, in their view, the same as the God of religion, He, in conformity with a traditional religious belief, may be said to be—and they, in fact, regarded Him as—the *efficient* cause of the world. But the question remained as to what its material cause should be. As regards this question, the Vaiṣnavites answered it, not uniformly, but in different ways. Thus Vallabha, the founder of the school of Pure Non-dualism *(śuddhādvaita)*, held that *saguṇa* Brahman or God is Himself the material cause of the world, besides being its efficient cause. And he went further in holding the view that the relation of the world and the finite selves to God is non-difference *(abheda)*. But this, apart from its other difficulties, obviously amounted to admitting pantheism, instead of theism which Vallabha, in common with other Vaiṣnavites, must have been anxious to vindicate. It is, perhaps, on this account, that Nimbārka, the founder of the *Dvaitādvaita* (dualistic-non-dualistic) school of the Vedānta, conceived the relation of the world and the finite selves to God as both difference and non-difference *(bheda-abheda)*, while agreeing with Vallabha in holding that God Himself is the material cause of the world. But this, far from making any improvement upon the situation, worsens it by involving the absurd suggestion that two contradictories, namely, difference and non-difference, may be admitted together or at one and the same time.

But then, to hold, as Maddhva, the founder of the Dvaita (dualistic) school of the Vedānta, held, that the world and the finite selves owe their origin, not to God, but to *prakṛti*, and that their relation to God is neither identity (*abheda*) nor identity-in-difference (*bheda-abheda*), but pure and uncompromising difference (*bheda*) is tantamount to the admission of deism which he, as a Vaiṣnavite, would certainly not prefer to theism. It is then left for us to consider whether Rāmānuja, the founder of the Viśiṣt-ādvaita school of the Vedānta and, perhaps, the foremost among the theistic absolutists, has really succeeded in accounting for the origin of the world and the finite selves and providing a satisfactory view of their relation to God. As regards the former point, he was in agreement with the Sāṁkhya in holding that it is not God, but *prakṛti* which is the material cause of the world, and that the world is the *pariṇāma* (modification) of *prakṛti*. But this gives rise to the question as to whether *prakṛti* is identical with or different from, *Saguṇa* Brahman or God. If the former alternative holds good, then God would be identical with the world and the finite selves, with the result that pantheism would come to hold its own. If, on the other hand, the latter alternative materializes, the world and the finite selves would present themselves to be different from, and indeed, in a sense, independent of, God, pointing towards the inevitability of deism, much to the disappointment of Rāmānuja himself.

As regards the question of the relation of the world and the finite selves to God, Rāmānuja, however, dealt with it in a way very different from that of other theistic absolutists. Thus he eschewed the use of the prevalent concepts of non-difference (*abheda*), difference (*bheda*), identity-in-difference (*bheda-abheda*), and employed the new concept of substantive-adjective in his understanding of the relation in question. Accordingly, he came to hold that the world and the finite selves are adjectives or qualities (*viśeṣas*) of God regarded as the substantive. And since adjectives or qualities are inseparable from the substantive concerned, the *jagat* and the *jīvas*, as Rāmānuja argued, are held in an inseparable relationship with God, which amounts to stating that God is *immanent in* them. But, then, the adjectives or qualities of a thing are not the same as, but different from, the thing itself. That being so, the *jagat* and the *jīvas*, being *ex hypothesi* the adjectives or qualities of God, as he argued further, must be different from the latter, which, according to him, means that God is, in a sense, transcendent from them. Thus did Rāmānuja try to prove God's immanence in, as well as His transcendence from, the world of nature and the world of finite selves and thereby vindicate theism, as distinguished from pantheism on the one hand and deism on the other.

But the main difficulty regarding Rāmānuja's present position seems to be due to the irresolvable uncertainty as to whether the relation of the world and the finite selves to God admits of interpretation in terms of the concept of substantive-adjective. Even granted that such interpretation is *logically* possible or, in other words, that God is *conceivable* as the Substantive and the *jagat* and the *jīvas* as His adjectives or qualities, it does not necesarily follow that the relation between God on the one hand and the *jagat* and the *jīvas* on the other is, in *reality*, expressible in terms of the concept of substantive-adjective. Thus Rāmānuja's fault here, as we have previously observed, would be analogous to that of the ontological argument for the existence of God.

It is, perhaps, fairly evident from the foregoing discussions that it is difficult, if not impossible, to justify theism on philosophical grounds. And, as we have seen above, the difficulty becomes all the greater when attempts are made, as have been made by the Vaiṣṇavites, to evolve theism out of absolutism, especially of the Upaniṣadic brand. But then, when philosophers devote themselves solely to the cause of religion, they do not pursue philosophy for its own sake, but use it as a means of the promotion of this cause. This is testified to by the very starting point of the philosophical investigations of the Vaiṣṇavites, which consists in their uncritical and rather dogmatic assertion that the Upaniṣadic concept of Brahman is the same as the concept of *Puruṣottama* (Supreme Person) of the Bhāgavata. Since *Puruṣottama* or God is determinate (*saguṇa*), they readily dismissed Śaṁkara's conception of Brahman as *nirguṇa* and interpreted the Upaniṣadic concept of *nirguṇa* Brahman as Brahman without inauspicious or unseemly qualities only. And Caitanya, the founder of the *Acintyabhedābheda* (unthinkable-identity-in-difference) school of the Vedānta, went further in holding that the concept of *nirguṇa* Brahman is not, as according to Śaṁkara it is, the highest development of the conception of reality, but, on the contrary, marks a lower stage in this process, the highest stage of which is marked by the concept of *saguṇa* Brahman.

Once the Vaiṣṇavites thus arrived at the theistic interpretation of Brahman, they found themselves in a position to understand the nature of God in terms of the qualities which were ascribed to Brahman in the Upaniṣads as well as the qualities which are ordinarily attributed to God. Thus Brahman in the highest divine form, according to them, is 'One without a second;' is *sat* (existence), *cit* (consciousness) and *ānanda* (bliss); is eternal and omnipresent. On the other hand, He is omniscient, omnipotent and possessed of a number of special powers. As such, He, as the usual religious belief goes, is the creator, preserver and destroyer of the world. As regards God's motive in His creation of the world, the Vaiṣṇavites generally hold that it consists in His desire to be *many* in expression of His sportive spirit *(līlā)* and for the sake of mere pleasure. This obviously represents a fantastic conception of the origin of the world. It is, therefore, no wonder that the views of the relation of the world and the finite selves to God, corresponding to this conception of their origin, should be and, as we have seen above, actually are lacking in rational justifiability.

We may bring our present enquiry to a close by adverting to the two main conceptions of Bhakti* which prevail among the Vaiṣṇavites, with a view to indicating the two distinct conceptions of the relation between God and the finite selves which are respectively involved in them. The two conceptions of *Bhakti*, it is important to note, correspond to the two distinct conceptions of the Lord and His *Śakti* or Consort which are distinguished by the Vaiṣṇavites. Thus Rāmānuja and Madhva conceive the Lord in the form of Viṣṇu or Nārāyana with Lakṣmī as His consort and emphasize His transcendent majesty (*aiśvarya*), greatness and glory. In consequence, the relation of His creatures, including finite selves, to Him should, according to them, be the same as that which subsists between the ruled and the ruler, between the

* Bhakti, according to the Vaiṣṇavites, is the way of spiritual realization.

servant and the master. And their attitude towards Him should naturally be that of submission, awe and reverence with hardly any room being left for their intimate living contact with Him. Vallabha, Nimbārka and Caitanya, on the other hand, conceive the Lord as Kṛṣṇa with Rādhā as His consort and, accordingly, insist on the all-importance of the human relationship between the Lord's creatures and the Lord Himself as friend, child or beloved. This relationship regarded as a way of spiritual realization is the realization of the Lord, not in His *aiśvarya-rūpa*, that is, the form in which He appears in His majesty, but in His *mādhurya-rūpa*, the form in which He appears as a human being amongst other human beings without transcending the limitations of ordinary manhood. Judged in this light, the attitude of finite selves towards God is that of love, affection and fellowship as opposed to that of submission, awe and reverence.*

III

INDIAN RELIGION AS THE WAY

INTRODUCTION

The result of our enquiry into Indian philosophy of the religion of God, as seems to have been evident, has hardly anything about it which can be said to be in favour of this kind of religion. The proofs of the existence of God, which have been offered by the schools of Indian philosophy concerned, are at best futile, and at worst inflict a shock upon the innocent belief in God, instead of reinforcing it as they were intended to do. And the views of the nature of God and of His relation to the world and especially finite selves which we have already come across seem to bear the reflection of the situation which ordinarily prevails in a patriarchal social or political organization. How can this kind of religion, which thus flourishes upon a crude and primitive form of anthropomorphism, then, fulfil its supposed promise of bringing heaven on earth? This question has in recent times been exposed to the challenge of a socio-economic programme of reform set in the background of atheism and materialism. But there is as yet no indication of the possibility of the conquest of the distance of heaven from this petty planet of ours.

We may then be well advised in looking back towards ancient wisdom, as distinguished from the intellectual sophistications of modern times, and just enquire into the real significance of Buddha's

* *Vide* my *Glimpses of Indian Wisdom*, Munshiram Manoharlal, New Delhi, 1972, pp. 12–13.

silence, among other things, over the question of the existence of God. It is often held that Buddha was exclusively interested in practical problems and, therefore, kept himself aloof from metaphysical questions such as the question of the existence of God which are predominantly theoretical. But this view seems to be the outcome of a rather narrow conception of metaphysics. Of course, Buddha made a departure from the metaphysical trend of the teaching of the Upaniṣads. But the doctrines taught by the Upaniṣads cannot be said to constitute the unexceptionable paradigm of metaphysical truths. On the contrary, there may be, and, in fact, there have been diverse ways of metaphysical thinking. And this points to the fact that some of Buddha's teachings, for example, the doctrine of dependent origination, while being unparalleled in the history of Indian philosophy, indeed are of paramount metaphysical import. Not only that; the very fact that quite a few outstanding schools of metaphysics flourished under the aegis of both the Hīnayāna and Mahāyāna divisions of Buddhism and were founded upon the teaching of Buddha is an unmistakable evidence of his absorbing interest in metaphysics of a kind.

It will not, therefore, do to hold that Buddha's silence over the question of the existence of God and allied questions was due to his lack of interest in metaphysics. On the contrary, it seems to have a deeper philosophical significance which it would be worthwhile to try to ascertain. In this connection, it is necessary to bear in mind that Buddha flourished at a time in the history of India when religion not only did not have an undisputed sway over the Indian people in general, but remained exposed to the serious challenge of atheism. And, although, as we have previously seen, Buddha made no secret of his inclination towards atheism, his deeper insight led him to view the conflict between belief in God and disbelief in Him in an altogether new way. The point which was particularly brought home to him was that both of these owe their origin to the view of the human situation in a false perspective. This is in need of explanation which may be given as follows.

Human existence may be said to differ from other kinds of existence in that, unlike the latter, it has a significance of its own which is in need of being unfolded. The question then is as to how this need can be fulfilled. As regards this question, atheism allied with materialism, far from making any attempt to answer it, would dismiss it outright on the alleged ground that human existence, in the ultimate analysis, is indistinguishable from other kinds of existence, and that it has no more a significance of its own than the latter can be said to have theirs. But in this the atheist and the materialist resort to a kind of humility which, far from conveying its usual sense of an excellent human quality, proves offensive to human dignity. Hence comes within sight the most glaring instance of the view of the human situation in a false perspective. But this is far from suggesting that to admit the present question and answer it in any way one likes would amount to viewing the human situation in the proper perspective.

Strictly speaking, the right view of the human situation in the present context would depend upon the determination of the mutual relation between man's *being* and his *doing*, between his *existence* and his *action* with special reference to the possibility of the fulfilment of the need for the unfolding of the significance of his existence. But this gives rise to the most difficult and yet the most important issue as to whether his *being* or existence should be regarded as the superordinate and his *doing* or action as its subordinate or *vice versa.* Now if the former alternative be admitted, it would obviously follow that in order for the supposed significance of his existence to be unfolded, man would have to depend upon a transcendent agency, instead of upon his own *doing.* This would easily, though not necessarily, lead to the admission of the religion of God, on the understanding that it is God who alone can know the real significance of human existence, and it is He who alone is competent to bring about the unfolding of the same.

But then, the matter cannot really end there. For, once the religion of God is thus invoked, the view that would naturally come to prevail is that the significance of human existence does not lie within man himself, but consists in his relation to God, and, consequently, that it rests with God to instil into human existence whatever significance is its due. Hence it is evident that just as atheism in its alliance with materialism liquidates the question of the intrinsic significance of human existence in one way, theism does the same in another, in demonstration of the curious phenomenon of the meeting of opposites. But then, whereas in the case of the former, the process of liquidation is the outcome of the abuse of humility, in the case of the latter it is the result of the abuse of humility as well as of its opposite, namely, conceit—humility on account of theism's initial denial of significance to human existence as such and conceit on account of its final recognition of the significance of human existence as divine.

Since both atheism set in the background of materialism, and theism, as seen above, are equally the outcome of the view of the human situation in a false perspective, it would be neccssary to steer clear of them in order for the right view of it to be reached. The requirement to this end, should, then, be, on the one hand, to admit as against atheism-cum-materialism that human existence has a significance of its own and, moreover, that it is in need of being unfolded. It should, on the other hand, consist in realizing, in disagreement with theism, that the demand of the human situation with respect to the significance of human existence is the subordination of man's *being* to his *doing* and not the converse of it. This—it may not be difficult to see—amounts to suggesting the prevention of transcendence from the human sphere by means of the ascription to man's *doing* of the function which theism may be said to ascribe to God—the function of unfolding the significance of human existence. Now if the successful performance of this function be—and there seems to be hardly any reason why it should not be—the ultimate goal of the life of man on earth, then it may well be regarded as the essence of religion in the sense of a unique form of humanism, at once independent of both belief in God and disbelief in Him.

Since it desists from referring, whether directly or indirectly, positively or negatively, to any transcendent *being*, and is primarly concerned with *doing* within the confines of the human sphere, the religion in question may simply be called the Way or, as we have suggested earlier, religion as the Way. This is precisely the kind of religion which Buddha seems to have envisaged and taught, although, be it noted, Buddhism is divided from the religion of Buddha just as Christianity is from the religion of Jesus. It seems, however, that atheism as such, on account of its total disregard of anything transcendent, is more favourable to religion as the Way than is theism which flourishes on the invocation of the transcendent. This is evident from the fact that Buddhism and Jainism, the two major schools of heterodox thought and the Sāṁkhya and the Mīmāṁsā among the schools of orthodox thought, which have espoused the cause of religion as the Way, are committed to atheism. Of course, the case of the Cārvākas, on the one hand, and that of the Nyāya-Vaiśeṣikas, the Vedāntists and the Yoga school on the other, are exceptional from the present point of view in as much as the former admit atheism without religion as the Way and the latter admit religion as the Way alongside the religion of God. But we need not go far to seek for an explanation of this twofold exceptional situation. In the first place, it needs to be observed that atheism is only favourable to, but is not necessarily bound up with religion as the Way. On the contrary, when it is allied with materialism, as it is in the case of the Cārvākas, unlike in the case of the Bauddhas and the Jainas, it necessarily excludes religion as such, no matter whether it is the religion of God or gods, or religion as the Way. Secondly, the religion of God and religion as the Way, if they were somehow brought together, do not admit of assimilation with each other as is well evident from Śaṁkara's demonstration of the inability of the former to survive along with the latter.

Let us now try to explain the nature of the significance of human existence to which reference has been already made. In this regard, it is first necessary to take special notice of the obvious fact that man's advent on earth is the beginning of his *empirical life* which lasts till the termination of his earthly existence. During the whole period between his birth and his death he goes on acquiring innumerable experiences of the cognitive, affective and conative kinds. These experiences, of course, are diverse from one another. But there is something common to them all, namely, the productivity of pleasure or pain as the case may be. But then, as Indian philosophers have generally held, there is hardly any pleasure which is not mixed up with, or eventually does not lead to, pain or suffering. The net result accruing from all human experiences, then, is suffering. And this, in their view, means that man's empirical life as such is the life of bondage, bondage and suffering being held by them to be inseparables. Of course, one may say that, from the present point of view, animals should also be regarded as being in a state of bondage. But that would not be true. The reason for this is that none can be said to be in a state of bondage if he does not have the *feeling* of being in that state, and that the subhuman species of animals do not seem to be capable of such feeling.

The consideration that human bondage is not mere bondage but *felt* bondage, and that man not only suffers, but is painfully aware of his suffering, however, is of paramount importance with regard to the spiritual goal of his life. And the importance, according to Indian philosophers, lies in that *felt* bondage attended with *felt* suffering inevitably gives rise to the desire for liberation *(mumukṣā)*, together with the termination of suffering. This is a unique discovery or realization, common to all schools of Indian philosophy with the exception of the materialist Cārvākas, which is indeed the basis of Indian religion as the Way. In any case, the view of the ultimate goal of human life is its freedom consequent upon the elimination of its accustomed bondage seems to be the result of a deeper and more authentic analysis of the significance of human existence than is the view of it as the achievement of pleasure or happiness or even God-realization. But before we proceed to enquire into the conceptions of liberation admitted by the different schools of Indian philosophy, it would be necessary to have somewhat detailed accounts of the various views human bondage that have found place within the field of Indian philosophy.

A

INDIAN VIEWS OF HUMAN BONDAGE

Be it noted at the outset that, with the exception of the Carvāka materialists and their allies, all the schools of Indian philosophy are agreed among themselves in admitting such a thing as human bondage. And, as previously observed, they hold in common that the suffering of man is the invariable concomitant of his bondage. But the question remains as to what is bondage due to or why human experience, whether cognitive or affective or conative, produces pain or suffering either directly in some cases or through the intermediary of pleasure or happinessi n others. As regards this question, its answer from the Christian point of view, as is well known, consists in stating that human bondage or the fall of mankind is due to the Original Sin, the sin committed by the remotest ancestor of the human race by disobeying the will of God. The secular version of the Christian explanation of human bondage has been offered in recent times by the existentialist thinkers, like J. P. Sartre, in terms of the view that man's fall is consequent upon his birth into the world without his consent. In this, as is obvious, the point of view of the religion of God is replaced by a sort of humanistic point of view in the understanding of human bondage or the fall of mankind. But then, the main defect of the former is allowed to remain unremedied in so far as the responsibility for man's fall, according to the latter, does not rest with himself, but with the circumstances of his birth over which he has no control.

But very different from the explanations of the origin of human bondage such as the above, is that which has emerged from the Indian way of thinking. All the schools of philosophy in India—of course, with the exception of the Indian materialists—are of the view that, despite whatever man's birth may have to do with his bondage, it is some grievous ignorance *(avidyā)* or other on his part which is the direct and immediate determining condition of this deprivation of his existence. And it is this view which has been differently presented by different schools of Indian philosophy with a view to accounting for the origin of human bondage. Thus the Nyāya-Vaiśeṣikas hold that delusion *(moha)*, which is a variant of *avidyā* (false apprehension), is the cause of *rāga* (attachment) and *dveṣa* (aversion), which, in their turn, bring about human bondage. It is due to his ignorance of the fact that sensual pleasures are inseparable from pain or suffering, that man becomes *attached* to this kind of pleasures and, in consequence, is thrown into the state of bondage and is condemned to suffer. Not only that; he is, as these philosophers observe, keenly desirous of rebirth in the expectation of the attainment of greater pleasures in a future life and, as a result, becomes entangled in bondage.

It needs to be noted, however, that the Nyāya-Vaiśeṣikas' account of the origin of human bondage is predominantly psychogenetic, and that they regard bondage not merely as *apparent*, but as *real*. The Sāṁkhya-Yoga, on the other hand, offer an ontologically oriented theory of human bondage on the basis of their dualism of *puruṣa* and *prakṛti*. Accordingly, they hold that, while the *puruṣa* is utterly disparate from *prakṛti*, the former loses sight of its separation from the latter due to non-discrimination *(aviveka)* on its part, with the result that it is thrown into a state of bondage. And this, in the view of the Sāṁkhya-Yoga, amounts to stating that the *puruṣa's* bondage is not *real*, but only *apparent*. Strictly speaking, the *puruṣa* cannot be said to be in a state of bondage any more than the appearance of the snake-in-the-rope can be regarded as a real snake. Nevertheless, even the appearance of the bondage of the self or the *puruṣa*, according to this combined system of Indian philosophy, is due to a kind of ignorance, which, although it is not *avidyā* in the Śaṁkarite sense, is yet false apprehension *(avidyā)* in the sense of non-discrimination.

The Advaita Vedānta of Śaṁkara agrees with the Sāṁkhya-Yoga in holding that bondage is not *real* but only *apparent*. But it holds this view for a reason radically different from that of the latter. The Sāṁkhya-Yoga is of the view that the self *(puruṣa)* is essentially, really or in itself *individual* or self-sufficient, but that, due to its failure to discriminate itself from *prakṛti* or its evolutes, it appears to be devoid of its essential feature and, consequently, to be in a state of bondage, while it really remains with its individuality or self-sufficiency absolutely unaffected. Śaṁkara, on the other hand, holds the diametrically opposed view that individuality or self-sufficiency, far from being the contrary of bondage, is synonymous with it, and that the *jīva* or the individual self is in a state of bondage on account of its *individuality*, which is due to the apparent concealment of the *absoluteness* of the Ātman, that is, Brahman by the cosmic principle of nescience called Māyā. Thus, while the Sāṁkhya-Yoga and the Advaita Vedānta of Śaṁkara hold in common that bondage is due to false apprehension in one form or another, their conceptions of bondage itself are contradictory to each other. This not only indicates the difficulty of determining the nature of bondage, but may even lead one to deny, as the Cārvākas may be said to have denied, that there may be any such thing as bondage.

While Śaṁkara, as seen above, equates the individuality of the self with its bondage, the Vaiṣṇavites, including Rāmānuja who is the foremost among them, find no fault with its individuality. On the contrary, they hold that the individuality of the self *(jīva)* and the absoluteness of Brahman are not only compatible with, but are essential to, each other. What then is at fault and indeed constitutes the bondage of the *jīva*, in their view, is its *egoity*, as distinguished from its individuality. The basis of the egoity of the *jīva* lies in its confinement within a material body. Thus confined, the *jīva* ascribes to itself the qualities of the body, revels in the fleeting pleasures resulting from the satisfaction of passing desires and, above all, remains oblivious of the glory and majesty *(aiśvarya)* of God. All this, according to the Vaiṣnavites, points towards the downfall or degradation of the individual self which is but another name for its bondage, and which is the ultimate result of its *avidyā* (false apprehension), together with its previous deeds *(karmas)*. Thus the theistic Vedāntists or the Vaiṣnavites have come to conceive bondage in a different way, but in agreement with the general view that it is, after all, the product of *avidyā* in some form or other.

The Mīmāṁsakas, like the Nyāya-Vaiśeṣikas and the Sāṁkhya-Yoga, regard human bondage as coextensive with man's empirical life as a whole. His birth into, and his consequent connection with, the world and his having a material body and the sense-organs inevitably give rise to his variegated experience, comprising cognition, pleasure, pain, desire, aversion, impression, merit and demerit. And for his self to have these diverse varieties of experience, according to these philosophers, is for it to be entangled in bondage. It seems at first sight, however, that bondage thus conceived cannot be said to be due to *avidyā* in any sense whatsoever. But it is not really so. The reason for this lies in that for the self to rest content as it usually does with its experiences, including pleasure and pain, is for it to remain oblivious of the fact that its relation to its body, its sense-organs and the external world is not essential, but adventitious and, consequently, that experiences resulting from this relation are really foreign to it and not, as is usually held, its essential equipment. And this suffices to indicate that bondage regarded as coextensive with empirical life is the outcome of *avidyā* (false apprehension)—of course, *avidyā* in an ontological and not in the psychological sense.

As seen above, the self's association with a material body, including the sense-organs, in the view of the Indian philosophers in general, plays a determining role in its degradation or bondage. But it is, perhaps, the Jainas who attached special importance to this association of the self in their explanation of the origin of its bondage. And in this they were at one with the Sāṁkhya-Yoga, on account of the fact that both were alike advocates of the uncompromising dualism of spirit and matter. Once it is taken for granted, as the Sāṁkhya-Yoga on the one hand and the Jainas on the other do grant, that the self is purely spiritual and as such is utterly disparate from, and, moreover, superior to, matter, both of them, of course, have no option but to hold that the self's association with a material body is tantamount to its degradation or bondage. But then, the question arises as to how this association, the possibility of which is *ex hypothesi* precluded, can at all take place. It is precisely this difficulty which, as we have already seen, the Sāṁkhya-Yoga seek to resolve by having recourse to such a thing as false apprehension *(avidyā)* in the sense of non-discrimination *(aviveka)*. And as regards the Jainas, they, as we shall see below, resort to a similar device in accounting for the origin of bondage.

According to the Jainas, the causes of bondage are wrong belief, non-renunciation or, let us say, attachment, carelessness, passions and the union of the self with the mind, body and speech. There is, obviously, no separate mention of false apprehension in this list. But that really does not matter. The 'passions', which find a suitable place in the list, while being distinct from false apprehensions, are apt to, and, in fact, invariably do, beget the latter. It is in view of this that the Jainas find themselves in a position to hold that the self, owing to its coming under the influence of passions, assimilates matter in the form of *karmas* and, in consequence, is tranished and thrown into a state of bondage. The *karmic* matter, according to the Jainas, is of four kinds: *mohanīya* (deluding) *karmas* which bring about the involvement of the self in *saṁsāra* (mundane affairs); *antarāya* (obstructive) *karmas* which offer resistance to the noble endeavours of the self; *jñānāvaranīya* (knowledge-obscuring) *karmas* which interfere with the prevalence of right knowledge and, lastly, *darśanāvaranīya* (faith-obscuring) *karmas* which stand in the way of the manifestation of right faith. Thus do the Jainas try to show how matter in the subtle form of the four kinds of *karmas* enters into the very being of the self through the gate-way of false apprehension *(avidyā)* engendered by passions, with the result that the self is degraded into a state of bondage. In this they, of course, are in agreement with the general Indian view that *avidyā* is a determining condition of the bondage of the self. But then, they are not in favour of the view of bondage as merely *apparent* which is held by the Sāṁkhya-Yoga on the one hand and the Advaita Vedānta of Śaṁkara on the other. On the contrary, they are at one with the Nyāya-Vaiśeṣikas and the Mīmāṁsakas in taking a more serious view of human bondage by holding that it is *real* and not merely *apparent.*

Lastly, we are required to have an account of the Buddhist view of human bondage. In this regard, it is first necessary to note that, in the view of Buddha and Buddhism, as in the view of several other schools of Indian philosophy, the life of bondage is indeed a life of suffering. That being so, the causes of human bondage, according to Buddhism, should naturally be the same as those of the suffering of mankind. Now there is no gainsaying the fact that at least some, if not all, of the causes of human suffering are external circumstances some of which are removable, while others may be irremovable, being beyond human control such as an earthquake. But then, the former, being removable, pose no difficult problem, and the latter being beyond human control and, consequently, irremovable, mankind has no option but to endure with patience and equanimity the suffering caused by them. So they, too, do not pose any serious problem. Moreover, neither of these two kinds of external circumstances can be said to be the causes of the universal suffering of mankind. An earthquake, for example, may cause the suffering of the people inhabiting a certain region of the earth, but not that of mankind in general at one and the same time.

But, as distinguished from the external causes of human suffering, there is another kind of its causes which are specially effective and indeed are universal and yet are too subtle to be easily detected. These are internally related to man and, in fact, are the phenomena of his mind. One of them, according to Buddha, is *avidyā* which, as we have already seen, is more or less univesally recognized by the orthodox schools of Indian philosophy as one of the causes of human suffering. Another, in his view, is *tanhā* (selfish craving) which, in an atmosphere dominated by *avidyā*, succeeds in misleading man on the way to suffering. *Avidyā* and *tanhā*, according to Buddhism, are then the main causes of human suffering as well as the bondage of mankind.

Buddhism did not, however, stop there; on the contrary it has devoted itself to further analysis of the mental atmosphere which may be said to be responsible for the degradation and suffering of the human race. And this brings us to the well-known Buddhist doctrine of ten fetters or the evil states of the mind. These are: (1) delusion of the self (*sakkāya-ditthi*), (2) doubt (*vicikicchā*), (3) belief in rites (*sīlabbata parāmāśā*), (4) lust (*kāma*), (5) hatred (*patigha*), (6) desire for rebirth on earth (*rūparāga*), (7) desire for rebirth in heaven (*arūparāga*), (8) pride (*māna*), (9) self-righteousness (*uddhacca*), and (10) ignorance (*avijjā*). In addition to these mental evils, Buddhism admits four *āsavas* or impurities of mind and their effects called *kileśas* (afflictions). Thus Buddhism presents an elaborate introspectionist view of the origin of the degradation and suffering of mankind, which stands in contrast with the purely environmentalist way of viewing the same. But while the latter view is usually accepted as the basis of the endeavours for the liberation of man and the elimination of his suffering, but with little success, the former is left absolutely neglected, owing to the perversity of the bondman to cling to his accustomed degradation with suffering as its invariable concomitant.

The foregoing account of the Indian views of human bondage may be brought to a conclusion with the following observations. In the first place, human bondage, as the predominant Indian view goes, is coextensive with the empirical life of man and as such is universal to mankind. So, in an ultimate analysis, all men, although this is not usually realized, are equal, being equally in bondage and being equally in need of freedom. Secondly, man has none else to blame except himself for his bondage in as much as it is his own *avidyā* in some form or other which, as the Indians hold, is the root cause of this deprivation of his existence. Thirdly, man's natural gift of craving (*tanhā*) takes the form of selfish desire for his own sensual pleasures under the influence of *avidyā* and as a result of the ignoring of the fact that there is no pleasure which is unmixed with, or eventually does not lead to, pain or suffering. In consequence, there ensues universal suffering of mankind alongside human bondage. Thus is presented the tragic situation of the human race. The question then, is whether this situation is a permanent feature of the history of mankind or whether there is an end to it. The Indian reply is optimistic and is conveyed through the various doctrines of liberation and the way to its realization.

B

INDIAN VIEWS ON LIBERATION (*MOKṢA*)

The liberation of man, according to the Indian way of thinking, is as realizable a possibility as his bondage is, as a matter of fact, the dominant feature and indeed the key-note of his empirical life. But in order that the right kind of measure may be adopted with a view to the realization of liberation, it would be absolutely necessary to ascertain how man's empirical life is at fault. As regards this, two diametrically opposed views are distinguishable in the field of Indian philosophy. One of them is based on an extremely individualistic and isolationist view of the self and consists in holding that its empirical life undermines its intrinsic individuality and isolation and thereby reduces it to a state of degradation and suffering which constitutes its bondage. The other view is, on the contrary, based upon the non-individualistic conception of the self and amounts to holding that the self's admission into empirical life is its fall from its intrinsic non-individuality and its consequent individuation which is synonymous with its bondage and is the ultimate source of its suffering.

Now the former of these two views is held by the Nyāya-Vaiśeṣikas, the Sāṁkhya-Yoga, and the Mīmāṁsā among the orthodox schools of Indian philosophy and Jainism among the heterodox ones. The latter is advocated by the Advaita Vedānta of Śaṁkara on the one hand and Buddhism on the other. Both these groups of philosophical schools should naturally hold and, as we shall see below, actually do hold—of course, for different reasons—that freedom from the bonds of empirical life through the means of the negation of experience is the *conditio sine qua non* of the achievement of liberation.

But, as distinguished from this view, there is another in the sphere of Indian philosophy which suggests, not the negation of experience, but its reconstruction or reorientation from a higher standpoint based on the understanding that individuality and its opposite are each an abstraction, and that reality lies in their interrelation. This view, as previously indicated, is held by the Vaiṣṇavites, including Rāmānuja in particular.

First as regards the Nyāya-Vaiśeṣikas, they hold that the self in itself is devoid of all kinds of experience and, consequently, that its *de facto* empirical life is, strictly speaking, foreign to it. This, in their view, is the reason why the self loses its characteristic peculiarity or individuality in its empirical life so as to be reduced to a state of bondage and suffering. So the way out of this predicament, signifying its liberation, should necessarily be found in the total negation of experience. Accordingly, the Nyāya-Vaiśeṣikas come to hold that liberation is a purely negative state, consisting in the destruction of the nine specific qualities of the self, namely, intelligence (*buddhi*), aversion (*dveṣa*), conation (*prayatna*), righteousness (*dharma*), unrighteousness (*adharma*), pleasure (*sukha*), pain (*duḥkha*), desire (*icchā*) and predisposition resulting from past experience (*saṁskāra*). The inclusion of *saṁskāra* in this list is, however, significant in that *mokṣa*, according to the Nyāya-Vaiśeṣikas, not only consists in the cessation of experience as such but also in the destruction of latent tendencies which may eventually develop into experience in the future in virtue of the self's connection with the mind (*manas*).

In spite of holding that liberation consists in the cessation of experience and also the destruction of the tendencies towards the emergence of experience, the Vaiśeṣikas in particular are of the view that *mokṣa* is a state of felicity that naturally belongs to the self. But this view amounts to the admission of an absurdity, because the self, being *ex hypothesi* absolutely devoid of consciousness in the state of *mokṣa*, can have no consciousness of felicity and because the recognition of felicity of which there is no consciousness is lacking in logical propriety. It is, perhaps, in view of this difficulty that the Naiyāyikas went further than the Vaiśeṣikas in holding that there is no transcendental felicity in the state of *mokṣa*, and that this state cannot be said to be pleasurable for the simple reason that where there is pleasure, there is desire for pleasure, together with its necessary consequence, namely, enslavement or bondage. That is the reason why the Naiyāyikas not only agreed with the Vaiśeṣikas in regarding *mokṣa* as freedom from suffering, but also differed from them in holding that it is freedom from happiness as well. In any case, the Naiyāyikas and the Vaiśeṣikas may be said to be advocates of the view of *mokṣa* as self-realization in opposition to Buddhism and the Advaita Vedānta of Śaṁkara, both of which, as we shall see later, conceive liberation to be a a state of self-annihilation. But then, the idea of the realization of the self viewed to be devoid of all kinds of consciousness and, consequently, indistinguishable from material objects has hardly any advantage over that of self-annihilation. This is well brought out by Jainism by means of the observation that it would be absolutely useless to strive after *mokṣa* if it were a state in which the self must needs be reduced to a condition in which it is not distinguishable from material objects such as 'pebbles'.

The Sāṁkhya-Yoga agrees with the Nyāya-Vaiśeṣikas in holding that *mokṣa,* negatively speaking, is freedom from suffering and, positively speaking, consists in the reaffirmation of the individuality, independence and autonomy of the self. In particular, it holds in common with the Nyāya-Vaiśeṣikas that *mokṣa* thus understood is realizable through the negation of experience. But, it is important to note, the Sāṁkhya-Yoga differs from the Nyāya-Vaiśeṣikas in understanding the relation of experience to the self. According to the Nyāya-Vaiśeṣikas, the self is a *substance,* to which the various items of its experience are related as *qualities,* so that its bondage, which consists in its empirical life is, as previously observed, *real.* The Sāṁkhya-Yoga, on the other hand, holds that the self is not the *substance*, but the *subject*, of its experience, and that its relation to its experience is *illusory*, resembling as it does the relation such as that of the surface of water to the trees which cast their reflections upon it. The idea underlying this view is, however, that liberation would be a realizable goal if bondage were illusory and not real as held by the Nyāya-Vaiśeṣikas and their allies in this respect. As regards this idea, its plausibility would depend upon the satisfactory explanation of the illusoriness of bondage. And as far as the Sāṁkhya-Yoga is concerned, its explanation, according to it, lies in holding that it is due to the failure on the part of the self (*puruṣa*) to discriminate itself from the not-self, that is, *prakṛti* and its evolutes. But this not only presupposes the objectionable doctrine of dualism of spirit and matter, but leaves unanswered the question regarding the *why* of the *aviveka* (non-discrimination) between the self and the not-self.

Moreover, the negation of experience, which, according to the Sāṁkhya-Yoga, is the necessary prerequisite of liberation, should leave the self in a condition in which it is, as in the view of the Nyāya-Vaiśeṣikas, indistinguishable from material objects. But the Sāṁkhya-Yoga tries to save itself from this obnoxious position by holding that consciousness is the essence of the self (*puruṣa*), and that the self regarded as essentially conscious is in a class apart from material objects. But then, the difficulty here is that consciousness in its usual sense is bipolar and indeed is a generic term standing for different kinds of experience and, consequently, that the denial of experience to the self cannot leave the self in a state of consciousness. So in viewing the self in itself and in the state of liberation to be essentially conscious, the Sāṁkhya-Yoga construes consciousness in a transcendental sense without offering any justification for taking this step. The only redeeming feature of the Sāṁkhya-Yoga view of liberation, however, lies in holding that liberation is a way of self-realization, instead of self-annihilation. Even so the question remains whether the self, the realization of which is held to constitute liberation, really deserves to be realized or not. The answer, with reference to the Sāṁkhya-Yoga itself should, of course, be in the negative in as much as the self in itself which, according to this combined school of philosophy, is absolutely insular, being detached from the physical world as well as from other selves, no more deserves to be realized than would the self which, as conceived by the Nyāya-Vaiśeṣikas, is indistinguishable from material objects.

We may next proceed to the consideration of the Mīmāṁsā view of the nature of liberation. To this end it is necessary to remind ourselves that neither Jaiminī, the founder of the Mīmāṁsā school nor Sabara, the commentator on the Mīmāṁsā-Sūtra attached any importance to the concept of liberation, and that they insisted on the supreme need for the performance of the duties prescribed by the Vedas with a view to the attainment of happiness in heaven. It was left for Kumārila and Prabhākara and their respective followers to deal with the question of liberation and the way of its achievement. Now Kumārila begins by observing that liberation, in order to be worth the name, must be something eternal, but that whatever is of a positive nature such as happiness in heaven is perishable. It should then, as he holds, be of a negative character, and must be due to the destruction of the self's relation to the world which binds it through the body, the sense-organs and the external objects of experience. Be it noted in this connection that Kumārila is here thinking of the destruction of the self's relation to the world (*prapañcasambandhavilaya*) and not, as held by the Advaita, Vedānta of Śaṁkara, the destruction or cessation of the empirical world itself (*prapañcavilaya*).

The destruction of the threefold bondage imposed upon the self by the world would obviously result in the negation of all kinds of experience, including cognition, pleasure, pain, desire, aversion, impression, merit and demerit. The inclusion of merit and demerit in this list is, however, of special significance. The reason for this is that, since merit and demerit, if they remain intact, are apt to bring about rebirth, together with a body and its necessary consequence in the shape of bondage, their destruction would put an end to rebirth and the production of bodies and thereby serve to eliminate the possibility of bondage. Hence it is evident that the Mīmāṁsā rules out the possibility of *jīvanmukti* (liberation during life on earth) and advocates the doctrine of *videhamukti* (liberation after death). Both Kumārila and Prabhākara are in agreement with each other in this respect. And the latter, like the former, holds that liberarion, consisting in complete freedom from the sufferings of empirical life, is consequent upon the destruction of the self's relation with the body and the sense-organs, following upon the destruction of the latter due to the disappearance of merits and demerits. And in consonance with this view both of them hold further that the state of liberation is absolutely vacuous, being not only devoid of all empirical experiences, including pleasure and pain, but also the so-called transcendental consciousness of bliss (*ānanda*) as conceived by the Vedānta.

Thus it is plain that the Mīmāṁsā, like the Nyāya-Vaiśeṣika and the Sāṁkhya-Yoga, admits a purely negative conception of liberation. Although it may be said to advocate the view of liberation as a way of self-realization, instead of self-annihilation, it, too, lays itself open to the objection of Jainism to which reference has been already made, because the liberated self as conceived by it is certainly one which by no means deserves to be realized.

Jainism, like the Sāṁkhya-Yoga and the Mīmāṁsā, is of the view that liberation is a state in which the self comes into its own or realizes itself by way of the reaffirmation of its purity, independence, autonomy and, in brief, its individuality which suffer deprivation in the course of its empirical life. Moreover, in agreement with the Nyāya-Vaiśeṣikas, it understands the nature of the self in terms of the category of substance and quality. But whereas, according to the Nyāya-Vaiśeṣikas, the relation of the qualities to the self is adventitious, in the view of Jainism, it is intrinsic or essential. Thus according to Jainism, the self has the innate or intrinsic qualities of infinite knowledge, infinite perception, infinite power and infinite bliss. But then, as previously observed, in the course of its empirical life such a thing as *karmic* matter comes into existence and flows into, and interpenetrates, it, with the result that its intrinsic qualities are obscured. Hence follows the deprivation of the self's purity, autonomy and individuality, amounting to its bondage attended with evils, including suffering.

The demand of the realization of liberation, according to Jainism, then, should, of course, be negation or destruction, but not the destruction of the self as held by Buddhism and the Advaita Vendānta of Śaṁkara, nor the *direct* negation of its experience as held by the Nyāya-Vaiśeṣikas, the Sāṁkhya-Yoga and the Mīmāṁsā, but the negation, destruction or 'burning' of the *karmic* matter which lies at the very foundation of its empirical life, together with its attendant evils. And once the *karmic* matter is liquidated, what follows is certainly the undermining of the importance, if not the negation, of its usual way of life. But this is far from suggesting that the state of liberation is vacuous. On the contrary, it is, as Jainism holds, precisely the state in which there happens the lifting of the veil which is spread over the essential qualities of the self by its empirical life as determined by the accumulated mass of *karmic* matter. And, in consequence, the self is restored to its pristine purity, autonomy and individuality so as to be able to show itself with its essential endowment of infinite knowledge, infinite perception, infinite power and infinite bliss.

Liberation thus conceived by Jainism may well be regarded as a way of self-realization. But then, the realization of the self held to be qualified by infinite knowledge, infinite perception, infinite power and infinite bliss is, obviously, another name for the attainment of divinity. And the elevation of the human self to the status of the divine being would bring about its dehumanization in one way just as its condemnation to the status of material objects would produce the same result in another. Strictly speaking, the Jaina conception of liberation, then, is not far removed from the conception of it as self-annihilation. In this connection it would, perhaps, be of interest to note that the affirmation of the reality of the Absolute on the part of the Buddhists of the Mahāyāna school in particular as well as Śaṁkara has led them to the conception of liberation as self-annihilation, and that the denial of the existence of God on the part of the Jainas has, on the other hand, led them to hold that the liberated soul were, as it were, the Deity discovered anew.

We are now required to deal with the two views, according to which liberation primarily consists in the undoing of the *individuation* of the self attended with its suffering, which is consequent upon its admission into empirical life. One of these, as previously mentioned, is held by Śaṁkara and the other by Buddhism. We may, for the sake of convenience, first enquire into the former of these two. Śaṁkara holds that the Self (Ātman) is essentially the Absolute, that is, Brahman. But, owing to its involvement in *saṁsāra* (mundane affairs), it presents itself in the false garb of individuals and undergoes suffering, which constitutes its bondage. Bondage in the view of Śaṁkara, as in the view of the Sāṁkhyā, then, is illusory. In this Śaṁkara, as observed earlier, is in agreement with the Sāṁkhya in presupposing that liberation may be a realizable goal provided only that bondage is illusory and not real. So the problem of liberation, in the case of Śaṁkara as in the case of the Sāṁkhya should be, and indeed is, that of the elimination of the illusion that is bondage.

But then, whereas the Sāṁkhya holds that the demand of the solution of this problem is for the negation of experience through the elimination of the relation of the self to the body, the sense-organs and the external objects, Śaṁkara is of the view that the demand is not merely for the negation of experience but for that of the empirical world itself. In this he seems to have thought of the need not only for the negation of experience but also for the negation of the possibility of the arousal of experience. But then, the demand put forward by him is obviously much too excessive to admit of fulfilment. In consequence, liberation would not only present itself to be difficult, if not impossible, of realization, but also a sheer nonsense. This will be further evident from the consideration of Śaṁkara's view of the destiny of the individual self *(jīva)* in the context of liberation with its demand for the negation of the empirical world.

The negation of the empirical world, which as seen above, is, according to Śaṁkara, the presupposition of the realizability of the liberation of the self, is, on his view, also a corollary of his conception of the Ultimate Reality, that is, Brahman. Since Brahman, as he holds, is a pure Unity, being devoid of all kinds of difference and distinction, the empirical world, characterized as it is by variety and diversity, must needs be unreal and stand negatived. And judged from the same metaphysical standpoint, the individual self must, likewise, be unreal and unavoidably subject to negation. The reason for this is that the apparent plurality of the individual selves and their apparent individuality are respectively contradictory to the unity and absoluteness of the Ultimate Reality. The negation or, as we should rather say, annihilation of the individual self, thus being, in Śaṁkara's view, an ontological necessity, must have a proper place in his scheme of religion, lest religion should, in his hands, prove guilty of the charge of irrationality. Accordingly, Śaṁkara came to hold that the realization of liberation is dependent on two fundamental conditions—the negation of the empirical world on the one hand and that of the individual self on the other.

It would, perhaps, be of interest to consider in this connection whether the negation of experience or of the empirical world as such should necessarily have its counterpart in the negation of the individual self. As far as Śaṁkara is concerned, the answer is, of course, in the affirmative. But then, the reason here is not that the negation of experience or the empirical world as such leads to the negation of the individual self, but that the two negations are equally necessary corollaries of Śaṁkara's view of the Ultimate Reality as the undifferentiated and non-individual Absolute. Should it then be held that in the absence of the Śaṁkarite type of the absolutistic conception of the Ultimate Reality, the negation of experience, far from conveying the demand for the negation of the individual self, should necessitate the affirmation of it in its essential features or features? This question seems at first sight to admit of an affirmative answer in the case of the Nyāya-Vaiśeṣikas, the Saṁkhya-Yoga, the Mīmāṁsā and the Jaina schools of Indian philosophy, all of which hold an individualistic, instead of an absolutistic conception of reality. But then, as we have already seen, their conception of the individual self in its essential feature is, in one way or another, tantamount to its negation. So it seems that the negation of experience or the empirical world goes hand in hand with the negation of the individual self.

There is no denying the fact, however, that there is something basically wrong about the empirical life of man, on account of which he is tragically situated in a state of bondage. But that should hardly be any reason for the negation of the empirical world or even experience and for taking the suicidal step of negating the empirical life of man, with a view to the elimination of human bondage. But it is precisely this twofold device which the majority of the schools of Indian philosophy have, either consciously or unconsciouly, implicitly or overtly, adopted and thereby have presented a dismal picture of the ultimate destiny of man in the name of holding out to him the prospect of his liberation. And in this regard the Advaita Vedānta of Śaṁkara figures most prominently on account of its display of logical subtlety of the highest order in its demonstration of the need for the liquidation of the individual self with a view to the realization of its liberation. Of course, the state of liberation, in the view of Śaṁkara, unlike in the view of the Nyāya-Vaiśeṣikas or the Mīmāṁsakas, seems to be the embodiment of the realization of the highest theoretical and practical goal of life, being pure, infinite and eternal existence *(sat)*, consciousness *(cit)* and, above all, blessedness (ānanda). But, strictly speaking, this, far from giving any indication of what human liberation is or should be, amounts to the reiteration of Śaṁkara's conception of the Ultimate Reality as undifferentiated and non-individual Brahman who usurps whatever is of fundamental value in the world of nature and the world of human beings and in whose abysmal depth both man and the world are eternally and absolutely lost.

Before we proceed to enquire into the Buddhist conception of liberation, we may have a brief account of the views which have been held by the Vaiṣnavite schools of the Vedānta on this subject. In this regard it is most important to note that the Vaiṣnavites are agreed among themselves in ruling out the annihilationist doctrine of liberation advocated by Śaṁkara. Liberation, in their view, is the way of self-realization, instead of self-annihilation. But then, they are equally opposed to the isolationist view of self-realization held by the Nyāya-Vaiśeṣikas, the Śaṁkhya-Yoga and others, according to which liberation consists in the realization of the self as an isolated being. This view, as the Vaiṣnavites hold, is based upon the misunderstanding of the individuality of the self as its egoity, due to the misleading influence of *avidyā*. So the primary requirement of the realization of liberation, according to them, is the elimination of the *avidyā* and the consequent understanding of the true nature of the individuality of the self. But then, while they hold in common that the self as an individual is by no means separate from, but is, on the contrary, related to Brahman, they differ from one another as to the exact nature of the relation between the individual and the Absolute that is Brahman.

As has been previously observed, the relation in question has been differently conceived by the different schools of Vaiṣṇavism and is characterizable as substantive-attributive (Rāmānuja), difference (Madhva), identity-in-difference (Nimbārka), pure identity or non-difference (Vallabha) or inconceivable-identity-in-difference (Caitanya). Accordingly, Vaiṣṇavism comes to hold that liberation is the realization of the individuality of the self understood in terms of its relation to Brahman in any of these ways. But this, no matter whether or not it provides any indication about the nature of human liberation, certainly serves to reiterate the Vaiṣṇavite views of the ontological situation of the individual self *vis-a-vis* Brahman. Of course, the relation between the individual self and Brahman conceived in any of these manners is, in the view of Vaiṣṇavism as in the view of Śaṁkara, pregnant with transcendental felicity or blessedness. But that points towards the valuational aspect of the ontological situation of the individual, and does not seem to have anything in particular to do with the practical problem of human liberation. What is especially noticeable about the Vaiṣṇavite conception of liberation lies in its being informed with a religious significance. In consequence, liberated life is conceived to be a life of self-surrender, of devotion (*bhakti*) to, and worship of, the Lord. But the question arises whether this really shows the way to the achievement of liberation or else the increase of the burden of bondage. Even so Vaiṣṇavism does a signal service to the cause of religion as the Way by putting its veto on both the annihilationist and isolationist doctrines of liberation.

It would, perhaps, be appropriate to begin our enquiry into the Buddhist view of liberation by mentioning, even at the cost of repetition, the main ideas concerning bondage and liberation which are equally shared by the major schools of Indian philosophy, including Buddhism. The first and the foremost of these ideas is that bondage pertains to, and indeed is inextricably bound up with, empirical life as such, and that it is due to a kind of *avidyā* (ignorance) on the part of the self that participates in empirical life. Necessarily connected with this idea is another, namely, that bondage is universal to mankind, the reason for this being simply that it is given to every man to live an empirical life, and that none can altogether avoid his admission into it. The third idea is that bondage is invariably, if not necessarily, attended with suffering. The reason for this seems to be that human bondage amounts to at least an apparent deprivation of the intrinsic dimension of man's existence and, consequently, that it brings about human suffering, it being understood that suffering is the subjective or psychological counterpart of the ontologicel phenomenon of existential deprivation.

Since bondage is universal to mankind and since it is invariably attended with suffering, there arises the fourth idea that all men, being situated in a state of bondage on account of their unavoidable admission into empirical life, are condemned to suffer. Any dispute about this implication of human bondage should, however, be unwarrented due to the ignoring of the fact that suffering, as the Sāṁkhya has rightly observed, is of many kinds and is brought about by many kinds of causes.* But despite the admission of the ubiquity of bondage and suffering in the world of human beings, there still prevails in the sphere of Indian thought the unusually optimistic idea that these two are open to liquidation, and that liberation is the legitimate culmination of human destiny and is within the reach of man. Besides these ideas which are common to all the schools of Indian philosophy, there is another equally shared by all of them, which consists in stating that empirical life being, *ex hypothesi* a life of bondage, it is absolutely necessary that it should pass through the crucible of some basic change or other in order that human existence may show itself to be the veritable testimony of the state of liberation. But it is at this point that the schools of Indian philosophy begin to differ from one another. As we have previously seen, they are certainly not unanimous as to the kind of change which empirical life is in need of with a view to the realization of liberation. We have also seen that they differ among themselves as to the nature of the state of liberation itself. And, as will be shown later, their difference from one another is equally pronounced with regard to the means of the realization of liberation (*mokṣasādhana*).

Now as far as Buddhism is concerned, it did not rest content with the usual view of human bondage as merely due to *avidyā*, but, as has been already mentioned, provided a detailed analysis of the complex subjective or psychological determinant of this tragic human situation. The fetters, *āsavas* and *kileśas*, which Buddhism for the first time laid bare through a deeper analysis of the human mind, constitute an entire inventory of the factors which form themselves into the egoity or selfishness of man in the usual circumstances of his life. And egoity, as Buddha himself observed, manifests itself in the search after one's own good in preference to that of others, and indeed is the offspring of the irrational or mistaken belief that one has a uniquely distinctive or peculiarly individual self of one's

* The Sāṁkhya distinguishes three kinds of suffering: (1) Ādhyātmika, comprising those that are due to physical disorder, mental disturbances brought about by emotions or passions, and the like; (2) Ādhidaivika, including those which are caused by men, beasts, birds, etc., (3) Ādhidaivika, being the category under which may be subsumed those sufferings that are due to supernatural causes, elements of nature such as heat and cold, aarthquakes, etc.

own to foster and preserve during life and even after death. This, in the view of Buddhism, points towards the essential feature of human bondage. But then, since it does not become man as a strictly human being to care for himself alone to the exclusion of his fellows, his usual egoity or selfishness is in need of being eliminated. And in order that this need may be fulfilled the mistake of the belief concerned should be removed by means of the counter-belief that there is no such thing as the self which is identically the same or permanent in itself so as to be regarded as fit to be fostered and preserved here and hereafter.

It follows, then, that, according to Buddhism, liberated life, negatively speaking, is a life denuded of selfishness or egoity. And since the self regarded as a permanent entity is, in the view of Buddha, but another name for the ego, the Buddhist conception of liberation may be said to amount to the rejection of eternalism and the affirmation of annihilationism. But then, Buddhism's denial of the reality of the self really consists in the rejection of the *ātma-vāda*, that is, the doctrine of the self as an entity advocated by the orthodox schools of Indian philosophy. And it may be said that it does not negate the self in every possible sense. On the contrary, as is evident from the dialogue between king Milinda (the Greek prince Menander) and monk Nāgasena, the self, according to Buddhism, is, like the body, not an *entity*, but a *complex*, consisting of five factors (*skandhas*) subsumable under two categories, namely, *rūpa* (physical form) and *nāman* or the psychological factor, comprising *vedanā* (sensation or feeling), *saṁjñā* (perception or idea), *saṁskāra* (conative disposition) and *vijñāna* (intellection or reasoning). But then, the question still remains whether this *structural* conception of the self, if it may be so called in distinction from the entitative conception of it, can hold its own or else is in need of being liquidated in the context of the realization of liberation. As this question seems to be of primary importance with regard to the understanding of the Buddhist view of liberation, it may be briefly consisdered as follows.

The structural conception of the self, while it certainly amounts to the negation of egoity signified by the entitative conception of it, is not free from, but, on the contrary, involves the admission of the self's *individuality*, in virtue of which one self is distinguishable from another or the preceding phase of a certain self may be recognized in distinction from its succeeding phase. That being so, just as one ego may come into conflict with another of its kind, there may arise a conflict between one individual and another and, moreover, what the preceding phase of an individual self may have done might be undone by its succeeding phase. In consequence, it is more likely than not that there would prevail an atmosphere no less unfavourable to the establishment of a state of liberation than would be the atmosphere created by the reign of egoism. It is, perhaps, in view of this difficulty that the earlier followers of Buddhism, the Hīnayānists, comprising the Sthaviravādins and the Sarvāstivādins, drew a distinction between permanent and temporary individuality, and, accordingly, held that the demand of the realization of liberation is the liquidation of permanent individuality, and that temporary individuality, because of its temporary character, is no hindrance to the achievement of liberation. But this certainly involves the failure to realize that, apart from the question of the worth the recognition of individuality in distinction from egoity, from the metaphysical point of view, this recognition seems to be of little consequence from the point of view of the practical problem of liberation. Strictly speaking, individuality, irrespective of its distinction between the permanent and the temporary, would be no less a hindrance to the realization of liberation than egoity may be. This seems to have been realized for the first time in the history of Buddhism by the Mahāsanghikas, and it is under their influence that the Śūnyavādin section of Mahāyāna Buddhism, like the Vedānta of Śaṁkara, came to dismiss the concept of individuality altogether, and thereby had recourse to annihilationism.

But then, as is testified to by the Brahmajāla and the Potthapāda Sūttas, Buddha himself sometimes held that *nirvāṇa* means neither existence nor non-existence nor both nor neither. Thus he steered clear of eternalism as well as annihilationism and thereby maintained an attitude of vagueness towards the question of the nature of liberation. And he was himself aware of this, as is evident from the report of his statement contained in the Pāsādika-Sūttanta, namely, that of the things he has not clearly explained, one concerns the state of *nirvāṇa*, and that his reason for not having done this was that enquiry into the nature of this state is vain and heretical. However that may be, Buddha seems to have realized that, no matter how the self should be viewed from the metaphysical point of view, individuality is as reprehensible as is egoity from the practical point of view, both being equally unfavourable to the possibility of the realization of the highest goal of life. That being so, the *mumukṣu* (aspirant for liberation), as Buddha seems to have thought, should assume the attitude of non-committal towards the question of the metaphysical status of the self by avoiding both eternalism and annihilationism and should think, feel and act as if he were selfless, *as if* his thoughts, feelings and deeds were not his own any more than somebody else's. This obviously serves a twofold purpose. On the one hand, it conveys the suggestion that the way to liberation lies through the elimination of selfishness which compels one to care for oneself to the exclusion of others. On the other hand, it brings about the resolution of the conflict between the Hīnayānists' resistance to the elimination of temporary individuality of the self and the Mahāyānists' all-out onslaught on individuality, by means of suggesting that this conflict, while being irresolvable on the metaphysical level, is out of place and indeed is non-existent from the practical standpoint from which alone it needs to be viewed.

From what has been observed above, it may well be presumed that there was no real conflict between the Hīnayānists and the Mahāyānists in the present context, and that the apparent conflict between the two was due to the fact that the former realized a certain aspect of the whole truth contemplated by Buddha, while the latter realized a certain other aspect of it. Thus the Hīnayānists dismissed permanent individuality which was really the same as the *ātman* of the orthodox schools of Indian philosophy and as such was considered by Buddha himself to be reprehensible. But then they failed to find anything wrong with the so-called temporary individuality. And it was left for the Mahāyānists to realize the further truth that individuality as such, like egoity, needs to be eliminated in order that there may be an end to human bondage which, according to Buddha, manifests itself in man's search after his own good in preference to the good of others.

Liberation, according to Buddha, should then, consist, negatively speaking, in eschewing the bondman's usual habit of seeking his own end in disregard of that of others and, positively speaking, in acquiring the freeman's habit of seeking only that good which he can share with his fellows. This points towards the ideal of Bodhisattvahood (and Buddhahood) in the realization of which, according to the Mahāyānists, consists the liberation of man. The liberation of man, according to Mahāyāna Buddhism, is then governed by the all or none principle, which means that there can be no such thing as individual salvation, and that either all attain salvation or none does. But this does not preclude the Hīnayānist idea of one's making personal endeavours for one's salvation with a view to becoming an *arhat* (liberated being). On the contrary, the liberation of all would remain an unrealizable goal if all do not make personal endeavours for their own salvation. But this amounts to only a partial representation of the situation. And the completion of its representation would consist in the realization that individual salvation, as distinguished from individual endeavour for salvation which is legitimate, is a contradiction in terms for the simple reason that individuality, as Buddha rightly observed, is incompatible with salvation. All this amounts to suggesting that there is really no conflict between the Hīnayānist ideal of Arhatship and the Mahāyānist ideal of Bodhisattvahood, and that, strictly speaking, the latter contributes to the completion of what is partially represented by the former.

It is curious to notice, however, that there prevailed a great deal of controversy as to the exact nature of the state of liberation *(nirvāṇa)*. And it was replete with many and various views which, according to De La Valee Poussin, may be brought under four categories, namely, that liberation is (1) a state of pure extinction or annihilation, (2) a state of happiness, (3) an inconceivable state and (4) a changeless state as in the Pali Canon. But these views are obviously the outcome of the failure to realize that the very idea of liberation as a *state* is based on the doctrine of eternalism, the rejection of which is essential to the Buddhist conception of liberation as *nirvāṇa*. So the question about the nature of the *state* of *nirvāṇa* is absolutely irrelevant or, as Buddha himself held, vain and heretical. Of course, *nirvāṇa*, negatively speaking, is the extinction of egoity and/or individuality. But, positively speaking, it is not a *state*, but a way of life, comprising the way of thinking, feeling and acting. So the question that may legitimately arise in connection with *nirvāṇa* cannot be said to concern the conception of it as a state, but should rather relate to the newly oriented way of life in the comprehensive sense, following upon the elimination of egoity and individuality. This gives rise to the whole question of the practice of *mokṣa (mokṣasādhana)* or rather *mokṣa* as a way of life, to the consideration of which we are now required to address ourselves.

C

INDIAN VIEWS OF MOKṢA AS THE IDEAL WAY OF LIFE

It is, of course, well-known that the Cārvākas and the allied materialists, advocates of the grossest form of hedonism as they were, dismissed the very idea of *mokṣa*. But it is perhaps not so widely known that amongst those thinkers in India who were neither materialists nor advocates of hedonism, there were some who condemned the concept of *mokṣa* as a pragmatic fiction, by stating that it can only provide solace to those who are afflicted with anxiety or sorrow or bereavement, but would be useless and even harmful if it were brought to bear upon the adventure of life. In any case, it cannot, as is further held, serve as a means of the elimination of the concomitants *(anubandhas)* of empirical life, including suffering due to *rāga* (attraction), *dveṣa* (aversion) and *moha* (delusion), which are regarded as constituents of bondage. Hence it is concluded that of the four kinds of ends of life *(puruṣārthas)* that are usually recognized, namely, *artha* (wealth), *kāma* (happiness), *dharma* (righteousness) and *mokṣa* (liberation), the first three should be sought for to the exclusion of the last. But then, as a result of a deeper analysis of the human situation, it was discovered that *artha*, *kāma* and *dharma*, despite their unquestionable worth, are more likely than not to be reduced to triviality, if not to positive disvalue, unless they are subjected to a process of humanization through the crucible of the supremely spiritual value of *mokṣa.** So the ideal way of life, to mature Indian thinking, does not consist in the production or acquisition of wealth, the attainment of happiness, the cultivation of righteousness or even all these three together. On the contrary, it is held to be a life of absolute freedom, freedom from the shortcomings of empirical life judged from the point of view of the genuine interests of man.

But then, since human life bears the promise of developing *knowledge* that is contemplation or meditation, *action* that is performance of duties, and *faith* with the feeling of devotedness as its essence, the question arises as to the relative importance of these aspects in liberated life. Stated more clearly, the question is whether liberated life is a life dedicated to the contemplation of an eternal verity or verities, ceaseless performance of duties, adoration and glorification of the object of faith, namely, the Deity, any two of these alternatives taken together or all of them in combination with one another. Of these possible conceptions of liberated life that which concerns the ceaseless performance of duties without knowledge or faith or with either or even both of them, but regarded, not as coordinate with, but merely as preparatory to, it does not find any place in the field of Indian philosophy.

Now, among the orthodox schools of Indian philosophy, the Sāṁkhya stands out as the advocate of an extremely noetic conception of liberated life in terms of the view that the ideal way of life is that which is imbued with the contemplation of the fundamental principles, that is, the twenty-five *tattvas*, including *prakṛti*, *mahat*, etc. and underlying the world as a whole and, is, in particular, impregnated with the clearest consciousness of the irreducible distinction between the spiritual principle *(puruṣa)* and matter *(prakṛti)*. In the scheme of ideal life thus conceived, there is, according to the Sāṁkhya, no room for the performance of duties, whether conditional *(kāmya)* or unconditional (akāmya), secular or religious (enjoined by the scriptures). The reason for this, according to the Sāṁkhya, is that the performance of these duties involves impurities such as that which follows from the destruction of life and that their results are perishable and by no means consist of any pure and unmixed felicity.

The Yoga, despite the fact that it is affiliated to the Sāṁkhya, holds, however, that certain practical measures, as distinguished from the so-called duties, need to be adopted as the means to the purification of the mind and the removal of the subtle tendencies and dispositions which are apt to interfere with the successful practice of contemplation or meditation. These, according to the

* *Vide* my *Glimpses of Indian Wisdom*, Munshiram Manoharlal, New Delhi, 1972 pp. 65-68.

Yoga, comprise certain physical aids such as bodily postures *(āsanas)* and certain activities of self-restraint *(yamas)* as well as of self-regulation *(niyamas)*. Besides, meditation on the Lord's glory and perfection, in the view of the Yoga, is conducive to dispassion *(vairāgya)* which is the necessary prerequisite of the discrimination of the essence of the *puruṣa*. Thus, according to Patañjali, the founder of the Yoga school of Indian philosophy, action is not altogether out of place in the planning of the ideal way of life. On the contrary, he is of the view that actions which are conducive to contemplation or meditation should be *compulsorily* performed—of course, not ceaselessly but only till the ideal of contemplative life is reached. And this makes no secret of the fact that liberated life, according to the Yoga system of Patañjali, is, after all, a life devoted to the contemplation of the truth about the nature of the self.

The Advaita Vedānta of Śaṁkara, like the Sāṁkhya and the Yoga, conceived liberated life as a life devoted to contemplation. But, whereas according to the latter, the object of contemplation or, let us rather say, direct and immediate intuition, is the essential self, that is, the self in distinction from the not-self, in the view of the former, it is the identity of the individual self with the Absolute Self or Brahman. As regards the role of action *(karma)* in liberated life, Śaṁkara is in agreement with the Sāṁkhya and the Yoga in holding that liberation as such is pure contemplation and is characterized by *naiskarmya* (actionlessness). But then, he, on the one hand, differs from the Sāṁkhya in not excluding action altogether from the planning of the ideal life and holding, on the contrary, that the performance of the various kinds of duties contributes to the purification of the mind *(cittaśuddhi)* which is essential to successful practice of contemplation. And, on the other hand, he differs from the Yoga by stating that the performance of duties is necessary in the case of those who are in need of the purification of their mind, but not in the case of those who are born pure of mind and whose mind is, therefore, in no need of being subjected to a purificatory process. Thus, according to Śaṁkara, action in the form of performance of duties, though useful in some cases, is not a necessary condition of the realization of the ideal of life, as it is in the view of the Yoga. On the contrary, he is of the view that morality is not the inescapable gateway through which one must have to pass in order to be initiated into liberated life, and that some may have the prerogative to live this life without ever having to bear the burden of morality.

Now, in the orthodox circle of Indian philosophy, the view prevailed that there are three chief ways leading to liberated life which are respectively known as *jñāna-mārga* (the way of knowledge or contemplation), *karma-mārga* (the way of action or rather conventional morality) and *bhakti-mārga* (the way of devotion born of faith).

These are not always regarded as mutually exclusive. But, as far as the Sāṁkhya, the Yoga and the Advaita Vedānta of Śaṁkara are concerned, liberated life as an accomplished fact, as we have seen above, is, according to them, purely noetic, being the contemplation of an eternal verity in independence of *action* (conventional morality) as well as *devotion*. But this extreme form of the noetic conception of liberated life is liable to many and various difficulties, some of which are as follows.

In the first place, the object of contemplation, as a matter of fact, is not the same in every case, but varies from one case to another, being the essence of the self *(puruṣa)* in the view of the Sāṁkhya and the Yoga and the identity of the individual self *(jīva)* with the Absolute Self or Brahman in the view of the Advaita Vedānta of Śaṁkara. And this obviously indicates that the present conception of liberated life is open to the charge of subjectivism and relativism. Secondly, the conception of the object of contemplation in either of the two cases derives from a purely *a priori* or dogmatic metaphysical theory and indeed is such that it deprives liberation of its true meaning in the name of of vindicating its reality. For the self conceived as detached from the world as well as other selves, which, according to the Sāṁkhya-Yoga, is the object of contemplation in liberated life, is unreal, being an arbitrary abstraction. And the identity of the individual self with Brahman, the contemplation of which, according to Śaṁkara, is the essence of liberated life, is tantamount to the former's annihilation, but is grossly misconstrued as its liberation.

Thirdly, the view of liberated life as conscious and yet as inactive seems to be a psychological impossibility, because all modes of consciousness, as the finding of psychology goes, are at least implicitly, if not overtly, conative. Not only that; life without its manifestation in action at any level of its development, should be indistinguishable from death. This, it may be of interest to note, points to the resemblance of the view of human liberation held by the Sāṁkhya-Yoga and the Advaita Vedānta of Śaṁkara to the quietistic view of the perfection of the human soul. According to Miguel de Molinos, one of the foremost advocates of quietism in the West, the wish to act is an offence against God; inactivity, on the other hand, brings the soul back to its principle, the divine being, and enables it to be transformed into the latter and thus pass through 'mystic death' so as to become perfect. But then, whereas quietism in the West is evidently an exaggeration and even perversion of the mystical doctrine of 'internal quiet', and is basically theological, its Indian version is free from all manner of theological bias and is built upon the foundation of metaphysics—maybe, metaphysics of a perverted kind.

But then, the quietistic conception of liberated life made no appeal to other orthodox schools af Indian philosophy. This was, perhaps, due to the growing awareness of the importance of action, especially in the form of performance of duties, with respect to the realization of the ideal of life. But the views of its importance in this respect were not uniform, but differed from one another. Some held that the performance of the unconditional duties directly contributes to liberation and, therefore, has a legitimate place in liberated life. Others, on the contrary, were of the view that conditional and unconditional duties are equally important, and that their importance lies, not in making any *direct* contribution to liberation, but in helping the emergence of contemplation in which liberation consists. Thus, according to the former view, action is coordinate with contemplation and so is, like it, part and parcel of liberated life. According to the latter, on the other hand, action is not coordinate with, but only subordinate to, contemplation, although, as in the view of the Yoga and unlike in the view of Śaṁkara, it is a necessary and not merely an optional aid to the realization of liberation.

It seems, however, that the recognition of the importance of action at all stages in the manifestation of life on the one hand, and the discernment of the sterility of mere contemplation on the other prepared the ground for the admission of a more concrete view of liberated life in the light of the idea of the *samuccaya* (coordination) of contemplation and action. Thus the Nyāya-Vaiśeṣikas assigned to *action* a place in liberated life alongside contemplation. This amounted to bringing about the dissociation of intellectualism from quietism and its alliance with voluntarism. Nevertheless, it needs to be borne in mind that it is action in the sense of the performance of only the unconditional duties prescribed by the scriptures, which, according to them, forms part of liberated life. But this is a preliminary indication of the feebleness of the voluntaristic aspect of their view of liberated life as compared with the noetic or intellectual aspect of it. And further indication to the same effect is provided by their view that the performance of the unconditional duties is *supplementary* to knowledge in the task of inculcating disinterestedness and dispassion in the individual and thereby making him fit for initiation into liberated life. But, as we shall see below, the result of their analysis of the role of knowledge in this task does not seem to warrant this view.

As has been previously mentioned, bondage attended with suffering, according to the Nyāya-Vaiśeṣikas, is due to error *(avidyā; mithyājñāna)* generated by the influence of attraction *(rāga)*, aversion *(dveṣa)* and delusion *(moha)*, with which experience is replete. That being so, knowledge of the true nature of things, of things as they are in themselves, should take the place of the erroneous apprehension of them in order that the realization of liberation may be possible. But then, mere knowlenge of this kind, as these philosophers realized, is of little consequence in this respect in as much as it cannot rule out the *possibility* of the occurrence of error. What then is necessary in their view is a process of meditation *(bhāvanā)* on the true nature of things, including the self, until it reaches its culmination in continued, uninterrupted and arduous concentration *(dhyāna)* upon the same. Thus does ordinary knowledge of things develop into intuitive apprehension of them, consisting in the final assessment of their true nature, implying the realization of what is substantial and valuable and what, on the other hand, is unsubstantial and worthless about them. And it is this valuational view of things which, according to the Nyāya-Vaiśeṣikas, serves to extinguish the passions, including *rāga*, *dveṣa* and *moha*, put an end to thirst for life or the will-to-live and rule out the possibility of error, and thereby enables the individual concerned to be initiated into liberated life.

Now the above account of the development of the knowledge of things, which, according to the Nyāya-Vaiśeṣikas, is the requirement of the realization of liberation, seems to be sufficient in itself and leave no room for any contribution to be made to the same end by *action* in the sense of the performance of unconditional duties prescribed by the scriptures. For, if the development of knowledge to the intuitive level can, and, according to these philosophers, actually does, put an end to passions and the possibility of error, nothing else remains to be done in order for one to begin to live a liberated life. It may be contended, however, that the performance of these duties may contribute to the reinforcement of the effect produced by the intuitive apprehension of things. But even then, the difficulty would be that since action goes on producing merits and demerits ceaselessly and since these inevitably lead to rebirth which, according to the Indian way of thinking in general, is opposed to liberation, the performance of the so-called unconditional duties should have no place in liberated life. And this seems to have been the reason why the Sāṁkhya-Yoga and the Advaita Vedānta of Śaṁkara conceived liberated life to be actionless and accordingly advocated a purely noetic view of liberation.

But as far as the Nyāya-Vaiśeṣikas are concerned, they seek to get rid of the present difficulty by asserting rather dogmatically that actions performed after the attainment of true insight not only do not produce any demerit, but cannot produce any merit either, so that the possibility of rebirth is ruled out. But even then they certainly leave unanswered the contention of the Sāṁkhya that the duties prescribed by the scriputres, in some cases, involve the destruction of life which is sinful, and, consequently, that the performance of these duties would aggravate bondage, instead of contributing to liberation. The main point here is that scriptural duties, for which the Nyāya-Vaiśeṣikas seek to find a place in the scheme of liberated life, pertain to conventional morality and that this kind of morality is confined within the bounds of empirical life and so is unable to serve as a means of transcendence from experience which is essential to liberation in the view of all those schools of Indian philosophy, including the Nyāya-Vaiśeṣika, which believe in the realizability of liberation.

It is, however, specially important to note in this connection that the doctrine of *karma* and the understanding of morality in a conventional sense, which are common to all the orthodox schools of Indian philosophy, really stand in the way of their conceiving liberated life as active, instead of as passive. The truth of this is aptly demonstrated in the quietistic view of liberation upheld by the Sāṁkhya-Yoga and the Advaita Vedānta of Śaṁkara. The Nyāya-Vaiśeṣikas, who, on the other hand, made an attempt to impart an activistic sense to liberation, succeeded only in emphasizing the all-importance of intellectual insight in liberated life and thereby lent an indirect support to quietism. The case of Mīmāṁsā in this regard is, however, of special interest in view of the fact that, among the schools of Indian philosophy, it is most enthusiastic about the importance of action (*karma*) in the conduct of the affairs of life, and yet that, as we shall immediately see, it differs from the Nyāya-Vaiśeṣika in treating action, not as coordinate with, but as auxiliary to knowledge or rather self-knowledge with respect to the realization of liberation.

As Yamunācārya has mentioned in his work entitled *Siddhitraya*, in addition to the well-known doctrine of *jñānayoga*, *karmayoga* and *bhaktiyoga*, there is another which may be designated as the doctrine of *anyatara*, according to which there are two alternative ways of the realization of the ideal of life, namely, (a) action regarded as primary and knowledge as auxiliary to it, and (b) knowledge regarded as primary and action as auxiliary to it, either of which may be chosen, depending on the aptitude and inclination of the individual who makes the choice. Now Kumārila, as Pārthasārathi Miśra informs us, holds that he who chooses the former alternative does that on the understanding that the *summum bonum* of life is not *mokṣa* (liberation), but *svarga*, that is, happiness in heaven which is, of course, perishable. And, as he further holds, he who chooses the latter alternative, clearly demonstrates thereby that, in his view, the ultimate goal of human life is *mokṣa* in the sense of freedom from experience, which is eternal. The Mīmāṁsaka view of the way to the realization of the ideal of life may then be said to consist in holding, on the one hand, that the predominance of action in human life may at best lead to perishable heavenly happiness, but is an obstacle to the attainment of imperishable freedom from experience which is *mokṣa*. On the other hand, it is conveyed through the statement that knowledge, including self-knowledge in particular, in its predominance over action, leads the individual in a different direction, enables him to transcend the limits of experience and finally finds him firmly established in imperishable liberated life. This, while falling apart from the noetic-quietistic conception of the ultimate goal of human life, is obviously conspicuous for its leaning towards it rather than towards the voluntaristic conception of liberation. Hence is evident the almost insuperable difficulty which the Indian way of thinking has to encounter in its attempt to extricate itself from quietism and rehabilitate action in liberated life.

Even so the question remains whether the inability of action to hold its own in liberated life is remediable and, if so, what the remedy in question should be. In reply, it may at once be pointed out that the remedy cannot lie in the elimination of knowledge from the way of life and the consequent establishment of the supermacy of action in it. The reason for this is simply that action without knowledge may be possible in the case of certain embryonic forms of life which certainly cannot be the pattern of the liberated life which is said to be the ideal culmination of human existence. So action, in order that it may form part of liberated life, must have to *coexist* with knowledge. But then, the difficulty of its coexistence with knowledge, which is often left unresolved, is, in the view of the Vaiṣnavite schools of the Vedānta, resolvable in the light of the realization of the whole truth about the respective roles of knowledge and action in liberated life, which is usually lost sight of.

The Vaiṣnavites, including Rāmānuja in particular, are in agreement with the Nyāya-Vaiśeṣikas in holding that knowledge of the true nature of things, and action in the sense of performance of unconditional duties without desire for the consequence are equally essential to liberated life. But then, each of these two and even both of them together are, in their view, inadequate as means of the realization of liberation. According to them, Śaṁkara failed to realize the inadequacy of knowledge in this respect, and the Nyāya-Vaiśeṣikas on the one hand, and the Mīmāṁsakas on the other also failed to realize that even both knowledge and action together are similarly inadequate. The remedy for this twofold inadequacy, as they came to hold, lies in Devotion *(bhakti)* to, and Worship *(upāsanā)* of, the Lord, necessitated by Faith which is the culmination of knowledge and action together. Thus the Vaiṣnavites arrived at the theological interpretation of liberation which is unique and unprecedented in the history of the ethico-religious thought in India and, in that sense, is un-Indian. With the exception of the Nyāya-Vaiśeṣikas, the various schools of the Vedānta and the Yoga, all the major schools of Indian thought are atheistic, so that the question of the theological interpretation of liberation did not arise in their case. And as regards the Nyāya-Vaiśeṣikas and Śaṁkara, despite the fact that they admitted the religion of God, they did not bring any theological consideration to bear upon their treatment of the problem of liberation. The Yoga, of course, attached considerable importance to meditation upon the glory and perfection of God with respect to the realization of liberation. But then, such meditation, in its view, is only an aid, like *āsanas*, *yama* etc., to the concentration on the true nature of the self which is held to constitute the very essence of liberated life. The Yoga may, therefore, be said to have been unconcerned with the theological interpretation of liberation as such. In view of all this, it seems that the Vaiṣnavites' exceptional preoccupation with this kind of interpretation of liberation is due to some foreign influence or other. But the discussion of the point raised here falls outside the scope of this work. We may better confine ourselves to a brief examination of the theological view of liberation held by Vaiṣnavism in general.

Now the admission of the religion of God on the part of the Vaiṣnavites does not seem to have provided the only reason or even the primary reason for their attempt to interpret liberation theologically as they actually did. For they had before them examples of those who admitted this kind of religion and yet found no reason for understanding liberation in theological terms. Their main consideration for having recourse to this way of understanding liberation may then be said to have derived from their reaction against quietism and consisted in their desire for the replacement of the passivist conception of liberation by the activist conception of it. But they found that no attempt to this end could succeed as long as knowledge and action are allowed, as they have been actually allowed by most of the orthodox schools of Indian philosophy, to remain unassimilable to each other. So, as they seem to have thought, the only way in which liberation could be restored to activity would consist in making use of the religion of God, instead of leaving it out of account as the Nyāya-Vaiśeṣikas, for example, have done, with a view to bringing about the assimilation of knowledge and action to each other. And this accounts for the Vaiṣnavite view that it is in devotion to, and the worship of, God that knowledge and action shed their usual independence of each other, reach the culmination of their development and are made holy in and through their transformation into love *(prema)* conveying the announcement of the advent of liberation.

Now the question arises whether knowledge and action must be, as Vaiṣnavism, in common with many other schools of Indian thought, tacitly assumes that they are, independent of each other, and whether their synthesis, which is essential to the possibility of liberation, should be held, as Vaiṣnavism holds it, to be miraculously brought about through the invisible intervention of God, following upon man's devotion to, and worship of, Him. As regards the first part of this question, it needs to be remembered that some of the schools of Indian philosophy did not consider it proper to assign, while others could not succeed in assigning, a place to action in liberated life. This was in either case due to the fact that they not only misconceived the knowledge concerned but also the action which could be regarded as contributory to liberation. All the orthodox schools of Indian philosophy conceived the performance of the so-called unconditional duties to be action of the highest order, no matter whether or not they treated it as competent to serve the cause of liberation. But then, since action in this sense, as the general Indian belief goes, is at best productive of happiness in heaven and at worst, as the Śaṁkhya pointed out, is sinful, it cannot be said to have anything to do with liberation. Moreover, the doctrine of *karma* allied with rebirth, as has been previously mentioned, militates against the alliance of action with liberation. But as far as Vaisnavism is concerned, it seeks to remove the latter difficulty by dogmatically asserting that the performance of the unconditional duties produces *eternal merit* which is recalcitrant, instead of being conducive, to the occurrence of rebirth and, consequently, is not prejudicial to the interest of liberation. And as regards the former difficulty, it has hardly any option but to suggest that the supervention of devotion to God upon the performance of the unconditional duties is the surest remedy for it. But this points towards the main difficulty of Vaiṣnavism's theological interpretation of liberation which may be stated as follows.

Vaiṣnavism's view that devotion to, and the worship of, God serves to resolve the conflict, and establish harmony, between knowledge and action bears a close resemblance to the Occasionalist view that the dualism of mind and body is resolved in virtue of the occasional intervention of God in the affairs which, strictly speaking, are the exclusive concern of man. It is, therefore, as fantastic, arbitrary and unwarranted as the latter. Since bondage, according to most of the schools of Indian philosophy, including the theistic schools of the Vedānta, is a peculiarly human phenomenon, liberation should be an exclusively human responsibility. And that being so, divine intervention in man's struggle for liberation is more likely than not to add further weight to his burden of bondage, instead of lifting it off his shoulder. This is, perhaps, the reason why the Nyāya-Vaiśeṣikas and Śaṁkara, in spite of the fact that they admitted the religion of God, refrained from interpreting liberation theologically. The real point in this connection is, however, that most of the difficulties to which the orthodox schools of Indian philosophy are open in respect of their treatment of the problem of liberation, as has, perhaps, been evident by now, are due to their misconception of the knowledge and the action which could be regarded as esssential to liberation. In view of this we are now required to enquire whether the heterodox schools of Jainism and Buddhism have succeeded in offering a satisfactory view of human liberation, free from the shortcomings of the orthodox views of it.

Jainism, like Buddhism, did not rest content with the ordinary Indian view that *avidyā* is the cause of human bondage, but, on the contrary, made a searching analysis of the human mind with a view to the discovery of the subjective or psychological factors which are apt to bring about this tragic situation of man. And its finding was that bondage is the outcome of an all-round ill-health of the human mind which affects its cognitive, affective and conative aspects and manifests itself in false apprehension, false belief and wrong conduct. Thus does Jainism arrive at a comprehensive view of the origin of human bondage. Now since bondage is the mental or, let us say, spiritual ill-health of the whole man, liberation, as Jainism seems to have thought, must consist in the restoration of the whole man to spiritual health. And the means to this end should naturally include right knowledge, right faith and right conduct, respectively the contraries of the causes of bondage, namely, false apprehension, false belief and wrong conduct.

But then, all these means, as Jainism insists, should be treated as equally important, and no attempt should be made, as has sometimes been made by the orthodox schools of Indian philosophy, to emphasize the importance of one of them to the neglect of the equal importance of the others, lest the task of the restoration of the bondman to perfect spiritual health should remain unfulfilled. It is perhaps with this idea in view that Jainism considers them collectively, instead of individually and separately, and calls them the threefold jewel (*ratha-ṭraya*).* Moreover, it has made many valuable suggestions in connection with its attempt to clarify its notions of right knowledge, right faith and right conduct. But it is not necessary for our present purpose to make an enquiry into these suggestions. What needs to be especially noted here is that Jainism made an earnest endeavour to arrive at a concrete and comprehensive view of liberated life by steering clear of the noetic-quietistic view of it such as that of the Sāṁkhya as well as the theological and pietistic view of it like that which is advocated by the Vaiṣnavite schools of the Vedānta.

In fact, Jainism not only eschewed the conception of ideal life as a state of quiescence, but was opposed to passivism in any form such as is represented by the Christian doctrine of beatific vision. On the contrary, it was conspicuous for its admission of the doctrine of eternal progress, according to which it is on its attainment of liberation that the soul becomes really active and, what is more, passes through an unending upward motion (*anantagati*) from its empirical situation (loka) towards a transcendental condition (aloka).

*According to Jainism, right conduct, which is one of the three 'jewels', should be free from three kinds of superstitious belief, one of which is deva-muda, that is, belief in gods followed by worship of them for the cure of diseases and the redress of other kinds of human suffering.

Hence it is evident that in the view of Jainism, liberated life is not life eternal as it is often conceived to be; it is, on the contrary, life that is marked by the defiance of the arrest of its temporality and the welcome of its return to its onward march without let or hindrance.

But then, the view of ideal life as eternal or else as ceaselessly temporal is, in either case, an ontological way of characterizing it which, no matter whether or not it is appropriate as a purely ontological doctrine, may only succeed in indicating what liberation is not, instead of what it is. The reason for this is that, on the former view of ideal life, the destiny of the individual would consist in his absorption in the undifferentiated and non-individual Absolute, amounting to his annihilation in the name of his liberation, or else his self-surrender to the Absolute theistically conceived as God, signifying not only the aggravation of his bondage, but his being permanently established in this tragic situation, instead of being liberated. And as regards the latter view which is Jainism's own, and which is our special concern at present, it consists in holding that the upward journey on the pathway of time which it is given to the liberated soul to undertake results in the fulfilment of its ultimate destiny by way of its attainment of godhead and its becoming a *paramātman* (Supreme Soul). Thus does Jainism have recourse to fanaticism in its conception of liberated life and, moreover, takes the unusual step of interpreting liberation in terms of an inverted theology. In any case, the liberation of man cannot be his transmutation into godhead, because, as has been previously indicated, that would mean his annihilation as a human being which certainly cannot constitute his liberation.

Lastly, as regards the Buddhist view of the ideal way of life, the best and the most suitable approach to it may be said to lie in the consideration of Buddhism's answer to the question regarding the essential constituents of liberated life in contrast with other typical answers to the same question. In this regard, it needs to be observed at the outset that Buddhism in its pristine form, as distinguished from Buddhism in its degeneration under various extraneous influences, including that of Brahmanism, was far from being pietistic and made no room, in liberated life, for *bhakti* (devotion) in the sense in which it is understood by the Vaiṣnavites. The reason for this is simply that *bhakti* cannot be regarded as a constituent of liberation except in so far as the latter is theologically interpreted, and that Buddhism being a godless religion, the interpretation of liberation in this manner is out of the question in its case. But this is far from suggesting that Buddhism leaves no room for feeling or sentiment in liberated life. On the contrary, as we shall see later, certain sentiments, according to Buddhism, are of primary importance to right conduct which, as a part of the Eightfold Path, is essential to liberation.

But granted that devotion, for the reason mentioned above, can form no part of liberated life, there is no gainsaying the fact that, not to speak of liberated life, human life even in the ordinary sense cannot be said to be a blind force, but is subject to the guidance of knowledge. That being so, liberated life must needs be, and, as Buddhism holds, indeed is imbued with knowledge. But the question naturally arises as to the kind of knowledge which may suitably find a place in liberated life. As regards this question, the answer of the majority of the schools of Indian philosophy consists in stating that the knowledge concerned is that of the essential nature of the self. But then, they differ from one another as to what the self essentially is, and yet, curiously enough, as Buddha realized, their divergent views are, after all, variants of one and the same doctrine called *ātma-vāda*, according to which the self is an entity in one sense or another. And for the self to be an entity, as he further realized, is for it to be an ego, which is but the self in bondage. Of course, the entitative conception of the self, as Buddha himself suggested, should, on this account, be replaced by the view of it as a complex of certain psychological phenomena. But this, however satisfactory it may be from the theoretical point of view, is unable to meet the practical demand of liberation. The reason for this, according to him, is that the self regarded as a complex of certain mental phenomena is, after all, an individual which is no more free from bondage than is the ego.

As far as the cognitive constituent of liberated life is concerned, it cannot, therefore, be the knowledge of the self in any sense whatsoever. But then, the awareness of egoity and/or individuality should not only find no place in liberated life, but should be extinguished with a view to the realization of liberation. That being so, liberated life must needs be impregnated with the *supposal* (as distinguished from knowledge) of the non-existence or extinction *(nirvāṇa)* of the self, which, as previously mentioned, steers clear of eternalism and annihilationism at the same time. But this is far from satisfying the unavoidable need for the presence of some definite kind of knowledge or other as a constituent of liberated life. What then should the knowledge in question be ? Buddha's answer is that it is the knowledge of his new discovery, well-known as the doctrine of the Four Noble Truths *(catvāri āryasatyāni)* : (1) there is suffering *(duḥkha)*; (2) it has a cause *(samudāya)*; (3) it can be suppressed (nirodha) and (4) there is a way *(mārga)* to its suppression.

Now it is no peculiarity of Buddhism, but is a common feature of the major schools of Indian thought, whether orthodox or heterodox, to hold that bondage and suffering are inseparables, and that liberation consists in the elimination of suffering, it being understood that its elimination is at the same time the elimination of bondage.

But this view, it is important to note, seems at first sight to be utterly divergent from the Christian view, according to which the endurance of suffering as signified by the bearing of the Cross is not only not incompatible with, but is definitely essential to liberation. Of course, there is a fundamental disparity between the Christian doctrine of vicarious suffering and the Indian view that every individual is the sole arbiter of his own destiny. Moreover, to undergo suffering merely for the sake of suffering is, perhaps, contrary to human nature and, as Buddha realized, is a positive hindrance to the realization of liberation. Even so the endurance of suffering may be a way and, indeed, the most spectacular way, of the ending of suffering. And this, perhaps, brings out the deeper significance of the Christian concept of the bearing of the Cross. So there seems to be no real conflict between the Indian and the Christian views of liberation.

But even granted that suffering is a concomitant of bondage, why should it be held, as Buddhism is most insistent on holding, that suffering, instead of any other concomitant of bondage that there may be, needs to be eliminated with a view to the realization of liberation ? The answer would consist in stating as follows. In the first place, suffering is of various kinds and is due to various causes, being *mental* such as jealousy, hatred, etc., *physical*, for example, old age, disease, and the like, together with natural calamities such as earthquake, pestilence, etc. In view of this, there can hardly be any individual who is altogether immune from suffering. Moreover, the influence of bondage upon man usually results in his being accustomed to endure suffering without grumble or protest, so that he may not be fully aware of the fact of his suffering. Hence it is evident that there is, perhaps, no evil which is as ubiquitous among mankind as is human suffering. Secondly, human bondage, as previously observed, is the deprivation of the essential dimension of man's existence, the valuational tangible counterpart of which is human suffering. Human suffering thus being the universal and basic and yet the tangible concomitant of human bondage, its elimination should naturally be regarded, as Buddhism regards it, as tantamount to the realization of liberation.

What, then, is the way to the termination of human suffering ? This problem, which is of no direct concern to Christianity, is, for obvious reasons, of fundamental importance to all the major schools of Indian philosophy, including Buddhism. But as regards the orthodox schools with the exception of the Mīmāṁsakas and the Vaiṣnavites, they treated it as ultimately *existential*, instead of as predominantly *practical* as it really is. Accordingly, the solutions which they respectively offered to it amounted, in one way or another, to the reaffirmation of the *ātma-vāda* which is condemned by Buddha and which, as we have already seen, in a sense, amounted to the admission of the annihilation of the individual, instead of its liberation. The Vaiṣnavites and the Mīmāṁsakas, on the other hand, recognized the inalienable practical aspect of the problem under consideration. But then, their solutions of it were affiliated to the *ātma-vāda* and, in consequence, presented themselves as travesties of human liberation, attuned to the spirit of the doctrine of annihilation. It was, of course, creditable on the part of Jainism to excel the Mīmāṁsakas and the Vaiṣnavites in its recognition of the predominantly practical character of the problem concerned. But it also was in agreement with the orthodox schools in advocating the *ātma-vāda* in a novel form, with the result that the solution which it offered to it was vitiated by fanaticism as well as the same fault as was committed by the orthodox schools.

Now, as far as Buddhism is concerned, it treats the present problem as characteristically practical—but certainly not practical in the sense that it is unconcerned with knowledge. On the contrary, the knowledge of the Four Noble Truths is its very presupposition. But then, the realization of the urgency of this problem and, in particular, the urgency of the need for its solution is not due to the mere knowledge of these truths, but is the outcome of meditation upon them. In other words, it is the meditation upon the Four Noble Truths which generates the urge for the adoption of the ways and means which are likely to bring about human liberation. In this connection it would be worthwhile to note that Indian thinkers in general are of the view that the shortcomings of intellectualism are remediable, and that the remedy in question lies in the development of knowledge into meditation, it being understood that the latter acquires the capacity to lead to action which mere knowledge lacks. This points towards the almost universal recognition of the efficacy of *yoga* in the philosophical atmosphere in India.

Once it was realized, as was realized by Buddhism, that meditation upon the Four Noble Truths is essential to liberation, this school of philosophy was, however, precluded from the search for an existential solution of the problem of liberation, instead of a practical solution of it. Of course, the concepts of Arhat, Bodhisattva and Buddha played no inconspicuous part in the Buddhist view of liberation. But these concepts were symbolic representations of the fulfilment of the supreme practical ideal rather than entities such as Brahman of the Advaita Vedānta, Viṣnu of Vaiṣnavism or the *Paramātman* of Jainism. In fact, what the individual self's realization of his identity with Brahman, for example, is to the Advaita Vedānta, one's having recourse to the Eightfold Path is to Buddhism. So it follows that in the view of Buddhism, liberated life primarily comprises the supposal of the non-existence of the self, meditation upon the Four Noble Truths and the pursuit of the Eightfold Path, together with its implications.

The Eightfold Path is precisely that which is meant by the Fourth Noble Truth concerning the way to the elimination of suffering. As previously mentioned, it comprises right belief, right resolve, right speech, right conduct, right livelihood, right endeavour, right mindfulness and right concentration. In this connection it would be necessary to observe that Buddhism differs from most of the orthodox schools of Indian philosophy and is in agreement with Jainism in not recognizing the performance of any specific duty or any duty of the conventional kind as part of the way to the termination of suffering. In this is expressed its realization of the truth that such duties are bound up with empirical life or life in bondage and, consequently, that their observance would amount to the maintenance of the *status quo* of bondage, instead of contributing to liberation. Apart from this, Buddhism further realizes that in respect of the spiritual adventure towards liberation, as distinguished from the moral struggle for living the life of bondage as well as possible, the question as to *what* action or actions should be performed is absolutely irrelevant, and the question that is supremely important is as to *how* an action or actions, which need to be performed, should be performed. This suffices to indicate that the demand of the realization of liberation is the performance of actions in conformity with certain principles of conduct as suggested by the *how* in preference to the observance of any precept or precepts as suggested by the *what*. Accordingly, all the constituents of the Eightfold Path are qualified by the adjective 'right' by which it is meant that whatever one needs to do with a view to the realization of liberation, one should do in conformity to a rule or rules, a principle or principles.

Now, of the items included in the Eightfold Path, all except two, namely, right belief and right knowledge, are concerned with action in one way or another, and so may be easily subsumed under the head 'right conduct'. And as regards the two items which fall in a different category, they may be said to be primarily concerned with the Four Noble Truths, the meditation on which, as has been previously observed, is essential to liberated life. So the Eightfold Path is, ultimately, reducible to the single path of right conduct, comprising actions performed in conformity with certain practical principles or principles of conduct. So the question arises as to what these principles exactly are.

As regards the question posed above, it cannot be ascertained whether Buddhism ever felt the need for raising it. But the fact is that it did not raise it, not to speak of its making any attempt to answer it. But then, the Buddhist doctrine of *nirvāṇa* considered as a whole is rich in enough material which may constitute the basis of the principles of conduct in question. And as far as one can judge, it provides for the formulation of as many as three such principles. The first and the foremost of these may be said to relate to what we have called the supposal regarding the non-existence *(nirvāṇa)* of the self. Accordingly, it may be stated thus : So act that your action is neither directly nor indirectly governed by ego-consciousness or, in other words, that your action were, as it were, everyone's action or no one's in particular. Allied with, and yet distinct from this principle, there may be another which does not concern ego-conciousness as such, but one of the basic manifestations of egoity which consists in fear of death and the desire for the prolongation of personal existence after death or personal immortality. That this desire is a potent factor in the determination of human bondage and a source of many of the evils with which mankind is afflicted was painfully realized by Buddha and he condemned it with all the force at his command. In view of this, another principle of conduct may be formulated as follows : So act that your action is neither directly nor indirectly governed by the fear of death and the desire for your personal immortality.

Now, human conduct in its conformity with the two principles formulated above would, perhaps, be good enough for the realization of *arhatship* which, strictly speaking, is preparatory to, but not identical with, liberation as symbolized by *Bodhisattvahood* or *Buddhahood,* which is liberation *par excellence.* The reason for this is that *arhatship,* while being conspicuous for its conquest over egoity, is still bound up with individuality, and that the imperative demand of liberation is the liquidation of individuality along with egoity. So in order that liberation may be an accomplished fact, there must happen a progress from *arhatship* to *Bodhisattvahood* through the elimination of individuality. And this calls for the admission of at least one more principle to which human conduct must conform with a view to the fulfilment of this end. In this regard there arises the need for the recognition of another basic manifestation of egoity and/or individuality on the one hand, and the realization of the deeper significance of Buddhism's emphasizing the importance of certain noble sentiments on the other.

The manifestation of egoity and/or individuality in question is none other than aversion to rejoice, and, in particular, to suffer, *with* one's fellows. But then, since life, as Buddhism holds, is marked by the preponderance of suffering over happiness or joy, aversion to suffer with others is much more calamitous to mankind and a much greater hindrance to the realization of liberation than aversion to rejoice with others. In view of this there arises a fresh demand for the conformity of human conduct to an additional principle which may be stated thus : So act that your action is neither directly nor indirectly governed by aversion to suffer with others or, to express the same thing in Christian terminology, aversion to bear the Cross. It is necessary to note in this connection, however, that neither

Buddha himself nor any of his followers has mentioned any such thing as aversion to suffer with others, not to speak of his condemning it as an obstacle to liberation. But Buddhism's insistence on the paramount need for the cultivation of the noble sentiments of benevolence towards all creation *(maitrī)*, compassion towards the distressed *(karuṇā)*, joy at others' happiness *(muditā)* and indifference to others' faults *(upekṣā)* is, obviously, attuned to the spirit of the principle of conduct just formulated.

It may be observed in conclusion that it is neither a new religion nor a set of new dogmas, but the principles of human conduct mentioned above which are the ultimate outcome of the reconstruction of the Buddhist view of liberation which we have attempted with a view to bringing out its true significance. Judged in the light of these principles of human conduct, human liberation consists in man's emancipation from the ill-effects of the insularity of his day to day life, comprising ignorance and an entire gamut of sordid proclivities such as hate, jealousy, anger, arrogance and conceit. Positively speaking, it is his initiation into a new way of life in which he is united with his fellows by the strongest of all ties, the tie of common humanity, resulting in the fulfilment of his obligation to mankind *(manuṣya-ṛṇa)* with which he was born, and the prospect of the dawn of wisdom and love and the blessedness of peace on earth.

Selected Bibliography

GENERAL

Barua, B. M. —A History of Pre-Buddhistic Indian Philosophy, University of Calcutta, Calcutta, 1921.

Bhandarkar, R. G. —Vaisnavism, Saivism and Other Minor Religious Systems, K. J. Trübner, Strasbourg, 1913.

Dasgupta, S. N. —A History of Indian Philosophy, Vols. I-V, Cambridge University Press, Cambridge.

Deussen, Paul —Outlines of Indian Philosophy, Karl Curtins, Berlin, 1907.

Haribhadra *Ṣaḍ-darśana-samuccaya* with Gunaratna's Commentary, Asiatic Society, Calcutta.

Hiriyana, M. —Outlines of Indian Philosophy, George Allen and Unwin, Ltd., London, 1932.

Hopkins, E. W. —Ethics of India, Yale University Press, New Haven, U. S. A., 1924.

Mādhavācarya —*Sarva-darśana-saṁgraha;* Eng. trans. by E. B. Cowell and A. E. Gough; Kegan Paul, Trench, Trubner & Co. Ltd., London, 1904.

Maitra, S. K. —The Ethics of the Hindus, University of Calcutta, Calcutta, 1925.

Maxmüller, F. —The Six Systems of Indian Philosophy; Longmans, Green & Co., London, 1928.

Radhakrishnan, S. —Indian Philosophy, Vols. I and II, George Allen and Unwin Ltd., London.

Śaṁkara —*Sarva-siddhānta-saṁgraha*, Eng. trans. by Prem Sundar Bose, Navavidhan Press, Calcutta, 1929.

Seal, B. N. —The Positive Sciences of the Ancient Hindus; Longmans, Green & Co., London, 1915.

Sinha, J. N. —A History of Indian Philosophy, Vols. I and II, Central Book Agency, Calcutta, 1956.

CĀRVĀKA

Haribhadra —*Ṣaḍ-darśana-samuccaya* with Gunaratna's Commentary.

Mādhavācārya —*Sarva-darśana-saṁgraha*, with Eng. trans. by E. B. Cowell and A.E. Gough.

Shāstri, D. —A Short History of Indian Materialism, Calcutta Book Co., Calcutta, 1930.

—*Cārvāka Shashti* (trans.), Calcutta Book Co.

Tucci, G. —A Sketch of Indian Materialism.

JAINISM

Haribhadra —*Ṣaḍ-darśana-samuccaya*, Asiatic Society, Calcutta.

Jaini, J. —Outlines of Jainism, Cambridge University Press, Cambridge, 1916.

Mallisena —*Syād-vāda-mañjari*, Chowkhamba Press, Banaras.

Mookerji, S. —The Jaina Philosophy of Non-absolutism, Bharati Mahavidyalaya, Calcutta, 1944.

Siddhasena Divākara —*Nyāyāvatāra* with Eng. Trans., Indian Research Society, Calcutta.

Stevenson, Mrs. S. T. —The Heart of Jainism, Oxford University Press, London, 1915.

Umāsvāmin —*Tattvārthādhigama-sūtra* with Eng. trans., The Central Jaina Publishing House, Arrah, Bihar, India.

BUDDHISM

Conze, E. —Buddhism, Its Essence and Development, Philosophical Library, New York, 1954.

Dharmakīrti —*Pramāṇa-vārttika; Nyāya-bindu.*

Keith, A. B. —Buddhist Philosophy in India and Ceylon; The Clarendon Press, Oxford, 1923.

Kern, H. —Manual of Indian Buddhism, Encyclopaedia of Indo-Aryan Research, Vol. III, Part VIII; K. J. Trübner, Strasbourg, 1896.

Murti, T. R. V. —The Central Philosophy of Buddhism; George Allen and Unwin Ltd., London, 1955.

Nāgārjuna —*Mūla-Mādhyamika-Kārikā.*

Obermiller, E. —History of Buddhism, 2 Vols.; Heidelberg, 1931-32.

Oldenberg, H. —Buddha, His life, His Doctrine, His Order; Williams and Norgate, London, 1882.

Rhys Davids, Mrs. C.A.F. —A. Manual of Buddhism, Sheldon Press, London, 1932.

" —Outlines of Buddhism, A Historical Sketch, Methuen, London, 1934.

Rhys Davids, T. W. —Buddhism, Its History and Literature, Rev. ed. G. P. Putman's Sons, New York, 1926.

Śāntirakṣita —*Tattva-saṁgraha.*

Stcherbatsky, Th. —Buddhist Logic, 2 Vols., Academy of Sciences of the U. S. S. R., 1932.

" —The Central Conception of Buddhism, Royal Asiatic Society, London, 1923.

Suzuki, D. T. —Outlines of Mahāyāna Buddhism, Luzac & Co., London, 1907.

Thomas, E. J. —History of Buddhist Thought; Kegan Paul, Trench, Trübner & Co. Ltd., London, 1933.

Valée-Poussin, L. de La —The Way to Nirvāṇa; Cambridge University Press, Cambridge, 1971.

Vasubandhu —*Vijñapti-mātratā-siddhi.*

Warren, H. C. —Buddhism in Translations, Harvard Oriental Series, Vol. III, Harvard University Press, Cambridge, Mass., 1915.

NYĀYA-VAIŚEṢIKA

Bhaduri, S. —Studies in Nyāya-Vaiśeṣika Metaphysics; Bhandrakar Oriental Research Institute, Poona, 1947.

Chatterjee, S. C. —The Nyāya Theory of Knowledge, 2nd ed., University of Calcutta; Calcutta, 1950.

Faddegon, B. —The Vaiśeṣika System, J. Müller, Amsterdam, 1918.

Ingalls, D. H. H. —Materials for the Study of Navya-Nyāya Logic, Harvard Oriental Series, XL, 1951.

Jha, Ganganath —The Nyāya Philosophy of Gautama; Allahabad University, Allahabad.

Keith, A. B. —Indian Logic and Atomism; The Clarendon Press, Oxford, 1921.

Kesavamiśra —*Tarkabhāṣā*, trans. by Ganganath Jha, Oriental Book Agency, Poona, 1924.

Praśastapāda —*Padārtha-dharma-saṁgraha* with *Nyāya-kandali* of Śrīdhara, trans. by Ganganath Jha, E. J. Lazarus & Co., Allahabad.

Udayana —*Kusumāñjali*, trans. by E. B. Cowell, Baptist Mission Press, Calcutta, 1864.

Vidyabhusan, S. C. —A History of Indian Logic, University of Calcutta, Calcutta, 1921.

Viśvanātha Nyāyapañchānana —*Bhāsā-parichheda* with *Siddhānta-Muktāvali*, trans. by Swami Madhavanda, Advaita Ashrama, Calcutta, 1940.

SĀṀKHYA-YOGA

Aniruddha —*Sāṁkhya-sūtra-vṛtti*.

Dasgupta, S. N. —Yoga as philosophy and Religion, Kegan Paul, Trench, Trübner & Co., Ltd., London, 1924.

Garbe, R. —Sāṁkhya and Yoga, K. J. Trübner, Strasbourg, 1896.

,, —The Sāṁkhya Philosophy, Eng. trans. by R. D. Vadekar, Poona.

Iśvarakṛṣna —*Sāṁkhya-kārikā*, Eng. trans. by S. S. Suryanarayana Śāstri, University of Madras, Madras, 1935.

Keith, A. B. —The Sāṁkhya System, Oxford University Press, London, 1918.

Patañjali —*Yoga-sūtra* with the *Bhāsya* of Vyāsa, Eng. trans. by Ganganath Jha, Theosophical Publication Fund, Bombay, 1907.

Sāmkhya-pravacana-sūtra, Eng. trans, etc. —Nandalal Sinha, The Sacred Books of the Hindus, Vol. XI, Allahabad, 1915.

Vācaspatimiśra —*Tattva-kaumudi*, Eng. trans. by Har Dutta Sharma; Oriental Book Agency, Poona, 1934.

Vijñānabhikṣu —*Sāṁkhya-pravacana-bhāsya.*

Woods, J. H. —The Yoga System of Patañjali, 2nd ed. Harvard Oriental Series, XVII, 1927.

MĪMṀĀSĀ

Bhatta, Kumārila —*Śloka-vārttika*, Banaras.

Jha, Ganganath —*Mīmāṁsā-sūtra* with *Sabara-bhāsya*, trans. Gaekwad Oriental Series, Vols. LXVI, LXX, LXXIII, Baroda 1933-36.

,, Prabhākara School of Pūrva-Mīmāṁsā, Indian Thought Series, No. VIII, Banaras Hindu University, Banaras, 1918.

Kane, P. V. —A Brief Sketch of Pūrva-Mīmāṁsā System, Aryabhushan Press, Poona, 1924.

Keith, A. B. —The Karma Mīmāṁsā, Oxford University Press, London, 1921.

Prabhākara —*Bṛhati* with *Ṛju-vimala*, Madras University Sanskrit Series, No. 3, Madras, 1934.

Sastri, Pasupatinath —Introduction to Pūrva-Mīmāṁsā, Calcutta, 1923.

VEDĀNTA

Bhattacharya, Asutosh —Studies in Post-Śaṁkara Dialectics, University of Calcutta, 1936.

Bhattacharya, K. C. —Studies in Vedantism, University of Calcutta, Calcutta, 1909.

Caitanya —*Daśa-mūla-śloka.*

Chaudhuri, Roma —The Doctrine of Nimbārka and His Followers, 3 Vols., Royal Asiatic Society of Bengal, Calcutta, 1940-43.

Das, R. V. —The Essentials of Advaitism; Motilal Banarasi Das, Lahore, 1933.

Deussen, Paul —The System of the Vedānta, The Open Court Publishing Co., Chicago, 1912.

Dharmarājadhvarīndra —*Vedānta-paribhāṣā*, trans. by S. S. Suryanarayana Sastri, Adyar Library Series, 134, Adyar, Madras, 1942.

Ghate, V. S. —The Vedanta, A Study of the *Brahma-sūtra* with the *Bhāsyas* of Śaṁkara, Rāmānuja, Nimbārka, Madhva and Vallabha; Bhandarkar Oriental Research Institute, Poona, 1926.

Gosvamin, Jīva —*Sat-sandarbha.*

Gosvami, Rūpa —*Laghu-bhāgavatāmṛta.*

Madhva —*Brahma-sūtra-bhāsya*
Bhāgavata-tātparya.

Nimbārka —*Vedānta-pārijāta-saurabha* (Commentary on the *Brahma-sūtra*).

Raghavendrachar, H. N. —Dvaita Philosophy and Its Place in the Vedānta, Mysore University, Mysore, 1941.

Rāmānuja —*Śrī-bhāsya*, trans. by G. Thibaut, The Sacred Books of the East, Vol. XLVIII, The Clarendon Press, Oxford, 1904.

Sadānanda —*Vedānta-sāra*, Ed. and trans. by M. Hiriyanna, Oriental Book Agency, Poona, 1929.

Śaṁkara —*Sārīraka-bhāsya*, trans. by G. Thibaut, The Sacred Books of the East, Vols. XXXIV, XXXVIII, The Clarendon Press, Oxford, 1890, 1896.

Sastri, S.S. Suryanarayana —*Siddhānta-leśa-saṁgraha* (trans.), University of Madras, Madras, 1935.

Srinivasachari, P. N. —The Philosophy of Bhedābheda, Adyar Library Series, No. 74, Madras, 1960.

,, —The Philosophy of Viṣiṣtādvaita, Adyar Library, Series No. 39, Madras, 1943.

Vallabha —*Aṇu-bhāsya* on the *Brahma-sūtra*
,, *Subodhinī* on the Bhāgavata.

Vidyabhusana, Baladeva —*Govinda-bhāsya* on the *Brahma-sūtra.*

Index

(Items listed in the table of contents are not included)

Bheda, 209, 211, 212-3, 214-5, 220, 224
Bodhisattva, 32, 253, 365
Bradley, F. H, 167
Brahmaçarya, 46, 273
Brahman, 24, 27, 28, 38, 40, 205, 206, 207, 208, 210, 211, 213, 214, 217-8, 222, 223-5, 231, 251, 268, 281, 282, 288, 313, 320, 321, 324, 325, 327, 334, 343, 354, 365
Brāhmana, 246, 247, 291
Brāhmanism, 138, 293, 362
Buddha, 20, 30-1, 44, 138, 163, 203, 231-2, 259, 286, 290, 294, 300-2, 328-9, 331, 347, 349-50, 351, 363, 364
Buddhi, 179, 183
Buddhism, 15, 18, 20, 21, 25, 28, 29, 31, 32, 33, 35, 36, 41, 44, 45, 47, 48, 53, 58-9, 78, 83, 100, 101, 138, 139, 145, 150, 152-4, 155, 157-8, 162, 163, 172, 177, 197-8, 202, 205, 233, 243, 252, 253, 258-9, 260-1, 262, 269, 274-5, 279-80, 285, 289, 293, 295, 297, 298, 331, 336-7, 338, 339, 342, 345, 346-51, 360, 362-8
Caitanya, 206, 212-4, 327, 328
Candragupta, 138
Candrakīrti, 274-5
Cārvāka, 18, 20, 25, 28, 44, 45, 48, 52, 53, 66-9, 77, 78-9, 83, 92-3, 98, 99, 118, 139, 235, 237, 257-8, 262, 268, 269, 279-80, 283-4, 291, 296, 297, 298, 331
Ceṣtā, 53, 97, 98
Christianity, 20, 244, 277, 289, 307, 331, 333, 361, 364, 367-8
Conceptualism, 150-1
Degrees of Reality, 226-7
Dehātmavāda, 139
Deism, 212, 316
Democritus, 143, 147, 174
Descartes, 23, 141, 164, 183, 193, 197, 223, 224, 310
Dewey, John, 118
Dharma, 33, 46, 159, 160, 163, 193-4, 195, 246n, 259-65, 351
Dharmakīrti, 199
Dharmottara, 119
Dhyāna, 356
Dinakara Bhatta, 254
Diṅnāga, 78, 199
Dravya, 73, 140, 141-8, 167
Dualism, 23n, 26n, 28, 37, 360
Duḥkha, 37, 44, 159, 228, 257, 339, 347n, 363-5
Ego, 19, 259
Eightfold Path, 252, 259, 362, 365, 366
Ekāntavāda, 185
Evolution, The Sāmkhya theory of, 176-81
Existentialism, 141
Fatalism, 19, 179
Gangeśa, 74, 102, 257n
Gārhasthyā, 46
Gauḍapāda, 205
Gautama, 73, 140, 270, 310, 315
Germany, 117
God, 28, 29, 39, 40, 64, 75, 139, 142, 148, 162, 177, 205, 207, 208, 209, 210, 215, 219, 220, 224, 250, 268, 269, 279, 281, 295, 297, 321-2, 325, 326, 328, 360
Greece (Greek), 133, 134, 150, 277, 279, 286, 289
Guelincx, 51
Guṇa, 140, 148-9, 167, 175-6, 181
Happiness *(Sukha)*, 36, 138, 257, 339
Hari, 213, 215
Heaven, 139
Hedonism, 139, 284-8
Hegel, 226, 232
Hīnayāna, 21n, 157, 199, 252, 253, 329, 349-50
Hinduism, 14, 21, 157, 158
Hume, David 69, 149, 292
Immortality, 19-20
Islam, 20
Iśvara, 225, 226, 281, 313, 322, 323

Iśvarakṛṣna, 73
Italy, 117
Jaimini, 33, 341
Jainism, 15, 20, 21, 22, 23n, 25, 32, 33, 41, 45, 47, 58, 59, 62, 63-4, 77-8, 83, 100-1, 103, 104, 105, 115, 118-9, 169, 184-96, 252, 253, 258, 259, 262, 268, 269, 275-7, 279-80, 286, 292, 293, 297, 298, 299-300, 331, 335, 336, 342-3, 360-2
James, William, 58, 59, 118
Jayanta Bhatta, 146, 310-1
Jesus, 289, 294, 331
Jīva, 207, 210, 216, 221, 307, 320, 322, 323, 324, 334, 344, 354
Jīvanmukti, 26, 46, 264, 342
Jñāna, 35, 36, 37, 42, 51, 52
Jñānakarmasamuccaya, 42
Jñānamārga, 43, 353-4
Jñānaprasthāna, 157
Jñānayoga, 43, 357
Judaism, 20
Kaivalya, 244, 245, 252, 253, 303, 319
Kāla (Time), 142, 144-5, 181, 195-6
Kāma, 46, 138, 351
Kamalaśīla, 199
Kāmyakarma, 41, 48
Kanāda, 53, 140, 141n, 148, 296n
Kant, 50, 60, 96, 133-4, 145, 146, 184, 242, 246-7, 255-6, 258
Karma, 36, 40-1, 42, 73, 140, 149-50, 167, 262, 353; The doctrine of, 11, 18-25, 48, 316, 317, 357
Karmamārga, 43, 353-4
Karmayoga, 43, 357
Karuṇā, 21, 259, 293, 368
Kātyayani-putra, 136
Kṛṣna, 207, 328
Kṣanikavāda, 150, 158, 159
Kṣatriya, 246, 247, 291
Kumāralāta, 157
Kumārila, 33, 34, 53, 80, 86, 87, 88, 89, 90, 93, 95-6, 100, 110, 166-73, 261, 263, 266-7, 304-6, 341, 342, 357
Lakṣmī, 327
Leibniz, 191, 192
Leucippus, 143
Libertarianism, 19
Līlā, 207, 219, 327
Liṅga, 66, 76, 77
Locke, John, 60, 164, 197
Lokasaṁgraha, 42
Lokāyata, 136-9, 252, 283
Madhva, 40, 58, 59, 206, 209, 214-6, 325, 327
Mādhyamika, 122, 123-4, 126, 127, 129, 158, 198, 199, 200, 203, 222, 228-32, 233, 238, 242, 274-5, 321
Mahābhārata, 39, 248, 282, 284, 292
Mahāsaṅghika, 349
Mahat, 179, 305
Mahāvīra, 290, 294
Mahāyāna, 13, 21n, 32, 157, 198, 199, 203, 230, 253, 329, 343, 349, 350
Maitra, S. K, 14
Maitreyanātha, 199
Maitrī, 259, 293, 368
Malebranche, 197
Manas, 142, 145-6, 171
Manu, 247-8, 249, 250, 264, 289, 292
Marx, Karl, 232
Mathurānātha, 257n
Māyā (Māyāvāda), 24, 131, 207, 213, 214, 216, 217-8, 220, 221, 224-6, 312, 313, 322, 324
Milinda, 348
Mill, J. S, 69, 257
Mīmāṁsā, 15, 20, 33, 34, 41, 45, 47, 53, 54, 56, 75, 77, 80, 81, 82, 83, 84, 85, 86, 87, 88, 91, 93, 97, 98, 100, 102, 105-6, 107, 108, 109-10, 111, 112, 113, 115, 117, 119, 120, 121, 124, 125-6, 166-73, 194, 205, 249, 250, 265, 269, 280, 295, 302, 304-6, 314, 331, 335, 336, 338, 341-2, 357-8, 364-5
Molinos, Miguel de, 354
Moral Law, 255-6, 258, 279-82, 317

Muditā, 259, 293, 368
Mukti (Mokṣa), 14, 46, 244, 245, 257, 296, 351, 352
'Mystic death', 354
Nāgārjuna, 232
Nāgasena, 348
Naimittika-karma, 37, 41, 249
Naiṣkarmya (karma-sanyāsa), 42, 264, 265, 282, 353
Nārāyana, 327
Nāstika, 11, 47-8, 49, 58
Navya-Nyāya, 102
Necessitarianism, 19
Negation (See *Abhāva*)
Nimbārka, 206, 209, 210-4, 237, 328
Nirvāṇa, 29-30, 31, 163, 244, 245, 259, 350-1, 363, 366-7
Nityakarma, 36, 249
Niyama, 15, 353
Nominalism, 150-1
Nyāya, 22, 23, 33, 34, 35, 36, 37, 38, 39, 47, 53, 54, 55, 56, 57, 58, 59, 62-3, 65, 69, 70, 74n, 75, 77, 79-80, 81, 82, 83, 84, 85, 86, 90, 91, 94, 95, 96, 97, 100, 101, 102, 103, 105, 106-7, 110, 111, 112, 115-7, 118, 119, 120, 127-8, 129, 130, 134, 140, 160, 166, 168, 169-70, 171, 172, 194, 237-8, 249, 250, 256-7, 258, 260, 261, 262, 263, 266, 267, 269, 279, 280, 281, 285, 295, 296, 298-9, 303, 306 308-11, 312, 313, 315-8, 319, 321, 331, 333, 335, 336, 338, 339-40, 342, 355, 356-7, 359, 360
Occasionalism, 360
Optimism, 29
Original Sin, 330
Padārthas, 140
Pantheism, 209, 210, 212, 325
Pariṇāmavāda, 178, 211, 215, 219, 237-42
Pariśeṣa (Elimination), 53, 72, 97, 98
Pārthasārathi Miśra, 34, 80, 100, 111, 171, 261, 305, 312, 357
Patañjali, 271-4, 311-2, 318-20, 321, 353
Pessimism, 44-5, 48, 243
Plato, 141, 150, 244, 289
Pluralism, 142, 156
Polytheism, 19-20
Prabhākara, 35, 57, 80, 86, 87, 88, 89, 90, 93-4, 100, 110, 124-5, 166-73, 255-6, 257, 258, 261, 263, 266-7, 304-6, 341, 342
Pragmatism, 117, 119, 120
Prakṛti, 28, 29, 37, 174-81, 184, 215-6, 219, 260, 303, 313, 325, 334, 352
Prapatti, 39
Praśastapāda, 248, 254
Pratisaṁkhyā-nirodha, 160
Pratītyasamutpāda, 158, 159, 162, 301
Predestination, 19
Probability, 139
Pudgala, 193
Purāṇas, 39, 58, 292
Puraṇa Kāśyapa, 136
Puruṣa, 28, 29, 37, 172, 174, 177, 178, 179, 181-4, 303, 319, 334, 352
Puruṣottama, 207, 209, 210, 215, 327
Pūrva-Mīmāṁsā (See Mīmāṁsā)
Rādhā, 328
Raghunātha Śiromani, 155
Rajas, 175-6, 319
Rāmānuja, 27, 40, 126-7, 128, 129, 206, 216-21, 250, 251, 264-5, 267, 268, 326, 327, 334, 358
Rāmāyana, 248
Ratnatraya (Triratna), 361
Realism, 150-1
Rebirth, 19, 20, 21, 22, 23, 25
Ṛṇa, 251, 368
Rome, 289
Ṛta, 236, 290
Rūpa, 160, 163, 348
Sabara, 33, 80, 87, 100n, 105, 171, 172
Sadasatkhyātivāda, 125-6
Sādhana, 36-44

Sādhāraṇa-dharma, 14, 247-8, 251, 262
Sākṣin, 112
Śalikanātha, 33
Samādhi, 162
Sāmānya, 73, 140, 150-3, 167
Samavāga, 54, 55, 57, 73, 76, 140, 155-6, 167
Sambhava, 53, 97
Śaṁkara, 27, 37, 207, 208, 209, 213, 214, 216, 217-8, 220, 221-7, 238, 251, 263, 268, 281-2, 287-8, 297, 312-4, 320-3, 331, 334, 336, 338, 339, 341, 343-5, 349, 353, 354, 355, 356, 357, 360
Śaṁkara Miśra, 91, 94n
Sāṁkhya, 14, 15, 18, 20, 22, 23, 24, 26, 28, 29, 32, 33, 34-5, 36, 37, 39, 41, 44, 45, 47, 48, 53, 63, 75, 83, 85, 90, 91, 93-4, 97, 98, 99-100, 102, 106, 108, 110, 111, 112-3, 117, 118, 119, 120, 121, 125-6, 128, 167, 172, 173, 174-84, 194, 205, 219, 233, 237, 238, 243, 262, 265n, 267, 292, 297, 302-4, 306, 325, 331, 333-4, 335-6, 338, 340-1, 342, 343, 347n, 352, 353, 354, 356, 361
Sāṁkhya-kārikā, 73n
Saṁsāra, 323, 336
Samudāya, 363
Samyoga, 54, 55, 57, 76
Sannikarṣa, 54-7
Śāntirakṣita, 199
Sanyāsa, 46, 246
Sartre, J. P, 141
Sarvāstivāda, 157, 158, 162, 344
Satkāryavāda, 178, 237-42
Satkhyātivāda, 126-7
Sattva, 175-6, 179, 319
Satya, 272
Schopenhauer, 175
Self-determinism, 19
Siddhasena, 100n
Śīla, 162
Skandha, 139, 348
Sophists, 138
Sound, 54, 73, 143
Space, *(dis)*, 142, 144, 181
Spinoza, 22, 96, 204, 212
Spiritualism, 45-6
Śrīdhara, 76, 91, 141n
Substance (See *Dravya*)
Śūdra, 246, 247,
Śūnya (Śūnyatā), 123, 198, 199, 228, 229, 321
Śūnyavāda, 13, 123, 166, 203, 204, 223, 228-32, 349
Svabhāva-vāda, 136, 235-6
Svalakṣṇa, 158
Syllogism, 69-74
Tādātmya, 167
Taittirīyopaniṣad, 45
Tamas, 175-6, 319
Tanmātra, 180
Tapas, 32
Tathāgata, 232
Tathatā, 198, 199, 202, 203
Theism, 19, 20, 27, 208, 209, 212, 216, 221, 222, 224, 232, 306, 325, 326
Theology, 306-7
Theravāda, 157
Transmigration, 19, 20, 21, 22, 23, 25
Udayana, 33n, 91, 92, 97, 101, 309
Uddyotkara, 74, 101, 141n, 146
Universals (See *Sāmānya*)
Upekṣā, 259, 293, 368
Vācaspati, 73n, 303, 315, 319
Vadideva Suri, 100n
Vaihinger, 187
Vairāgya, 213, 353
Vaiśeṣika, 15, 17, 22, 23, 33, 34, 35, 36, 37, 38, 39, 47, 53, 74, 76, 77, 83, 84, 85, 86, 90, 91, 94-5, 96, 97, 101, 102, 103, 105, 106-7, 110, 111, 112, 115-7, 118, 119, 120, 127-8, 129, 130, 139-56, 158-9, 160, 166, 168, 169-70, 171, 172, 179, 180, 194, 237-8, 260, 261, 262, 263, 266, 267, 269, 279, 280, 281, 295, 296, 306, 308-11, 312, 313, 315-8, 319,

321, 331, 333, 335, 336, 337, 338, 339-40, 342, 355, 356-7, 358, 359, 360
Vaiṣnavism, 15, 27, 39, 40, 41, 206, 296, 323, 325-8, 334-5, 358, 359-60, 361, 362, 364-5
Vaiśya, 246, 247
Valée-Poussin, De, la 351
Vallava, 58, 59, 206-10, 237, 325, 328
Vānaprastha, 46, 246
Varadarāja, 74, 101
Varnāśramadharma, 14, 41, 246-7, 252, 262
Varuna, 39
Vasubandhu, 157, 199
Vātsyāyana, 33n, 73-4, 146, 270-1, 310
Veda, 14, 39, 41, 46, 47, 49, 75, 77, 135, 137, 213, 262, 264, 271, 291, 292, 296, 298, 341
Vedānta, 34, 35, 36, 47, 48, 56, 58, 75, 77, 80, 81, 82, 83, 84, 85, 86, 88, 89, 90, 91, 93, 95-6, 98, 99, 100, 107n, 109, 110, 111-2, 113-4, 117-8, 119, 120, 121, 194, 228, 231, 232, 263, 270, 281, 295, 307, 342, 358, 360, 361
Vedānta-paribhāṣā, 81n, 88n, 93n
Vibhāṣā, 157
Videhamukti, 26, 27, 33, 46, 342
Vijñāna-mātra, 199, 202
Vijñānabhikṣu, 177, 284-5, 303-4, 319
Viśeṣa, 73, 140, 154-5, 167
Viṣṇu, 207, 213-4, 215, 327, 365
Viṣṇupurāṇa, 39
Viśvanātha, 102
Vivartavāda, 225, 237-42
Vyāpti, 66-9, 76, 81, 236, 310
Vyāsa, 312, 319
Xenophanes, 316
Yadṛchhāvāda 235, 236
Yama, 353, 358
Yamunācārya, 357
Yaśomitra, 302
Yoga, 23, 24, 36, 37, 47, 75, 83, 93, 94, 128-9, 177, 199, 237, 238, 271, 292, 306, 308, 309, 318-20, 333-4, 335, 356, 358-9
Yogācāra, 17, 45, 101, 103, 123-4, 125, 129, 141, 149, 157, 158, 164, 165–6, 196-203, 229, 231, 233
Zeno, 150

For Product Safety Concerns and Information please contact our EU
representative GPSR@taylorandfrancis.com
Taylor & Francis Verlag GmbH, Kaufingerstraße 24, 80331 München, Germany

www.ingramcontent.com/pod-product-compliance
Lightning Source LLC
Chambersburg PA
CBHW071146300426
44113CB00009B/1098
9781032572536